T0334031

ROMAN ARTISANS AND THE URBAN ECONOMY

This book offers the first comprehensive study of economic conditions and economic life in Roman cities during the late Republic and early Empire. By employing a sophisticated methodology based upon comparative evidence and contemporary economic theory, the author develops interlocking arguments about the relationship between four key attributes of urban economic life in Roman antiquity: the nature and magnitude of consumer demand; the structure of urban labor markets; the strategies devised by urban artisans in their efforts to navigate their social and economic environments; and the factors that served to limit both the overall performance of the Roman economy and its potential for intensive growth. While the author's methodology and conclusions will be of particular interest to specialists in economic history, other readers will profit from his discussion of topics such as slavery and manumission, the economic significance of professional associations, and the impact of gender on economic behavior.

CAMERON HAWKINS is Assistant Professor of History at Queensborough Community College, City University of New York. His published work focuses on the social and economic history of the Roman world during the late Republic and early Empire.

ROMAN ARTISANS AND THE URBAN ECONOMY

CAMERON HAWKINS

Queensborough Community College

CAMBRIDGE
UNIVERSITY PRESS

CAMBRIDGE
UNIVERSITY PRESS

University Printing House, Cambridge CB2 8BS, United Kingdom

Cambridge University Press is part of the University of Cambridge.

It furthers the University's mission by disseminating knowledge in the pursuit of education, learning, and research at the highest international levels of excellence.

www.cambridge.org
Information on this title: www.cambridge.org/9781107115446

© Cameron Hawkins 2016

First published 2016

Printed in the United States of America by Sheridan Books, Inc.

A catalogue record for this publication is available from the British Library.

Library of Congress Cataloging-in-Publication Data
Hawkins, Cameron, 1973– author.
Roman artisans and the urban economy / Cameron Hawkins (assistant professor, Department of History, Queensborough Community College).
Cambridge, United Kingdom ; New York, New York : Cambridge University Press, 2016.
LCCN 2016015480 | ISBN 9781107115446 (hardback)
LCSH: Rome – Economic conditions. | Cities and towns – Rome – History. | City and town life – Rome – History. | Artisans – Rome – History. | Consumption (Economics) – Rome – History. | Labor market – Rome – History. | Slaves – Emancipation – Rome – History. | Production (Economic theory) – Social aspects – Rome – History. | Rome – History – Republic, 265–30 B.C. | Rome – History – Empire, 30 B.C.–284 A.D. | BISAC: HISTORY / Ancient / General.
LCC HC39 .H38 2016 | DDC 331.7/94–dc23
LC record available at https://lccn.loc.gov/2016015480

ISBN 978-1-107-11544-6 Hardback

coniugi carissimae parentibusque optimis

Contents

Figures

Tables

Acknowledgments

This book has been a long time in the making. Now that it is finally complete, I take great pleasure in expressing my gratitude to those who helped along the way.

Thanks are due first to the advisors of the dissertation project from which this book emerged: Richard Saller, Cam Grey, Jonathan Hall, and Walter Scheidel. Each offered valuable guidance not just during the process of writing the dissertation itself but also while I struggled to refine my arguments for presentation in this book.

I am no less grateful to the many friends and colleagues who have provided support over the years, some from the earliest days of graduate school. Too many to count offered advice, help, and commiseration. Those who went above and beyond the call of duty in this respect include Adam Darlage, Fanny Dolansky, John Deak, Jodi Haraldson, John Hyland, Sharon Hyland, Paul Keen, Tania Maync, Matt Perry, and Phil Venticinque.

In the later stages of the project, I was lucky to benefit from the feedback of several scholars who share my interest in economic history, some of whom read the developing manuscript in whole or in part. These include Fredrik Albritton-Jonsson, Alain Bresson, Miko Flohr, Claire Holleran, Emanuel Mayer, Corey Tazzara, and the two anonymous reviewers at Cambridge University Press, all of whom I am very pleased to acknowledge for their assistance. My students over the years have also contributed to the final form of the project more than they know by offering me the opportunity to explore ideas with them in class, and I thank them for their patience.

I presented early versions of many of the specific arguments in this book at workshops or conferences, where the feedback and questions I received often prompted me to modify my views. I am most grateful to the organizers of those conferences or panels I found especially stimulating. Alain Bresson, Elio lo Cascio, and François Velde organized a conference called *Growth and Factors of Growth in the Ancient Economy*, which took place at the Federal Reserve Bank of Chicago in January 2011; there, I had the opportunity to present the core of what is now Chapter 3, which elicited a number of critical and productive questions from the audience. Elements of Chapter 2 formed the basis of a talk I delivered at a panel on Roman labor markets at the 2012 ESSHC in Glasgow; I am grateful to Miriam Groen-Vallinga for inviting me to participate. My central arguments in Chapter 4 benefitted tremendously from discussions with historians of early modern Europe during an ESF-sponsored conference in Oxford, *Urban Economic Life in Europe and the Mediterranean from Antiquity to the Early Modern Period*, organized by Miko Flohr and Andrew Wilson. Finally, I learned much about current research on workshop archaeology and labor markets at a 2013 conference at Ghent University on *Work, Labor, and Professions in the Roman World*, organized by Koenraad Verboven and Christan Laes.

Several stages of my project also benefitted from institutional research support. The Franke Institute for the Humanities provided a fellowship to support work on what became Chapter 2, and organized a productive workshop in which I was able to present my ideas to scholars from a range of disciplines. The Introduction to the book was conceived and written during a delightful visit to Ghent University, where I spent a short time as a visiting scholar with *Structural Determinants of Economic Performance in the Roman World*, a research network sponsored by the FWO; I am profoundly grateful to the directors of the network for providing the intellectual space necessary for me to stand back and survey my project, and to Paul Erdkamp for the opportunity to present a lecture based on that project to students at the Vrije Universiteit Brussel.

Finally, my deepest gratitude goes to my family. Without the unflagging support of my parents, Blaine and Lois Hawkins, this book would not have been written. Nor would it exist had it not been for my partner, Emily Jusino, who has invested almost as much time in the project as I have myself, and who sustained me when I had all but lost hope of finding my way out of the woods. Thank you.

Introduction

At some point after the middle of the first century BCE, Marcus Vergilius Eurysaces commissioned a costly and visually striking funerary monument for himself on the eastern fringe of the city of Rome, near the intersection of the Via Labicana and the Via Praenestina (Figure I.1). Built from travertine and over thirty feet high, it bore an innovative decorative scheme evoking the world of work and business. The three surviving facades confront the viewer with the circular mouths of replicas of the kneading machines used in the city's larger bakeries, arranged in three horizontal rows. Above these, just below the tomb's upper story, runs a frieze depicting several scenes associated with bread and bread-making: on its south face the frieze depicts the receipt and milling of grain; on the north face, the work in the bakery itself; and on the west face, the weighing of the final product. Finally, the visual program of the monument is complemented by an inscription proclaiming: "This is the monument of Marcus Vergilius Eurysaces, baker, contractor, public servant."[1]

The scale and cost of the monument demonstrate that Eurysaces enjoyed success in his profession. Other artisans were not so fortunate. Although those who failed to prosper in the urban economies of the Roman world are more difficult to detect – they were, after all, unlikely to commemorate their failures on a monument – they do make occasional appearances in the evidentiary record, even if only in oblique ways. Our legal sources, for instance, leave little doubt that financial collapse was a very real risk for slaves who had been entrusted with capital by their masters to develop and operate a business: during the second century BCE, the praetors at Rome developed legal remedies designed to permit creditors of a slave whose business had become insolvent to recover their money

---

[1] For a recent and thorough discussion of this monument, see Petersen 2003.

Figure I.1 The tomb of Eurysaces (Photo: Cameron Hawkins)

from the slave's master.[2] Much later, in the second century CE, Artemidorus of Daldis recorded the story of a carpenter from the city of Cyzicus in Anatolia in his handbook on the interpretation of dreams, *Oneirocritica*. According to Artemidorus, the carpenter's dream that his colleague had died proved to be an evil omen of his own impending financial ruin: shortly after this dream, the carpenter was forced to abandon his workshop and leave Cyzicus because he could not pay back his creditors.[3]

These brief anecdotes provide representative examples of our direct evidence concerning the experiences and fortunes of the artisans who lived and worked in the cities of the Roman world during the late Roman Republic and early Roman Empire. They communicate vital information, particularly in the case of Eurysaces' monument, which implies that Eurysaces enjoyed success largely because he could produce bread at a scale suitable for state contracts. Yet, at the same time, these sources raise more questions than they answer about the nature of urban economies in the Roman world, the opportunities and challenges they created for artisans, and the strategies artisans devised to navigate these economies successfully. For instance, while observers in the ancient world recognized that the concentrated demand produced by urban environments could create opportunities for those with skill or ambition, the contrast between the fortunes of Eurysaces and the carpenter from Cyzicus implies that those opportunities held potentially serious risks. Likewise, although the scenes of working life preserved on Eurysaces' monument leave little doubt that his enterprise operated on a scale that demanded the help of numerous workers and even suggest that his bakery gave rise to internal divisions of labor, they say little about what Eurysaces' efforts to recruit and manage his workforce entailed.[4]

Given the nature of the evidence, historians who study artisans and urban producers in the Roman world have followed two trajectories. First, scholars have researched production and distribution in those industries that have left strong traces in the archaeological evidence (some of which, strictly speaking, took place in suburban or rural contexts rather than urban). These include the pottery industries responsible for producing the coarsewares and finewares that circulated widely in the Roman world, as well as more utilitarian items such as ceramic shipping containers, tiles,

---

[2] In particular, see Aubert 2013: 201–2 and Chiusi 1993 on the *actio tributoria*, which receives extensive treatment on the part of the Roman jurists.
[3] Artem. 4.1.   [4] For a brief discussion of divisions of labor within bakeries, see Ruffing 2008: 374.

or bricks;[5] industries that produced marble sarcophagi;[6] and, increasingly, those that gave rise to sizeable physical installations, like the fulling industry.[7] Studies of this sort have revealed much about the organization of individual industries, even if the nature of the evidence makes it difficult to grapple with questions concerning strategies on the level of the individual workshop. Second, scholars have also explored what representations like those of Eurysaces can tell us about the self-fashioned identity of artisans and other members of sub-elite groups in Roman cities and about the value artisans attached to hard work and professional success.[8] Work in this vein has done much to read past Cicero's notorious argument that most urban trades belonged to what he called the "sordid" rather than the "liberal" arts (*quaestus sordidi* and *quaestus liberales*, respectively) and to demonstrate that artisans in particular took pride in their skill, in the proceeds of their labor, and did not hesitate to celebrate their successes.[9] At the same time, it has also worked to situate artisans in their social contexts by shedding light on the kinds of personal and professional relationships that gave structure to their working lives.

By comparison, historians have only recently focused in detail on the questions that Artemidorus' anecdote and Eurysaces' monument raise about the nature of the Roman economy and about the strategies artisans developed to manage their enterprises.[10] While it has now been over a decade since Jean-Jacques Aubert encouraged ancient historians to develop a detailed and comprehensive model of business management in antiquity,[11] we are still in the very early stages of this project. As a result, we still know much less about the factors that shaped the decisions of urban producers than we do about those that shaped the decisions of wealthy landholders like Cicero or even about those that shaped the decisions of the tenants and smallholders who constituted the bulk of the rural population in Italy and other regions of the empire. This gap in our knowledge is problematic for two reasons. First, a study of artisans and their business

---

[5] Aubert 1994 discusses the management and organization of a number of different ceramic industries. Cf. also Fülle 1997 for a detailed discussion of *terra sigillata* production.

[6] Ward-Perkins 1992 is the standard work. See, more recently, Birk 2012, who attempts to produce a more nuanced analysis of the organization of workforces in this particular industry.

[7] Flohr 2007, 2011, and 2013.

[8] Much of this work was inspired by Veyne 2000, which explores the culture of the so-called *plebs media*. For the state of the art, see Tran 2013. Cf. also Knapp 2011: 5–52 and Mayer 2012.

[9] Cic. *Off.* 1.150–1.

[10] E.g., Venticinque 2010 and Holleran 2012: 194–231. For examples that approach the problem from an archaeological perspective, see Birk 2012 (marble workers) and Flohr 2013, esp. 96–180 and 242–87.

[11] Aubert 2001: 106–8.

strategies can enrich our understanding of the practical circumstances that gave rise to the thought-worlds of the "invisible Romans" that form the subject of Robert Knapp's recent book – broadly speaking, those members of Roman society who, unlike the elite, did not produce extensive literary reflections about their world.[12] Second, because artisans' strategies reflected the economic environments in which they were embedded, an analysis of those strategies can contribute directly to the debate about the structure and performance of the Roman world's economy.

Argument

In this book, I intend to fill that gap by making three principal arguments about artisans, their strategies, and the economic environment in which they worked. In the first place, I show that even though urban environments in antiquity did give rise to concentrated markets for the products and services of artisans and other urban producers, those markets were fundamentally unstable, because consumer demand at all levels of the socioeconomic spectrum remained both seasonal and uncertain. Second, I demonstrate that artisans responded to the instability of urban product markets in two main ways: (1) they sought to buffer themselves against the risks that arose from seasonal and uncertain demand by devising business strategies designed both to minimize their fixed and ongoing costs and to ensure that they had the flexibility to respond to elevated periods of demand by stepping up production when necessary; (2) they compensated for potentially high transaction costs in what was a tight market for skilled labor by embedding their production strategies either in relationships of trust (which often arose in the context of professional associations), or in relationships of power that bound freed slaves to their former masters. Third, I suggest that an understanding of artisans' strategies can be used to address persistent questions about the performance of the Roman economy, especially its potential for intensive growth during the late Republic and early Empire. Those strategies point to subtle but important contrasts between the world of antiquity and the world of seventeenth- and eighteenth-century Europe – contrasts which suggest not only that the urban market structures of the Roman world were underdeveloped in comparison with those of early modern Europe but also that the Roman economy was unlikely to have experienced ongoing growth during the first and second centuries CE.

[12] Knapp 2011.

By making these arguments, I contribute to current scholarship on the social and economic history of the Roman world in two ways. First, by drawing a connection between artisans' strategies and the nature of the economic environment in which they worked, I add some fresh perspective to the ongoing debate about the structure of economic life in antiquity – that is, about how economic behavior and social relations intersected with and influenced one another. The basic parameters of this debate continue to be shaped heavily by Sir Moses Finley's substantivist model, which was itself influenced by the work of sociologists such as Max Weber and Karl Polanyi. Crudely put, Finley held that individuals in the Greek and Roman worlds tended to prioritize concerns about social and political status over economic goals emphasizing material gain and that even though they were linked to extensive markets, they nevertheless embedded a considerable amount of economic exchange in relationships based on reciprocity or hierarchies of status. Much of the dialogue in ancient history over the past thirty years has revolved around efforts to assess whether or not Finley's models need to be nuanced or even replaced by those based more strongly on methodological individualism and to elaborate on the consequences that this might hold for our understanding of economic life in antiquity.[13]

In Chapters 2–4 in this book, I make the case that while social relations and the ideologies on which they were based did affect the behavior of artisans in the Roman world, much of the evidence suggests that artisans made strategic use of social relations based on power hierarchies or trust in their efforts to respond to the challenges generated by the seasonal and uncertain demand for their products and services. As we shall see, social relations and ideologies exerted their strongest structural effect upon behavior within the household, where they affected the division of labor between (mostly male) artisans and their wives. The economic lives of women have become a major focus of interest in recent years, both at the level of the household and at the level of the Roman economy more broadly. While the early work of Susan Treggiari focused on how gender affected the kinds of work performed by women, more recently historians have grappled explicitly with the problem of family dynamics in a society in which households weighed the demands of gender ideologies against the hard, practical need to earn a living. Scholars have offered valuable insights

---

[13] Good discussions of the development and state of this debate can be found in Morris 2002, Manning and Morris 2005b, and Bang 2008: 17–36.

about the implications that gendered divisions of labor hold for our understanding of living standards and economic growth, but much remains to be said about how and to what extent women who belonged to artisanal milieus contributed to their households' well-being.[14] I stress that even though artisans could be flexible and adaptable when they deployed the labor of their wives and sons, the importance they attached to specific kinds of work performed by their wives – namely, to several kinds of household tasks crucial to a household's economic success – limited women's participation in work directed explicitly toward market production and income generation.

In other respects, however, artisans made strategic use of social relations in order to navigate successfully the economic environments in which they worked. This was true above all in the case of coercive social relationships based on slavery. Historians are well aware that Roman slaveholders found numerous ways to exploit the labor of slaves and freedmen in urban enterprises, whether by employing slaves directly as managers of a workshop or as members of its staff, or by placing slaves in charge of semi-autonomous businesses.[15] Likewise, slaveholders could also derive benefits from slaves whom they freed. The dominant approach to Roman manumission stresses that slaveholders freed slaves in order to exploit the opportunities of urban markets indirectly, namely by relying on freedmen to manage urban businesses as their agents or managers, or as junior partners in joint enterprises.[16] Yet even though Sandra Joshel pointed out some years ago that many of the freed slaves who are identified as artisans in the Roman funerary inscriptions seem to have been manumitted by other craftsmen rather than by wealthy slaveholders, few serious attempts have been made to assess why and in what contexts artisans themselves acquired, trained, and manumitted slaves, or to tease out the implications of Joshel's observations for our understanding of urban labor markets.[17] I resolve this tension by showing that artisans took advantage of their ability to assert ongoing control over former slaves in order to retain access to skilled labor, while offloading many of the risks of seasonal employment onto their freedmen themselves.

Relationships built on trust and reciprocity likewise offered artisans considerable scope for strategic action. Scholarly interest in the economic

---

[14] Treggiari 1979 is the classic study. For work focusing on women and household strategies, see especially Scheidel 1995 and 1996a, Saller 2003, and Groen-Vallinga 2013.

[15] For an overview of the economics of slavery in ancient Greece and Rome, see Bradley 1994: 57–80, Osborne 1995, and Scheidel 2008.

[16] See especially Mouritsen 2011: 206–47.   [17] Joshel 1977, esp. 205 and 619–20.

aspects of trust and reciprocity in the Roman world was stimulated
originally by studies of peasant agriculture in the ancient Mediterranean,
which sought in part to explore how peasant cultivators constructed networks of mutual support as a form of insurance against the ever-present
danger of harvest failure and famine.[18] Historians have built on this
approach by examining the extent to which individuals relied on trust
and reciprocity not just to secure support in times of crisis, but rather to
structure their social and economic strategies more broadly. This is true not
only of those who continue to study peasant communities in antiquity[19]
but also of those interested in the economic behavior of members of other
social groups. In particular, Koenraad Verboven has recently stressed that
members of the Roman socioeconomic elite relied heavily on relationships
of friendship and patronage anchored in trust (*fides*) to provide security for
their economic transactions and to overcome limitations of Roman
business law that may otherwise have stifled economic activity.[20] Nor
have the social strata of artisans and businessmen been overlooked. Paul
Veyne's work, for instance, has explored the connections between trust,
reputation, and business dealings among members of the *plebs media*.[21]

Other historians, drawing on comparative studies of sociability in later
historical periods, have resumed study of the voluntary associations (cultic,
professional, or otherwise) to which many members of the Roman world's
urban population belonged and which fostered networks of trust,
reciprocity, and mutual support.[22] Yet despite this renewed interest in
the social worlds of Roman artisans and businessmen, we have only just
begun to piece together an understanding of how urban producers took
advantage of relationships of trust and reciprocity as they negotiated
economic life in Roman cities. Much of the work on the intersection
between social and economic life in voluntary associations has
concentrated on the material and social support these associations could
provide both for artisans or businessmen and for the inhabitants of Roman
cities in general, whether by providing short-term loans, offering assistance
with funerary rites and expenses, or allowing members to engage
collectively in both urban politics and relationships of patronage with
the wealthy and powerful. Historians have probed whether or not association members used the relationships they cultivated with one another to
articulate business strategies, but in most cases they have concentrated on

---

[18] Garnsey 1988: 41–63 and Gallant 1991: 153–68 remain fundamental.
[19] See, most recently, Grey 2011.   [20] Verboven 2002.   [21] Veyne 2000.
[22] For the most important general treatments, see below, Chapter 2, n. 13.

long-distance traders, who relied on strong social ties to collect information about markets and to structure agency relationships.[23] I extend this work by showing how artisans employed relationships of trust based upon reputations to solve serious problems of coordination without incurring the costs and risks necessary to create large firms.

Second, because these questions of economic structure cannot be divorced from the overall performance of the Roman economy, my arguments in the following chapters also contribute to the scholarship on economic growth in the Roman world, which remains one of the most pressing problems confronting historians of the late Republic and early Empire. At issue are three key points with a profound bearing on how we conceptualize standards of living in antiquity: (1) how the per capita output of the economy measured up to the outputs of other preindustrial systems; (2) whether the Roman economy experienced sustained growth in productivity above and beyond those changes provoked by Roman conquests in the second and first centuries BCE and by the wealth that those conquests transferred to Italy; (3) how equitably the output of the Roman economy was distributed among members of different social and economic strata.[24]

We have not yet reached a consensus on any of these points. Views about per capita output range from conservative estimates that the economy of Roman Italy at its peak (if not of the empire as a whole) was capable of performing at the same level as the more developed areas of northwestern Europe ca. 1500 CE,[25] to more optimistic claims that Roman Italy was capable of generating a per capita output comparable to that of the same area in the late seventeenth or eighteenth centuries.[26] Opinions on long-term change in per capita output also vary substantially, although two models in particular deserve to be singled out. The first is a model of one-off growth generated by Rome's political integration of the Mediterranean world, which accelerated the diffusion of Hellenistic innovations from east to west and prompted a period of intensified urbanization in the western provinces. Because this model emphasizes causal factors that occurred relatively early – chiefly, during the second century BCE – it implies not

---

[23] See, for example, Bang 2008: 239–68 and Broekaert 2011 on associations of traders. Venticinque 2010 focuses instead on urban craftsmen in Roman Egypt.

[24] For a short introduction to the basic issues, see Scheidel 2012a: 2–5. Scheidel 2009 and Wilson 2009 offer lengthier discussions.

[25] Scheidel and Friesen 2009: 64 and 74.

[26] Grantham 1999: 222–5; Lo Cascio and Malanima 2009; Temin 2013: 243–61. Jongman 2007: 600 also seems to prefer an estimate that places the performance of the Roman economy "at the upper end of what could be achieved in preindustrial economies."

only that growth had likely stagnated by the early Empire but also that demographic expansion may have started to erode any gains in per capita output that the economy had generated in the late Republic. An alternative model posits that per capita output, incomes, and living standards continued to grow throughout the first and second centuries CE until this growth was ultimately interrupted by a sudden shock – possibly by the Antonine plague in the late second century CE or by the political and economic upheavals associated with the "crisis" of the third century.[27]

These disparate views persist largely because we are still navigating the serious empirical and theoretical challenges that obscure the trajectory of the Roman economy from our view. The empirical problems are the consequence of a dearth of evidence that prevents us from quantifying critical parameters like the population of the Roman Empire or the total output of its economy in any precise way. Historians instead make inferences about economic change on the basis of disparate categories of evidence that may serve as proxy data. Recent work, for instance, has emphasized the construction and interpretation of archaeological time-series. One of the most well-known series charts the number of (known) shipwrecks in the Mediterranean century by century, but archaeologists and historians have also exploited time-series reflecting several other phenomena that may reflect changing economic performance: lead and copper pollution deposited in Greenland ice sheets, archaeological evidence pointing to changing levels of meat consumption, osteological markers of health and stature in human remains, dedicatory inscriptions reflecting building activity, and the spread of technical innovations such as waterwheels. On occasion, our fragmentary documentary evidence can be pressed into service for this purpose, as demonstrated by recent studies on wages and incomes. Crucially, these proxies do not always line up in ways that permit easy conclusions about long-term developmental patterns: while the shipwreck time-series seems to suggest that the volume of maritime trade in the Mediterranean peaked in the first century BCE, the archaeological evidence for meat consumption shows that animals were slaughtered for food at a higher rate in the late second century CE than was the case in earlier periods.[28]

---

[27] On the basic contrast between the two models, see Temin 2013: 233–4. Scheidel 2009 advances a cautious argument for a spurt of one-time growth that had already begun to taper off by the late Republic or early Empire (but cf. Wilson 2009 for a criticism of this position); Jongman 2007: 611–15 believes that per capita growth continued into the second century CE.

[28] On these various different time-series, see Jongman 2007, Scheidel 2009, and Wilson 2009.

These problems of evidence are compounded by serious theoretical challenges. As Walter Scheidel has stressed, the most pressing of these is our need to determine whether any particular kind of data can be interpreted as a proxy for intensive growth – that is, for genuine increases in per capita output – rather than as evidence for extensive growth driven by population expansion or for the ability of members of certain social groups to claim a larger share of the economy's total output for themselves. For example, if heavier lead and copper pollution in the Greenland ice sheets does reflect increased smelting activity, then this could point to a change in the per capita consumption of goods manufactured from metal, or to an increase in production designed to accommodate the needs of a growing population, or to some combination of the two possibilities. Likewise, the increase in building activity in the Greek East in the early Empire may say more about unequal wealth distribution and the tendency of the municipal elite to engage in competitive euergetism than it does about economic growth.[29] No less pressing is our need to construct coherent models that make explicit claims about what kind of phenomena could have stimulated or depressed growth in per capita output, especially over the long term. Ancient historians have identified several phenomena that may be related to economic change – trade, specialization, technological development, access to training – but as of yet few have offered compelling reasons to think that these, operating alone or in conjunction with one another, were able to generate ongoing and sustained changes in per capita productivity well into the second century CE.[30]

Although my analysis of artisans and their economic behavior in the Roman world may not solve these problems decisively, it offers a useful perspective on the performance of the Roman economy because the structural features I address throughout the book shed light on the level of market coordination it attained. The importance of market coordination as a driver of growth in preindustrial contexts is emphasized by George Grantham, who has added considerable nuance to conventional models of preindustrial economic change, most of which depend heavily on a Malthusian-Ricardian framework.[31] These conventional models stress that sustained growth in per capita output in preindustrial contexts was constrained by the interplay between incomes and demography. On the one hand, improvements in per capita incomes in preindustrial contexts tended to produce increased population growth. On the other, because

---

[29] See especially Scheidel 2009: 47, 49–50, and 65.
[30] For a discussion of potential factors driving growth, see Saller 2005.   [31] Grantham 1999.

increased population growth ensured that the marginal returns of labor were certain to decrease unless economic actors could intensify agricultural production, it also ensured that standards of living were certain to erode. In the kind of system described by this model, intensive growth can only occur if a demographic shock reduces the population, or if technological innovations enhance labor productivity. More importantly, that growth is ultimately unsustainable and reversible in the absence of further technological innovations, since improved per capita incomes will eventually stimulate enough population growth to eat away all relative gains and degrade living standards to their previous level.[32]

Without denying that this model offers a powerful explanation for economic change at certain critical moments in Europe's past, Grantham believes that few historical societies exhausted the limits of their resources and that the kinds of bottlenecks envisioned by the Malthusian-Ricardian model have been rare. He proposes instead that most observable changes in productivity in preindustrial European economies should be attributed to endogenous changes in market structure. In his view, thin markets operated to constrain intensive economic growth in preindustrial contexts by deterring individuals from making the investments in material or human capital necessary to specialize intensively in production for the market: not only did individuals embedded in thin markets run the risk that marketing costs would be high enough to prevent them from earning returns on specialized investments, but they were also reluctant to rely on potentially unstable market mechanisms to acquire the food and other necessities that they would cease to produce themselves if their own activities were to become more specialized. Preindustrial economies therefore often possessed reserves of untapped productivity that could be unleashed under the right circumstances, even without decisive changes in technology. In particular, either the emergence of thicker markets or a decrease in marketing costs could reduce the risks associated with specialized production while raising its potential returns and thus stimulate entrepreneurs to invest more heavily in specialized training or in productive capital. In turn, as increasingly specialized producers became more dependent on the market to meet their own consumption needs, they created "thick market externalities" – that is, they injected positive feedback into the system by enhancing the overall demand for goods and services in the economy, and thus the potential for more increasing returns to specialization. In theory, such a system could be self-sustaining until

---

[32] Temin 2012 offers an accessible account of Malthusian models.

reaching a point of stable equilibrium: a thickening market eventually ensures that specialization begins to exhibit decreasing rather than increasing returns, and for that reason a point will be reached at which it no longer pays to undertake production at increasingly specialized levels barring major technological innovations.[33]

In Grantham's model, urbanization and institutional factors lowering the costs of long-distance trade serve as the two main drivers of thicker markets. By concentrating consumers of agricultural output, urbanization reduces marketing costs and signals to producers in the countryside that increased specialization in production for the market can yield significant rewards. Institutional factors promoting connectivity and trade, on the other hand, lower marketing costs by enabling producers to move goods to market more easily and to find distant buyers for increasingly heterogenous and specialized goods. Although there can be no doubt that these drivers were important, Jan de Vries's recent work indicates that changes in household consumption goals can be even more decisive in creating the thick markets that can generate increasing returns to specialization. For de Vries, changes in household consumption goals transformed the economy of northwestern Europe between 1650 and 1850. In his view, the key development in this process was the emergence among both working- and middle-class households of new ideals of comfort, fashion, and respectability, all of which stimulated the regular and enthusiastic consumption of services, new foodstuffs (such as coffee, sugar, and tea), and increasingly fashion-sensitive manufactured goods. These ideals served as signals for entrepreneurs to invest in the capital and skills necessary to meet growing demand and at the same time motivated working- and middle-class households to direct time and labor away from leisure or production for self-consumption and toward income-generating work in order to fund their purchases. Growth in both consumer demand and real productivity was thus sustained even in the face of stagnant or declining real wages, since the reallocation by women of their labor from household production to production for the market increased the disposable income available to the members of their households.[34]

The models of Grantham and de Vries point to two ways in which a study of artisans and their strategies might help us understand questions about the performance of the Roman world's economy. In the first place, because they link market thickness so closely to changes in per capita economic output, they suggest that an analysis of market thickness in

---

[33] The core of the model can be found at Grantham 1999: 215–22. [34] De Vries 2008, esp. 71–2.

antiquity should be able to provide some sense of the output that the Roman economy was capable of producing. Second, because they explicitly identify factors that provoked intensive economic growth in other pre-industrial contexts, these models can also help us assess the likelihood that the economy of the late Republic and early Empire could generate improvements in per capita income. While I will touch briefly on the first of these two points in the following chapters – primarily to note that market structures do not seem to have been as thick in antiquity as in the early modern period – I will have considerably more to say about the second, since it is probable that a strong reorientation of consumption goals like the one responsible for economic expansion in the early modern period did not take place in antiquity.

Scope and methods

The subjects of my analysis, to whom I refer loosely as "artisans" or "entrepreneurs," were for the most part urban workers who applied skill in order to transform or enhance raw materials or semi-finished goods, or who performed skilled services.[35] This definition overlaps closely with how the ancients themselves conceptualized an *artifex*, who could be a doctor just as easily as a blacksmith.[36] Skill was an important concept for artisans in the Roman world themselves, since it served as a key element in self-identity, just as in the early modern context.[37] More importantly – at least from an economic perspective – the acquisition of skill itself demanded an investment on the part of the artisan or the artisans' parents, guardians, or owners.[38] As we shall see in later chapters, that investment was substantial relative to the household earning power of most inhabitants of the Roman Empire. For that reason alone, artisans' strategies are a significant index of economic performance, since the training on which they depended points to the ability of their economy to sustain potentially costly divisions of labor.

[35] That is, the individuals who fall into the "building," "manufacture," and "skilled service" categories in Joshel 1992: 69–76.

[36] Julian, *Dig.* 38.1.25.2, clearly categorizes doctors with "other craftsmen." For further comments on ancient conceptions of medicine as a craft (*artificium* or *techne*), see Kudlien 1970: 3–4, Nutton 1995, and Pleket 1995.

[37] For the importance of skill to the identities of ancient artisans, see esp. Tran 2011. For the early modern context, see Farr 2000: 3–5.

[38] Here I follow George Grantham's suggestion that what set artisans apart from other workers was "the irreversible investment in acquiring the skills that made specialised workers more productive than unspecialised ones" (Grantham 1999: 217).

This definition unavoidably embraces workers who differed widely not only in occupation but also in wealth and in social or juridical status, just as the definitions used by early modern historians likewise incorporate both poor journeymen and wealthy, entrepreneurial masters. As far as distinctions of wealth are concerned, I focus primarily on those who enjoyed some degree of economic autonomy – that is, those who spent at least some of their time working directly for clients as primary contractors or as subcontractors, and who thus made decisions about organizational issues or labor management. Freeborn, freed, and slave artisans could all belong to this category, but in practice much of our evidence refers to freeborn or freed artisans who had the ability to leave some trace of themselves in our sources. I also limit the discussion primarily to artisans who earned their livings by working in the towns and cities of the empire. I do engage from time to time with material reflecting craftsmen who produced goods in rural or semi-rural contexts, such as those who made bricks, tiles, and much of the pottery that was manufactured in bulk and shipped over long distances, including *terra sigillata*.[39] Although these artisans are highly interesting in their own right, some of the basic parameters of their operations differed from those of urban craftsmen in ways that argue against incorporating them into the same general framework. Direct proximity to the market was often critical in many urban trades, where craftsmen often made goods to order. This was not necessarily true in the case of rural or semi-rural production, where products tended to be more homogenized, and where access to raw materials was a more important consideration than immediate proximity to the consumer market.[40]

In geographical and chronological terms, my study privileges the city of Rome during the late Republic and early Empire. In part, this decision is dictated by the importance of Rome in this period to the ongoing debates about market integration and growth in the ancient economy. At the same time, it is also shaped by the nature of the surviving source material. As the following chapters will show, evidence for artisans and their economic strategies is scattered among different kinds of sources, most of which

[39] Some of these industries have received recent and detailed treatments of their own. See, in particular, Graham 2006 on bricks, and Mees 2002 on *terra sigillata*, particularly the lines produced in Arezzo. See also Fülle 1997: 142–3, who argues that "at least a part of the manufacture of Italian *terra sigillata*" took place in a rural context. On p. 145 he notes that production in Arezzo itself was probably sub-urban rather than urban.

[40] See Schwarz 1992: 31–4, on the way that comparable factors affected the distribution of industries in eighteenth-century England.

provide only fragmentary pieces of information. Literary evidence tends to reflect the concerns of its socially and economically privileged authors and touches on the economic lives of artisans only incidentally (if at all). The same, unfortunately, is often true of our legal evidence. Funerary and dedicatory inscriptions preserve the voices of artisans themselves, but like the monument of Eurysaces, they do so in a selective and incomplete way. Archaeological evidence offers an invaluable guide to the physical contexts of production and to the nature of artisans' products, but only in certain circumstances offers insight into the organization of production or the business strategies adopted by individual craftsmen. Because of these difficulties, it is often necessary to exploit several categories of evidence simultaneously, and in this sense Rome of the late Republic and early Empire offers the best overall prospects for generalization.

That said, my focus on Rome is not exclusive. Throughout the text, I suggest that urban artisans in the Roman world faced challenges that were broadly consistent in character from city to city, since these challenges arose primarily from structural features like seasonality that were endemic to preindustrial economies. Moreover, I also suggest that the institutional and organizational environments in different regions of the empire were comparable enough to each other that the strategies developed by artisans in Egypt or Asia Minor did not differ radically in character from those employed by artisans in central Italy. For these reasons, my analysis does incorporate evidence pertaining to local conditions outside of Rome itself. I also adduce some material from sources produced earlier or later than my core period of interest when that material is particularly relevant to my argument. In such cases, I take care to demonstrate that the phenomena recorded by the sources can also be detected in evidence from the late Republic or early Empire. In Chapter 2, for example, Augustine's discussion of subcontracting networks within the silversmithing trade provides a particularly vivid description of how production was organized in a particular industry. Even though his comments reflect conditions of the fifth century CE, earlier sources suggest that what Augustine observed in the silversmiths' quarter of his own day would have been equally familiar to a Roman of the first century CE.

From a methodological perspective, the nature of the evidence presents serious challenges. As should be clear from my discussions of Eurysaces' monument, Artemidorus' story about the carpenter from Cyzicus, and the difficulties encountered when we attempt to discuss economic performance, our evidence is sparse enough that approaches based heavily on traditional close readings of individual sources have only a limited ability to resolve questions about either artisans' strategies or the nature of the economy in which they worked. Generalization can be challenging enough when historians struggle to determine whether an isolated piece of evidence was preserved because the behavior or process it documents was typical, or precisely because that behavior or process was exceptional enough to excite notice; it becomes even more difficult when our sources fail to explain the behavior of individuals by linking it explicitly to specific features of the social or economic environments in which those individuals were embedded. Artemidorus' anecdote about the carpenter is a case in point: not only does it fail on its own to communicate any sense of how likely artisans were to fall into debt, it also offers no indication of the economic conditions or business practices that may have prompted an artisan to accumulate debt in the first place. For these reasons, ancient historians interested in generalization must anchor their analyses in strong, theoretical frameworks that permit them to make claims not only about the typicality of behavior recorded in the evidence but also about potential causal relationships that the surviving sources leave unexplored or unarticulated.

In the following chapters, my efforts to generalize about artisans' strategies and the nature of the Roman economy draw strongly upon the theoretical framework associated with New Institutional Economics (NIE). Broadly speaking, NIE is distinctive primarily because it breaks away from some of the basic assumptions of neoclassical economics. In particular, it rejects both the assumption that economic actors have ready access to the information they require to make economic decisions and the idea that transactions can be negotiated and enforced without cost. Instead, NIE invokes the concept of transaction costs – the time and resources individuals must expend in order to locate and gather information about potential partners, negotiate relationships or agreements with those partners, and enforce the terms of those agreements.[41] In certain contexts, these costs can be severe: as Clifford Geertz famously observed in his analysis of the bazaar, often "information is poor, scarce, maldistributed, inefficiently communicated, and intensely valued."[42]

Within the framework of NIE, the economic behavior of individual actors is shaped strongly by their institutions and organizations. Institutions are conceptualized as clusters of rules or expectations that

---

[41] For a good introduction to the utility of NIE in the study of past societies, see Acheson 2002 (from whom I adapt the definition of transaction costs that I present here). For discussions of NIE with specific reference to Graeco-Roman history, see Frier and Kehoe 2007 and Bang 2009: 195–9.

[42] Geertz 1978: 29.

arise in a variety of ways: some are matters of social or cultural convention, which are propagated and enforced informally through the politics of reputation and social pressure; others are more formal in the sense that they are created and enforced by a coercive authority, such as the state. Organizations such as firms or voluntary associations, on the other hand, are structures created by economic actors who seek to better coordinate their activities with one another. Both institutions and organizations can affect behavior profoundly by shaping individuals' conceptions of what kinds of actions are possible or desirable. NIE also stresses, however, that both often have a more instrumental effect, in that they help individual actors structure transactions with one another by mitigating potential sources of friction – whether by compensating for asymmetrical access to information or by allowing actors to articulate and enforce specific rights or privileges. Crucially, as Geertz also recognized, actors often seek to develop strategies that exploit the full range of organizations and institutions at their disposal. In that sense, NIE offers a useful tool for conceptualizing ways in which actors might embed economic decisions in different kinds of social relationships. If, for instance, transaction costs associated with exchanging goods or services on the market are high – whether because the quality and value of goods or services are difficult to assess or because partners to a transaction have few remedies available to them in the case of fraud – then individuals may conceivably choose to deal only with partners whom they already trust or over whom they exercise some power.[43] Thus, in Geertz's economy of the bazaar, individual *bazaaris* conduct most of their transactions with partners to whom they have firm and long-lasting reciprocal ties.[44] It is precisely because NIE links the social and economic spheres of behavior in such a way that it can generate fresh insight into persistent questions concerning economic behavior in antiquity, the structure of the ancient economy more broadly, and the relationship between those two variables.

Comparative evidence offers an additional tool for negotiating the limitations of our evidence. Comparative evidence works best not when it is used to fill in gaps in our own material, but rather when it is used in the same way as a robust body of theory – namely, to identify potential causal connections between phenomena that would appear unrelated to one another were we to rely on inductive approaches alone. For that reason, comparative evidence is most useful when drawn from studies of historical

[43] For further discussion, see the references cited above in n. 41, and especially Acheson 2002.
[44] Geertz 1978: 30–1.

or contemporary societies that are documented extensively and similar enough to the society under investigation for historians to identify those parallels or differences that were likely to have been most significant.[45]

In the following chapters, I rely primarily on comparative evidence drawn from studies of artisans and urban economies in northwestern Europe during the late phase of its early modern period, the seventeenth and eighteenth centuries. These studies match the criteria articulated above in important respects. One key consideration is that documentary evidence pertaining to artisans has survived more extensively from this period than from any other in preindustrial Europe. Historians of the seventeenth and eighteenth centuries are therefore able to draw upon sizeable collections of wills, probate documents, letters, journals, and administrative records produced by guilds or trade corporations, and they have used this material to generate detailed accounts of the social and economic conditions in which artisans lived and worked. These accounts emphasize not only issues of identity and group consciousness but also issues of more direct relevance for my own project, such as market conditions, social and economic institutions and organizations, and artisans' production strategies. Given the rich character of the primary evidence on which they are based, these accounts offer access to comparative evidence of a quality that cannot be matched by material from other preindustrial societies.

Just as importantly, studies of northwestern Europe during the seventeenth and eighteenth centuries are particularly fruitful as sources of comparative evidence for Roman historians because they draw attention to potentially meaningful similarities and differences between the urban economies of antiquity and those of the early modern world. On a general level, the urban economies of antiquity shared important structural characteristics with those of early modern Europe in spite of obvious differences between the two historical contexts. One important difference is the fact that Roman Italy was a genuine slave society in the late Republic and early Empire, whereas seventeenth- and eighteenth-century Europe was not.[46] More subtle, yet equally profound, were differences in how both state power and the social and political status of merchants affected economic behavior in each historical context.[47] Yet, in both contexts, large urban centers coexisted alongside smaller towns in what remained heavily agricultural economies; technologies of communication and transportation

---

[45] On the utility of comparative evidence and its appropriate application, see Skocpol and Somers 1980, esp. 176–81. For specific discussions of the benefits (and potential limitations) of the comparative approach in ancient history, see Erdkamp 2005: 7–11 and Bang 2008: 37–60.

[46] See Bradley 1994: 10–30 on the nature of Rome's slave society.   [47] Bang 2008: 49–60.

remained dependent on wind or animal power; urban manufacture and production were predominantly rooted in relatively small workshops and reliant on human muscle and skill rather than on machines or technology; and, in both, urban populations were stratified by wealth in ways that fostered segmentation in product markets, especially in cities that became centers of display for members of imperial or national elites. These broad similarities therefore provide a baseline from which to assess the potential impact of structural phenomena that were peculiar to antiquity, such as the prevalence of chattel slavery.[48]

In a more specific sense, because northwestern Europe arguably achieved a level of market integration in the seventeenth and eighteenth centuries that pushed the limits of what was possible in a preindustrial context, studies of this period are especially valuable as a heuristic device for the analysis of both artisans' strategies and urban economies in the Roman world. As I discuss in more detail in subsequent chapters, artisans in early modern Europe tailored their business strategies to suit an economy that remained deeply affected by seasonality and uncertainty in spite of the relatively high level of market integration it had reached by the end of the period. In the Roman world, in which central Italy was the only region that may have approached comparable levels of market integration during the late Republic and early Empire,[49] the challenges artisans faced as a consequence of seasonality and uncertainty were, if anything, more severe than in the early modern period; for that reason, artisans in antiquity found it no less necessary to adapt their production strategies to these pressures than did their early modern counterparts. Furthermore, by focusing on the key institutions and social practices that permitted Europe in the seventeenth and eighteenth centuries to attain a high level of market integration, the work of early modern historians such as Grantham and de Vries makes it possible for us to test the specific claim that Roman Italy may have achieved a comparable degree of market integration – chiefly, by inviting us to examine whether or not phenomena comparable to those responsible for producing the sustained growth of Europe's long eighteenth century were at work during the late Roman Republic and early Roman Empire.

---

[48] Grantham 1999, esp. 222–5 and Erdkamp 2005: 7–11 both offer strong justifications for the use of early modern Europe as a comparative model for the Roman Empire.

[49] See nn. 25 and 26 above for the state of debate on this particular issue. Even Scheidel and Friesen 2009: 64 acknowledge the possibility that Italy and the Aegean may have approached the same level of development as early modern Europe, even if the rest of the Roman Empire did not.

Structural outline

I have divided the book into four main analytical chapters. Chapter 1, "Seasonality, uncertainty, and consumer demand in an ancient city," offers a basic sketch of the rhythms of economic life in Rome and other cities of the empire. I show that the demand for artisans' products and services in the cities of the Roman world, like the demand for comparable products and services in European cities of the seventeenth and eighteenth centuries, tended to be both seasonal and uncertain. Seasonal demand was, in the first instance, a product of patterns of seasonal travel and temporary migration, which ensured a higher concentration of consumers at all levels of the socioeconomic spectrum in most large cities at some times of the year than there was at others. At Rome, peak season began at the end of autumn or in the first days of winter and extended until the early summer. The seasonality of demand was accentuated further by seasonal fluctuations in the price of grain, which affected consumer spending power, and by the impact exerted by the weather on both the shipping season and on the building trades, both of which provided substantial employment for unskilled workers in particular. Uncertainty in segments of the market catering to the wealthy tended to be a product of the particularized consumption habits of aristocratic clients, who commissioned substantial amounts of goods on a bespoke basis, whereas in others it was a product of inter-annual harvest variability, which altered the purchasing power of consumers from one year to the next. I also stress that uncertainty in these latter segments was more severe in ancient Rome than in many early modern cities, both because most Romans were less well-off in real terms than their early modern counterparts and because their consumption habits did not necessarily encourage them to purchase manufactured goods on a regular and consistent basis.

Chapter 2, "Specialization, associations, and the organization of production," examines how seasonal and uncertain demand affected industrial organization in the ancient world. Thanks to the nature of the markets in which they sold their goods and services, artisans were reluctant to incur the fixed costs necessary to establish large and integrated firms. Instead, they organized production by collaborating with one another in complex subcontracting networks. They were able to adopt disintegrated production strategies largely because professional associations (*collegia*) supported the private-order enforcement of transactions, and therefore served as governance structures capable of mitigating transaction costs. From this perspective, *collegia* offered mixed prospects for growth in productivity: although their private-order enforcement functions helped foster increasingly intensive specialization in certain industries, their exclusive natures meant that these benefits were not available to all actors in the urban economy.

In Chapter 3, "Manumission and the urban labor market," I explore the apparent tendency on the part of Roman artisans to manumit skilled slaves with some regularity. I show that artisans manumitted skilled slaves in exchange for labor services (*operae libertorum*) in order to reconcile two specific and mutually contradictory goals: (1) to minimize their regular and fixed outlays on labor as much as possible; (2) to ensure access to the skilled help they needed if they were to take advantage of periods of elevated demand by temporarily expanding their output. Their use of manumission in pursuit of these goals reflects, among other things, a market in skilled labor that remained tight relative to comparable markets in the early modern period and which generated high transaction costs for artisans who sought to control labor costs by hiring workers on short-term contracts as necessary. That tight market was partly caused by the absence of organizations capable of circulating skilled labor on a regional level; in turn, it also exacerbated the opportunity costs of apprenticeship (already high relative to household income), made parents and guardians less likely to invest in apprenticeships for their sons, reinforced the comparative weakness of markets in skilled labor, and ultimately limited the possibilities for specialization and thick market externalities to provoke sustained growth in productivity.

Finally, the artisan family is the subject of Chapter 4, "The artisan household and the Roman economy." Here, I suggest that the artisan household was in some sense a flexible and adaptive structure. In particular, artisan fathers typically sought to establish sons in careers of their own rather than to employ them personally, primarily as a response to the nature of urban product markets. Because fathers could not always offer their sons regular employment, they sought to enhance their sons' productivity by finding careers for them outside the household, especially if they did not control business assets of substantial value to pass down to their sons as heirs. Conversely, the adaptability of artisan households was limited by consumption goals that were closely connected to ideologies of gender, and which stressed the value of work performed by women within, and in order to meet, the needs of the household. These consumption goals ultimately ensured that women in the Roman world allocated less time to income-generating work than did those in early modern Europe and that opportunities for the kind of intensive growth explored by de Vries in the context of the long eighteenth century were unlikely to develop in antiquity.

CHAPTER I

Seasonality, uncertainty, and consumer demand in an ancient city

Late in the second century CE, Artemidorus of Daldis composed a handbook on the interpretation of dreams in the hope of establishing both a theoretical framework for his craft and a body of empirical data capable of guiding the interpretations of others. To that end, if we can believe his claims, he not only read widely in related topics but also conducted firsthand research, interviewing diviners personally and analyzing dreams for clients in urban marketplaces in Asia Minor, Greece, and Italy.[1] More importantly, Artemidorus believed strongly that professional diviners could make sense of a client's dream only by taking into account the dreamer's personal qualities – things like gender, age, status, and even occupation.[2] For that very reason, he was careful to distinguish between the various meanings any given dream could hold for clients of different backgrounds. As a result, his handbook therefore reflected the concerns and anxieties of men and women who not only lived in the cities of some of the most important regions of the Roman Empire (including at least one truly metropolitan city, Ephesus) but also spanned the social spectrum, from slaves to the municipal elite.[3]

Artisans and craftsmen featured prominently enough among Artemidorus' clients that he produced interpretations tailored specifically to members of this particular social group. On the basis of these interpretations, we can reconstruct some sense of the questions that artisans posed when they visited professionals like Artemidorus – questions that are not necessarily reflected in surviving texts authored by artisans themselves, which largely take the form of graffiti, inscriptions, and the occasional written contract. Unsurprisingly, many of Artemidorus' interpretations

---

[1] Artem. 1.pr.

[2] On the importance of occupation, see Artem. 1.9. For a good example of this analytic in practice, see Artem. 1.17. For discussion, see Harris-McCoy 2012: 15–18.

[3] See Artem. 3.66, where he explains that although he normally writes as Artemidorus of Ephesus, in this particular case he chose to honor his mother's home by styling himself Artemidorus of Daldis.

suggest that artisans sought meaning in their dreams out of anxiety about their general prospects for long-term career success. Sometimes these dreams could signal impending ruin, as Artemidorus noted in the case of the unfortunate carpenter from Cyzicus.[4] Other dreams portended a brighter future, and Artemidorus records that artisans who dreamt that they possessed strong and muscular forearms could anticipate success in their trades, as could those who dreamt of having sexual intercourse with their mothers. While the import of the first dream was probably self-evident, Artemidorus tells us that the second was propitious because artisans often spoke metaphorically of their crafts as their "mothers," and hence intercourse with their biological mothers in their dreams symbolically denoted ongoing engagement with their businesses in the future.[5]

More interesting are those interpretations in which Artemidorus evokes artisans' anxieties about their economic fortunes in the immediate future and over the short term. These interpretations, scattered throughout the body of the text, imply not only that artisans worried constantly about whether or not they would receive any business at all from clients but also that the volume of such business could seem frighteningly erratic and unpredictable. On a very basic level, Artemidorus' interpretations reflect artisans' concerns over the availability of work simply by signifying periods of activity or unemployment. Thus, it was propitious for an artisan to dream that he had more than two ears, since this dream indicated that he would receive orders from many clients. Conversely, it was bad for an artisan to dream of fishing: since one could not fish and work at the same time, this dream clearly foretold an upcoming period of idleness.[6]

At the same time, however, Artemidorus' work alludes to the essential unpredictability of the markets in which artisans sold their products and services. The fact that artisans consulted interpreters like Artemidorus is an indirect reflection of that unpredictability, inasmuch as it signaled artisans' desire to eliminate uncertainty about the future. More pointedly, several of Artemidorus' interpretations engage more or less directly with that unpredictability. It seems significant, for example, that Artemidorus could rarely predict how long a period of unemployment would last. The primary exception is found in his discussion of what an artisan could expect in

---

[4] See Introduction, n. 3.   [5] Artem. 1.42, 1.79.
[6] For dreams about unemployment, see, e.g., Artem. 1.13; 1.54; 2.3. (The dream about fishing can be found at 2.14.) Cf. Pleket 1987, as well as Aubert 2001: 107 and n. 35. For dreams about good prospects for employment, see, e.g., 1.24 (where an artisan dreams of having more than two ears) and 1.42. Finally, for dreams about the viability of one's occupation more generally, see, e.g., 1.70.

his immediate future if he were to dream that he was an *ephebe* – a young man on the cusp of manhood. While this dream could be auspicious for some clients, for artisans it was particularly foreboding: it portended a full year of unemployment.[7] In all other cases, however, Artemidorus' interpretations predict changes of a more erratic nature in the volume of work an artisan could anticipate. Thus, when artisans dreamt that they were dressed in white clothing, this too signified an upcoming dearth of work, but the costlier the clothing the artisan wore in his dream, the more serious that period of unemployment was likely to be.[8] By the same token, dreams that were auspicious for an artisan often predicted sudden (and perhaps ultimately ephemeral) improvements in job prospects. I have already noted Artemidorus' interpretation of a case in which an artisan dreamt that he had more than two ears, which implied an unexpected windfall in business. To that, we might add his interpretation of a case in which an artisan dreamt that he had more than two hands. This dream signified that the dreamer would soon have a great deal of work to do – more, in fact, than he could manage on his own.[9]

The world evoked by Artemidorus' interpretations – in which urban craftsmen and artisans worried constantly about their ongoing prospects for work – invites comparison with Francis Place's comments about the nature of London's economy in the late eighteenth and early nineteenth centuries. Place, a London tailor, had to contend with the kind of volatility hinted at in Artemidorus' predictions about artisans' prospects for employment. When he wrote his autobiography in the 1820s, Place did so as a man of leisure who had retired after enjoying an astonishing amount of success in his tailoring business. That success, however, had been anything but inevitable, and he remembered periods in which he had worried about the stability of the nascent business he ran from the small apartment that doubled as workplace and residence: "my employment was very irregular sometimes sinking down to almost nothing – at other times all I had was wanted at the same time." Not only did this volatility make it difficult for Place to exploit fully those opportunities that came his way – he frequently lacked ready cash with which to hire temporary help in order to alleviate his workload – the irregularity of his business also interfered with his ability to pay his bills, since his revenue stream was uncertain.[10]

The parallels between Place's reminiscences and the anxieties detectable in Artemidorus' dream interpretations suggest that further comparison between the economic conditions in the Roman world and those in the

---

[7] Artem. 1.54.   [8] Artem. 2.3.   [9] Artem. 1.24, 1.42.   [10] Place 1972: 173–4.

cities of early modern Europe may establish a context for the concerns expressed in Artemidorus' handbook. In what follows, I explore this possibility by using recent studies of urban economies in the early modern period in order to structure an analysis of the urban economies of the Roman world. In the first section of this chapter, I lay out a basic model of consumer demand in early modern cities. As we shall see, product markets in the cities of northwestern Europe were generally anything but stable well into the nineteenth century, even if conditions had started to change somewhat for the better in segments catering to working- and middle-class consumers in the early 1700s. Instead, consumer demand for many goods and services varied considerably over the course of a given year. Not only was that demand highly seasonal in character, it was also frequently subject to uncertainty even during peak moments of its seasonal cycle. As a result, many urban producers were forced to respond to problems much like those that plagued Francis Place. I then adopt this model as a heuristic device for examining the rhythms of economic life in the cities of the Roman Empire. In the second section of the chapter, I show that demand was no less seasonal in most ancient cities than in the early modern context. In the third section, I shift my focus to uncertainty. Here, I suggest that in antiquity urban demand for artisans' products and services was likely more susceptible to uncertainty than in seventeenth- and eighteenth-century Europe, for two main reasons: (1) many urban residents in the Roman world enjoyed less purchasing power than did even unskilled workers in cities like London and Amsterdam; (2) those city dwellers who did enjoy some prosperity did not necessarily develop consumption habits that would have encouraged them to purchase manufactured goods on a regular and consistent basis. In the cities of the Roman world, seasonality and uncertainty therefore combined to ensure that consumer demand in urban economies seemed very unpredictable indeed to artisans who turned to professionals like Artemidorus to find meaning in their dreams.

Consumer demand in early modern cities: an overview

In this section, I survey recent research on the urban economies of early modern Europe and identify structural features of those economies that can guide our analysis of demand in the cities of the Roman world. Two structural features stand out and, as we shall see in later sections, generate powerful new insights into our understanding of ancient urban economies. First, seasonality profoundly influenced the rhythms of demand in the cities of the early modern world well into the nineteenth century, both by constraining the purchasing power of individuals or the intensity with which producers and distributors could carry out certain activities over the course of the year, and by generating distinctly seasonal rhythms of travel and migration to and from cities. Second, that demand was also subject to a high degree of uncertainty, both because members of certain social groups engaged in highly particularistic forms of consumption, and because others were vulnerable to fluctuations in food prices that limited their purchasing power. Together, these aspects of the economic environment affected demand in multiple segments of the urban economy. Most notably, they posed as many challenges for artisans and craftsmen who manufactured goods for the emerging middle- and working-class markets as they did for those who catered to the wealthy.

Seasonality imposed a distinct shape on demand in most sectors of the early modern economy, including manufacture. Simply put, seasonal fluctuations – whether climatic or social – could produce considerable peaks and troughs in consumer demand over the course of any given year, and even though they were to some degree predictable, they were not entirely regular. Climatic seasonality made its impact felt in three main ways. First, the seasons naturally dictated the growth cycles of staple food crops, many of which exhibited seasonal changes in prices. Grain crops, for instance, were generally at their most affordable immediately after the harvest, but grew more expensive over the winter, spring, and early summer as stores were gradually exhausted. The severity of those price changes depended, among other things, on the level of integration of local markets: in London they were lower than elsewhere because of the capital city's primacy in Great Britain's urban system, but in other cities they remained more pronounced. Notable swings in grain prices were naturally more serious for the less affluent than for the wealthy, and rises in the price of grain and bread cut into the purchasing power of both working-class consumers and some of the "middling" types during the lean months leading up to the next harvest.[11]

Second, climatic seasonality limited the ability of craftsmen who practiced their trades outdoors to work during certain months of the year. Winter was a lean time for builders and shipwrights in early modern Europe, since cold weather could dramatically slow or even halt

---

[11] Persson 1999: 65–72 discusses seasonal oscillations in grain prices in early modern Europe; Chartres 1985: 457, on the other hand, argues that fluctuations of this nature are difficult to detect in the case of England during the late seventeenth century.

their activities.[12] Seasonal changes in the weather also affected trades that
depended on agricultural produce for their raw materials – not only the
food processing industries, in which the harvest was a critical event in the
annual calendar, but also the textile industries, which relied on seasonal
supplies of wool, cotton, and flax.[13]

Third, shipping schedules remained closely tied to the seasons until well
into the nineteenth century, when the advent of steamships freed ocean-
going vessels from the distinctly seasonal sailing patterns imposed by wind
and tide. Patterns of this sort are particularly well attested in seventeenth-
and eighteenth-century London. The Port, though quiet from November
through February, experienced two noticeable peaks in inbound shipping:
one in the spring, when ships arrived from the Americas, and the other in
early autumn, when shipping from the West Indies complemented
American and European traffic.[14] Not only did this sailing schedule
generate cycles of employment and unemployment along the docks for
the stevedores and longshoremen who unloaded ships' cargoes, it also
affected demand for artisans and manufacturers who sold products to
seaborne merchants. It also probably affected local market conditions in
other ways that are difficult to trace, by altering the supply of raw materials
or imported luxury goods that competed with the products of local
artisans.[15]

Social patterns of seasonality also shaped the rhythms of demand in early
modern cities. At the most basic level, the uneven distribution of
important liturgical and secular holidays throughout the calendar year
generated distinct patterns in consumption habits, particularly among
wealthy consumers. The Christmas gift-buying season in early modern
London generated not only a clear and seasonal peak in business
in December for many craftsmen but also an equally clear trough in
demand in January.[16] Just as frequently, holidays in most European cities
served as contexts for conspicuous consumption and display among
members of wealthier social groups, and therefore generated considerable
demand for the goods and services of numerous artisans who made or
repaired clothing and important accessories. By treating records detailing
the number of journeymen employed in any given month as proxy data for
prevailing levels of demand, Michael Sonenscher demonstrated some years
ago that the holiday calendar created pronounced peaks in demand for

---

[12] Sonenscher 1989: 138 and 203–4; Schwarz 1992: 109. Cf. Sonenscher 1989: 24 on seasonality in the
French glazing trade.
[13] Schwarz 1992: 103.   [14] Schwarz 1992: 107–8.   [15] Stedman Jones 1984: 36–7.
[16] Schwarz 1992: 106–7.

both wigmakers and tailors in eighteenth-century Rouen. For tailors, those peaks occurred just before the Easter season and the Feast of All Saints. Seasonal peaks in demand were even more pronounced for wigmakers, who were very busy indeed at three particular times of the year: between the beginning of the New Year and Lent, between Easter and Pentecost, and between the Feast of All Saints and Christmas.[17]

Patterns of travel and temporary migration generated social seasonality of a more pervasive kind because they could alter the size and composition of a city's overall consumer base in ways that affected demand for the products and services of a wide range of urban manufacturers at certain times of the year. London serves as a particularly good and well-documented example of an early modern city in which this kind of social seasonality was strongly pronounced, particularly among wealthier clients. By the seventeenth century at the latest, Londoners referred to the months between late autumn and early summer as "the Season." Because the Court was in residence in the capital and Parliament was in session at this time of year, London exercised a magnetic attraction on members of the English aristocracy and gentry: elected politicians came to London to discharge their duties; aristocrats to make their appearances at court; the gentry to mingle with high society. Many of these part-time residents and visitors not only maintained townhouses in the city but also arrived with sizeable retinues in tow. All were keen to purchase manufactured goods of high quality in London, and members of their retinues generated some demand for goods and services in their own right. The Season affected even the consumption patterns of the wealthier full-time residents of the capital, whose social calendars became busier at this time of year and who consequently felt increased pressure to engage in conspicuous consumption.

If the onset and height of the Season produced a regular and predictable surge in the demand for goods and services within London, then its dissipation in high summer and early autumn produced an equally predictable slump in business. The fashionable districts of the city emptied out as the Court relocated to its summer residence, Parliament went into recess, and members of high society and wealthy Londoners alike left the heat of the city for more pleasant summer retreats. Demand for manufactured goods and services in the capital fell off dramatically, and

---

[17] Sonenscher 1989: 159, 162–3.

many craftsmen found themselves un- or underemployed until the Season began anew.[18]

Within these seasonal rhythms – which were broadly predictable – the demand for the products and services of many artisans in early modern cities was also subject to considerable uncertainty. For those who catered to a wealthy clientele, that uncertainty was produced by the particularistic consumption habits of customers who sought to make claims about their own status, taste, and refinement. While clients at this level of the social spectrum purchased some ready-made goods off the shelf, they were more likely to commission pieces tailored at least in part to their individual specifications. Since the artisans who catered to their needs therefore worked primarily on a bespoke or made-to-order basis, trade in this level of the market was dominated by short-term fluctuations in demand that remained erratic and unpredictable even within broader seasonal peaks in overall consumption. In these circumstances artisans could easily experience long periods of little or no activity, punctuated by periods in which they were overwhelmed by a sudden windfall of orders. Francis Place's complaint about the irregularity of his employment fits clearly into this particular context, but he was far from alone. Adam Smith noted that masons and bricklayers in particular were heavily dependent "upon the occasional calls of [their] customers" and often found themselves out of work because of the unpredictable and episodic character of their employment, and although he did not elaborate on circumstances in other lines of work, he did suggest that many other craftsmen experienced this same uncertainty (if perhaps not to quite the same degree).[19] Among these we should include most artisans who worked in the upmarket segments of the urban luxury trades – painters, sculptors, goldsmiths, jewelers, coach makers, and fine tailors.[20]

From the middle of the seventeenth century onward, markets for artisans began to expand in important ways thanks to new consumption patterns among the "middling" populations of Europe – merchants, shopkeepers, artisans, and other professionals who catered to the needs of the wealthy – and even, to some extent, among the working classes. Large sectors of the clothing, footwear, and food processing trades were affected

---

[18] Schwarz 1992: 104–7; Green 1995: 34–6. On p. 35, Green includes a graph of one nineteenth-century tailor's monthly accounts, which shows that his earnings could be more than twice as high in May as they were in August. Stedman Jones 1984: 34–5 argues that the Season remained clearly defined throughout much of the nineteenth century.

[19] Smith 1994: 119 (Bk. I, Ch. X, Pt. I).

[20] Earle 1989b: 114–15; Sonenscher 1989: 137–8; Schwarz 1992: 118.

early on by this process. For example, by the mid-eighteenth century the furniture trades in London were experiencing growing demand from the upper middle classes.[21] Historians continue to debate the precise causes of this development, but at least three mutually reinforcing processes appear to have been at work. First, changing ideas of luxury and comfort among the middle classes increased demand for a range of relatively inexpensive and replaceable manufactured goods that served less as stores of value than as goods to be enjoyed in their own right. Second, changes in market structure and household organization released previously underemployed labor into the market (particularly the labor of women and children), while simultaneously driving the substitution of goods purchased on the market for goods produced in the home. Third, changes in the organization and technology of production generated incremental decreases in the real costs of durable manufactured goods.[22]

Because these new patterns of consumption increased demand for goods that were simultaneously less expensive and more standardized than those produced for the upmarket trade, they made possible the development of markets that were less subject to uncertainty than those dominated by wealthy clients who purchased made-to-order items. That said, it took some time for markets of this nature to mature, and most historians conclude that true mass markets, in which manufactured goods were purchased by a wide cross-section of the population on a regular basis, were a product of the nineteenth century.[23] Until then, the markets catering to middle- and working-class customers not only failed to outstrip dramatically those catering to the wealthy in terms of size but they also remained subject to important uncertainties of their own. Not only was much of the income of the artisanal and working class still seasonal, inter-annual variability in crop yields in the seventeenth and eighteenth century generated considerable variation in food prices from year to year, and made the purchasing power of members of these social groups unstable.[24]

For most manufacturers in early modern cities, demand was therefore quite variable over the course of any given year, both in segments of the market catering to elite clients and in segments catering the growing number of middle- and working-class consumers. Artisans contended not only with seasonal fluctuations in demand – whether produced by the

[21] Earle 1989b: 21–2; Kirkham 1988; Schwarz 1992: 186–207.
[22] See, e.g., Weatherill 1988; Earle 1989b: 269–301; Fairchilds 1993; de Vries 1993, 1994, and 2008, esp. 71–2; Farr 2000: 62–70.
[23] For a general overview, see Farr 2000: 62–81.
[24] On seasonal variations in crop prices, see above, n. 11.

weather's impact on transportation and production, or by forms of social seasonality capable of changing consumption patterns in dramatic ways – but also with uncertainty arising from the aggregate behavior or purchasing power of the urban population. As we shall see in the following two sections, these observations offer a valuable heuristic device for exploring the economic conditions that were likely typical of cities in the Roman world, in which factors comparable to those responsible for seasonal and uncertain demand in the early modern period were almost certainly at work.

Seasonality and demand in Roman cities

Ancient historians are increasingly sensitive to the fact that seasonality affected not only the political, military, and religious calendars of Rome and other ancient cities but also urban economic life.[25] Yet, at the same time, we are only just beginning to understand how pervasive its impact could be. In a world that remained fundamentally agrarian in character, and in which medium- to long-distance trade depended heavily on oar- or sail-powered ships, the seasonal rhythms of both the weather and the agricultural calendar dramatically molded urban life.

In what follows, I consider how climatic and social aspects of seasonality structured the demand for the products and services of artisans and other skilled workers in the cities of the Roman world. As we shall see, cities in the ancient Mediterranean were no less susceptible than those in early modern Europe to distinctly seasonal changes in prevailing levels of urban demand. Evidence that this was the case in Rome itself is particularly suggestive, but our sources also imply that conditions were broadly comparable elsewhere in the empire. Although the individual factors responsible for creating seasonal rhythms in urban demand did not affect all sectors of the economy equally, few artisans were immune to such rhythms, whether they catered to a wealthy clientele or to consumers from low and middling income groups.

The model I outlined in the previous section suggests that factors of two kinds could generate patterns of seasonal change in demand for artisans' goods and services in Roman cities: first, climate and its impact on production and transportation; second, seasonal changes in social behavior that altered overall patterns of consumption, sometimes on a dramatic

---

[25] For the impact of seasonality on urban economic life, see Brunt 1980; Aldrete and Mattingly 1999; and Erdkamp 2008.

scale. Of the climatic factors in play, the growth cycle of cereal crops – especially wheat – was potentially the most significant. Although cereals ripened and were harvested only once per year in much of the Mediterranean, they formed the basis of most ancient diets. Demand for these crops was thus inelastic, and remained high over the full growing season. While the supply of grain tended to be abundant immediately after the summer harvest, by the following spring it was often in relatively short supply. Not surprisingly, the price of grain therefore exhibited a strongly seasonal pattern of its own, and prices could easily double over the course of the year.[26] Inhabitants of Rome itself may have enjoyed some protection from seasonal changes in prices from the Augustan period onward as the imperial government made greater efforts to provide a stable food supply, but as we shall see in more detail later, prices remained volatile even in the capital. In practical terms, this meant that the ability of consumers from low and middling income groups to purchase goods and services other than foodstuffs did not remain constant throughout the year but rather decreased more or less in proportion to the seasonal rise in grain prices[27] – and that the artisans who catered to them faced a correspondingly constricted product market in the spring.

Seasonal changes in the climate likewise could alter the rhythm of numerous trades and industries by imposing limitations on maritime shipping. The weather created a clear and pronounced shipping season across much of the Mediterranean, which extended from late May until mid-September, with shoulder seasons on either side from mid-March to mid-November. Shipping did not halt over the winter, but the volume of maritime traffic in the Mediterranean declined notably during the off-season. While some regions of the Mediterranean were more affected by the weather than others – the route from Egypt to Rhodes, for instance, seems to have been practical all year round – winter conditions typically created distinct hazards for shipping. Rain and offshore fog frequently combined to create poor visibility along the coasts, making navigation difficult and increasing the odds of shipwreck. Storms at sea also endangered square-rigged ships at this time of year. The story of Paul's journey from Myra to Rome aboard

---

[26] For more discussion, see Erdkamp 2005: 147–55. The key pieces of ancient literary evidence for the Roman period are Cic. *Verr.* 2.3.214–15 and Julian *Mis.* 369b. Also relevant in this context are several data points from the Classical and Hellenistic Greek world and from Roman Egypt, although the value of some of these data points is contested. For details, see Erdkamp 2005: 149 n. 18.

[27] Erdkamp 2005: 148. Cf. Schwarz 1992: 106 on the way in which bread prices affected purchasing power in early modern London.

a grain freighter late in the year illustrates some of the perils: an unexpected northeast gale took hold of the vessel somewhere off south-western Crete and forced its crew to run helplessly before the wind; they passed cables around the exterior of the hull to prevent its seams from rupturing, they jettisoned most of the cargo and much of the tackle, and after fourteen days at sea they were finally able to run the ship aground on Malta. Our legal sources show that investors were less willing to offer maritime loans to shippers in the winter because of these well-known dangers, and demanded higher rates of interest when they did.[28]

The economic impact of reduced maritime traffic would have been felt most keenly by the laborers who unloaded ships in harbors and moved goods from wharves into nearby warehouses. At Rome, it also affected the employment prospects of the bargemen, animal handlers, and porters who moved goods to Rome from its two harbor towns, Ostia and Puteoli, whether overland or along the Tiber River.[29] But reduced shipping in the off-season likewise would have constricted demand for the services of artisans and craftsmen in ways that are not necessarily immediately obvious. Craftsmen who worked in shipbuilding and its ancillary trades presumably noted seasonal fluctuations correlated to the sailing season. So too did those who made a living by working on goods imported by sea. The industrial-scale fulleries in Rome and Ostia, for instance, may have existed primarily to soap and rinse either cloth or worked clothing from overseas before it entered the local market,[30] and the reduced volume of shipping in the winter meant that these establishments had far less business in the winter months than during the peak of the sailing season.

Early modern evidence shows that seasonal changes in the weather could also greatly reduce the volume of work at certain times of the year in trades practiced outdoors. In the cities of the ancient world, seasonal changes in the weather most demonstrably affected the building trades. Mediterranean winters were naturally not as harsh as those in northern Europe, but cold and wet weather did slow building activities for a few months every year (particularly in districts further north). The Roman penchant for working in concrete and mortared brick exacerbated that pattern. While discussing the work conducted on Rome's aqueducts throughout the course of the year, Frontinus argued in the first century

---

[28] For the practicability of the Rhodes-Egypt route even in the winter, see Dem. 56.29–30. The story of Paul's voyage can be found in *Acts* 27.13–42. On the sailing season in antiquity, see Casson 1974: 150; Sirks 2002: 147; Morley 2007: 28–9. Sirks 2002 explores the impact of seasonality on investors' willingness to finance maritime loans.

[29] Aldrete and Mattingly 1999: 192–204.   [30] Flohr 2011: 92–3.

CE that Roman mortar and concrete did not set well when subjected to frost or extreme temperatures. For that reason, he recommended that building activities on the aqueducts be conducted between the beginning of April and the beginning of November, with a short hiatus during the hottest part of the summer.[31] Because mortar and concrete had been in widespread use in Italy since the second century BCE at the latest, building in general was a highly seasonal occupation throughout the late Republic and early Empire.[32] The same was likely true of brick manufacture, an important subsidiary to the building trade (though much of this was conducted in rural contexts): in later historical periods, wet weather halted production in brickyards.[33]

No less important than the impact of seasonal climatic changes were patterns of social seasonality, which likewise demonstrably changed levels of consumer demand in the Roman world. In the first place, most cities in the ancient world celebrated dozens of important religious festivals every year, if not more. In the same way that major holidays in the early modern period triggered specific kinds of consumption – whether by encouraging people to purchase new wigs or clothes or to have their old items serviced – festivals in antiquity could also temporarily accelerate certain kinds of consumer behavior and generate localized peaks in demand for artisans in specific trades. Participants in religious festivals were often expected to wear distinct or celebratory clothing, whether togas in Rome or various different kinds of festival outfits in the Greek-speaking parts of the empire. Marc Kleijwegt has suggested that although some sanctuaries in the Greek-speaking parts of the empire had their own workshops to capitalize on the demand for holiday clothing, much of that demand was presumably met by private enterprise.[34] Artisans capable of manufacturing this kind of clothing undoubtedly saw notable increases in their business in the lead-up to major festivals, as did artisans like fullers, dyers, and menders, all of whom provided important services to people who already owned the appropriate garments.

Our sources occasionally offer insight into specific holidays that generated sharp spikes in the demand for various goods and services at Rome itself. On March 17, the Romans celebrated the Liberalia. Older women made and sacrificed honey-cakes to the god Liber on behalf of anyone who was willing to pay for the service, and one suspects that their trade must

---

[31] Frontin. *Aq.* 2.123.
[32] On concrete and mortar in Roman building, see Anderson 1997: 145–51. The seasonal character of the Roman building trades is widely recognized: see, e.g., Brunt 1980: 93; S. D. Martin 1989: 73.
[33] Campbell 1747: 169.   [34] Kleijwegt 2002.

have been rather brisk. Moreover, because they wore ivy wreaths, they generated business for the *coronarii*, the artisans who specialized in preparing wreaths and garlands made of flowers and other materials.[35] Finally, Cicero and Ovid both note that on the Liberalia it was customary for Roman youths to celebrate their transition from boyhood to manhood. Because they did so by assuming the *toga virilis*, the traditional garment of the Roman citizen,[36] early March was busy for craftsmen involved in producing and cleaning clothing.

In late December the Saturnalia and the Sigillaria provoked a notable surge in consumer demand by encouraging gift exchange between friends, family members, and individuals who were bound together by patronage.[37] When and how the Sigillaria emerged as a festival in its own right remains obscure: in the late Republic, the Saturnalia ran from December 17 to 19, but by the first century CE five or possibly even seven days were devoted to the festival, the final two of which were perhaps the Sigillaria proper.[38] The giving of gifts was nonetheless an integral component of both festivals. Some gifts that were exchanged were traditional items that "symbolised relations of trust and solidarity and had little if any commercial value":[39] clients gave candles to their patrons, and children often received the small figurines (*sigilla*) from which the Sigillaria derived its name.[40] Yet because gift-giving and gift exchange were mechanisms for either conspicuously displaying one's own status (*dignitas*) and generosity (*liberalitas*), or discharging obligations imposed by patronage relationships,[41] some of the gifts exchanged during the Saturnalia were quite valuable. Thus, although most of the *sigilla* that changed hands were made of clay, some may have been made of more precious materials such as ivory, silver, or gold.[42] Moreover, in the fourteenth book of his *Epigrammata*, Martial catalogs many other gifts given during these celebrations, ranging from small amounts of food given to slaves by their masters, to precious manufactured

---

[35] On the role of women at the Liberalia, see Varro *Ling.* 6.14 and Ov. *Fast.* 3.761–70. Pliny the Elder mentions *coronarii* at *HN*. 21.68, and several are attested in the inscriptions at Rome: see von Petrikovits 1981: 93 for references. I thank Fanny Dolansky for bringing these sources to my attention.

[36] Cic. *Att.* 6.1.12; Ov. *Fast.* 3.771–90.

[37] By the fourth century CE, the festival of the January Kalends seems to have displaced the Saturnalia and Sigillaria as the main occasion for gift-exchange in the Roman world. This delayed the bulk of the gift-giving a few days, but probably did not alter the basic pattern of gift exchange. See Libanius *Or.* 9.8; Asterius of Amasea 4.3.1, 4.4.1–3, and 4.6.1.

[38] Leary 1996: 3–7.   [39] Verboven 2002: 78–9. Cf. Leary 1996: 5–6.

[40] See Varro *Ling.* 5.64 on the tradition of giving candles to patrons. Sen. *Ep.* 12.3 describes *sigilla* as gifts appropriate for children.

[41] Verboven 2002: 71–115; cf. Harrison 2001: 306–7.   [42] Leary 1996: 5–6.

objects like furniture or gold and silver plate awarded by the wealthy to their favorite clients. Ovid and Juvenal likewise suggest that Saturnalia gifts could be quite costly, and show that while some wealthy Romans gave away goods of their own for which they no longer had any use, others instead purchased high-end merchandise specifically as gifts.[43] If we can take the *scholia* on Juvenal at face value, a temporary market was set up in Rome to cater to the elevated demand for gifts at this time of year.[44] Although some of the items that were purchased as gifts were clearly antiques that were traded in the second-hand market, many artisans too would have experienced dramatic increases in the volume of their business as the December holidays drew near and clients either purchased new goods or hired the services of artisans to repair older items in preparation for giving them away.[45]

Our sources also suggest that artisans catering to high-end and low-end segments of the market alike faced shifts in demand arising from seasonal patterns of travel and temporary migration, which produced regular oscillations in the size and composition of urban populations. The evidence is best for Rome itself: several brief remarks in our literary sources imply that the resident and transient populations of the capital peaked in the early months of the year and dwindled in the summer and autumn. Pliny the Younger, for instance, remarks that January was a month in which Rome was normally crowded not just by senators (many of whom were undoubtedly present to attend the annual elections of the city's magistrates) but also by throngs of other people.[46] By contrast, our sources indicate that Rome's streets and public places were comparatively empty in the summer and autumn. In a letter to his friend Arrian, Pliny noted that legal business was especially slow in July; in part, this was surely due to the many holidays that prevented courts from convening in this particular month, but the context in which Pliny makes his comments nevertheless suggests that even on days when the courts were open, advocates were less likely to be called to service than at other times of the year.[47] That impression is only reinforced by Seneca the Younger, who had lampooned the deified emperor Claudius half a century earlier as a man so enamored

---

[43] For wealthy Romans giving goods of their own as gifts, see Luc. *Sat.* 14–15. For the purchase of gifts during the Saturnalia (many of which were perhaps antiques) see Ov. *Ars.* 1.400–36, along with the comments of Hollis 1977: 106–7, and Juv. 6.153–60.

[44] *Schol. in. Iuv.*, 6.154.   [45] For the market in antiques, see Mart. 9.59.

[46] Plin. *Ep.* 2.11.10, with the comments of Talbert 1984: 144–5.

[47] Plin. *Ep.* 8.21.2. For the holidays in July, see Scullard 1981: 158–69, with the caveat that this work deals with a somewhat earlier period.

with court proceedings that he frequently sat in judgment in front of the temple of Hercules for entire days in July and August; his remark would have had little bite unless legal business was, under normal conditions, not particularly heavy during these months.[48] Finally, Suetonius informs us that the emperor Augustus mandated two official recesses during late summer and autumn months. The Senate took its annual recess in September and October, when only a small quorum of senators chosen by lot was required to remain in the city to deal with any pressing business;[49] the rest were free not to attend the regular senate meetings, and presumably many of them left town, retreating to estates in the Roman *suburbium* or in nearby regions of Italy.[50] Likewise, Augustus arranged for the courts to close for November and December of each year.[51]

The lack of coincidence between the senatorial and judicial recesses is at first glance puzzling, but the late date for the official judicial recess merely formalized a marked slowdown of judicial business that began in September. At the beginning of every year from the Augustan period onward, new jurors (*selecti*) were drawn from the *album iudicum* in which the names of candidates eligible to serve as members of the standing criminal courts or as judges in private suits were recorded. Because judicial business needed to be concluded before the new jurors assumed their duties, a judicial recess in September and October would have made no sense; it was more efficient to deal with outstanding legal business introduced in the summer as soon as possible and to move the official recess to the end of the year, particularly since increasingly large numbers of the *selecti* in the first century CE were drawn from Italy and from the western provinces and may have appreciated the opportunity to return home at the beginning of November rather than at the end of December.[52] The need to conclude judicial business before new jurors were empaneled had already motivated the creation of the *lex Acilia* in 123 BCE, stipulating that the praetor should not allow cases to go to trial after September 1 precisely so that outstanding cases could be discharged before the end of the year.[53] Assuming that this law was still in effect in the

[48] Sen. *Apocol.* 7.

[49] Suet. *Aug.* 35.3. For further discussion see Balsdon 1969: 79 and Talbert 1984: 211.

[50] D'Arms 1970, esp. 48–55, discusses the pleasure estates that the Roman aristocracy maintained on the Bay of Naples. Spring was a popular time for visiting this area, and some historians have accordingly suggested that there may have been a further recess of the Senate at this time of year.

[51] Suet. *Aug.* 32.3.

[52] On the selection of individuals from the *album iudicum* and on their geographic origins, see Bablitz 2007: 91–100.

[53] Balsdon 1969: 79–80. My argument in this paragraph relies heavily on his analysis of the judicial calendar.

early Empire, the tempo of legal business at Rome – already slow in the summer – decreased further in September in the first and second centuries CE (much as it had in Cicero's day) even though the official recess did not begin for two more months.[54]

Evidence for specific factors that prompted people to move in and out of Rome not only strengthens the case for seasonal ebbs and flows in the capital's population but also emphasizes that these ebbs and flows affected consumer demand for artisans catering to clients at all levels of the socio-economic spectrum. First, Rome was both a destination for and a source of seasonal migrant laborers, whose movements to and from the capital enlarged the city's population in the months leading up to the harvest and slowly depleted it later in the year. Artisans catering to low- and middle-income segments of the market therefore enjoyed a larger consumer market in the winter, spring, and late summer than they did during peak harvest periods in early summer and autumn, even if fluctuations in the demand generated by that market were partly mitigated by changes in the price of grain following the harvest itself.

The seasonal migration of laborers to Rome was driven primarily by the rhythms of agricultural work in the countryside. Although earlier generations of scholars believed that peasant cultivators had been largely displaced from many areas of Italy by increasingly large aristocratic estates, it now seems clear that small farms remained an important and vital element of the agricultural economy throughout our period.[55] More importantly, the proprietors or tenants of these farms faced challenges that were not only common to peasant agriculture in comparative contexts, but also capable of generating seasonal migration. The most pressing of those challenges arose from cultivators' efforts to balance the land and labor at their disposal. Generally, peasant cultivators in a wide range of historical contexts have often struggled to enlarge the amount of land at their disposal because of poor access to liquid capital. At the same time, many also found that the natural growth experienced by their families during certain phases of their households' life cycles left them with more labor than they could deploy productively on their own plots, particularly during slack points in the agricultural calendar, once the heavy work of the harvest, the vintage, and the sowing of the next crop ended. Apart from

---

[54] Cic. *Att.* 1.1.2, with the comments of Balsdon (see n. 53 above).

[55] Dyson 1992: 28–34 offers a good overview of what we know about land distribution in the late Republic and early Empire. While some areas were dominated by large estates, others continued to be home to many small farms. Cf. Launaro 2011, esp. 165–83. Generally speaking, both systems of land use probably coexisted with one another for much of our period.

eroding the overall labor productivity of a cultivator's household, this imbalance also strained its resources. In these circumstances, members of peasant families have often turned to seasonal migration, both to increase their productivity beyond what is possible on their own farms, and to provide extra insurance against the risk of a poor harvest by diversifying their income.[56]

While the number of rural Italians who may have migrated seasonally for comparable reasons every year in Roman Italy is uncertain, it was likely to have been large. Comparative evidence from other preindustrial contexts demonstrates that peasant cultivators' seasonal migration can be truly massive in scale. During the nineteenth century, for example, more than 100,000 people in Italy left farms in predominantly upland regions every year to seek seasonal work in the agricultural heartland of central Italy, in northern towns, or in Rome itself. Even if Italy was not as densely populated in antiquity as it was in the nineteenth century, we can nevertheless estimate that tens of thousands of rural Italians left their farms in search of additional work at certain times of the year, particularly during the slack period in the agricultural calendar.[57] Potential destinations for these workers included not only agricultural estates in nearby regions where the harvest happened somewhat earlier or later than in their home territories but also Rome itself and some other towns in Italy and in the nearby provinces. From time to time, such migrants surface in our sources. During the first century CE, agricultural workers crossed into Sabinum every year from Umbria to help with the harvest.[58] Much later, in the fifth century CE, Germanus of Auxerre encountered a party of workmen (probably builders) as he was crossing from Gaul into Italy. These workers were returning to their homes after temporarily migrating to work in Gaul; the timing of their journey, which took place before the feasts of Saints Gervasius and Protasius on June 19, suggests that they were peasants returning to their farms in time for the harvest after seeking paid work elsewhere during the spring.[59]

Cities like Rome were not only destinations for seasonal migrant laborers from the countryside; they were also home for workers who temporarily migrated from city to country to help with farm operations that demanded enormous quantities of labor in relatively short periods of time. Neville Morley has argued that most estates in the immediate vicinity

---

[56] Erdkamp 1999; Erdkamp 2005: 55–87; Erdkamp 2008: 424–33.
[57] For discussions of seasonal migration and its relationship to peasant cultivation in the early modern world, see Lucassen 1987, esp. 95–9, 116–19, and 235–60.
[58] Suet. *Vesp.* 1.4.   [59] Constantius, *Vita S. Germani* 31.

of Rome produced highly perishable commodities like fruit that needed to be transported to market as quickly as possible.[60] Inhabitants of the capital may have left town in some numbers at certain times of year to assist with the harvest of these commodities, much in the same way that inhabitants of early modern London left town to help gather hops in late August and early September on a truly astonishing scale.[61] Nor should we necessarily rule out the possibility that inhabitants of Rome ventured further afield to pick up work as farmhands during the grain harvest and the vintage, when wages in the countryside were especially high. Numbers are impossible to estimate with any accuracy – though it is worth noting that something like 35,000 Londoners left town every year in the nineteenth century to pick hops – but the fourth- and fifth-century Christian tombstones from Rome suggest that even residents of the capital who normally worked as skilled artisans and craftsmen frequently sought temporary harvest work. Because these tombstones record not only the precise date at which the individual commemorated died but also the duration of his or her marriage (often down to the month or even the day), we can reconstruct a seasonal profile of marriage patterns in Rome and, to a lesser extent, elsewhere in Italy. As Brent Shaw has demonstrated, a notable seasonal spike in the frequency of marriage occurs precisely in those months of the year with the lowest demand for agricultural labor. In the comparatively slack months of December and January, the number of attested marriages in the sample from Rome is almost four times higher than in June and July, both of which were busy agricultural months. Clearly, the pattern demonstrates an ongoing attachment on the part of residents of Rome to the rhythms of the agricultural calendar, and one explanation for that attachment is temporary migration into the countryside for seasonal work on the part of members of the urban populace.[62]

Second, wealthy consumers – whether they were residents of Rome or visitors – also moved in and out of the city in patterns that generated distinctly seasonal rhythms of demand from the perspective of artisans who catered to them, with a peak in the winter and spring, and a corresponding trough later in the year. Wealthy residents of the capital migrated temporarily because of the annual cycle of disease-related mortality in Rome and because of the demands of the agricultural calendar; both factors prompted them to leave the capital throughout the summer, and to return

---

[60] Morley 1996: 83–107.   [61] Stedman Jones 1984: 90–2.

[62] Shaw 1997: 69–75. Shaw does not suggest directly that the marriage pattern was a product of temporary seasonal migration, but he argues that it was a consequence of the economic demands of the agricultural labor cycle.

only late in the autumn. The annual cycle of disease and mortality is documented best in Christian tombstones of the fourth and fifth centuries CE. Because Christian commemorators in this period often engraved precise dates of death on tombstones, historians have been able to generate profiles of seasonal mortality for the city, which reveal a dramatic upswing in deaths between July and November, peaking in late August and early September. A number of diseases and parasites became increasingly dangerous during these months, when warm temperatures not only created ideal climatic conditions for their transmission but also made the unsanitary conditions of the city even more pronounced and noticeable than they were at other times of the year. Those pathogens include typhoid, tuberculosis, and malaria (particularly the more lethal form, falciparum malaria).[63] There is no reason to believe that these were any less dangerous (nor any less seasonal) in the late Republic and early Empire,[64] when Rome was already notoriously unhealthy at this time of year: our literary sources demonstrate that members of the landowning elite of the late Republic and early Empire were fully aware of the danger posed by increased morbidity in the city when falciparum malaria was at its peak, even if they did not understand its precise causes. Unsurprisingly, several writers betray a strong preference for leaving the capital at this time of year whenever possible. In this respect they differed little from wealthy inhabitants of Rome in the medieval and early modern periods, who left the city in droves in the summer to avoid disease.[65]

The demands of the agricultural calendar amplified seasonal migration away from Rome in the summer and autumn on the part of its wealthy inhabitants, many of whom derived the bulk of their income from landed estates elsewhere in Italy. Although most managed their estates indirectly through overseers, to whom they entrusted the day-to-day operations of their properties, at least some estate owners supervised critical operations on their properties in person. In his treatise on agriculture (composed during the first century CE), Columella exhorted his peers to devote as much of their own time to estate management as possible rather than to

---

[63] Scheidel 1994; Scheidel 1996b: 139–63; Shaw 1996; Scheidel 2003.

[64] According to Lamb 1995: 146–53, there was some climatic change between the early Empire and late antiquity: summers in Europe and in the Mediterranean appear to have become warmer and drier until roughly 400 CE. These changes may well have affected local patterns of morbidity. But Sallares 2002: 101–3 argues that climatic conditions in Italy during the Roman period were already more favorable for the spread of falciparum malaria than they were in the cooler early modern period, when the disease was nevertheless widespread. As a consequence, it is safe to assume that the seasonal impact of disease was severe even in the late Republic and early Empire.

[65] Sallares 2002: 205; Scheidel 2003: 166–7.

entrust too much to the judgment of their overseers, many of whom were slaves.[66] This is obviously a prescriptive declaration rather than a descriptive one, and undoubtedly only a few aristocrats spent as much time managing their properties in person as Columella advocated. Nevertheless, the correspondence of Pliny the Younger suggests that it was not unusual for wealthy landowners to supervise at least some tasks themselves. Although Pliny left many aspects of estate management in the hands of his subordinates, he nevertheless intervened in the operations of his property personally when prompt attention was crucial for ensuring that critical agricultural tasks were carried out at the appropriate time of year. In one letter Pliny seeks permission from Trajan to leave Rome to rent out some of his property in person so that he would have new tenants in time to prune the vines.[67] In another, he describes how he responded to a poorer-than-anticipated grape harvest by meeting with dealers who had purchased the right to collect it well in advance of its maturation: he met with them on his estate to offer them rebates as compensation for their losses.[68]

As Pliny's letters demonstrate, the vintage was arguably the most crucial moment of the agricultural calendar for wealthy Roman estate owners, many of whom generated the bulk of their income from sales of grapes or wine.[69] As such, many may have been present on their estates at this particular time. The vintage took place in October in most of Italy, along with the sowing of the coming year's cereal crop, and thus coincided well with the Senate's official recess. Other moments also may have drawn landowners away from Rome temporarily, such as the harvest of cereal crops, which could begin as early as late June and continue through mid-July (and ran even later in the north), and the tending of olive trees in August and September.[70] Members of Rome's middling groups who possessed country estates had even greater incentives than did senators or equestrians for leaving Rome during critical moments of the agricultural year. Since they were less likely to own slaves who served expressly as bailiffs, their personal supervision would have been important for the success of crucial farm operations.

Furthermore, because wealthy visitors to Rome were more likely to be present in the early parts of the year than in summer or autumn, their

---

[66] Columella, *Rust.* 1.pr.11–12. [67] Plin. *Ep.* 10.8.5; Talbert 1984: 211. [68] Plin. *Ep.* 8.2.
[69] See, e.g., Plin. *Ep.* 8.2 and 10.8.
[70] The key primary sources are Columella, Palladius, and the *Menologium Rusticum Colotianum*. These are conveniently summarized by White 1970: 194–5. See also Frayn 1979: 47–56. Finally, see Mattingly 1996: 221 for a discussion of olive trees and the times of year during which it was most critical to tend to them.

movements in and out of the capital only exacerbated the seasonal peaks and troughs in demand confronting artisans who catered to the high end of the market. Rome attracted visitors from an extraordinarily wide catchment area because, as the imperial capital, it housed both significant cultural and religious monuments as well as important political institutions. Rome's cityscape was a reason in and of itself for non-residents to visit the city, and many visitors presumably came to contemplate its monuments and other physical manifestations of empire.[71] Its political landscape exercised an equally powerful appeal. From the Augustan period onward, Rome housed the imperial court, but long before this it had been the capital of a burgeoning empire. As such, it had long been a natural center of gravity for different kinds of travelers, and it continued to be so even after the imperial court became more peripatetic in the second century CE.[72] Those travelers ranged from citizens who hoped to strike up relationships of patronage or marriage alliances with members of the senatorial and equestrian elite, to suppliants and ambassadors who came from all over the Roman world (and also from points beyond) to speak with members of the Senate or the emperor himself.[73] Much of this travel would have been seasonal in character, not just because visitors themselves often had reasons to remain at home during certain times of the year – a reluctance to travel by sea in the winter, for instance, or a desire to be present for critical agricultural operations on their estates – but also because they would have timed their movements to coincide inasmuch as possible with the presence of the Roman political elite.

Much additional travel to Rome by wealthy potential consumers was stimulated by its role as the judicial capital of the empire, which drew members of both Italian and provincial elites to the city in distinctly seasonal patterns. As we have seen, the jurymen who were registered in Rome's *album iudicum* were drawn increasingly from men who were not necessarily native to the capital itself from the first century BCE onward. Italians were the first to enter judicial service in this way, but by the middle of the Julio-Claudian period jurors were increasingly drawn from the western provinces of the empire.[74] To some extent, enlistment into the *album* may have been purely honorific; nevertheless, some of our sources show that men from the

[71] Purcell 2000: 405–12.

[72] See Talbert 1984: 140–1 and 152 for comments on the tendencies of emperors to spend increasing amounts of time outside of Italy.

[73] Purcell 2000: 405–12; Millar 1977: 375–85.

[74] It is clear that by Pliny the Elder's day the *album* included men from the provinces (*HN*. 33.30). See Bablitz 2007: 91–100.

provinces did come to Rome to preside over civil cases or to serve on juries.[75] Inevitably, they were men of wealth: the majority of those who were enlisted into the *album* belonged to the senatorial and (from the first century BCE) equestrian orders, and even when Augustus expanded the membership further down the social hierarchy, he extended it only to those who possessed property worth at least half of the value of an equestrian census.[76] Most of these men came to the capital at the beginning of the year and served for a ten-month term (though they might leave at the end of August if they were assigned no further cases after September 1); an additional number, however, remained in Rome only temporarily and returned home if they were not chosen as one of that year's *selecti*.[77] For that reason, their movements in and out of Rome were essentially a form of seasonal migration.

Other Italian and provincial elites came to Rome as litigants rather than as jurymen, but their movements too were shaped largely by seasonal factors. Magistrates in the *municipia* and *coloniae* of Italy enjoyed some independent jurisdiction over civil suits, but it was limited by legislation that transferred certain cases to the capital. The *lex Rubria*, for instance, limited the ability of local magistrates in Gallia Cisalpina to preside over those cases that might produce *infamia* or a change in juridical status for the litigants, and over those in which sums greater than 15,000 *sesterces* were at stake.[78] No direct evidence of comparable laws survives from other Italian cities, but such regulations must have been widespread (if not universal). That view is strengthened by the survival of epigraphic evidence demonstrating comparable provisions in the charters of *municipiae* or *coloniae* in other parts of the empire.[79] The specifics of the limitations imposed on magistrates undoubtedly varied from city to city – a Flavian-period law from the town of Irni in Spain, for instance, places a relatively low limit of 1,000 *sesterces* on the competency of that town's local magistrates – but in the end these limitations all diverted the wealthiest litigants in Italy to Rome.[80] This pattern may have been interrupted from

---

[75] E.g., Plin. *HN.* 29.18.

[76] See Brunt 1988: 194–239 on the conflicts in the late Republic over the role of equestrians in the judicial process, and 231–6 for the composition of the *album* in the Principate. For Augustus' inclusion in the *album* of the so-called *ducenarii* – men who possessed estates worth 200,000 HS, or half the equestrian census – see Suet. *Aug.* 32.3.

[77] Bablitz 2007: 92–3 provides the most recent discussion of the selection procedure.

[78] *FIRA* i², 19f. See A. H. M. Jones 1960: 75–7; Brunt 1988: 225–6. Cf. Johnston 1999: 120–1.

[79] These include fragments of a *lex Coloniae Genetivae*, several passages in the *Digest*, and one in Paul's *Sententiae*. See González's comments on Chapter 84 of the *lex Irnitana* for details (González 1986: 227).

[80] Brunt 1988: 233; Johnston 1999: 120–1.

time to time in the second century CE when both Hadrian and Marcus Aurelius appointed *iudices* with broad powers to assist the praetor by overseeing civil cases in Italy, but even then there must always have been a residual flow of litigants to the capital.[81] That flow was seasonal in nature not just because of the rhythm of judicial business in Rome itself but also because many of these litigants would have been reluctant to go to court during critical moments of the agricultural calendar. When Marcus Aurelius decreed in the second century CE that litigants could not compel adversaries who were busy with "agricultural business" to appear in court during the harvest or vintage, he probably codified an already existing preference.[82]

I conclude this section by noting that Rome was hardly the only city in the empire in which artisans working at multiple levels of the market faced seasonal peaks and troughs in the demand for their services, even though evidence for conditions outside of the capital is patchy. In the first place, the conditions that triggered seasonal migration to and from Rome itself were present to some degree in and around most large cities in antiquity. Funerary epigraphy suggests that seasonal fluctuations in morbidity and mortality were common in other Italian towns, though the patterns could differ from those visible at Rome: in towns in southern Italy, mortality peaked at roughly the same time of year as in Rome, but in the north – where the climate was much colder – mortality peaked in the winter rather than summer.[83] In Egypt, the deadly time of year was not just the summer, but also November and December.[84] There is also some evidence that the climate of Carthage and the North African coast was thought to be unhealthy and dangerous in the summer, though here the funerary epigraphy does not demonstrate a clear seasonal trend in actual mortality.[85] Conditions were likely worse in large cities with high population densities (where poor sanitation would have been most problematic) than elsewhere. But whenever contemporary observers were aware of seasonal fluctuations in mortality (or at least believed that these existed),

---

[81] On the *per omnem Italiam iudices*, see SHA *Hadr.* 22.13 and *Ant. Pius* 2.11. Marcus Aurelius likewise appointed subordinates to oversee the administration of justice in Italy: SHA *Marc.* 11.6. One factor that might have contributed to residual flow into the capital was the *revocatio Romae*. See A. H. M. Jones 1960: 75–6.

[82] Ulpian, *Dig.* 2.12.1 and 2.12.3.   [83] Shaw 1996: 125–9.   [84] Scheidel 2001: 1–117.

[85] There is no entirely convincing explanation for why the Carthaginian inscriptions show no pronounced spike in mortality during the summer, even though contemporaries believed the climate to be unhealthy during those months. Either our evidence is inadequate for some reason that is not apparent, or Carthage benefitted from a climatic peculiarity that ameliorated conditions somewhat in the summer. For further discussion see Scheidel 1996b: 155–63; Shaw 1996: 130–1.

and whenever they had the economic means to relocate, they turned to seasonal migration to minimize their chances of succumbing to illness, much like the Roman aristocracy itself.

Economic factors also generated seasonal migration in and out of other large cities, among both the wealthy and the less affluent. The great regional capitals of the empire were home to large-scale landowners who possessed one or more country estates some distance away from the city and who therefore split their time between urban and rural residences, timing their movements around the agricultural calendar. In Egypt, for instance, members of the Alexandrian elite often owned agricultural properties in the Nile valley, where they must have spent at least part of their time.[86] Likewise, Rome was surely not the only city that served both as a magnet for country-dwellers searching for seasonal work and as a source of laborers who could be recruited to help with the harvest by estate owners within the immediate hinterland. Much of this movement remains undocumented, but occasionally our sources do refer to it, even if only obliquely. According to Pausanias, for example, the town of Patrae in the northwest Peloponnese had twice as many women as men during the second century CE because it was a local center of textile production, employing women in large numbers. Women may have migrated to the town from the countryside every year in search of work.[87] We are also told by a very late Roman source, Joshua the Stylite, that a Saracen army in 502 CE captured 18,500 prisoners when it raided the districts around Carrhae and Edessa in Syria, most of whom had left town to help with the harvest.[88] Although this evidence obviously pertains to a later period, the kind of temporary relocation for harvest work it reports must have been a regular feature of life in the Roman world.

Although other large cities in the empire did not exert the same degree of political gravity as Rome, they too attracted their fair share of visitors during certain seasons of the year. Not only did they house members of the provincial elite (who, no less than their Roman counterparts, could offer valuable patronage), they were also home to monuments of historical significance and centers of religious devotion. They therefore prompted visits from travelers engaged in *theoria* – that is, travel for the specific purpose of visiting monuments, shrines, and temples, not entirely unlike pilgrimage in later periods of European

---

[86] Bowman 1986: 155.   [87] Horden and Purcell 2000: 352–9; Erdkamp 2005: 90–1.
[88] M. Kaplan 1992: 58 and 274, with sources. On migration and seasonal harvest work in North Africa, cf. Shaw 2013: 3–33.

history.[89] While we cannot quantify the scale of this kind of tourism, it was likely extensive, especially among wealthier elements of the Italian and provincial populations. It could profoundly boost local economies: festivals at some religious centers served as periodic regional markets, which could draw business from a wide geographical area. Even at the relatively unimportant temple of Artemis at Perge in Pamphilia, visitors dedicated various devotional objects to the goddess, many of which they probably purchased from local manufacturers.[90] More importantly, as with other forms of travel, the rhythms of *theoria* were linked closely to the sailing season, particularly in major coastal cities. Inscriptions from Samothrace offer some sense of those rhythms in an earlier historical context: they record the initiations into the Samothracian mysteries of visitors from Thrace, Macedonia, the Cyclades, and Asia Minor during the classical Greek period, most of which took place between April and November, during peak sailing season.[91]

Lastly, Roman rule itself generated important patterns of movement within individual provinces by concentrating judicial authority in the hands of provincial governors. Justice was often dispensed on a local level in the provinces by town magistrates or councils, but the case of Irni in Spain shows that there were limits on the jurisdiction of the local magistrates in provincial *municipia*, just as in Italy.[92] A certain volume of legal business between either Roman citizens or *municipales* of Latin status in the provinces was therefore channeled from the local level to the provincial governor, particularly when those cases were contested by wealthy litigants over sizeable sums. Moreover, as the representatives of Roman authority, governors also exercised considerable jurisdiction over non-Romans within their provinces. Representatives of provincial communities and individual provincials alike approached governors in large numbers to deliver petitions or to ask for their intercession in local disputes.[93] Since governors typically circulated between the major population centers in their provinces to hold assizes, local communities also periodically and temporarily played host to visitors who came from wide catchment areas to speak before the governor's court and who, in the process, generated considerable demand for the products and services of local inhabitants. In an oration he delivered in the Phrygian city of

---

[89] For a general account of tourism in the ancient world, see Casson 1974: 229–329. For discussions of *theoria* and the degree to which it can be likened to pilgrimage, see Elsner 1992 and Rutherford 2001. Kleijwegt 2002: 117 n. 152 conveniently draws together citations to older scholarship.
[90] Kleijwegt 2002: 119–20, with references.   [91] Dillon 1997: 29.   [92] *lex Irnitana* 84.
[93] Crook 1967: 85–7; Johnston 1999: 120; Lintott 1993: 43–69.

Celaenae in the second half of the first century CE, Dio Chrysostom illustrates the way in which a governor's periodic assizes could affect the economies of such towns:

> What is more, the courts are convened here on alternate years, and they draw together countless multitudes of people – litigants, judges, orators, princes, servants, slaves, pimps, muleteers, dealers, prostitutes, and artisans. Thus, those with goods to sell secure a very great price, and nothing in the city wants for employment, neither the draught animals, nor the houses, nor the women.[94]

Along with the other root causes of seasonality, movements of this sort ensured that overall levels of consumer demand in ancient cities oscillated between peaks and troughs that affected artisans in broad swathes of the economy simultaneously, even if specific trades remained subject to their own individual rhythms.

Consumption and uncertainty in the ancient world

The evidence for the impact of seasonality on urban economies is compelling, and it strongly indicates that demand was anything but regular over the course of a given year in most cities of the Roman world. As we have seen, however, demand in the product markets of early modern European cities was characterized not just by seasonality but also by uncertainty. In this section, I demonstrate that the same was true in antiquity. The nature of our evidence makes this argument easier to support in the case of product markets that catered to the wealthy, but indirect arguments suggest that demand in product markets catering to the less affluent segments of urban populations was equally uncertain.

In upmarket segments of the urban economy, many artisans in the Roman world worked on a bespoke basis for individual clients, much as their early modern counterparts did. At this level of the market, clients tended to be interested in consumption as a means of expressing their own status and refinement, and they therefore preferred items of high quality, often tailored on some level to their own specifications.[95] For that reason, they purchased many of their goods made-to-order, and artisans who catered primarily to such clients therefore contended with erratic and ultimately unpredictable demand, even if it was stronger in a general

[94] Dio Chrys. *Or.* 35.15.
[95] Olson 2008: 97–9 and 106–10 explores some of these issues in the context of women's clothing and adornment.

sense in high season than at other times of the year. Apuleius' account of
the circumstances that led him to commission work from the carpenter
Cornelius Saturninus is particularly interesting in this respect: aside from
being one of the few literary texts to reveal something about the nature of
the transactions that took place between an artisan and his or her clients, it
also shows how heavily artisans who catered to the bespoke market relied
on serendipitous orders placed by wealthy consumers. In his *Apologia*,
composed and delivered in 158 or 159 CE, Apuleius describes how he
commissioned a number of pieces from Saturninus, a renowned carpenter
in the African city of Oea; these included a devotional statue and small toys
or models of uncertain purpose.[96] Apuleius implies that he had placed his
order on impulse: having noticed a number of interesting objects on
display in Saturninus' workshop, he was impressed by the artisan's skill
and technique, and decided to commission pieces for himself. This
anecdote illustrates that although an artisan like Saturninus might well
do his best to tempt potential customers into his shop by making high-
quality samples of his work visible to the public, he nevertheless remained
highly dependent on the idiosyncratic and ultimately uncertain preferences
of individual buyers. The same basic model of production helps to explain
the organization of the most well-preserved statuary shop in our
archaeological record, a small establishment in the Anatolian city of
Aphrodisias. The sculptors who worked in this shop attracted impulse
buyers by performing some of their work in an open room adjoining
a heavily trafficked plaza, where passers-by could observe them.[97]

For most artisans in antiquity who manufactured goods that were
heavily tailored to individual specifications, bespoke production was
generally the rule. Portrait sculpture and portrait painting obviously fall
into this category, as does the manufacture of high-quality footwear, fitted
to the measurements of individual customers.[98] But a range of other goods
likewise was manufactured by artisans to suit the individualized needs of
their clients, particularly in smaller cities of the empire in which the
aggregate demand generated by elite consumers was lower than in large

---

[96] Apul. *Apol.* 61.
[97] Rockwell 1991: 140–1. In his view these sculptors were advertising pieces for sale that they had
produced on speculation, but van Voorhis 1999: 117 argues instead that they were probably working
mostly on commission.
[98] High-quality footwear was probably made-to-measure in classical Athens. See Burford 1972: plate 3:
in this vase painting, a shoemaker is depicted cutting out the sole of a shoe to the measurements of
a young boy's foot. Likewise, in the quality trade in early modern Europe, shoes could still be made-
to-measure, though sizes were becoming increasingly standardized (e.g., Schwarz 1992: 195). There is
no reason to think that the process was any different in the Roman world.

cities like Rome or Alexandria. Gold artifacts stand out in particular. Cicero (in an admittedly highly rhetorical context) could assume that a Roman senator who needed to replace a gold ring in a provincial town would commission one directly from a local craftsman.[99] Likewise, a papyrus document from the Fayum records a contract in which a customer not only commissioned a pair of serpent-shaped bracelets from a local goldsmith but also advanced him the funds to purchase the gold.[100] High-quality woodworking offers another good example: few pieces of the wooden furniture preserved by carbonization in Herculaneum show signs of standardization that might indicate serial production, and Stephan Mols has argued on that basis that woodworkers in the city tailored pieces of furniture to the particular needs and specifications of individual clients.[101] While this conclusion applies to surviving pieces of hanging and freestanding storage furniture, it also extends to other important wooden display pieces that have not been so well preserved, such as the dining couches (*lecti tricliniares*) used by the wealthy to entertain guests in the typical Roman *triclinium*.[102]

Even in larger cities, where a concentrated elite generated a comparatively high level of aggregate demand for manufactured goods and possibly satisfied at least part of it by purchasing ready-made articles from shops or from merchants who visited their homes,[103] many artisans worked on commission even when their products did not need to be tailored to individual specifications. The comic poet Plautus could assume in the second century BCE that jewelers often accepted work from their clients on commission, as did embroiderers, who were hired by private customers to add decorative elements to clothing.[104] And although what was true in the second century BCE need not have been true in the more intense

---

[99] Cic. *Verr.* 2.4.56.

[100] *BGU* IV 1065, with the comments of Whitehorne 1983. The details of the financial transaction associated with the commission remain confusing and difficult to understand, but fortunately they are not nearly as significant for my present purposes as are the document's implications for the widespread nature of bespoke production in the Roman world.

[101] Mols 1999: 58 and 112.   [102] Ulrich 2007: 232–5.

[103] Holleran 2012: 241–57 discusses the various contexts in which the wealthy purchased goods, including privately in the home, at auction, and in luxury shops. For a good example of a shop stocking ready-made goods, see Paul (quoting Scaevola), *Dig.* 34.2.32.4. Scaevola's *responsum* refers to a businesswoman (*negotiatrix*) who owned a retail shop selling silver articles for women. Also interesting in this context is Martial's satire of a shopping trip (9.59), but this is problematic since in a number of instances Martial is obviously imagining antiques being displayed for sale rather than new manufactured goods. All that said, these sources make it impossible to determine how frequently shops of this nature were patronized by the wealthy as opposed to less-affluent consumers.

[104] Plaut. *Men.* 426–7, 541–5.

economic climate of the first or second century CE, later evidence suggests that goldsmiths and jewelers in the late Republic and early Empire were just as likely to produce goods in response to the orders of individual clients as they had been in Plautus' day. The jurists of the imperial period, for example, assumed that goldsmiths often worked to meet specific orders, whether they made use of their own raw materials or worked with gold supplied by their clients.[105]

Naturally, the building trade offers the paradigmatic example of a bespoke industry. Admittedly, some evidence testifies to a degree of speculative building: a legal *responsum* delivered originally by Papinian and quoted by Ulpian and the compilers of the *Digest* describes a partnership between Flavius Victor and Bellicus Asianus, who developed and then sold funerary monuments.[106] Speculation of this nature, however, was apparently rare. Instead, most artisans in the building trades worked on projects similar to those described by Cicero in his correspondence to his brother Quintus: distinct jobs let out by individual proprietors who wanted specific building or repair work done.[107] For this reason, most builders in antiquity depended no less "upon the occasional calls of [their] customers" than did those in eighteenth-century England.[108] The same was no doubt true of the various specialists who finished the interiors of new structures (whom we shall revisit in Chapter 2).

While we can therefore conclude that particularistic consumption habits among the wealthy generated considerable uncertainty for artisans who catered to this clientele, it is more difficult to judge the nature and extent of uncertainty in the demand for manufactured goods among sub-aristocratic inhabitants of ancient cities. The aggregate demand generated by these consumers was considerable: Rome alone possessed a population of close to one million people in the early Empire, the vast majority of whom did not belong to the wealthy elite, and a handful of other cities possessed populations on the order of a hundred thousand or more (chiefly, Alexandria, Antioch, Carthage, Ephesus, and Pergamum).[109] Yet the potential size of this market does not necessarily imply that the demand it generated was regular or stable. In what follows, I make the case that consumers of neither low nor middling wealth generated predictable and regular demand for manufactured goods and services. Instead, that

---

[105] Gaius, *Dig.* 19.2.2.1; Ulpian, *Dig.* 19.2.13.5; Alfenus, *Dig.* 19.2.31; Pomponius, *Dig.* 34.2.34.pr.
[106] Ulpian (paraphrasing Papinian), *Dig.* 17.2.52.7.
[107] S. D. Martin 1989: 45–52; Anderson 1997: 75–95.
[108] Cf. Mattingly and Salmon 2001b: 9. The quoted passage is from Adam Smith; see above, n. 19.
[109] Erkamp 2012: 243–5 compiles most of the relevant estimates.

demand remained highly uncertain – more so, perhaps, than the demand generated by comparable social groups in the early modern period. For city-dwellers who possessed only limited resources, purchasing power served as the primary obstacle limiting their ability to engage in the regular consumption of goods and services. Above all, low purchasing power rendered them vulnerable to unpredictable fluctuations in the price of food, and as a result their demand for the products and services of artisans and entrepreneurs was likely subject to considerable uncertainty, since the funds remaining after they met their basic needs could change dramatically from year to year, or even in some cases from week to week. On the other hand, if fluctuations in food prices did not necessarily affect the spending patterns of urban consumers who enjoyed higher levels of material security so dramatically, demand at this level of the social spectrum nevertheless remained uncertain because it was dictated partly by consumption patterns that did not necessarily encourage the regular and predictable purchase of manufactured goods.

I begin by considering the purchasing power commanded by sub-aristocratic inhabitants of cities in the Roman world. Our evidence for wages and prices in Roman antiquity is limited, but it nevertheless suggests that most adult males who depended on wages were hard-pressed to earn enough to support their families, let alone enough to purchase manufactured goods with any regularity. On the basis of Diocletian's edict of maximum prices, Robert Allen has argued that unskilled workers in the early fourth century earned enough to fund consumption at a level of 1.10 times the basic cost of subsistence. Although the relationship between the wages articulated in the edict and those actually paid to workers is unclear – if, for instance, the edict was designed to curb wages, then it effectively underreports what workers could earn – it remains true that the real incomes implied by these figures were dramatically lower than those enjoyed by unskilled laborers in London or Amsterdam during the seventeenth or eighteenth centuries; in Allen's estimate, these workers were capable of earning as much as 3.0–3.5 times what they required to maintain their families at a bare-bones level.[110] On the basis of surviving wage and price data in Egyptian papyri of the second and third centuries CE, Walter Scheidel has likewise argued that the real incomes of rural workers in Roman Egypt were extremely poor, particularly when situated in a comparative context. Scheidel estimates that the annual wages of a typical unskilled rural worker in Roman Egypt were not even high enough to cover the costs of the "bare-bones" basket of goods

---

[110] Allen 2009, esp. 339–42.

required to support a family at subsistence level, but instead covered only about 70–80 percent of the total costs of a household's basic needs during the second century CE.[111]

At first glance, it is difficult to say how accurately Allen and Scheidel capture the purchasing power of unskilled laborers elsewhere in the Roman world during the late Republic and early Empire. To cite just the obvious concern, Italy itself and certain other highly urbanized areas of the empire are generally thought to have enjoyed better economic conditions in the late Republic and in much of the early Empire than was the case either in Roman Egypt or in late antiquity.[112] Moreover, living standards in Rome itself may have been enhanced by the public grain dole, which could alter the consumption patterns of the capital's urban populace in significant ways. From the Augustan period onward, the dole itself was distributed free of charge to some 200,000 male citizens who were registered among the *plebs frumentaria*; each received five *modii* of wheat per month, which in theory could have met the basic subsistence requirements of one adult, with some left to spare. While the right to collect the dole was, strictly speaking, a privilege of citizenship and residency and thus not based on need, members of low and middling income groups derived more benefit from it than did the wealthy. The dole thus theoretically made it possible for some members of the urban poor and middling groups to shift their own household expenditures away from basic subsistence and towards other forms of consumption.[113]

Even so, it is important not to overemphasize the standards of living enjoyed by the bulk of Rome's inhabitants. Although we possess no reliable wage data for private employees in the capital, most household heads in

---

[111] Scheidel 2010, esp. 433–5. Two important assumptions are embedded in these calculations: (1) unskilled workers in both the ancient and early modern contexts each worked for roughly 250 days each year; (2) the daily wage in Roman Egypt was roughly 1 *drachma* per day. Wages in Egypt may have been somewhat higher than this on average (see Rathbone 2009: 314–17, and especially table 15.3), and so too may have been the number of days spent working by the average city-dweller – apprentices in Roman Egypt, for example, enjoyed only a few weeks' worth of holidays throughout the year. Yet even if we assume that an unskilled worker in Roman Egypt earned a wage of, for example, 1.2 *drachmai* per day, and that he worked for 360 days per year, his resultant annual income – roughly equivalent to 1.22 times the cost of a household's basic subsistence needs – would have remained quite low relative to that enjoyed by laborers in northwestern Europe during the early modern period.

[112] On conditions in Italy, see especially Scheidel 2007a. Cf. Lo Cascio and Malanima 2009: 395–6 and 412–15.

[113] For the most recent discussion of the public grain distributions in Rome, see Erdkamp 2005: 240–4. Rickman 1980 also remains fundamental. That Augustus established 200,000 as a notional limit for the *plebs frumentaria* seems clear from several ancient sources, including his own *Res Gest.* 15, as well as Dio Cass. 55.10.1. Our evidence does not directly reveal whether or not that number was later increased by one of Augustus' successors.

Rome could not hope to approach the level of purchasing power commanded by unskilled workers in northwestern Europe during the seventeenth and eighteenth centuries, even with the assistance of public grain handouts. This is illustrated best by the purchasing power enjoyed by praetorian guardsmen. Because of their importance to the imperial household's security, guardsmen were compensated at a rate that was undoubtedly generous by metropolitan standards, even before factoring in perquisites such as donatives and discharge bonuses.[114] At best, the relative purchasing power represented by guardsmen's annual wages (exclusive of perquisites) may have just matched the purchasing power of the unskilled wage in London or Amsterdam during the early modern period. Although the precise daily rate of guardsmen's pay is disputed, their annual earnings fell within a relatively well-defined range of 675–750 *denarii* (i.e., 2,700–3,000 *sesterces*) for much of the first century CE.[115] Since grain prices during this period could not have been any lower than about six *sesterces* per *modius* (a Roman measure equivalent to roughly 6.8 kg of wheat), civilian household heads capable of generating an annual income at the upper end of this range would have been able to support a family at a level of consumption equivalent to roughly 2.53 times the cost of basic subsistence. If that worker was also a member of the *plebs frumentaria*, and was thus eligible to receive public grain handouts, his total earnings would have funded consumption for a family at a level equivalent to roughly 2.84 times the cost of basic subsistence – still somewhat short of the level of consumption enjoyed by household heads in northwestern Europe during the early modern period, albeit not by much.[116]

---

[114] For a brief, recent overview of the functions of both the praetorian guard and the urban cohorts, see Rankov 2007: 44–8. Rathbone 2007: 158–65 presents a good summary of military wages and the perquisites enjoyed by soldiers.

[115] Tac. *Ann.* 1.17 and Dio Cass. 53.11.5 are our two main ancient sources for the pay of praetorian guardsmen. In a speech attributed to the mutineer Percennius, Tacitus implies that regular legionaries earned ten *asses* (i.e., 10/16 of a *denarius*) per day in 14 CE, while members of the praetorian guard earned two *denarii*, for an annual salary (at 360 days to the year) of 720 *denarii*. Dio Cassius, on the other hand, claims that Augustus paid his guardsmen at double the rate he paid other soldiers. Modern commentators generally assume on this basis that Augustus effectively doubled the rate at which praetorian guardsmen had been paid in late Republican legions; since that rate was already 1.5 times base legionary pay, it implies that praetorians under Augustus earned 675 *denarii* over a 360-day year. The highest estimate for annual praetorian wages, 750 *denarii*, is derived by assuming praetorian and regular legionary wages exhibited the same ratio to one another as did the bequests left by Augustus in his will to each member of the praetorian guard (250 *denarii*) and to each member of the legions (75 *denarii*). For a classic discussion of these problems, see Brunt 1950: 50–6. For a more recent overview, see Rathbone 2007: 158–61.

[116] On the price of grain in Rome during the first century CE, see Duncan-Jones 1982: 345–6, and Rickman 1980: 239–40, along with the more recent comments of Rathbone 2009: 308 and Scheidel 2010: 444. I have calculated purchasing power by assuming that a "bare-bones" subsistence basket

Yet if praetorian guardsmen were indeed paid well relative to typical urban residents, even before the value of donatives and discharge bonuses is factored into the equation, then the relative purchasing power of an average Roman worker would have been substantially smaller. How much smaller is of course difficult to say. The annual earnings of members of the urban cohorts offer one potential metric. Members of the urban cohorts played an important policing function in Rome itself and in other important cities, and while they remained less privileged than praetorian guardsmen, their compensation too was likely meant to be relatively generous. For that reason, their wages may be broadly representative of what some skilled workers – or even the most highly paid of the unskilled, if they could secure regular work – could hope to earn in a year. While we lack precise figures for the daily pay rate for soldiers of the urban cohorts, their annual earnings almost certainly fell between 337.5 and 375 *denarii* (or 1,350 and 1,500 *sesterces*) until the reign of Domitian.[117] An income at the upper end of that range would have enabled a household head to support a family at a level roughly 1.27 times basic subsistence without assistance from public grain handouts, or at 1.57 times basic subsistence if he was also registered among the *plebs frumentaria*.[118] A Roman worker in these circumstances would have enjoyed considerably more purchasing power than a comparable worker in rural Egypt, but he could not have hoped to match the purchasing power commanded by unskilled workers in London or Amsterdam during the seventeenth and eighteenth centuries.

On a more schematic level, the parametric models constructed by historians in recent years likewise suggest that most city-dwellers in the Roman world did not possess the same kind of purchasing power as unskilled workers in northwestern Europe during the early modern period. Several scholars have constructed such models in order to estimate both the GDP of the Roman Empire (aggregate and per capita) and patterns of wealth

---

was valued at roughly 428 kg of wheat-equivalent for an individual, and 1,341 kg of wheat-equivalent for a household; these figures are essentially those employed by Scheidel 2010: 433–5. The purchasing power represented by an income of 750 *denarii* per year would have amounted to roughly 3,400 kg of wheat-equivalent (assuming wheat prices of 6 *sesterces* per *modius* of 6.8 kg). Individuals belonging to the *plebs frumentaria* would have received an additional 408 kg of wheat from the state every year.

[117] On these figures, see Brunt 1950: 55 and Rathbone 2007: 161.

[118] Domitian increased legionary base pay by a third, to 300 *denarii* per year (see Suet. *Dom.* 7.3 and Dio Cass. 67.3.5, with the discussion of Brunt 1950: 54). It is generally thought that he boosted the pay of praetorian guardsmen and members of the urban cohorts by a comparable proportion at the same time (so Brunt 1950: 56). Whether or not this represented an increase in purchasing power is unclear, since it is difficult to track changes in wheat prices (cf. Rathbone 2009: 310–12).

distribution among its population.[119] To date, Walter Scheidel and Steven Friesen have produced the most comprehensive model of this sort by constructing parallel series of high and low estimates for the Roman Empire's GDP based on expenditure, income, and the relationship between per capita GDP and both subsistence requirements and unskilled wage rates. In their view, these parallel series imply, in the first place, that the Roman Empire at its height enjoyed a per capita GDP of roughly 1.75 times the per capita costs of bare subsistence.[120] While it is possible that areas of the Roman world enjoyed greater levels of output than this, it seems unlikely that even Roman Italy achieved a level of economic performance commensurate with what was typical of England and the Netherlands from roughly 1600 onward.[121] Second, Scheidel and Friesen also conclude that wealth was distributed in such a way that something on the order of 84–90 percent of the Roman world's inhabitants lived either just above, at, or below subsistence level, much like unskilled workers and their family members in rural Egypt. They do suggest that urban populations had a higher-than-average concentration of households commanding middling or respectable incomes, which they define as incomes generating at least 2.4 times the amount required for basic subsistence; yet even if one-eighth to one-quarter of the residents of a city such as Rome did fall into this bracket, many of them still would have possessed less purchasing power than unskilled workers and their families in later historical periods.[122]

The sparse real-wage data and the parametric models therefore both suggest that the purchasing power of most urban residents in Roman cities remained limited, even in aggregate. Because most households in Rome hovered closer to the margins of subsistence than was the case in north-western Europe during the early modern period, fluctuations in food prices

---

[119] In addition to the model developed in Scheidel and Friesen 2009, see especially Hopkins 1995–1996: 44–8; Bang 2008: 85–93; Lo Cascio and Malanima 2009: 396–401. Cf. the contributions made by Goldsmith 1984; Temin 2006; and Temin 2013: 243–61.

[120] Scheidel and Friesen 2009: 73–4. They work with a mean per capita GDP of 680 kg of wheat-equivalent per year, and with a mean basic per capita subsistence requirement of 390 kg of wheat-equivalent per year.

[121] Scheidel and Friesen 2009: 64 and 74 present some basic figures for economic performance in England and the Dutch Republic, which ultimately derive from Maddison 2007. In particular, Maddison estimates that the Dutch Republic generated a per capita output of roughly 3.45 times the cost of subsistence in 1600, and that England had essentially reached this level by 1688. More recently, Lo Cascio and Malanima 2009 have disputed these figures and have argued instead that the economic performance of Roman Italy may have been much more similar to the performance of some seventeenth- and eighteenth-century European economies than other historians believe. Scheidel and Friesen 2009 argue in their postscript that Lo Cascio and Malanima overestimate the total GDP of the empire.

[122] Scheidel and Friesen 2009: 75–91. See esp. 85 and 88–91.

probably left such households with very little surplus income to spend on non-essential goods and services when food prices were unexpectedly high. The severity of the uncertainty experienced by artisans and by other workers who catered to these consumers was therefore heavily dependent on whether or not both the political institutions of a given city and the wider market structure in which that city was embedded mitigated unpredictable fluctuations in the price of basic staples, whether inter-annually or over the course of a given year.

How effectively market forces could mitigate price fluctuations in the Roman world is a matter of some debate.[123] That said, recent discussions of the structure of the market in foodstuffs have emphasized that those forces could not always respond to food shortages as quickly or as efficiently as consumers desired. Peter Bang, for instance, has recently argued that prices even for important commodities like wheat and wine not only fluctuated significantly in the short term within individual towns in the Egyptian province of Arcadia during the fifth century CE but also diverged sharply across towns near one another. In his view, strongly integrated markets did not exist in the Roman world on the inter-regional or even regional level, with the exception of those that may have emerged along certain well-demarcated transportation routes.[124]

The price series from fifth-century Arcadia is much more detailed than most of our evidence from antiquity, and thus it is difficult to demonstrate that the temporal and spatial price fluctuations visible in Arcadian towns were typical elsewhere in the Roman world, or in the late Republic and early Empire. Bang argues that his conclusions are broadly generalizable, not just because transportation and communication remained limited in important ways by the Mediterranean shipping season but also because the agents and institutions most capable of transforming the market in the late Republic and early Empire failed to do so. In his view, large landowners, who had a great deal of agricultural surplus at their disposal and the desire to convert it to cash, stood to gain more by hoarding their grain until prices were high in order to exploit their market power than they did by creating more integrated market structures. For its own part, the imperial state was less interested in improving overall conditions of trade than in delivering

---

[123] For an optimistic view, see Kessler and Temin 2008.
[124] Bang 2008: 131–201, and in particular 153–73. For an alternative view of price formation in Roman Egypt in general, see Rathbone 1997. Note that while Rathbone argues for more homogenous prices on a regional level, his model nevertheless leaves room for some inter-annual fluctuations in prices arising from variability in the inundation of the Nile.

tax grain from Egypt to Rome and in exploiting commerce in general via taxation.[125]

Paul Erdkamp likewise advocates a model in which markets in foodstuffs remained only partly integrated in the Roman world, and in which fluctuations in food prices within a given year or across years remained persistent. Because the communication technologies of the Roman world were less capable of disseminating homogenous information over large geographical areas than were those of early modern Europe, the extent of market integration varied extensively by region. Some market integration certainly occurred in core areas of the Mediterranean, especially when they were linked to trade routes designed to meet the needs of Rome itself. On the other hand, markets in primary foodstuffs in areas less well connected to the overall network (for instance, inland regions) tended either to integrate only at a regional level, or (in the worst cases) to remain seriously underdeveloped. Although the Roman world's grain markets therefore compared favorably in some respects with those of the early modern European economy, they did not quite reach the same level of overall performance.[126] Ongoing food insecurity in less well-connected regions hindered further system-wide market development, and probably also ensured that uncertainty continued to plague demand in the urban product markets of these regions.

Because no urban population in the Roman world was better protected against severe fluctuations in food prices than that of Rome itself, the evidence for ongoing price volatility in the capital is particularly striking. Both the city's institutions and the market in which it was embedded mitigated price fluctuations in at least two specific ways. First, because it was both the home of the largest agglomerated urban population in the Mediterranean world and the hub of a Mediterranean-wide network of shipping routes designed to facilitate the movement of tribute grain from the provinces to the center, Rome undoubtedly attracted many merchants, traders, and grain producers seeking a market for their goods. These would have contributed to the food supply by adding to the grain that was traded privately on the market. Second, because the imperial state collected more grain in tax revenue from the provinces than needed for the dole, it could release the excess onto the open market, possibly in sufficient quantities to help stabilize otherwise volatile food prices.[127] Yet, in spite of these

---

[125] Bang 2008: 173–90.   [126] Erdkamp 2005: 175–205 and 322–30. Cf. Morley 2007: 94–6.
[127] Erdkamp 2005: 249–55. Cf. Garnsey 1988: 231–9 for a slightly different view. Lo Cascio 2006 observes that the Roman state (in the person of the emperor) was in essence the Roman world's

advantages, the urban population of Rome nevertheless remained susceptible to ongoing variability in the costs of food. To cite the most well-
known evidence, Tacitus observed that the crowd at Rome, which was
accustomed to buying food day-by-day, remained concerned above all with
the smooth operation of the city's food supply. The extant material does
not permit us to track fluctuations in prices with any real precision, but our
literary authors nevertheless draw frequent enough attention to anxieties
expressed by Rome's populace about food prices to suggest that such
fluctuations remained a reality.[128] Given the low overall purchasing
power commanded by the sub-elite population in most Roman cities,
those fluctuations imply that the demand most city-dwellers generated
for manufactured goods and services was therefore even more uncertain
than the demand generated by consumers in the early modern period.[129]

If we can conclude that volatile food prices and low overall purchasing
power rendered the majority of urban residents in Rome and in other cities
of the empire unable to generate regular and predictable demand for
manufactured goods and services even in the aggregate, it remains more
difficult to gauge the level and intensity of the demand for manufactured
goods generated by members of urban middle-income groups. At first
glance, there are some grounds for optimism about their overall purchasing
power, and hence about their potential to generate predictable levels of
demand. These individuals constituted somewhere between one-eighth
and one-quarter of the population of any given city, and earned at least
2.4 times the cost of basic subsistence. They included the better-paid
members of the military, successful businessmen of various kinds (artisans,
wholesalers, bankers, merchants, etc.), as well as those who derived the
majority of their wealth from the direct or indirect exploitation of agricultural properties. The purchasing power of members of this social group
was potentially less vulnerable to fluctuations in food prices than was that
of members of lower-class social groups, for two reasons: (1) they were
shielded in part from such fluctuations because of their relative prosperity;
(2) they could smooth their consumption when they were short on cash by
securing shop credit from retailers and manufacturers.[130]

Here too, however, caution is necessary, since there are reasons to believe
that members of this social group did not generate the kind of regular and
predictable demand for manufactured goods and services that gradually

largest landowner and took in considerable grain in direct revenue above and beyond what it
collected in tax; this too was arguably released onto the market.
[128] Erdkamp 2005: 147–50.   [129] Cf. Erdkamp 2013b: 267–9.
[130] For more discussion about shop credit, see Chapters 2 and 4.

began to mitigate demand uncertainty in product markets catering to working- and middle-class consumers in the seventeenth and eighteenth centuries. More specifically, Jan de Vries has argued that the growth of demand in these markets was catalyzed by new and historically specific forms of consumption that did not necessarily have analogs in the Roman world. These forms of consumption were rooted both in a growing aware-ness of the ways in which the utility of individual goods could be increased in combination with other goods, and in an increasing appreciation for relatively inexpensive and replaceable goods that were valued more for their fashionability than for the intrinsic value of their materials. De Vries' argument concerning the first of these two processes is based on the concept of "consumption clusters." This idea stresses that members of working- and middle-class families actively developed ways of articulating identity by combining new goods together in novel ways – by using, for instance, specialized tableware to consume tea mixed with sugar – thus expanding both the range and the quantity of comestible and durable goods that they purchased on the market. His argument concerning the second idea hinges on the increasing "breakability" of many of the consumer goods that enjoyed widespread circulation in the seventeenth and eighteenth centuries; put simply, these goods were designed to have a relatively short useable life – that is, to be consumed in the proper sense rather than to be treated as stores of value. Together, the emergence of "consumption clusters" and the increasing breakability of many of the manufactured goods produced in the early modern period prompted working- and middle-class consumers to make frequent and regular purchases of manufactured items drawn from an ever-widening repertoire of goods.[131]

There are some signs that individuals belonging to different social groups in the ancient world may have constructed rudimentary con-sumption clusters of their own. In his recent monograph on changes in Roman material culture during the late Republic and early Empire, Andrew Wallace-Hadrill studies the kinds of consumer goods manufactured for an increasingly broad clientele from the first century BCE onward. Many of these articles were employed in domestic contexts, consumed primarily by purchasers interested both in personal luxury, and in using that luxury to advertise claims about status and identity. Though based originally on Hellenistic Greek models, most of these goods came to be produced locally from the first century BCE onward

---

[131] De Vries 2008: 31–7 (consumption clusters) and 129–33 (breakability).

in Italian variations and idioms, and to varying standards of quality and workmanship. Finds from Pompeii, for instance, demonstrate that standing bronze candelabra were popular, along with the bronze lamps that they supported. The most elaborate of these were crafted in the form of standing figures possessing internal oil reservoirs and bearing torches in which the wicks were seated, but most were simple upright poles supported by three feet and decorated with common motifs such as acanthus leaves. Comparable articles existed in other, less costly, materials: candelabra could be made from iron instead of bronze, and lamps, tableware, and articles of toilette could be ceramic rather than metal.[132] More recently, Emanuel Mayer has argued that comparable processes in funerary and domestic art began during roughly the same period of time as inhabitants of Roman cities began commissioning decorated tombs and beautifying their living spaces in towns such as Pompeii.[133]

More importantly, Wallace-Hadrill and Mayer both propose that these new forms of consumption were not the exclusive province of the elite but were also enjoyed by members of several other social groups. Mayer has stressed not only that much of the extant funerary and domestic art was commissioned by members of the social strata to which wealthy businessmen, merchants, and artisans belonged but also that the iconography of much of this funerary art reflects a desire on the part of members of this social group to express their own distinct identity and values.[134] Likewise, Wallace-Hadrill argues on the basis of find locations that the increasingly popular material goods circulating from the first century BCE onward were acquired by some members of middling income groups. For example, many of the bronze vessels in Pompeii, though hardly everyday items, were found in houses that were neither the largest nor the most lavish.[135] On these and on comparable grounds, Wallace-Hadrill concludes that the spread of this new culture of consumption was driven primarily by the desires of several different constituencies in Italy and beyond to articulate their own particular understandings of status and membership in the broader community of the Roman Empire. The municipal elite of Italian towns formed one such

---

[132] Wallace-Hadrill 2008: 356–440.

[133] Mayer 2012: 100–65 (funerary art) and 166–212 (domestic art).

[134] *Ibid.*, and esp. 110–20 (on tomb iconography evoking work and success); 120–37 (an increasing emphasis on emotional depictions of love and loss in epitaphs, reliefs, and statuary); 142–65 (the evocation on sarcophagi of myths signaling tragic death or loss).

[135] Wallace-Hadrill 2008: 376–7 and 402–6.

constituency. Although its members had been granted Roman citizenship as a consequence of the Social War in the 80s BCE, in practice most remained excluded from political office in Rome itself until they began to penetrate the imperial aristocracy in larger numbers in the middle of the following century. For individuals in this position, membership in the larger imperial community could therefore be best expressed through consumption as a marker of identity. The same was possibly true of members of a second constituency, namely freed slaves, who were likewise marginalized socially and politically, even though a very few came to control great wealth. Members of the middling ranks of society – particularly soldiers and military colonists – formed a third constituency. Here, the consumption of various kinds of goods served as a marker of the inherent status and dignity of the Roman citizen, which Augustus emphasized as part of his "restoration" of the Roman Republic. Finally, as Italians took their new forms of consumption with them beyond Italy, they prompted comparable developments among a final constituency: wealthier members of Rome's provincial population.[136]

That consumers apart from the elite were participating in new forms of material culture and consumption is significant, since it may have promoted a degree of mild but intensive growth in the first centuries BCE and CE by thickening product markets enough to encourage elevated levels of specialized production in Italy itself. Yet, at the same time, certain features of this new culture of consumption set it apart from comparable changes in the early modern period. First, many of the goods that formed the focus of the new culture of consumption were either made from materials of high intrinsic value (such as bronze candelabra and serving vessels, or decorative items made from iron), or were irregular and exceptional purchases, such as elaborately decorated tombs. These are not the kinds of goods that feature heavily in the consumption clusters at the heart of de Vries' analysis, and which ultimately fueled the growth of early modern consumer markets by stimulating increasingly regular purchases – that is, goods made from lower-cost materials and sensitive enough to changes in fashion that their useful lifespans were limited. Second, the social reach of many of these new forms of consumption remained limited. The primary consumers of new material goods in Wallace-Hadrill's account, for example, belonged solidly among the wealthier members of sub-elite urban strata when they did not

---

[136] Wallace-Hadrill 2008: 356–440 and esp. 435–40. On the motivations for (and cultural implications of) the spread of new material goods and their consumption to provincial populations, cf. Woolf 1998: 169–205.

belong to the urban elite itself. Pottery may represent the main exception: although pottery could be considered a "downmarket" version of more expensive work in metal, ceramic objects quickly developed artistic repertoires and distinctions in quality of their own, and they enjoyed both widespread circulation and (potentially) relatively limited lifespans.[137] Until archaeological research sheds more light on this problem, however, it seems best to conclude that members of middling economic groups in the Roman world did not necessarily seek to purchase manufactured goods with the intensity necessary to mitigate fundamental uncertainties in demand in a dramatic way.

Finally, recent research on the commercial structure of Rome itself dovetails with the view that the purchasing power of most urban residents remained limited and erratic, and that the demand they generated for manufactured goods was thus subject to considerable uncertainty (particularly relative to conditions in the early modern period). Claire Holleran has recently stressed that the commercial structure of the capital was dominated not just by *tabernae* – the ubiquitous small shops familiar from Pompeii, Ostia, and other well-preserved archaeological sites, and quite common in Rome itself – but also by street trading.[138] While this pattern was of course true in later European cities as well, two points are worth stressing. First, our evidence suggests that most artisans continued to engage in both production and retail. Although there were important exceptions in some industries (as we shall see in more detail in the next chapter), the retail side of manufacturing businesses does not seem to have given rise to the same level of specialization in antiquity as in a city such as London or Paris in the early modern period.[139] The nature of demand for manufactured goods offers one potential explanation: if that demand were neither as intense nor as regular as it was in other historical contexts, then we would not necessarily expect to find evidence for widespread and regular specialization or investment in retail by manufacturers. Second, it is possible that street trading was even more crucial in Rome than in early modern cities, in which fixed and well-appointed retail shops became increasingly important during the seventeenth and eighteenth centuries.[140] If so, then this was surely because street

---

[137] Wallace-Hadrill 2008: 386–91.
[138] Holleran 2012: 99–158 (*tabernae*, but note the evidence that some of these were likely residential units); 194–231 (street trade).
[139] On this phenomenon, see Sonenscher 1989: 31–4.
[140] For a general survey, see Farr 2000: 56–61. On conditions in eighteenth-century London, where the retail trade may have been more developed than on the continent, see Earle 1989b: 106–42 and Schwarz 1992: 57–73.

traders faced less overhead than shopkeepers, and could therefore price their wares lower. Since most urban consumers possessed limited and unpredictable purchasing power, the low price points at which hawkers and street traders could deliver basic goods were crucial if those consumers hoped to stretch the buying power of each *denarius*.[141]

From this perspective, what seems most significant about our evidence from the Roman world is not that it is broadly consistent with the view that demand was uncertain as well as seasonal for most urban artisans – that, after all, is expected given the prevalence of comparable problems in later periods – but rather that demand in Roman cities was probably more susceptible to these problems than was demand in the early modern European economy in the late stages of its preindustrial history. The economic environment of the Roman world must have seemed anything but predictable to the artisans who lived and worked within it, even though the Roman economy – as we shall see in later chapters – gave rise to complex subdivisions of labor in certain sectors. The anxieties reflected in Artemidorus' analyses of artisans' dreams therefore seem well-founded. What remains to be seen is how the profile of demand in ancient cities both affected artisans in the day-to-day operations of their businesses and interacted with other structures to generate either market opportunities or business challenges.

---

[141] See Holleran 2012: 216 on the low overheads carried by street traders, and on their ability to offer correspondingly low prices.

CHAPTER 2

Specialization, associations, and the organization of production

In the early fifth century CE, Augustine sought to explain what he believed to be a flaw in traditional polytheism by invoking the production of silver tableware as a metaphor for the tendency of pagans to assign highly specialized functions to individual gods.[1] In the process, he unintentionally provided a detailed account of how production was organized in a specific industry:

> We laugh indeed when we see pagan gods distributed by the whimsy of human opinion to tasks divided amongst them, just like contractors who bid to collect miniscule amounts of tax revenue, or like craftsmen in the quarter of the silversmiths, where one vessel passes through the hands of many artisans in order to come out perfect, even though it could have been completed by one perfect artisan. But it was thought necessary for a multitude of artisans to be consulted for no other reason than this, namely so that each artisan might learn one part of an art quickly and easily, and so that they would not all be compelled, slowly and with difficulty, to become perfect in a whole art.[2]

Augustine's comments are rightly taken as indicating that the artisans who worked in this particular industry had developed a sophisticated division of labor in which individual artisans specialized vertically in discrete stages of a complex production process.[3] Yet, at the same time, those comments obscure the answers to two important questions about the nature of the Roman economy. The first is the extent to which the divisions of labor he observed were based on intensive rather than extensive forms of human capital – that is, on human capital developed by artisans who had invested in costly and time-consuming training in specialist skills.[4] Augustine notes that the silversmiths who organized production on the basis of divisions of labor

---

[1] This chapter expands on Hawkins 2012.   [2] Aug. *De civ. D.* 7.4.
[3] Drexhage et al. 2002: 247; Ruffing 2008: 371; Wilson 2008: 395 and 405–6.
[4] On the distinction between intensive and extensive human capital, see Kim 1989, esp. 693–4.

did so in part so that each could quickly acquire training in a particular skill or process rather than learn the "entire art," but this means little without greater information concerning the range of skills necessary to produce a "perfect" vessel and the time it would have taken a single individual to perfect any one skill, let alone all. Thus, while one interpretation of Augustine's evidence might be that the silversmiths he observed had achieved efficiencies by reducing the amount of skill and training needed by each craftsman in the production chain, an alternative interpretation might stress instead that each specialist had invested intensively in mastering a relatively narrow but technically demanding skill that could only be acquired with long practice.[5]

The second important question obscured by Augustine's comment concerns the governance structure the silversmiths developed to coordinate the work of multiple specialists. Modern commentators have tended to assume that Augustine was describing a particular kind of governance structure, namely an individual firm or workshop, in which an owner or manager brought together the various specialists needed to produce complex goods.[6] Here too, however, alternative readings are possible, and Augustine's comments may in fact be more consistent with a model in which the silversmiths relied on a series of subcontracting agreements to coordinate their work: if anything, Augustine's reference to the "quarter" or "street" of the silversmiths (the *vicus argentarius*) conjures to mind not an integrated workshop, but rather the kind of artisanal district known from many early modern cities, in which the proprietors of highly specialized enterprises produced complex goods by subcontracting with one another for intermediate goods and services.[7]

These two questions are intimately related, since an economy's ability to support divisions of labor based on intensive human capital often depends directly on entrepreneurs' access to organizations or institutions that facilitate governance, especially when those divisions of labor reflect separate processes in a vertical chain of production.[8] Individuals generally choose to invest in the training necessary to develop intensive human

---

[5] Wilson 2008: 395, for instance, describes this as an example of "deskilling," when it may instead suggest that this particular industry had produced a large enough body of accumulated and practical knowledge that an individual silversmith could simply not master all of the relevant processes without years and years of training and experience. Cf. the comments of Becker and Murphy 1992: 1145–7 on the relationship between knowledge and specialization.

[6] Drexhage et al. 2002: 247; Wilson 2008: 405–6.

[7] See especially Hall 1962: 119. Ruffing 2008: 375–83 provides an overview of much of what we know concerning the topography of craft production in the Roman world.

[8] For theoretical considerations supporting this point, see Becker and Murphy 1992: 1142–5.

capital in the hope of earning a higher future income, but they can be deterred from doing so if they anticipate difficulty putting intensive skills to reliable and productive use. While thin or unstable product markets can discourage individuals from investing in specialized training by generating a strong perception that highly specialized workers will not find opportunities to profit from their skills, so too can institutional or organizational obstacles that make it difficult for individuals to develop governance structures that help coordinate production.[9]

In this chapter, I explore the linked problems of intensive specialization and coordination in the Roman world. While artisans and entrepreneurs in the Roman world developed vertical divisions of labor that relied on intensive investments in human capital in several industries, they coordinated the activities of specialist workers not by developing integrated firms, but rather by organizing subcontracting networks in which they contracted as necessary with one another for intermediate goods and services. Although this strategy was largely a response to seasonal and uncertain demand, which made integration costly, it was possible only because artisans could mitigate transaction costs by using their professional associations (*collegia*) as governance structures. Professional *collegia* therefore affected the performance of the Roman economy in complex ways. They established conditions for growth by supporting a higher degree of specialization in the urban economy, but because they were fundamentally exclusive in character, they were incapable of sustaining long-term improvements in productivity.

Collegia, transaction costs, and the theory of the firm

Even though professional *collegia* were widespread in the Roman world, there is still considerable debate about the precise nature of their impact on economic life in antiquity. By drawing on the theoretical insights of scholars who study economic organization from a transaction cost perspective, I suggest in what follows that we can gain traction on this problem by emphasizing one specific aspect of associational life in antiquity: the ability of a *collegium*'s members to regulate their private relationships with one another. This particular aspect of associational life in antiquity helps us to imagine how and why artisans employed *collegia* rather than firms as governance structures to coordinate the work of highly trained specialists.

---

[9] Kim 1989 and Lio 1998 present the basic theory. Cf. Grantham 1999 for a more general account of the relationship between coordination failures and specialization.

By the end of the Republican period at the very latest, professional *collegia* could be found in cities across the Roman Empire. Both in Italy and in the provinces of the Greek East, they had already enjoyed a lengthy history alongside other associations dedicated to the worship of a particular deity or founded on household, neighborhood, or ethnic affiliations.[10] These associations probably remained prominent in urban contexts in the late Republic and early Empire despite the Roman state's periodic pronouncements that *collegia* could not form without explicit authorization (symbolized by the grant of the *ius coeundi*, or the right to assemble). Although the Roman authorities were not enthusiastic about unlicensed *collegia* and sometimes took steps to suppress them, provincial and civic magistrates often tolerated them insofar as their members did not become involved in civic unrest.[11] Furthermore, under either Augustus or one of his early successors, the Roman state created an important exception to its general prohibition of unlicensed *collegia* by permitting so-called *collegia tenuiorum* (associations of the "rather humble") to assemble once a month and maintain a common treasury for funding funerals even without the formal authorization of the *ius coeundi*. In practice, this exception made it possible for urban residents to organize a wide range of groups and associations as *collegia tenuiorum*, including professional *collegia*.[12]

Because of their apparent and widespread popularity, these professional *collegia* have long interested ancient historians, who have sought to understand their place in the economic and social life of the ancient world. Broadly speaking, professional *collegia*, like other kinds of associations

---

[10] Our sources, both Greek and Latin, use a bewildering array of terms to refer to associations. I follow van Nijf 1997: 9 in using "*collegium*" as a catch-all term for a phenomenon which, despite regional and temporal variations, nevertheless exhibited important and ongoing continuities. For a good introductory discussion of taxonomy and membership, see Kloppenborg 1996: 18–26. Whereas previous scholarship tended to classify Latin *collegia* into functional categories (professional, religious, and funerary), scholars now see the different kinds of *collegia* as manifestations of the same basic organizational form, all of which appealed to roughly the same strata of the Graeco-Roman population. Cf. Harland 2003: 28–52.

[11] The question of the attitude of Roman authorities toward unlicensed associations has spawned considerable discussion. Liu 2005 argues that Roman authorities as a whole took a dim view of unlicensed associations but that the degree to which they tolerated them depended heavily on the attitudes of local provincial and civic magistrates. Others believe that the Roman authorities were far more lax in practice, particularly in the provinces, and that suppression of unlicensed associations occurred only sporadically. See de Ligt 2000, Arnaoutoglou 2002, and Arnaoutoglou 2005. Venticinque 2015 argues that relations between *collegia* and state were complex and could involve fine negotiation.

[12] The primary legal source for *collegia tenuiorum* is an excerpt from Marcian's *Institutes*, *Dig.* 47.22.1. pr. For professional associations and religious associations operating as *collegia tenuiorum*, see Verboven 2007: 873–4.

structured around neighborhood affiliation or religious practices, provided a social context in which members of the sub-elite strata of ancient urban populations could satisfy important social needs. First, professional *collegia* offered opportunities for sociability and conviviality. Most scheduled regular feasts and banquets, funded partly by individual members' contributions and partly by benefactors' generosity. Many also created sophisticated internal hierarchies that offered their members scope for competitive displays of status and social differentiation by permitting them to transform wealth into important forms of social capital. Second, religious ceremony was an important component of social life in all associations, not just those organized for religious or cultic purposes. The members of ancient professional associations often paid communal devotions to the imperial cult, to the *genius* of a particular craft, or to deities closely linked to specific professions. Third, all *collegia* offered important forms of social and financial support. Due to the nature of our evidence – much of which derives from inscriptions – funerary activities stand out as a particularly striking example: *collegia* often provided funeral services for those of their members who had no other form of social support or added pomp to funerals conducted by the families of the deceased. Finally, *collegia* made it possible for their members to interact with the broader structures of the civic community in ways that would have been difficult for them as individuals: together, members of *collegia* dedicated altars to civic deities or to the imperial cult; they engaged in relationships of patronage by commissioning monuments honoring important citizens in exchange for material benefits; and they participated collectively in civic ceremonies or religious processions. Like medieval and early modern guilds, *collegia* functioned as organizations in which moderately prosperous to relatively wealthy artisans could not only stake out a place for themselves within the association itself but also cultivate a sense of belonging and respectability that enhanced their standing in the broader civic community.[13]

On the other hand, there is less consensus among historians concerning professional associations' impact on economic life in the Roman world. Some clearly offered their members important and tangible benefits, though in many cases these benefits were confined only to associations

---

[13] The most important of the recent general treatments are van Nijf 1997, van Nijf 2002, Harland 2003, Tran 2006, and Verboven 2007. Flambard 1987 is also rewarding. Liu 2009: 247–77 examines these issues in the context of professional *collegia* of *centonarii*, workers in low- to medium-grade woolens. The importance of social and religious activities within even professional *collegia* was also recognized over a century ago by Waltzing 1895–1900, I: 161–333.

that had received formal recognition from the state in the form of the *ius coeundi*. From the mid- to late second century CE onward, for example, members of *collegia* that had received the *ius coeundi* could claim immunity from compulsory public services if they demonstrated that their associations offered public utility (*utilitas publica* or *utilitas civitatis*).[14] Likewise, beginning in the reign of Marcus Aurelius, *collegia* that had received the *ius coeundi* also became corporate bodies in a juristic sense and therefore obtained important legal capacities that were normally reserved for individuals: the ability to own property, manumit slaves, enter into litigation, and form contracts as corporate bodies. Jinyu Liu has recently argued that the state may have been likely to grant the *ius coeundi* to associations in order to form contracts with those that provided goods or services of special interest to its own goals: in particular, she suggests that artisans who worked in low- to medium-grade woolens (the *centonarii*) may have received official recognition for their *collegia* by arguing that incorporation would make it easier for them to supply textiles to the military. For artisans who joined such *collegia*, the chief benefit of the arrangement was greater opportunity to compete for a share of state contracts by subcontracting work from the association itself.[15]

More generally, much of the debate concerning *collegia* and economic life continues to be driven by responses to Sir Moses Finley's claim that "the communal activity [of professional *collegia*] was restricted to religious, social, and benevolent affairs," and that *collegia* themselves were distinctly different from medieval and early modern guilds, to which they are frequently compared. As is well known, Finley argued that professional *collegia* were neither "guilds trying to foster or protect the economic interests of their members" nor "regulatory or protective agencies in their respective trades."[16] Onno van Nijf's recent and comprehensive criticism of Finley's position suggests that its main weakness is its insistence upon a rigid dichotomy between the social and religious functions of *collegia* on the one hand and their economic functions on the other. Relying on recent studies in which historians have shown that social, religious, and economic functions were heavily entwined in the guilds or trade corporations of medieval and early modern Europe, van Nijf argues

---

[14] Liu 2009: 97–124 deals with these general issues in the context of *collegia centonariorum*.
[15] Liu 2009: 115–22. Cf. Wilson 2001: 291 and especially van Minnen 1987: 53–4, who notes that in Roman Egypt requisitions by the state were often mediated by professional associations. For further discussion, see Venticinque 2015.
[16] Finley 1999: 81 and 138. Cf. Burford 1972: 159–64. This view can be traced back to at least Waltzing 1895–1900, I: 161–333, and especially 181–95.

that there is no reason to think that professional *collegia* in the ancient world were any different. He adduces evidence purporting to show not only that *collegia* in the eastern Roman Empire did in fact serve a regulatory function in the economy, chiefly by governing relationships among their members, but also that they supported the "economic interests of their members" by staging collective demonstrations. In his view, the only reason that we do not see *collegia* engaging in this sort of behavior more often is that our evidence, consisting mostly of honorific or commemorative inscriptions, is unlikely by its very nature to reflect these kinds of activities.[17]

While van Nijf offers a valuable counterpoint to Finley's claims concerning the impact of *collegia* on economic life in the Roman Empire, his argument nevertheless elides an important distinction between Roman *collegia* and many medieval and early modern guilds. As Finley himself noted, the guilds of medieval and early modern Europe and the *collegia* of the Roman world interacted with state power in dramatically different ways. Shaped by a medieval ideology stressing the importance of corporatism as a structuring principle in civic life, medieval and early modern guilds typically functioned as formal, state-sanctioned institutions that set some of the basic ground rules of economic activity in late medieval and early modern cities. Although the fortunes of individual guilds rose and fell throughout the early modern period, guilds generally enjoyed regulatory authority and nominal monopolies over the practice of their trades by virtue of municipal or royal concessions. They exercised this authority (with varying degrees of diligence and success) by promulgating and enforcing corporate statutes that were, in theory, binding not only upon their members but also upon all those who sought to practice trades that impinged on any given guild's privileges.[18] Roman *collegia*, on the other hand, were typically unable to regulate economic life in the same way. Although some individual *collegia* may have purchased monopoly rights over narrow sectors of the economy in their cities from the civic authorities, such occasions seem to have been the exception rather than the

---

[17] Van Nijf 1997: 12–18.
[18] Guilds that possessed regulatory powers over their trades were widespread in early modern Europe (particularly in France and in the Holy Roman Empire), but not universal. In France, for instance, some towns and suburbs remained unincorporated. In England, trade corporations (the so-called livery companies) were already well in decline in the eighteenth century and had increasingly little to do with the regulation and management of the various trades. Farr 2000: 20–32 provides a general overview of the corporations. On France, see Sewell 1980: 16–39 and Farr 1988: 35–59. On the declining role of the livery companies in England, see Schwarz 1992: 209–21 and Berlin 1997: 83–8.

rule.[19] During the early Empire, the vast majority of professional *collegia* remained private associations. Individual artisans were free to join or not as they saw fit, and membership was not mandatory.[20]

Yet in some sense it was precisely in their role as private associations that professional *collegia* may have most strongly affected economic life, simply because their members relied heavily on norms propagated within these organizations to regulate their relationships with one another, both in their private and business lives. According to the jurist Gaius, members of *collegia* had been entitled to make whatever laws or pacts with one another they wished since the days of the Twelve Tables in the mid-fifth century BCE, so long as they did not violate public law.[21] Thus, from a very early date, professional *collegia* could structure economic relationships among their members, despite a limited ability to exercise formal regulatory functions in the economy. The pact made by a number of salt-dealers in the Egyptian city of Tebtunis during the middle of the first century CE offers a clear example of this principle in action. These individuals agreed to parcel out trading areas by lot, abide by clearly specified minimum prices, and assign to one of their own members the responsibility of gathering and paying all necessary taxes. While this agreement was once thought to reflect the operations of a cartel that had purchased monopoly rights from the state, it is now recognized as a private arrangement between individuals who constituted a small professional association and who governed their transactions with one another by mutual consent.[22]

The transaction cost approach pioneered by Ronald Coase offers a conceptual framework for understanding how and why artisans' ability to regulate their relationships privately within *collegia* may be crucial to our understanding of these organizations' economic significance.[23] More specifically, Roman artisans may have been able to use the private regulatory functions of *collegia* to transform these organizations into

---

[19] See, e.g., *IGR* 4, 352, with the comments of van Nijf 1997: 15. The inscription seems to provide evidence for a monopoly over money-changing in Pergamum granted by the state.

[20] The idea that *collegia* lacked formal regulatory functions is not new. In addition to Finley 1999: 81 and 138, see Waltzing 1895–1900, I: 181–95 and MacMullen 1974: 75–7. Van Minnen 1987: 60–72 collects evidence from Roman Egypt that is relevant to this issue and discusses it in the wider context of the Graeco-Roman world. Carrié 2002: 311–15 argues that membership in *collegia* became compulsory after Diocletian's reforms to facilitate the state's collection of taxes and *munera* (but see Sirks 1993: 161–2 and Garnsey 1998: 77–87 for the contrary view); on 328–9, however, he holds that even then *collegia* assumed no other formal regulatory functions.

[21] Gaius, *Dig.* 47.22.4.

[22] *P. Mich.* V 245. On this text, see the comments of van Minnen 1987: 64–5, in addition to those of van Nijf 1997: 13–14.

[23] Coase 1937 and Coase 1960, esp. 16.

governance structures with which they could coordinate the efforts of multiple specialists who had invested heavily in intensive human capital. By providing organized governance structures, both firms and networks permit entrepreneurs to circumvent problems that would make it difficult or undesirable for them to coordinate production were they to contract instead with specialists whenever necessary. Networks, however, can do so in ways that permit entrepreneurs to adapt more effectively to seasonal and uncertain demand than can firms.

In its most basic form, the transaction cost approach seeks to explain why some entrepreneurs choose to coordinate production by entering into arms-length contractual exchanges to secure intermediate goods and services, and why some instead coordinate production by embedding transactions in organized governance structures, such as firms or networks.[24] This approach departs from neoclassical models of economic behavior by assuming that economic actors almost never have easy access to the information about potential partners or about the economic environment that would permit them to make fully informed decisions. From this perspective, contractual exchange – especially arms-length contractual exchange between anonymous partners – is far from frictionless, and individuals typically incur transaction costs whenever they enter into exchange relationships. These are conceptualized as the direct and opportunity costs that arise because of the time, energy, and resources that individuals must expend to complete important components of an exchange, such as vetting potential economic partners, negotiating agreements in the face of potential uncertainties, and enforcing the terms of any resultant contracts.[25]

The magnitude of these costs depends largely on how effectively the institutional environment buffers an entrepreneur against sources of friction that might otherwise impede contractual exchange. Access to effective and predictable legal institutions can be particularly decisive, since these can mitigate problems of contract enforcement that might otherwise discourage exchange altogether. In practice, however, even effective and predictable legal institutions can be ill suited to enforcing certain kinds of transactions. When, for instance, future economic conditions are difficult to anticipate, individuals often find it impossible to frame contracts in ways that anticipate all possible contingencies, and

---

[24] Framed in this way, the model is historically specific in that it presupposes a context in which contractual exchange is supported by extant institutions. In that sense, it is, in theory, wholly applicable to the Roman world.

[25] See Acheson 2002 and Ensminger 1992: 1–32 for brief introductions to many of these issues. Frier and Kehoe 2007 discuss ways in which they might inform our approach to the ancient evidence.

instead leave their agreements at least partly open-ended. Disputes arising from these kinds of contracts can be particularly difficult for courts to resolve.[26] The same is true for transactions in which product quality is crucial to one or both partners, since quality requirements are often difficult to articulate in the terms of a contract.[27] Some of the most severe transaction costs arise when one partner exploits these limitations of contract enforcement by opportunistically reneging on an agreement or by attempting to renegotiate the terms of a contract in his or her own favor when it is least convenient for the other partner to do so.[28]

In classical formulations of the transaction cost approach, economic actors will seek to develop organized governance structures to coordinate production when high transaction costs interfere with (or even obstruct) their ability to do so by relying on arms-length contractual exchange. Those structures include firms and networks, each of which permits entrepreneurs to mitigate some transaction costs, provided that they are willing to incur certain organizational costs in their place. The firm can be defined as "an integrated and durable organization of people and other assets, acting tacitly or otherwise as a 'legal person,' set up for the purpose of producing goods or services, with the capacity to sell or hire them to customers, and with associated and recognized corporate legal entitlements and liabilities."[29] As a structure of governance, the firm enables an entrepreneur or director to coordinate production by internalizing transactions that would otherwise take place between independent actors through contractual exchange – namely, by incorporating them into a single organization, under a clear managerial hierarchy. An entrepreneur who coordinates production in this way will incur certain costs: some of these arise because large and complex organizations can be less responsive to sudden changes in market conditions, while others reflect the need to create internal incentive structures to replace the high-powered market incentives that motivate independent contractors to find new ways of improving quality or reducing prices. At the same time, however, the entrepreneur can rely on his own authority to reduce or eliminate some of the more severe transaction costs (like those related to the enforcement of contracts) that might make coordinating production through contractual exchange difficult or even impossible.[30]

---

[26] Klein 1996. Cf. Gibbons 2005: 236–8.

[27] For the theory behind this claim, see Baker et al. 2002: 58–61.   [28] Farrell 2005: 464–5.

[29] Hodgson 1999: 235–41 and esp. 238.

[30] Here, I simplify a complex body of scholarship characterized by a variety of theoretical approaches to the firm. For good, recent overviews of that scholarship, see Gibbons 2005 and Zenger et al. 2011. Despite the differences in the theoretical orientations adopted by theorists of the firm, however,

Like firms, networks also allow entrepreneurs to coordinate production without incurring many of the transaction costs typical of arms-length contractual exchange. While entrepreneurs who rely on network forms of governance coordinate much of their production through contractual exchange, they embed those exchanges within relationships of trust that persist beyond a single transaction. In their simplest form, these relationships involve bilateral relational contracts grounded on ties of trust and reciprocity between individual entrepreneurs, who rely upon one another to be honest and to show forbearance in their transactions when unexpected circumstances arise. The trust crucial to this kind of relational contracting is generally underpinned by a specific economic consideration, namely the extent to which parties to a contract believe that they stand to gain from ongoing cooperative exchange. So long as both parties anticipate that they will benefit from additional interactions with one another in the future, they will possess an incentive to honor the terms of their agreements.[31] Complex and multilateral relationships of trust, however, can arise in well-defined and exclusive networks that support organized mechanisms for the private enforcement of contracts. Entrepreneurs who coordinate production within a private-order enforcement network do incur costs, both direct and indirect: they typically pay membership fees; they face opportunity costs if they refuse to contract with partners outside the network; and they must often resolve disputes internally rather than by invoking formal legal institutions. That said, these networks confer important advantages. For one thing, members can continue to benefit from the high-powered market incentives associated with contractual exchange, even if the pool of potential partners is constrained by the boundary of the network. More importantly, because private-order enforcement supports powerful reputation mechanisms, entrepreneurs who use them to coordinate production can also mitigate the costs of enforcing contracts. Members of private-order enforcement networks rely heavily on individual reputations to identify reliable partners and also to signal to others that those guilty of negligent or opportunistic behavior are not to be trusted. Conversely, members who engage in questionable

Gibbons 2005: 236 notes that "the shared message of all four theories can be stated as follows: if contract imperfections are wreaking havoc under one governance structure, consider changing to another (e.g., integrate a transaction formerly conducted under non-integration)."

[31] McMillan and Woodruff 2001: 2430–2. The work of Clifford Geertz on economic strategies in Moroccan bazaars is also highly informative: see Geertz 1978 and Geertz et al. 1979: 197–235. For theoretical discussions of relational contracting (particularly as they relate to the boundaries of the firm), see Baker et al. 2002 and Gibbons 2005: 236–8.

behavior often find that others become reluctant to enter into exchange relationships with them, and thus have considerable incentive to honor their agreements. For these reasons, private-order enforcement networks can generate more trust and transactional security than the bilateral relationships typical of looser forms of network organization.[32]

Since much of the relevant literature focuses on the trade-off entrepreneurs must make between the transaction costs imposed by arms-length contractual exchange and the organizational costs associated with alternative modes of governance, it stresses that entrepreneurs choose to coordinate production in a manner that minimizes these total costs. Crucially, however, entrepreneurs often face an equally important trade-off in the realm of production costs:[33] although they can generate economies of scale by integrating production within a firm, they do so at the cost of transforming variable costs into fixed costs. Entrepreneurs can realize economies of scale so long as they can decrease per-unit production costs by increasing their output without increasing all of their inputs commensurately – as is the case when they can expand output by making more intensive use of their workspace rather than by renting larger (and costlier) facilities. Yet, at the same time, entrepreneurs must incur fixed costs that they would otherwise avoid by relying on disintegrated strategies of production – that is, on strategies based either on arms-length contractual exchange or on contractual exchange mediated by a network. Among other things, while entrepreneurs who coordinate production via contractual exchange pay for the services of specialists only when necessary, those who integrate production within a single firm must assume the regular and ongoing costs of paying specialists on a permanent basis.

On a practical level, this trade-off means that entrepreneurs may avoid creating integrated firms when their economic environment makes it dangerous to bear extensive fixed costs, even if integration could reduce their transaction costs. Although the economies of scale generated by firms will tend to outweigh the fixed costs arising from integration when product markets are stable enough for regular and predictable levels of output, the reverse will often be true when demand is uncertain or seasonal, as was the case in most urban product markets in the Roman

---

[32] Richman 2004 offers a recent and in-depth theoretical and empirical investigation of networks of this kind, which draws extensively on earlier scholarship dealing with so-called private law (on this, see esp. Bernstein 2001). In some disciplines, networks of this sort are classified as "hybrid" governance structures (e.g., Zenger et al. 2011: 117–18).

[33] A point not always appreciated by theorists of the firm, who tend to obscure the issue of production costs in their analyses. See Coase 1988: 38 for brief remarks about this problem.

world.[34] When entrepreneurs cannot easily anticipate the specific needs of their clients, for example, they can find it prohibitively costly to maintain specialists whose services are required only occasionally. Likewise, when demand for a particular product or service is seasonal in character, entrepreneurs may find it equally costly to maintain enough production capacity throughout the year to meet peak levels of demand, especially if the magnitude of that demand is difficult to predict.[35] In these circumstances, a network often represents the only viable, organized governance structure for entrepreneurs who are unwilling or unable to coordinate production by relying on arms-length contractual exchange. Individuals' ability to reap gains from intensive specialization – along with the ability of specialization and divisions of labor to generate intensive growth in the economy as a whole – can therefore depend heavily on whether they can create stable-enough networks to mitigate transaction costs and to coordinate decentralized or disintegrated production effectively.[36]

In light of the seasonal and uncertain demand characterizing most urban product markets in antiquity, many artisans in the Roman world probably found it impractical or undesirable to develop large firms, even when the scope of the market made possible the emergence of divisions of labor based on intensive human capital. For that reason, we should expect to see evidence that artisans who succeeded in cultivating such divisions of labor did so by coordinating the work of specialists without integrating them into one enterprise. While some may have done so by relying on arms-length contractual exchange, many may have chosen instead to use *collegia* as network-based governance structures, particularly since – as the example of the Tebtunis salt merchants illustrates – members seem to have used these organizations to regulate relationships with one another. In the next two sections, I explore this hypothesis in more detail. First, I show that artisans in some industries did indeed develop divisions of labor based on intensive human capital, even though they did not organize integrated firms. Second, I suggest that there are good reasons for believing that artisans used *collegia* as governance structures in order to coordinate

---

[34] For a concise statement of the advantages of decentralized production, see the work by Sabel and Zeitlin 1997: 20–1, which summarizes the much longer arguments of two earlier publications: Piore and Sabel 1984; Sabel and Zeitlin 1985. See also Sonenscher 1989: 135–8; Schwarz 1992: 32–3; Farr 2000: 52–6.

[35] Mead 1984: 1096.

[36] This statement is essentially a specialized application of the more general model articulated in Becker and Murphy 1992. It is also closely related to the ideas about coordination and specialization developed in Grantham 1999.

subcontracting relationships, precisely in those industries in which divisions of labor based on intensive human capital flourished.

Specialization, subcontracting, and disintegrated production in the Roman world

It has become increasingly clear that urban artisans of the seventeenth and eighteenth centuries rarely developed large and integrated firms. Instead, when artisans exploited divisions of labor to manufacture complex goods, they were more likely to coordinate production by contracting with other producers for intermediate products and services. This was true even though artisans catered to several different segments of the market by producing goods that can be lumped for conceptual purposes into three main categories.[37] Undifferentiated goods were those that were manufactured to standardized forms, exhibited little variation from piece to piece, and were frequently made of inexpensive materials so that they could be sold at relatively low prices; they include articles like low-end footwear, inexpensive clothing, and basic furniture. Although artisans who manufactured these goods often broke production down into a series of steps that required minimal dedicated training, they tended to put out individual steps to subcontractors who worked in their own homes instead of employing numerous unskilled or semi-skilled workers in their own premises.[38] High quality, bespoke goods occupied the other end of the spectrum. The value of goods in this class depended not just on costly materials but also on the skills of workers who specialized intensively in specific intermediate processes or techniques. The coach-building industry offers the paradigmatic example. While coachbuilders themselves often constructed the chassis of their vehicles, they relied on other specialists for a whole range of intermediate and high-quality products and services: blacksmiths produced axles, wheels, and springs; leatherworkers fitted out the harness and other trimmings; and artisans of various other kinds took care of painted, carved, and gilded decoration. Significantly, coachbuilders and other high-end artisans tended not to maintain such specialists as permanent employees, but rather commissioned specific components or services from subcontractors to

---

[37] For general discussions of subcontracting in the early modern economy, see Farr 2000: 52–6, Sonenscher 1989: 135–8, Schwarz 1992: 31–3, Lis and Soly 2008, and Riello 2008. I have adapted the typology of goods articulated here from Riello 2008: 262–3.

[38] These strategies are documented particularly well in London. See Schwarz 1992: 179–207.

meet the needs of individual clients.[39] Finally, so-called populuxe goods
occupied a wide band in the intermediate segments of the market. These
tended to be fashionable items like watches, umbrellas, and quality
furniture, all of which could exhibit some variety in form or decoration,
even though they often came ready-made and in standard configurations. The manufacture of many of these goods demanded collaboration
by multiple craftsmen, each of whom had specialized intensively in
particular materials, processes, or techniques, but here too
entrepreneurs only rarely developed firms to coordinate production.[40]
The furniture industry of the eighteenth century seems to have been the
main exception to this rule: in this industry, entrepreneurs like Thomas
Chippendale in London created large firms that united a number of
different specialists in one establishment, where they manufactured
both customized high-end goods and a wide range of more standardized
products for the emerging middle-class market.[41]

Although institutional and cultural factors contributed to the
proliferation of subcontracting in the early modern period, much of this
subcontracting can nevertheless be explained in terms of the economic
considerations discussed in the previous section. On the institutional level,
in those cities where guilds and trade corporations exercised monopoly
privileges over the production and sale of finished or semi-finished goods,
individual artisans or entrepreneurs could not always employ craftsmen
belonging to different guilds directly and were instead compelled to
coordinate production through subcontracting arrangements.[42]
The cultural value artisans themselves attached to proprietorship and
independence also came into play, as it encouraged many to set up shop
on their own account.[43] Yet a strong case can be made that subcontracting
would have been widespread even in the absence of these factors, precisely
because the seasonal and uncertain character of demand in most urban
product markets meant that artisans who established large firms assumed
considerable risk when they incurred the fixed costs necessary to maintain
integrated production. That point is underlined by the continued scarcity
of integrated firms in London during the eighteenth century: even though
local London guilds had ceased to function as regulatory bodies early in the
century and could not prevent artisans from developing integrated firms,
most artisans and entrepreneurs who manufactured complex goods

---

[39] On coachbuilding in particular, see Campbell 1747: 229–33, Collyer 1761: 105–9, Earle 1989b: 23–4,
and Styles 1995: 113–14.
[40] See esp. Fairchilds 1993; cf. Pfister 2008: 36–44.   [41] Kirkham 1988: 57–81.
[42] Sonenscher 1989: 137–8.   [43] Riello 2008: 268–9.

nevertheless chose to contract with specialists for intermediate goods and services rather than draw those specialists together in individual enterprises.[44] Those who did experiment with vertical integration did so in industries in which the demand for specific products underwent exceptional changes that rendered the market less unstable. Thus, Thomas Chippendale and his colleagues in the London furniture industry were able to create integrated businesses partly because wealthier members of the urban middle classes developed a taste for furnishing entire rooms with matching pieces that could be delivered promptly; these customers generated enough demand for quality, ready-made furniture that manufacturers could afford to internalize some of the separate processes involved in its production.[45] Shoemakers in Marseilles, on the other hand, were able to develop large firms mostly because they expanded the geographical range of their market into the growing colonies, where demand outstripped local output by a dramatic margin.[46]

Because artisans in the early modern context responded to seasonal and uncertain demand by relying heavily on subcontracting relationships, it seems likely that artisans in antiquity responded to comparable pressures by coordinating production in similar ways. In this section, I argue that the nature of urban demand deterred most artisans in the Roman world from developing integrated firms, even when they stood to benefit by cultivating divisions of labor. First, I suggest that the seasonal and uncertain character of urban product markets made sustained output risky for artisans who manufactured a wide range of goods – undifferentiated, bespoke, and populuxe – and that those risks were further exacerbated by the importance of credit transactions and the consequences of insolvency in the Roman world. Second, I show that artisans in many of the industries that gave rise to divisions of labor (and especially those that depended on intensive human capital) chose to coordinate production not by creating firms, but rather by structuring subcontracting agreements with other artisans.

Integration and its discontents

Artisans who manufactured undifferentiated goods in the Roman world – inexpensive articles such as basic household tools or furniture, ceramic coarsewares, and simple but functional pieces of clothing or footwear –

---

[44] Schwarz 1992: 32–3 and 206–7. More generally, see Farr 2000: 52–6. [45] Kirkham 1988: 57–81.
[46] Sonenscher 1989: 180–1.

enjoyed not only access to a potentially large market but also the luxury of producing at least some ready-made goods for inventory. Despite these apparent advantages, however, two features of the economic environment discouraged them from developing integrated firms. First, and as we have already seen, annual variability in crop yields and grain prices ensured that the overall purchasing power of most city-dwellers in the Roman world (and, consequently, the demand these consumers generated for undifferentiated goods) remained unpredictable from year to year. For that reason, artisans who gathered the human and material assets necessary to sustain a regular output of undifferentiated goods within a large firm risked being unable to recoup their investments in materials and in labor in the short term. Most would have been unwilling to bear that risk, unless they had access both to low-cost storage for their goods and to ready sources of long-term credit. Second, many of the artisans who produced goods in this class competed for customers with retailers who acquired and sold goods that had been manufactured in the countryside by peasant householders during slack periods of the agricultural calendar. Because peasant householders often undertook production of this sort as a supplement to agricultural work instead of as a primary source of income, they could sell their goods to distributors at relatively low prices,[47] which distributors could pass on to consumers. Domestic textile production of this sort is best attested in Roman Gaul, where landlords like the Secundinii purchased rural textiles or collected them from their tenants and sold them to traders at the farm gate.[48] In Italy, comparable products may have been moved from the countryside to the market in Rome by traders who circulated among the regular periodic markets in Italy's smaller regional centers. Not only were these markets (*nundinae*) timed to facilitate the movement of traders from one to another, they also served as a dendritic system, funneling products from rural Italy into Rome itself, where regular *nundinae* also took place; once in the capital, those products were most likely purchased by stallholders or by street vendors who operated with very little overhead and specialized in retailing low-cost goods.[49] The need to match the low prices of rural goods undoubtedly

---

[47] Erdkamp 1999.
[48] Wild 1999 discusses both the production of textiles in Gaul and the probable role of the Secundinii in the process. Drinkwater 1982, on the other hand, argues that the Secundinii played a much more active role as clothiers who bought and sold textiles on a large scale. Finally, Wilson 2001 suggests that Timgad in North Africa served as a node for the processing and distribution of rurally manufactured textiles, albeit to a higher segment of the market.
[49] On the *nundinae*, see de Ligt 1993, esp. 111–17; Morley 1996: 166–74. For distribution systems in Rome itself (*nundinae*, permanent installations, stallholders, and street vendors), see Holleran 2012.

prompted urban manufacturers to minimize their fixed costs; subcontracting offered a means of economizing not only on regular wage payments but also on rent.

As was the case in the early modern period, Roman artisans who manufactured high-quality and bespoke goods generally worked to specifications provided by clients with particularized tastes.[50] Because most of these goods were made to order, artisans working at this level of the market were rarely able to produce for inventory. More importantly, in those industries in which the quality of the final product depended on the ability of artisans to combine disparate materials and techniques, demand was uncertain not just because entrepreneurs could not predict how many orders they would receive but also because they could not predict precisely what combination of skills or materials would be necessary for any given project. Some sense of the different materials and processes that could be employed in a single project can be extracted from an honorific inscription commissioned in 105 BCE to commemorate the completion of a building project in Puteoli. The text of the inscription, the so-called *lex parieti faciundo*, articulates some of the conditions under which a building contractor was awarded a contract to construct a dividing wall opposite the town's temple of Serapis on the site of an earlier, decrepit structure. Included in the wording of the decree are detailed specifications not only for the materials and decorative elements of the wall itself (which was to be provided with copings, plastered, and painted with lime) but also for those of a new monumentalized wooden doorway intended to bisect it, complete with pillars, wooden moldings, and a tiled roof.[51] Since projects such as this involved considerable variation, it was impractical for artisans in building industries to maintain integrated firms of craftsmen specializing in all possible combinations of consumer preferences;[52] as we shall see in more detail below, the same was true in other industries geared toward the production of complex goods.

Articles such as bronze vessels, fashionable clothing, and mid-grade statuary can be conceptualized as the equivalent of early modern populuxe goods. These often exhibited some variation in form or in decoration even

---

[50] Earle 1989b: 114–15; Sonenscher 1989: 137–8. Cf. Coquery 1997 on the importance of the aristocratic hôtel in driving demand in Paris.

[51] *FIRA* III² 153.

[52] For early modern *comparanda*, see, e.g., Styles 1995: 114. Storper and Christopherson 1987: 104–6 discuss the problem in a more general sense.

though they were otherwise made to common specifications;[53] they also tended to be marketed at higher price points than undifferentiated goods, even if they were made of materials that ranged widely in cost and quality. Although artisans who produced goods in this class could smooth production over time by stockpiling at least some semi-finished goods more easily than artisans in bespoke trades, those who relied on divisions of labor were not necessarily insulated enough from the instability of most product markets to bear the fixed costs of integrated production. The potential importance of variation at this level of the market meant that artisans who manufactured relatively complex goods in this category, like those who worked for the high-end market, could not always predict exactly the balance of skills necessary for a single production season.[54] At the same time, producers of goods in this class also faced the possibility that the broadly seasonal and uncertain nature of agricultural production could alter the consumption patterns of even relatively prosperous urban residents in unpredictable ways.

The problems artisans faced because of seasonal and uncertain demand were only exacerbated by the importance of credit in the urban economy and by the potentially severe consequences of insolvency. Shop credit was a ubiquitous feature of life in the cities of early modern Europe, in which artisans and retailers not only extended credit to clients at all levels of the socioeconomic spectrum but also depended heavily on credit extended to them by their own suppliers and subcontractors. Undoubtedly, the same was true in the Roman world. As early as the second century BCE, the comic playwright Plautus joked about the expensive tastes of well-dowered wives, who – at least in the view of the wealthy bachelor Megadorus in *Aulularia* – bought so many goods and services on credit that a husband was likely to find artisans and retailers crowding the atrium of his townhouse, demanding payment for goods and services rendered.[55] The Roman jurists confirm that shop credit was a common feature of urban life, and they also demonstrate that artisans and retailers themselves typically purchased goods and services on credit from their own suppliers. Papinian, for example, discusses a relatively straightforward case in which

---

[53] On commonalities in form among Roman manufactured goods, see Wallace-Hadrill 2008: 361–71.

[54] This problem was increasingly pressing in the early modern period for artisans who produced populuxe goods, since fashions could change quickly (see, e.g., Schwarz 1992: 32). Fashions may have been less volatile in the ancient world, but there too particular iconographic schemes might wax and wane in popularity. For a good discussion of the relationship between standardization and consumer preference, and of how that relationship affected the manufacture of one particular product in this category (marble sarcophagi), see Birk 2012.

[55] Plaut. *Aul.* 505–19.

a father bequeathed to his son a purple-seller's shop, along with the shop's stock-on-hand and its slave employees.[56] The recipient of the legacy became embroiled in an argument with the estate's primary heir; the point of contention was whether or not other assets and liabilities that had been associated with the shop during the testator's lifetime were included in the legacy. Importantly, these included not only a sum of money set aside to buy additional stock but also what Papinian terms the business' *debita* and *reliqua* – that is, debts owed by the shop's slave managers to their suppliers and outstanding accounts payable consisting of shop credit extended by these same managers to the establishment's clients.

In practice, artisans who extended shop credit often found that clients did not settle their accounts quickly. This was especially problematic for those catering to affluent clients, who were likely to demand credit on long terms. When Cicero, for instance, asked his friend Gallus to purchase a collection of statues on his behalf, he sought to secure terms of credit from the seller Avianus that would permit him to defer payment for a full year.[57] In these circumstances, artisans needed to minimize ongoing fixed costs as much as possible so that they could devote most of their ready money to debt management. Otherwise, the costs of insolvency could be severe: because creditors in Roman law were able to execute on outstanding debts by seizing and auctioning off a defaulter's entire estate, producers who allowed their credit to become too extended risked losing all of their assets.[58] This may be precisely the kind of situation envisioned by Artemidorus of Daldis in his anecdote about the fate of the carpenter from the Greek city of Cyzicus, who was forced to abandon his workshop and emigrate from the city when he defaulted on debts to his creditors.[59] The Roman jurists offer valuable evidence that reflects a somewhat different context, preserved in a series of complex discussions concerning the so-called *actio tributoria*, which was created by the Roman praetors to deal specifically with situations in which slaves running semi-autonomous businesses on the basis of a *peculium* – a separate account awarded to them by their masters – defaulted on their debts. At that point, creditors could ask that the praetor order the slave's master to distribute the entire contents of the *peculium* among them to make good on the slave's debts. The existence of this remedy implies that semi-autonomous businesses

---

[56] Papinian, *Dig.* 32.91.2.
[57] Cic. *Fam.* 7.23.1. For the challenges artisans faced because of aristocratic clients and their demands for credit in the early modern period, see Styles 1995: 115 and Coquery 1997.
[58] Buckland 1921: 637–41. [59] Artem. 4.1.

run by slaves – some of which are envisioned by the jurists as artisanal enterprises – not only incurred debts from multiple suppliers but also became insolvent with some frequency. One suspects that the same was true for the businesses of free artisans who did not carefully manage their fixed costs and their credit relationships.[60]

Roman artisans and disintegrated production – bespoke goods

Given the pressures generated not just by seasonal and uncertain demand but also by the importance of credit and the potentially serious consequences of insolvency, Roman artisans arguably had strong reasons to shun integrated production, even when they worked in industries that could support divisions of labor based on intensive human capital. Our evidence for the organization of production confirms that expectation by showing not only that several industries gave rise to specialization in specific processes or techniques but also that entrepreneurs coordinated production in these industries by relying on subcontracting agreements rather than by creating integrated firms. This strategy is particularly well attested among artisans who produced for the bespoke and quality segments of the market, but as we shall see below, it can be detected in our evidence for production at other levels of the market as well.[61]

The building industry, which had grown particularly complex by the late Republic and early Empire, serves as the paradigmatic example of how production was organized in bespoke segments of the market. As noted above, the *lex parieti faciundo* of 105 BCE offers some sense of the materials and processes employed by builders. Even though construction in brick or concrete and agglomerated masonry became increasingly prevalent from the second century BCE onward, skill in dressing stone and working timber remained important for builders as well, as did skill in crafting

---

[60] Technically speaking, the slave needed to be engaged in regular business on the basis of his *peculium*, and the master had to be aware of this fact. See, in general, *Dig.* Title 14.4 and Buckland 1908: 233–8. Ulpian, *Dig.* 14.4.1.1, specifically mentions artisans as the sorts of slaves who might run semi-autonomous businesses (he lists launderers, tailors, and weavers as examples). The case of the slave who has acquired goods of some sort on credit is discussed by Ulpian, *Dig.* 14.4.5.18. Ulpian is interested here in a rather narrow legal question – if a creditor has handed over property for sale that is still in existence (e.g., raw materials that have not yet been consumed), who is the owner? The answer depends on the terms in which that property was handed over, and one of the possibilities that Ulpian envisions is a case in which it has been handed over in the expectation of future payment – that is, essentially on terms of credit. For the ubiquity of credit relationships in early modern England and the dangers they posed to artisans if they were not managed carefully, see Earle 1989b: 112–23. Finally, I discuss the *peculium* arrangement in more detail below.

[61] For other discussions of specialization, see Ruffing 2008: 370–5 and Wilson 2008.

a wide range of interior and exterior decorative elements in different materials, including marble, wood, plaster, and paint.[62] Several other pieces of evidence not only complement this sense of the industry's complexity but also indicate that it gave rise to a number of specialized trades, many of which required considerable skill and training. Some of this material is pictographic: the best-known example, a fresco from the Villa di San Marco at Stabiae, presents a scene of several men engaged in the construction of a building and shows individuals carrying out distinct tasks, such as stonemasonry and stucco work.[63] Comparable forms of specialization are envisioned by the Roman jurist Ulpian, who mentions in passing that slaves who had acquired specialized skills as plasterers or stonemasons were sometimes loaned out for use by their owners.[64] Finally, some of our inscriptional and papyrological evidence identifies men who specialized in specific trades within the construction industry. Stonemasons, plasterers, and stucco workers feature prominently in these sources, which also mention men who specialized either in work that demanded particular materials, such as marble, or in finishing work rather than in basic construction.[65]

More importantly, our evidence implies that most of the entrepreneurs and craftsmen who worked in this industry chose to operate specialized enterprises and coordinate with one another through subcontracting relationships rather than to develop comprehensive firms. On the most general level, the jurist Venuleius assumed that building contractors maintained only minimal permanent workforces of their own and recruited both unskilled and skilled workers as necessary for specific jobs. In his view, a conscientious builder was one who realized that he "should by no means hurry, gathering together craftsmen from all sides and employing a mass of workmen, nor on the other hand be satisfied with one or two," and instead made decisions about how much manpower he would employ by carefully assessing both the building site and the time-frame of the contract.[66] Although Venuleius himself unfortunately offers no further details about how building contractors organized production, other evidence strongly suggests that the craftsmen engaged by such

---

[62] For some of the varieties and techniques employed in the building trades, see Ulrich 2007: 59–201, DeLaine 2001, and DeLaine 2003: 724–7.

[63] Ruffing 2008: 371–2 briefly summarizes the main visual depictions of specialized builders at work.

[64] Ulpian, *Dig.* 13.6.5.7.

[65] The columbarium of the Statilii Tauri alone contains commemorations dedicated to several different kinds of building specialists: *CIL* 6.6283–6285 (*fabri*), 6.6363–6365 (*fabri tignarii*), 6.6318 (*marmorarius*), 6.6354 (*faber structor parietarius*).

[66] Venuleius, *Dig.* 45.1.137.3.

contractors were often specialists who operated their own enterprises, some of whom may have let out contracts themselves to other artisans.[67] In some cases, the physical remains of structures themselves point in this direction. Lynne Lancaster has observed that distinctive brick linings can be identified both on the vaulting of two groups of rooms in Trajan's market complex and on the vaulting of a group of rooms in the forum of Caesar, which was itself renovated during the construction of Trajan's forum; in her view, those linings can be understood as the handiwork of a building crew managed by a single, innovative craftsman, who accepted contracts to work alongside other craftsmen and their crews on different portions of the imperial forums in the early second century CE.[68] Funerary inscriptions commissioned by builders likewise suggest that independent specialists could be engaged at different stages of a building project for specific tasks, whether by a primary contractor or by the owner of the property. When Tiberius Claudius Celadus (probably either a freedman of the emperor Claudius or the descendant of one of Claudius' former slaves) commissioned a funerary monument for himself in the Roman suburb of Velitrae during the first century CE, he identified himself as a *redemptor intestinarius* – an independent contractor who specialized in interior finishing work.[69] Likewise, the monument of Caius Avilius December indicates that he worked in Puteoli as a *redemptor marmorarius*, a contractor who may have specialized in worked marble.[70]

On rare occasions, our literary sources also provide incidental glimpses of a building industry characterized not by large and integrated firms, but by specialists who worked alone or at the head of small enterprises, and who contracted with one another for any services they required. In his work on mental illness (or *mania*), the Cappadocian physician Aretaeus mentions a carpenter who specialized in interior woodwork and who suffered from periodic fits of madness. According to Aretaeus, the carpenter performed the technical aspects of his trade flawlessly while he was at work inside a house, and could "deal with those who let out the work (*ergodotai*), strike agreements with them, and exchange his work for fair pay." Yet if he left the house for any reason, then "once he was out of sight of the slaves and away from both the work and the place where he performed it, he went wholly mad."[71] The *ergodotai* envisioned here may have been the owners of the properties in which the carpenter was engaged

---

[67] For hiring practices in the building industry in general, see Lancaster 1998: 305–8 and DeLaine 2000: 121–3.

[68] Lancaster 1998, esp. 303–8.   [69] *AE* 1925.87.

[70] See, *AE* 1925.87 and *CIL* 10.1549, respectively. Cf. Anderson 1997: 110–11.   [71] Aret. *SD* 1.6.6.

to work, but it seems just as likely that they had themselves accepted contracts for construction or renovation and had subcontracted with other artisans for specialized services. The slaves, on the other hand, almost certainly belonged to and worked for the carpenter himself. A comparable picture of the building industry emerges from a series of letters written by Cicero to his brother Quintus more than a century before Aretaeus' text. After visiting Quintus' house on the Palatine in 56 BCE, Cicero wrote to his brother to reassure him that the renovations he had commissioned were in progress. Cicero had discovered the *redemptor* Longilius working hard alongside several builders whom Longilius either maintained as a permanent workforce or had recruited to work on the project. In a letter dated two years later, however, Cicero noted that while work was still ongoing on Quintus' property, it had been entrusted to other *redemptores* who specialized in interior finishing.[72] Cicero unfortunately makes no further mention of Longilius, and although this may mean that Quintus had entered into direct contracts with the *redemptores* applying the finishing touches to the house, it is not impossible that Longilius himself was still involved as the primary contractor.

While the scale and complexity of building operations may imply that the industry operated in a way atypical for artisan businesses as a whole, our evidence for the production of high-quality bespoke goods in precious and semi-precious metals indicates that artisans in these industries also specialized intensively as demand for their products expanded and coordinated their activities with one another by relying upon subcontracting agreements rather than integrated firms. Like building, the production of most high-value objects in precious metals incorporated several distinct processes by the late Republic and early Empire, many of which were complex enough to demand considerable training and experience. This had long been true of the production of monumental statuary, which spawned distinctions no later than the classical Greek period between the process of creating or manipulating the wax models from which molds were invested and the process of casting itself.[73] Yet the manufacture of smaller high-quality articles, often in gold and silver, also prompted artisans to refine and elaborate several techniques and processes. Goldsmiths and silversmiths could create a vessel either by casting it as a solid piece or by raising its body by hand from sheet metal (probably the more common

---

[72] On Longilius, see Cic. *QFr.* 2.6.3. On the other contractors, see Cic. *QFr.* 3.2.3 and 3.3.1. For further discussion, see Pearse 1974: 122–3, S. D. Martin 1989: 54, and Anderson 1997: 103–4.

[73] Mattusch 1996: 193–4. See the same volume, 8–19, for a more general discussion of statue-making techniques.

technique). After raising the body of a vessel, they planished its surface by striking it with overlapping blows from a small hammer. They could then employ one or more of the following decorative techniques: engraving; embossing; soldering separately crafted *appliqué* elements onto the vessel's body; inlaying the vessel with gilding or *niello*; and applying relief decoration by striking the vessel with specialized tools, either from inside (*repoussé*) or on its outer surface (chasing). Artisans next added elements such as the base and the handles, often cast or wrought separately and then soldered to the body of the vessel. Finally, they applied finishing touches. Even these final finishing stages of manufacture could be complex, since they demanded careful polishing and burnishing with a variety of different tools and materials, whether by hand or on the lathe.[74]

The demand for high-quality tableware seems to have provoked specialization in many of these individual processes. By the late Republican period, distinctions between different kinds of specialists among artisans who manufactured gold and silver plate were obvious enough that Cicero mentioned two broad categories of such specialists (*caelatores* and *vascularii*) in a wholly non-technical context in his prosecution of Verres, the former governor of Sicily. After claiming that Verres had confiscated masses of gold and silver plate from the inhabitants of several Sicilian cities, Cicero sought to persuade his audience that Verres had also "established an enormous workshop in the palace of Syracuse, where he ordered all artisans to assemble – those who engrave vessels (*caelatores*) and those who make them (*vascularios*) – and he himself had many artisans of his own."[75]

Even finer grades of specialization can be detected in the funerary inscriptions from Rome itself, where a concentrated body of wealthy consumers generated a particularly strong demand for high-quality metalwork. Although the surviving inscriptions date largely from the early Empire, the divisions of labor referenced may have existed already in Cicero's day. In addition to mentioning *vascularii* and *caelatores*, our inscriptions also reveal the existence of several other artisans specializing in individual technical processes or decorative techniques: *flaturarii*, or casters, who could in some cases manufacture tableware or flatware but more commonly produced components such as handles and bases by casting them in molds made from models; *crustarii*, who manufactured decorative elements applied to the surface of metal vessels by *appliqué*;

---

[74] Strong 1966: 7–13; Sherlock 1976: 11–23; Tassinari 1993: I, 225–30; Pernot 2004: 173–5.
[75] Cic. *Verr.* 2.4.54.

artisans skilled in a technique known as *ars toreutice*, possibly related to embossing, chasing, or *repoussé*; specialists known as *excusores* (or *exclusores*), whose precise function is obscure; *inauratores*, or gilders, who applied gold leaf to a range of products, including silver tableware; and, finally, *tritores*, or polishers, who finished items made of precious metals.[76]

In early modern London, where demand for high-quality metalwork was also strong, and where artisans likewise specialized heavily in individual processes, techniques, or in the manufacture of specific items, metalworkers had developed subcontracting strategies of considerable complexity no later than the eighteenth century. The ledgers produced in the 1740s and 1750s by the London goldsmith Edward Wakelin, for instance, show that he regularly employed at least eight subcontractors when filling orders for his own clients, all of whom maintained workshops of their own: a box maker; a burnisher; a caster; a second caster who moonlighted as a polisher; a silver turner; two chasers; and a specialist polisher.[77] Our evidence from the Roman world suggests that many artisans who specialized in distinct processes likewise operated their own enterprises and coordinated their efforts with one another through subcontracting arrangements rather than in integrated firms. Sandra Joshel has noted that it was common for Roman artisans either to represent themselves in their epigraphy or to be commemorated by others not only in terms of their occupations but also in terms of the district of the city in which they worked; in her view, these references to the location of work were intended to indicate that they were proprietors of their own establishments.[78] At least one *vascularius* was commemorated in this way – a freedman whose monument read "Marcus Atius Dometius, the freedman of Marcus Atius Anteros, and *vascularius* on the Sacred Way. He lived for sixty-two years, and was heir to a sixth part [of his patron's estate]."[79] Likewise, the engraver (*caelator*) and former slave Lucius Furius Diomedes commemorated his deceased wife in an epitaph designed in part to advertise his own status as the proprietor of an engraving workshop: "Lucius Furius Diomedes, freedman of Lucius and engraver on the Sacred Way, [put up this monument] for his wife Cornelia Tertulla, daughter of Lucius Cornelius." Two casters (*flaturarii*), both former slaves like Diomedes, are commemorated in essentially the same way, which suggests that they also ran autonomous enterprises.[80] Moreover, the fact

---

[76] Frank 1940, 5: 212–14; Strong 1966: 15–16; Von Petrikovits 1981: 83–119 and 120.
[77] Clifford 2004: 30–7. [78] Joshel 1992: 106–12. [79] *CIL* 6.37824.
[80] For the inscription commissioned by L. Furius Diomedes, see *CIL* 6.9221. The two inscriptions referring to *flaturarii* are *CIL* 6.9418 and 6.9419a.

that all of these craftsmen seem to have maintained premises on the Sacred Way (the *sacra via*) corroborates ancient claims that this particular street was known for its high-end shops.[81] In doing so, it emphasizes that Augustine's comments on specialization are more consistent with a model in which artisans collaborated with one another through subcontracting agreements than with one in which they created large and integrated firms: in Augustine's description, the context of production is not the individual workshop, but rather what he calls the *vicus argentarius*, or silversmith's district – that is, a neighborhood or street that was potentially much like Rome's Sacred Way, in which individual craftsmen specializing in various branches of production set up shop.[82]

Although our evidence for the intensity of specialization and the organization of production in other high-end industries is more scattered, we can nevertheless infer the existence of additional subcontracting, particularly when items were complex enough to demand the services of specialists who worked in different types of materials and techniques. The construction of a chariot or carriage required at a bare minimum the services of artisans who specialized in making the body, wheels, metal fittings, and leather suspension (when present); more elaborate examples also demanded artisans with a range of decorative skills.[83] A funerary inscription from Rome refers to an artisan who made his living by painting chariots, and while we cannot know whether or not he worked as an independent contractor, we do know that wheelwrights maintained their own workshops in antiquity, much as they did in later historical periods.[84] The high-quality bedframes from Herculaneum possess components and decorative elements made from a range of different materials (wood and bronze for the frames, gilding and inlay for the decorative elements); our inscriptions mention artisans who specialized in their manufacture (the *fabri lecticarii*), but these too perhaps subcontracted for intermediate parts or services as necessary. More generally, the production of high-quality wooden furniture and decorative items, much like the production of metalwork, involved a number of discrete processes that could have given rise to distinct specialities, including the creation of a carcass or frame by a joiner or cabinetmaker; the production of turned elements on

---

[81] See Joshel 1992: 107 and especially n. 32 on the high-end shopping districts of the city, along with Loane 1938: 113–21.

[82] August. *De civ. D.* 7.4.

[83] See Greene 1986: 38 for a brief overview of Roman vehicles and their construction.

[84] The chariot painter is attested in *CIL* 6.9793. For the wheelwright's shop, see Papinian, *Dig.* 43.10.1.4.

a lathe; and decorative processes, such as carving and inlay.[85] Greek and Latin sources periodically mention individuals who specialized in some of these processes, particularly carving and turning. They even suggest that such specialists operated as independent contractors rather than as members of integrated firms. There is some evidence that turners maintained workshops of their own, and the carpenter Saturninus, who features in Apuleius' *Apologia*, may have been a specialist carver: Apuleius does not explicitly identify him as such, but he describes most of the articles in Saturninus' shop as "carved."[86]

Roman artisans and disintegrated production – undifferentiated goods

Even though we possess only fragments of evidence about how artisans organized enterprises dedicated to the production of undifferentiated goods, those fragments are rewarding. They suggest that although some entrepreneurs who produced these goods not only exploited divisions of labor but did so within firms, the circumstances that permitted them to engage in integrated production were atypical. Fullers and bakers, for example, both broke down their production processes into relatively simple tasks that could be performed by workers who acquired the necessary skills quickly and on the job rather than via formal and intensive training. Some fullers delegated the unskilled and laborious chores of soaping and rinsing to subordinates, while they themselves handled the skilled components of the work personally – principally, the finishing stages of the process, in which the fuller raised, sheared, and polished the nap of a garment.[87] Likewise, Eurysaces' monument depicts both skilled and unskilled aspects of the baking and milling trade: while many of the men portrayed on its relief are engaged in the relatively skilled tasks of shaping loaves or managing the ovens, others are shown performing the menial work of turning mills or kneading machines with the help of draft animals.[88]

That said, fulleries and bakeries of this sort were atypical of businesses that produced undifferentiated goods. Because both tended to be more capital intensive than other enterprises, the entrepreneurs operating them had strong incentives to develop firms whenever they developed divisions

[85] Mols 1999: 91–110. For the *faber lectarius*, see *CIL* 6.7882.
[86] On turners, see Bagnall 1993: 85 and n. 252, who cites *P. Genova* I 24 (4c); Apul. *de Mundo* 1. Saturninus is implicitly described by Apuleius as someone who carves in Apul. *Apol.* 61.
[87] Flohr 2011; Flohr 2013: 96–121 and 242–87. For further discussion of labor in fulleries, see Chapter 3.
[88] Petersen 2003 provides an excellent discussion of the decorative elements on Eurysaces' tomb.

of labor. Yet the conditions that permitted them to develop divisions of labor are instructive in and of themselves, since they highlight the role played by demand in the organization of production. Large fulleries are attested best at Rome and Ostia, where fullers not only equipped establishments with multiple treading stalls and rinsing vats but also created rationalized workflows based on clear divisions of labor. What made these establishments possible was the unusually strong demand in the metropolis for imported textiles, all of which needed to be cleaned before they were sold to final consumers.[89] Proprietors of baking establishments, on the other hand, sold products for which demand was relatively inelastic. That inelastic demand mitigated the financial risks they faced when making the investments necessary to integrate the milling and baking processes – a step which afforded them better control over their supplies by reducing the risk that flour (always more perishable than grain) would spoil in transit.[90] Many of the surviving bakeries in Pompeii and Ostia are sizeable establishments in which workers both milled grain and baked bread: at Pompeii alone, there are thirty-one extant bakeries, twenty of which possessed animal-driven mills for grinding the grain; those without on-site milling facilities of their own may have specialized not in day-to-day bread, but rather in pastries or in other high-end products for which demand was not necessarily so regular.[91]

The less heavily a particular trade depended on fixed capital, and the less stable the demand for its products, the less likely an artisan was to coordinate the production of undifferentiated goods within a firm when it became possible to exploit divisions of labor. For these reasons, most of the entrepreneurs who manufactured goods of this class in the Roman world would have relied on subcontracting arrangements. The shoemaking industries of the seventeenth and eighteenth centuries offer a potential example of how subcontracting may have worked at this level of the market. Shoemakers in the early modern period performed most of the skilled aspects of their process in the workshop – typically, the initial cutting of the material and the final closing of the shoe, both of which required dedicated training. At the same time, they contracted out those stages of the work that did not require direct supervision and that relied on skills that could be acquired on the job, often to home-based workers.[92] The same may well have been true in antiquity. We possess no clear

[89] Flohr 2011: 93.   [90] Pelizzon 2000: 123.
[91] For a survey of the archaeological evidence for Pompeian bakeries, see Mayeske 1972.
[92] Riello 2006: 172–6.

evidence concerning the organization of the shoemaking trade in the late Republic and early Empire, but for what it is worth, Xenophon notes that the shoemaking trades of the fourth century BCE had already given rise to divisions of labor, not all of which demanded intensive skills, and not all of which required the shoemaker's direct supervision.[93]

Roman artisans and disintegrated production – populuxe goods

Much of the evidence for artisans' efforts to coordinate the production of populuxe goods is archaeological, and for that reason it can be difficult to interpret. Here too, however, there are indications of divisions of labor, at least some of which were based on intensive training in specialized skills. More importantly, although some of the evidence may point to integrated firms, there are reasons to believe that these remained unusual at this level of the market, even though many of these goods could be manufactured to partly standardized patterns. Instead, when entrepreneurs who manufactured goods of this class experimented with divisions of labor, they too appear to have coordinated production by subcontracting for intermediate goods and services rather than by creating integrated firms.

Recent studies of various durable goods made of marble suggest that the artisans who manufactured them not only developed some divisions of labor but also coordinated at least part of their production processes in integrated firms. The layout of the marble-working facilities at Simitthus in Tunisia offers the best evidence for a system of production organized along these lines. Here, in a structure originally constructed to house convicts condemned to hard labor in the nearby imperial marble quarries, a large workshop was established early in the third century CE for the production of small and relatively standardized marble objects, including tableware, ritual vessels, and statuettes. No evidence exists to shed light on the specifics of how workers were recruited and organized – were they wage workers, contractors, or slaves? – but the physical layout of the building implies that they collaborated closely with one another in what may have been a large-scale and integrated unit of production. Portions of the old barracks were converted into work areas for craftsmen who specialized in certain aspects of the production process: marble blocks were cut in the western sections of the facility; various stages of carving occurred in the central chambers; and finishing and polishing work took place in rooms at the north end.[94]

---

[93] Xen. *Cyr.* 8.2.5.   [94] Wilson 2008: 409.

Likewise, certain stages of the production of decorated sarcophagi may have taken place in firms operated by entrepreneurs who coordinated workflows designed to exploit divisions of labor. Quarries in Asia Minor supplied much of the marble used in the production of these sarcophagi, which became increasingly popular across the Mediterranean world between the first and third centuries CE. In at least some cases, several of the preliminary stages of production took place at the quarry, where the process was standardized in the sense that workmen not only shaped and hollowed sarcophagi out before shipping them but also roughed in basic decorative elements in standard configurations, which could later be customized by other craftsmen at the ultimate point of sale.[95] The details of how work at the quarry was organized remain unknown, but one can imagine a workflow in which craftsmen organized in individual firms or working groups took it in turn to perform the various stages of the initial production process.

Even if we assume that integrated firms did emerge in these particular industries, however, we ought not to take them as a model of how urban artisans typically coordinated the production of goods targeted at the middle or populuxe segments of the market. Notably, the examples discussed above concern production in suburban or extra-urban contexts, where part of the logic of production was driven by proximity to the necessary raw materials. As scholars have suggested, the costs associated with transporting and shipping large pieces of marble over long distances created some scope for entrepreneurs to economize on these costs by performing part of the work at the quarry before shipment. Sarcophagi in particular were presumably much easier to transport after craftsmen hollowed them out and removed additional surface material by roughing in common decorative elements, but access to convict labor meant that the entrepreneurs who coordinated the production of smaller consumer goods at Simitthus could economize sufficiently on costs to deliver competitively priced products to urban markets.

Nor was it necessarily common for craftsmen working in other kinds of suburban or extra-urban industries to coordinate production by organizing large firms, even when they clustered together near the sources of their raw materials. Although some basic divisions of labor seem to have emerged among the craftsmen who manufactured the various series of fine and semi-fine pottery that circulated in the Mediterranean, those craftsmen generally seem to have coordinated production in workshops that

---

[95] Ward-Perkins 1992: 25–6 and 30–7.

remained largely disintegrated, even if they were spatially concentrated. Only in the case of Campanian ware, which flourished between the middle of the third and first century BCE, might we plausibly detect large units of production: Morel has argued that the forms of this pottery became simplified and standardized during the second century BCE, perhaps because they were produced mostly by large workforces of relatively untrained slaves who flooded the market in Italy in the wake of Roman campaigns in the eastern Mediterranean.[96] Yet thanks to recent and ongoing research on the red-gloss or *terra sigillata* pottery that was manufactured near Arezzo during the first centuries BCE and CE, it seems increasingly clear that the large workshop was never characteristic of pottery production in general. *Terra sigillata* has been critical to the efforts of historians to understand how entrepreneurs in this industry organized production, primarily because most pieces were stamped with the name of an individual who was involved in some capacity in its manufacture. Since many of the individuals named in these stamps seem to have been the slaves or freedmen of only a few slaveholders, most historians in the twentieth century interpreted the stamps themselves as evidence that entrepreneurs organized the production of *terra sigillata* in large slave-based enterprises featuring some divisions of labor.[97] That view, however, has recently fallen out of favor. In his systematic overview of our evidence for pottery production at Arezzo during the first centuries BCE and CE, Gunnar Fülle argues instead that the stamps actually name *officinatores*, individuals who worked as potters either on their own or with the help of a small workforce. In cases where several of these *officinatores* were slaves belonging to a common master, they probably operated independent units of production that were not necessarily contemporaneous with one another. Thus, instead of coordinating production in large firms, the potters who made much of the *terra sigillata* did so in relatively small units of production clustered together in groups of nucleated workshops near important clay beds. In Fülle's view, we ought to envision a complicated set of arrangements in which a landlord leased out the right to work clay beds on his estate to numerous individual *officinatores* who shared access not just to the clay but also to installations like levigation tanks and kilns.[98] The same basic model appears compatible with evidence from Gallic production sites of the first centuries BCE and

---

[96] Morel 1981: 87–97; cf. Carandini 1981: 256.
[97] E.g., Gummerus 1916: 1487–90; Frank 1920: 166–71.
[98] Fülle 1997. On nucleated workshops and rival modes of organizing pottery production, see Peacock 1982: 12–51.

CE, where many of the potters were possibly free craftsmen (albeit free craftsmen who probably remained dependent in some way on local landowners).[99] It seems probable that the production of other major styles of pottery was organized in essentially the same way.[100] To the extent that the industry gave rise to vertical divisions of labor, it did so by generating a need for specialists who could fire and manage the kilns on which multiple potters at any given site relied. Although our evidence says nothing about how such specialists were recruited and compensated, it is possible that they either were maintained by the landlord who owned the clay bed or provided services on contract to the individual *officinatores* who placed their goods in the kiln for firing.[101]

Evidence for the production of populuxe goods in urban contexts proper suggests that most artisans in these segments of the market coordinated production by subcontracting rather than by establishing integrated firms. This may have been true even in the case of artisans who either finished partially pre-fabricated marble sarcophagi or manufactured them from intact blocks of marble. Stine Birk has recently argued that several individual craftsmen often had a hand in carving individual marble sarcophagi at the point of sale and that working groups in this industry altered their size and composition in response to individual commissions. If she is correct, then this could reflect either the kind of short-term employment relationship discussed in more detail in Chapter 3, or subcontracting relationships between sculptors.[102] The recently excavated artisans' quarter in the regional Gallic center of Augustodunum is no less interesting. Here, the layout of the city's workshops suggests that the bronzeworkers who manufactured mid-range goods not only specialized in certain aspects of the production process but also coordinated their efforts with one another through subcontracting arrangements rather than firms. On the basis of their analyses of both the structures and the artifacts unearthed in the quarter, excavators have identified some thirty-eight workshops dedicated to the production of bronze goods. The alloys in use suggest that the artisans who worked in these shops produced a range of articles intended for customers in their immediate urban environment and in the wider territory of the Aedui (for whom Augustodunum served as a regional capital): tools, decorative yet functional items such as cloak brooches, and various kinds of household or ritual vessels. Crucially, the excavations revealed a distinction between two kinds of workshops: those possessing

[99] Whittaker 2002.   [100] Fülle 1997: 121–7.   [101] See esp. Fülle 1997: 145–6.
[102] Birk 2012: 25–33.

the tools and space to engage in casting as well as in some of the cold-working or modeling stages of production, and those lacking dedicated casting facilities. While the precise ways in which these workshops functioned together remain unclear, their spatial arrangement indicates that production was probably split between those workshops with casting facilities and those without.[103] Subcontracting, though not the only potential explanation for this pattern, is the most plausible.

Finally, the story of the silversmiths' riot at Ephesus in *Acts* can also be read as evidence for specialization and subcontracting relationships in the manufacture of populuxe goods, albeit goods of relatively high value. According to the author of *Acts*, the riot was instigated by Demetrios, a silversmith who manufactured small devotional shrines for dedication to Artemis.[104] Although no exemplar of the items he produced himself has survived, his shrines probably resembled one or both of two extant objects in other materials that were produced in a comparable context: a terracotta statuette of Artemis ensconced in a niche, and a fragmentary miniature temple constructed in marble.[105] If so, then Demetrios' clients were most likely pilgrims who visited Ephesus in large numbers to pay cult to Artemis in her great temple and who made votive offerings to the goddess in the process.[106] While Demetrios' shrines were therefore objects demanding the work of skilled artisans – some of whom possibly specialized in different aspects of the production process – they were nevertheless also objects that could be manufactured to relatively standardized patterns, and in batches rather than on a bespoke basis. The story in *Acts* nevertheless suggests that Demetrios organized his business like those artisans who manufactured artifacts in precious metals for bespoke segments of the consumer market – by subcontracting from other skilled craftsmen, rather than by coordinating the labor of specialists within a firm. Not only does the author of the text describe Demetrios as someone who "furnished no small amount of business to the artisans" of Ephesus, he also implies that most of these other artisans ran independent enter-prises: when Demetrios decided that he needed the support of the other Ephesian silversmiths to denounce Paul's efforts to proselytize in the city, he first needed to "gather them together," presumably from their

---

[103] Pernot 2004: 184–6.   [104] *Acts* 19.23–8.
[105] For a discussion of what Demetrios may have been manufacturing, see Trebilco 1994: 336–7 and Kleijwegt 2002: 120 and n. 166. Coleman 1965 discusses an example of the surviving terracotta devotional items; for the fragments of the miniature marble shrine, see Oberleitner 1978: 56, #20.
[106] Casson 1974: 287. See also Trebilco 1994: 338 and n. 211.

various places of work, where some employed workforces of their own.[107]

The persistence of subcontracting in this particular instance is especially striking, because it was precisely in industries manufacturing goods for comparable market niches that artisans of the eighteenth century were able to experiment aggressively with vertical integration. Thomas Chippendale is the most prominent of these entrepreneurs, but other artisans also developed comprehensive firms for manufacturing either furniture or other goods aimed at middling segments of the market.[108] Although Chippendale's own enterprise continued to rely to some extent on subcontractors, it nevertheless drew together in one firm a heterogenous collection of workers who participated in the manufacture of high-end and populuxe furniture, including joiners, cabinetmakers, turners, carvers, chairmakers, and upholsterers. While the increasing complexity of the production chain itself may have made governance within a firm more desirable than subcontracting, the crucial development that gave rise to such firms was the emergence among the upper segments of the English middle class of a relatively stable level of demand for high-quality but increasingly standardized goods. In these circumstances, it became possible for entrepreneurs to manufacture increasingly for stock, and the economies of scale that could be captured by integrating production within individual firms began to outweigh the risks associated with additional fixed costs.[109]

The case of Demetrios strongly suggests that comparable developments were rare in antiquity. Ephesus was a prosperous and large city by ancient standards: not only was it the hub of the communication and transport network in Roman Asia, it also had a population of up to 100,000 people in the first century CE. Moreover, the temple of Artemis – described by Antipater of Sidon as one of the wonders of the world in the second century BCE – retained its fame in the early Empire,[110] and Artemis herself enjoyed an increasingly widespread cult with devotees all across the Mediterranean.[111] The popularity of the cult and the fame of the temple drew visitors from all over the Roman world. Many of these came as pilgrims, creating a sizeable market for the votive products made by Demetrios and other Ephesians. In light of the

---

[107] Cf. van Minnen 1987: 56–8 and Drexhage et al. 2002: 111. It may be going too far to see Demetrios as the manager of a putting-out system rather than an important figure in a basic subcontracting network.

[108] For some examples, see Pfister 2008: 48–50.

[109] Kirkham 1988: 57–81. Cf. Schwarz 1992: 199–200.   [110] Plin. *HN.* 36.95–97.

[111] E.g., Paus. 4.31.8. See Oster 1990 for further discussion of Ephesus' importance as a religious center.

standardized and pre-made nature of the items Demetrios probably sold, it seems surprising that he continued to rely on a disintegrated production network to coordinate the work of specialist craftsmen, even if pilgrimage (dependent on the ability of visitors to arrive by sea) was a highly seasonal phenomenon.[112] One potential explanation for Demetrios' ongoing reliance on subcontracting is that the inter-annual demand for his products during the seasonal peak of the pilgrimage season remained highly uncertain. In that sense, Demetrios' production strategies underscore the ongoing fragility of the market segments devoted to populuxe goods in antiquity; these appear to have remained less developed and less stable than those of the early modern period, and thus more susceptible to the seasonal fluctuations and uncertainties characteristic of the Roman world's urban economies.

Professional *collegia* and private-order enforcement in the Roman world

My argument thus far has stressed that artisans in the Roman world generally coordinated production by subcontracting with one another when industries supported divisions of labor rather than by creating integrated firms. In that sense, it has not yet addressed an important question: were these artisans able to rely on arms-length contractual exchange when forming subcontracting agreements, or did they find it necessary to develop organized networks that could mitigate transaction costs by functioning as governance structures?

By demonstrating that network forms of governance were common in other contexts in which subcontracting was the norm, comparative studies of the early modern period provide initial grounds for believing that artisans in antiquity too may have relied heavily on network governance, especially in industries dedicated to the production of goods for which quality remained important. Historians of early modern Europe are increasingly sensitive to the fact that artisans and entrepreneurs in the periods they study sought to mitigate high transaction costs, especially in economic environments unfriendly to the development of large and integrated firms. Sometimes, the strategies they devised relied upon formal institutional innovations designed to ease some of the transaction costs that could otherwise inhibit deepening divisions of labor. Ulrich Pfister, for example, has argued that export-based trades geared toward the production

---

[112] Dillon 1997: 29.

of complex goods like timepieces expanded in various areas of Europe from the sixteenth century onward, partly because entrepreneurs and artisans were able to coordinate production by taking advantage of the powers of search and inspection that state authorities often granted to guilds. In these industries, artisans and entrepreneurs advocated for the creation of new, specialized guilds, some with their own independent inspection mechanisms and some under the purview of a larger "umbrella" guild. In both cases, the power of guild or municipal authorities to inspect workshops and set common product standards mitigated transaction costs by establishing industry-wide and legally enforceable quality thresholds.[113]

In other contexts, however, early modern entrepreneurs relied instead on networks for governance. As noted above, both bilateral and multi-lateral networks made it possible for artisans and entrepreneurs to cultivate trust-based relational contracts that allowed them to rely on their partners to honor their obligations. Edward Wakelin's ledgers provide a vivid illustration of the potential importance of bilateral relational contracting. They show that although Wakelin's primary subcontractors all accepted work from other clients, most maintained long-standing relationships with Wakelin himself and accepted subcontracted work from him for several years. Even in the 1760s, when Wakelin partnered with John Parker and expanded the business to the point where he bought goods and services from dozens of subcontractors, he continued to rely upon a select few as his regular suppliers.[114] Other artisans embedded their contractual exchanges more heavily in multilateral networks, formal and informal. Gervase Rosser has noted that both formal craft guilds and informal associations of craftsmen in medieval Europe not only provided artisans with badly needed social credibility in the eyes of clients and peers but also mediated working relationships among their members.[115] The same held true in the early modern period, in which artisans coordinated production by relying on networks ranging from informal associations grounded on cabaret culture to formal guilds that included most of the specialists working in a given industrial sector.[116]

In this section, I argue that artisans in the Roman world likewise developed governance structures anchored in networks in their efforts to coordinate production, especially when they produced bespoke or

---

[113] Pfister 2008, esp. 40–4.   [114] Clifford 2004: 32–5 and 70–102.   [115] Rosser 1997.
[116] On the cabaret as locus of informal networks, see Garrioch 1986: 186–7; on "umbrella" or "sectoral" guilds, see Pfister 2008: 33, along with his comments on the silk industry in Bologna at 32–4 and 42–4.

populuxe goods that demanded contributions from craftsmen who had specialized intensively in individual processes or techniques. Although the limited direct evidence for relational contracting in antiquity emphasizes bilateral relationships, our information concerning the structure of Roman professional *collegia* nevertheless implies that artisans used these organizations as governance structures, especially in industries that fostered complex divisions of labor based in intensive human capital. More precisely, it indicates that professional *collegia* exhibited strong similarities to so-called private-order enforcement networks, in which members rely on the politics of reputation to mitigate transaction costs.

Transacting in Rome's artisan economy

The specific transaction costs that made network governance desirable for artisans in the ancient world are easiest to envision in the case of artisans who produced bespoke goods for upper segments of the market. These costs arose primarily because artisans working in these trades could not always use the legal system to enforce arms-length contractual exchanges, because they did not always find it practical or desirable to craft detailed and specific agreements that could be vindicated readily in court. Since contracts generally need to spell out the mutual obligations of contracting parties in considerable detail to be legally enforceable, they are not well suited to conditions in which producers require flexibility to respond to their clients' changing demands, and in which future contingencies are difficult to anticipate.[117] Conditions of this sort in the ancient world were caused by the particularized and somewhat heterogenous tastes of clients who commissioned goods to their own specifications, and who sometimes intervened in the production process to give feedback when they became dissatisfied with a particular project's progress, or when they developed new ideas about the goods they had ordered. This dynamic is illustrated nicely in a letter written by Cicero to his brother Quintus in the autumn of 54 BCE. Cicero noted that he had recently visited several of Quintus' estates, where he had inspected a number of ongoing construction projects commissioned by his brother. At Quintus' Manilian estate, where a contractor named Diphilus was supervising the construction of a villa and its outlying buildings and amenities, Cicero had examined several

---

[117] See Farrell 2005: 463 and 466 on the problems of anticipating risks *ex ante* in this kind of economy and the weaknesses of formal contracts in situations where unexpected circumstances are likely to arise.

aspects of the central villa itself. In addition to demanding that Diphilus should replace a recently positioned colonnade, which in his view had been laid out poorly, he also decided that some features of the building – its ceilings, as well as the position of one of the baths – were unsatisfactory from an aesthetic or practical standpoint, rather than because of poor workmanship, and instructed Diphilus to make several changes.[118] The project as a whole was complex enough that Diphilus had almost certainly engaged the services of several different subcontractors to complete individual stages of the villa's construction and decoration; for that reason, he himself had to alter the parameters of his agreements with his subcontractors to accommodate Cicero's requests. In these circumstances, artisans in antiquity – like artisans confronted by comparable problems in other contexts – probably would have sacrificed enforceability for flexibility by choosing to transact with one another on the basis of broad and general mutual understandings rather than highly specific contracts.

Yet even when artisans engaged in transactions that were straightforward enough to be articulated in a relatively clear and unambiguous way, certain terms could nevertheless be difficult to specify in a way that made them readily enforceable at law. In particular, although it was simple for an artisan who did not anticipate encountering any unforeseen changes to specify that subcontractors deliver their products or perform their services by a given date, it remained difficult to specify the desired quality of those products or services in terms that could be enforced in court. Certain characteristics of a product could of course be specified (such as the nature and grade of the materials from which it was to be constructed, its basic dimensions, and so forth), but workmanship always retained a subjective component that could not be described precisely in a contract – at least, not precisely enough that a judge could easily determine whether or not a subcontractor had lived up to his obligations, and therefore deserved to be paid.[119]

The challenges that the notion of quality posed for the Roman legal system can be seen in the opinions delivered by jurists who attempted to grapple with them. Two relevant strands of legal thinking can be singled out. First, Roman jurists clearly struggled to define quality in a way that would enable judges to resolve conflicts that periodically erupted between

---

[118] Cic. *QFr.* 3.1.1–2, with the comments of S. D. Martin 1989: 54.
[119] Cf. Barzel 2005, esp. 361, who notes that in situations like this contracting parties are likely to embed their transactions in long-term relationships.

building contractors and their clients, who were typically entitled to inspect and approve the completed work (a procedure known as *probatio*).[120] While this procedure was an implicit component of building contracts formed under *locatio-conductio*,[121] clients could also presumably write comparable clauses into building contracts formed by *stipulatio* and into contracts for the purchase of other kinds of goods or services. When a contract did feature an implicit or explicit clause guaranteeing the client's right to *probatio*, it could give rise to a legal action on the part of the client, if he or she deemed the work deficient and could not persuade the contractor to correct it, or on the part of the contractor, who might contest the client's assessment. In either case, it became the judge's responsibility to determine whether or not the contractor had discharged his obligations fully. This was an uncomplicated matter if the contractor had deviated from specifications dealing with dimensions or materials, but if the dispute had arisen because the client and the contractor disagreed on the quality of the workmanship, the judge in all probability could only apply the standard of the *arbitrium boni viri* – that is, the "judgement of a good man" – probably by soliciting views of other builders on the standards that were normal in the trade. How this worked in practice is difficult to say, but Susan Martin finds it "unlikely that in normal circumstances an employer could demand an extremely high level of skill."[122] Second, comparable problems are reflected in the jurists' discussions of *imperitia*, a concept which they developed to deal with the possibility that an allegedly skilled worker might damage the property of another in the course of his work – typically, property that belonged to and had been entrusted to him by his client. Like *probatio*, the concept of *imperitia* raised questions about how to assess a characteristic that was fundamentally difficult to measure – in this case the degree of skill that an artisan or craftsman had brought to bear on a particular piece of work. Although the Roman jurists were well aware that craftsmen who practiced any given trade exhibited a wide range of proficiency,[123] in practice it was difficult to make fine distinctions between different grades of skill. And, in any case, since legal cases that revolved around *imperitia* hinged primarily on whether or not a particular artisan had damaged property specifically because of his lack of skill (instead of some flaw in the material), most judges were presumably tasked only

---

[120] On this procedure, see S. D. Martin 1986 and 1989: 103–13.   [121] S. D. Martin 1986: 322.
[122] S. D. Martin 1986, esp. 325. Cf. S. D. Martin 1989: 109–13.   [123] E.g., Ulpian, *Dig.* 46.3.31.

with determining whether or not that artisan cleared some minimal threshold of competence.[124]

Because of these limitations in Roman contract law, artisans who contracted with one another risked forming agreements that created considerable scope for various kinds of opportunistic behavior, and thus for high enforcement-related transaction costs. At the most basic level, artisans who let work out often dealt with subcontractors who had complicated production schedules of their own, featuring orders from clients who had commissioned finished products, as well as orders from other craftsmen seeking either to purchase intermediate goods or services, or to supplement their production capacity by subcontracting components of large orders to others. In these circumstances, artisans risked that their subcontractors might give priority to other orders, and thus either deliver necessary goods or services late or skimp on quality to meet their deadlines.[125] Alternatively, subcontractors might refuse to comply with the changing needs of those from whom they had accepted work because rearranging their production schedules would impose excessively high short-term costs. In more extreme cases, one partner to a transaction could even try to profit unfairly at the other's expense by exploiting unanticipated developments to force the renegotiation of an agreement in his or her favor. An artisan who had hired work out could potentially use a dispute over quality as a pretext to refuse full payment to a subcontractor, or could pass on the lion's share of costs associated with changing an order-in-progress to a subcontractor who had invested too much time and energy in a given project to walk away empty-handed. Subcontractors, for their own part, could withhold important goods or services at critical moments in the hope of forcing those with whom they had contracted to make further concessions on price, particularly when they possessed skills vital to one stage of the production process and were difficult to replace.[126]

Transaction costs of this sort were more likely to be a problem for artisans who produced bespoke or populuxe goods than for those who

---

[124] The juristic development of *imperitia* is explored in detail by S. D. Martin 2001. For her comments on the standards that were typically employed, see esp. p. 124, where she invokes remarks by Gaius and Ulpian on the degree of skill possessed by slaves by way of analogy (for which see Gaius, *Dig.* 21.1.18.1 and Ulpian, *Dig.* 21.1.19.4).

[125] See Styles 1995: 115–16, with particular reference to London goldsmiths.

[126] Farrell 2005, esp. 464–5, offers a good overview of these problems in a discussion of disintegrated production in contemporary Italy and Germany. See also Bernstein 2001: 1748–9, who discusses comparable problems in the American cotton industry. Finally, see Sabel and Zeitlin 1997: 20–8 for commentary on other recent historical societies.

made undifferentiated items and who may have let out specific tasks to home-based and relatively unskilled workers. Because a low price point was often the key selling feature of undifferentiated goods and because their manufacture could be broken down into simple steps, the artisans who produced them found that the quality of subcontracted work did not need to be carefully controlled. At the same time, artisans who produced these goods benefited from favorable labor market conditions that gave them considerable clout over subcontractors and reduced the threat of opportunistic behavior. In the early modern context, where underemployment was often endemic among the urban populations of large cities, the market in unskilled and semi-skilled labor tended to be thick and transaction costs correspondingly low: because workers in these segments of the market were plentiful and could be replaced easily and at short notice, the consequences of broken contracts were often not severe, and subcontractors had insufficient leverage to force opportunistic renegotiations of their agreements.[127] In the Roman world, labor market conditions in the unskilled and semi-skilled segments may have been somewhat unfavorable for urban artisans in the second and first centuries BCE, when the political obligations of Roman citizens and the military obligations of both Roman citizens and Italians potentially interfered with their ability or willingness to participate in those markets.[128] Coupled with relatively low slave prices, those market conditions may have provoked some integration in certain industries (as, perhaps, they did in the case of Campanian ware – see above). By the end of the first century BCE, however, conditions were rapidly changing. Slaves became more expensive as the pace of imperial conquest abroad slowed, and urban labor markets thickened as a professional army replaced the military levy of the Republic and as popular participation in the political process began to decline, especially in the unskilled and semi-skilled segments. For that reason, artisans who manufactured undifferentiated goods during the early Empire were probably able to coordinate production in disintegrated subcontracting networks without developing sophisticated structures of governance.[129] By contrast, artisans who

---

[127] Schwarz 1992: 32–3 and 179–207 gives a basic overview of subcontracting networks in industries dedicated to the production of undifferentiated goods in early modern London. Cf. Pfister 2008, esp. 49–50, who notes that "[a]gency problems … presented few obstacles to industrial growth" when "proto-industries produced low-quality goods embodying low skills and a simple division of labour."

[128] Scheidel 2008: 119.

[129] On the transformations that probably took place in urban labor markets after the Augustan transition, see Scheidel 2005 and 2008. On the production of Campanian ware – which may have relied on relatively large working groups of slaves – see Morel 2007: 504–9.

manufactured populuxe and bespoke goods not only had to monitor the quality of subcontracted goods and services more closely but they also depended on skilled workers, who could be difficult to replace on short notice if they violated their agreements. The consequences of production problems arising from high transaction costs were also potentially greater for these artisans than for those who produced undifferentiated goods. If their subcontractors missed a deadline, delivered substandard work, or otherwise held up their production schedules, those who produced bespoke goods could find themselves compelled to apologize to frustrated clients in order to retain their custom.[130] Those who primarily made populuxe goods could easily miss an optimal seasonal window for selling their products if subcontractors failed to deliver goods as promised.[131]

Collegia and private-order enforcement

In circumstances of this sort – that is, when transaction costs associated with contractual exchange tend to be high, and when the nature of the economic environment militates against the development of large and integrated firms – artisans and entrepreneurs in a variety of different historical settings have turned to bilateral or multilateral forms of network governance to coordinate the work of specialists. Although our evidence from the Roman world is not comprehensive enough to permit us to track relational contracts between individual artisans in detail, there are nevertheless hints that relationships of this sort were widespread. For example, the contracts Demetrios formed with other Ephesian silversmiths were unlikely to have been arms-length transactions. Instead, the author of *Acts* presupposes that Demetrios had persistent and long-standing commercial relationships with most of these subcontractors – relationships that explain how he could persuade several of them individually to leave their workplaces and congregate for the impromptu meeting that ultimately evolved into a near riot.[132]

Even more interesting is a small subset of the apprenticeship documents from Roman Egypt, which reveals the existence of relational contracting among several weavers in Oxyrhynchus during the middle of the first century CE. These documents do not pertain to subcontracting relationships in any direct sense, but because apprenticeship agreements often

---

[130] See, e.g., Clifford 2004: 68 and Riello 2008: 256, both of whom cite examples of such an apology.
[131] Cf. Sonenscher 1989: 23, who characterizes most chances for sales in such economies as the product of serendipitous "short-term arrangements, fleeting opportunities and brief associations."
[132] *Acts* 19.25.

generate enforcement-related transaction costs that are comparable in many ways to those within subcontracting arrangements, they nevertheless offer some insight into the strategies artisans employed to mitigate those costs. Instructors have an interest in ensuring that they can not only recoup the costs of the time, energy, and resources that they invest in training their apprentices but also derive some gain by profiting from their labor; therefore, their apprentices' reliability and quality are both important. From the point of view of apprentices and their family members, the potential risks are more pressing: not only can apprentices find themselves abused by their masters – the Roman jurist Julian, for example, writes of one instance in which a Roman shoemaker blinded a freeborn apprentice in one eye by striking him with his last – unscrupulous instructors might also elect to impart only skills directly useful to their own immediate business needs, instead of providing general instruction. The latter risk is particularly insidious because apprentices themselves are not always capable of assessing the quality of their training.[133] Apprenticeship is therefore a high-stakes transaction that exposes a particularly valuable "long-term enterprise" to the "malfeasance, mistakes, and failures" of others: namely, the apprentice's future long-term productivity and, in some cases, even his health.[134]

For these reasons, it is highly significant that artisans in Roman Egypt who apprenticed their sons to other craftsmen sought security for these transactions not only by drafting formal contracts but also by embedding their apprenticeship agreements in personal networks of trust. The weaver Pausiris, for example, placed three of his sons as apprentices in the workshops of other artisans, all of whom were weavers themselves. A formal contract pertaining to one of these three agreements has survived. It shows that the weaver Apollonios agreed in 53 CE to accept Pausiris' son Dioskos as an apprentice and, like many contracts of this type, it contains clauses of interest both to the master and to the pupil's family. Apollonios sought to ensure that Dioskos would remain in his service long enough to compensate him for training costs, whereas Pausiris protected his own interests and those of Dioskos by requiring Apollonios to teach Dioskos

---

[133] On apprenticeship and its risks in general, see Smits and Stromback 2001, esp. 68–93. For Julian's account of the injured apprentice, see Ulpian, *Dig.* 9.2.5.3. Cf. Lucian of Samosata's account of the corporal punishment to which he was subjected in his short career as a stonemason's apprentice (Luc. *Somn.* 3).

[134] See C. Tilly 2005: 36–8 for brief comments on *quality of relations* and *stakes of relations*. The quoted passage is from C. Tilly 2005: 4.

"the whole craft of weaving, as he himself knows it."[135] The contract was then buttressed by penalty clauses stipulating fines to be paid if either party violated its respective obligations.[136] Yet because the quality of an apprentice's training could be difficult to measure, Pausiris chose not to rely exclusively on contracts to ensure that his sons were trained properly, but instead sought to generate extra security by carefully selecting instructors already known to him from past transactions. Thanks to an official notice filed for tax purposes, we know that Dioskos was not the first son whom Pausiris apprenticed to Apollonios: four years earlier, he had apprenticed his oldest son to the same weaver.[137] Similarly, in 62 CE, Pausiris placed the youngest of his three sons as an apprentice in the workshop of another weaver, Epinikos son of Theon, who was already known to him – a few years previously, Pausiris had accepted Epinikos' nephew as an apprentice of his own.[138]

At the same time, there are also solid grounds for believing that neither Demetrios nor the Oxyrhynchite weavers relied on simple bilateral relational contracts when they subcontracted with other artisans or framed apprenticeship agreements, but instead formed relational contracts that were embedded in larger networks. A recently published papyrus, dated to the year 62 CE, leaves no doubt that Oxyrhynchus was home to an organized *collegium* of weavers that had recently appointed a president during the period when Pausiris, Apollonios, and Epinikos arranged their apprenticeship contracts.[139] Likewise, inscriptional evidence from Ephesus attests to a *collegium* of silversmiths in the city during the first century CE.[140] Although there is no proof that Pausiris and his associates belonged to the weaver's association in Oxyrhynchus, nor that Demetrios and his subcontractors belonged to the Ephesian silversmiths' association, it is distinctly plausible that they did.

The likelihood that these craftsmen regularly transacted with other members of professional associations suggests that artisans in the Roman world relied heavily upon *collegia* as governance structures to mitigate transaction costs and to coordinate production, particularly in industries that gave rise to intensive specialization. That possibility is reinforced by

---

[135] *P. Wisc.* I 4. The other apprenticeship agreements are attested indirectly in official documents that were filed for tax purposes when parents or guardians placed children in apprenticeships: *P. Oxy.* II 310 (printed in full by Biscottini 1966: 260) and *P. Mich* III 170–2.

[136] These clauses are typical of apprenticeship documents from Roman Egypt in general. See Bergamasco 1995 and, more briefly, Bradley 1991: 106–16.

[137] *P. Mich.* III 170.   [138] *P. Mich.* III 171 and 172.   [139] *P. Oxy.* LXXVI 5097.

[140] Many of the relevant inscriptions are cataloged by Zimmermann 2002: 137.

theoretical and empirical work, some of which indicates that artisans in other contexts have relied on comparable professional associations or networks for building trust and enhancing relational contracts in ways that effectively smooth transactions. Networks of this sort operate primarily by supporting private-order enforcement functions based on reputation. When these networks work well, individuals who renege on their agreements with other members find that news of their malfeasance circulates among the membership as a whole and that they may consequently find themselves excluded from future transactions not just by the aggrieved party but also by others in their common professional circle. In some cases, they also find themselves excluded from other benefits open only to members, such as participation in communal social or religious functions. For these reasons, relational contracts can serve as a particularly effective governance structure when embedded in private-order enforcement networks and can readily substitute for governance structures based on vertical integration within firms: because the costs (professional and otherwise) incurred by those who default on their obligations can be high, participants in the network can trust that fellow members will generally honor their obligations.[141]

The importance that artisans in the early modern period attached to personal reputation is relatively uncontroversial,[142] and in all probability reputation was no less important to their counterparts in the ancient world. In the Roman context, the key concept was *fides* – a complex value that carried connotations of trust, obligation, loyalty, and reliability and was indivisible from an individual's personal reputation (*existimatio* or *dignitas*). In normal circumstances, the importance Roman aristocrats attached to their *dignitas* kept them honest in their dealings with one another.[143] Comparable mechanisms operated in the classical Greek world, where they not only helped to maintain general social norms but also structured economic transactions such as lending

---

[141] On bounded networks of this type, see Richman 2004: 2345–6 and Greif 2006: 450–1 (for basic theory) and 58–90 (a specific case study). Cf. C. Tilly 2005: 43–5, on the importance of network boundaries in "trust networks." McMillan and Woodruff devote much of their 2001 study to exploring the difference between spontaneous and organized private-order enforcement. Ogilvie 2011: 268–9, though skeptical of some aspects of the theory, acknowledges that these networks can have an effect (though they also impose costs). Finally, Gil and Hartmann 2009 provide empirical support for the way in which these networks can reduce the incentives for vertical integration.

[142] See, e.g., Sonenscher 1989: 135 and 214; Kooijmans 1995; Rosser 1997; Riello 2008: 270–1.

[143] Verboven 2002: 35–48 and 170–8. See also MacMullen 1974: 65, who describes *stipulatio* as a "personal promise that committed one's community standing to a bargain."

and borrowing.[144] Significantly, scholars have argued recently that *fides* and comparable values were not the exclusive concerns of the Greek and Roman elites, but rather structured relationships among a broad cross-section of the population at large. From time to time, our sources even indicate explicitly that reputations and the trust they generated were just as important among merchants and traders as they were in more aristocratic circles.[145]

The membership profiles of Roman professional associations offer an additional reason to believe that artisans may have organized certain *collegia* to help coordinate production. More specifically, when artisans organized *collegia* in industries in which coordination problems were most likely to arise – that is, in industries with scope for intensive specialization in individual processes necessary for the production of complex goods – they seem to have taken steps to ensure that their members included practitioners of the various specialized trades important to that industry. The strongest evidence that they did so pertains to the building industry. The jurist Gaius noted that the term *faber tignarius* – which, in its most straightforward sense, simply meant "carpenter" or "framer" – was used in practice to refer "not only to those who hew timber, but to all who work as builders."[146] Later juristic sources would define the word *structor* in the same way and use it in the general sense of "builder."[147] The inclusiveness of these terms suggests that *collegia fabrum tignariorum* and *collegia structorum* were associations in which one could find artisans who practiced a number of different specialized trades directly related to the building industry,[148] even if those who worked in trades geared toward certain kinds of interior decoration may have formed organizations of their own.[149]

---

[144] See Millett 1991, esp. 24–52, and D. Cohen 1991, respectively. The terminology in these and other works is slightly different than the usage I adopt here and conceptualizes reputation mechanisms in terms of reciprocity bolstered by honor and shame.

[145] Veyne 2000: 1187–94 makes this argument about the *plebs media* in a general sense; Verboven 2007 argues that the "moral matrix of friendship" that operated in aristocratic Roman society – especially the elements of *liberalitas, gratia,* and *fides* – also operated in the social environment of professional associations. On trust and reputation in associations in the Hellenistic World and in Graeco-Roman Egypt, see Gabrielsen 2007 and Venticinque 2010, respectively.

[146] Gaius, *Dig.* 50.16.235.1.   [147] *Cod. Just.* 10.66.1.

[148] Cf. Pearse 1974: 122–3. See also Garnsey 1998: 79, who thinks that the association of *tektones* attested in late antique Sardis probably "brought together a number of different specialists connected with the building trade."

[149] We find occasional references, for instance, to *collegia* of *fabri subaediani,* who are generally taken as artisans who worked on the interiors of buildings. See, e.g., *CIL* 6.9559. It may be that these associations included craftsmen like plasterers, painters, and so on. The only inscription in which the term is qualified is 6.7814. Here, we find a freedman named Lucius Valerius Pharnaces, who worked as a "*marmorarius subaedanus* [sic]" – perhaps an interior decorator specializing in marble.

The size and composition of the *collegium fabrum tignariorum* at Ostia likewise suggest that associations of builders incorporated artisans who specialized in a number of different trades vital to the construction industry. In 198 CE, this association produced what is one of the best-preserved membership lists (*alba*) that we possess. It preserves the partial names of 323 men who belonged to the association, which may have had some 350 members in all. Many of the men named in the inscription shared a *nomen* with one or more other members, and while some of these shared *nomina* may be purely coincidental – especially in cases in which members bore *nomina* indicating that they or their ancestors had been manumitted by members of the imperial family – others may indicate that the individuals concerned were either relatives, or patron and freedman, or freedmen who had been manumitted by a common master. Yet when we consider those members whose *nomina* are clearly not associated with the imperial family, roughly 35 percent bear names that are unique within the membership list, and some 70 percent bear names shared with only one or two other members. In Pearse's view, this pattern indicates that most members were the proprietors of small firms[150] – precisely what we would expect to find if the association did indeed draw its members primarily from artisans who operated specialized enterprises geared toward certain stages of the construction process. That conclusion is reinforced by a comparable pattern of names in the *album* produced at Portus by the local *collegium fabrum navalium* (shipwright's association): 64 percent of those members whose names were not connected to the imperial family either bore *nomina* that are unique within the sample, or had names that they shared with only one or two other members.[151] Since shipwrights, like builders, worked in an industry demanding the coordination of different specialists, it seems reasonable to interpret this pattern as evidence that the shipwrights in Portus incorporated men operating small and specialized firms into their association.[152]

Lastly, it is worth noting that in Lugdunensis, the *tectores* (plasterers) were either wholly or partly affiliated with the *fabri tignarii* – at any rate, they shared the same *genius* (*CIL* 13.1734).

[150] Pearse 1974: 130–9. I have corrected some minor errors of arithmetic in his original figures, but those corrections do not alter his basic point. For the *album* itself, see *CIL* 14.4569.

[151] *CIL* 14.256.

[152] See van Nijf 2002: 314–15 for an alternative interpretation of the pattern of *nomina* in this inscription. Van Nijf suggests that the *collegium fabrum tignariorum* in Ostia, along with comparable organizations elsewhere, served more as an honor society than as a professional association and that it recruited many of its members not from men affiliated with the building industry, but rather from "a wider segment of the urban 'middle classes'." Certainty about the composition of the association's membership is impossible given the state of our evidence, but it is worth noting that van Nijf bases this argument partly on the view that the building industry itself was dominated by

In other industries too, artisans structured *collegia* in ways seemingly designed to draw together specialists who collaborated in the production of specific goods. In most cities, for instance, artisans in the textile industry created either a *collegium centonariorum* or a *collegium* of *vestiarii*, but not both; this suggests that they organized themselves in large umbrella organizations that drew together different kinds of specialists, although fullers and dyers sometimes appear to have had associations of their own (possibly because they performed much of their work for private clients).[153] In the town of Brixia in northern Italy, what appear to have been informal groups of wool-combers, wool-carders, and perhaps felters produced a handful of inscriptions during the first century CE. Thereafter, they vanish from our evidence, and Liu has suggested that they became incorporated into the local *collegium centonariorum* with other wool workers.[154] Even in Saittai in the interior of Asia Minor, which has produced extensive epigraphic evidence for associations of textile workers, artisans tended to form organizations with relatively inclusive names, such as the linen-workers or the wool workers.[155] Here as well, the most economical hypothesis is that artisans who practiced a particular specialty joined the association that was most closely allied to their own business activities.

Lastly, many artisans who produced goods in precious and semi-precious metals also organized themselves into *collegia* housing specialists in several branches of their particular industries. Some metalworkers admittedly formed *collegia* based on relatively narrow trades, like the *anularii*, who were perhaps jewelers in a general sense (and not just "ring-makers"), or like the gilders and workers in gold leaf who formed the *collegium brattiarii inauratores*. These artisans' services were widely sought after by private clients or by artisans who worked in a range of different industries, including (in the case of the gilders) furniture-making and interior decorating.[156] Notable for their absence, however, are groups of important specialists involved in the various branches of largework in metal, like engravers (*caelatores*) and the artisans who manufactured plate in gold, silver, or bronze

---

a handful of powerful families and their freedmen. That may have been true of the *collegium* of the *lenuncularii*, or lightermen, which he cites as a parallel, but building – with its complex divisions of labor – was a different sort of industry entirely.

[153]   Liu 2009: 75–83.
[154]   Liu 2009: 146–7. The inscriptions in question are *CIL* 5.4501; *AE* 1927.100; *CIL* 5.4504 and 5.4505.
[155]   For Saittai, see Zimmermann 2002: 146–52, and esp. the table on 150–1.
[156]   For the *anularii*, see *CIL* 6.9144. On the workers of gold leaf and gilders, see *CIL* 6.95, along with the comments of Mols 1999: 109–10 on their role in the furniture-making business.

(*vascularii*).[157] Presumably, these artisans joined one of the larger *collegia* of metalworkers in Rome – which included the *collegium* of ironsmiths, the *collegium* of goldsmiths, and a *collegium* of bronzesmiths[158] – as did an engraver in the Mauretanian town of Caesaria, whose funerary inscription indicates that he had joined the local association of silversmiths.[159]

More interestingly, the evidence for associational life in antiquity suggests that the members of *collegia* typically structured their associations to support strong and organized private-order enforcement functions. This evidence presents some serious interpretative challenges: although the charters produced by several associations survive in whole or in part, these span an enormous geographical and chronological range, and they pertain to associations organized on the basis of religious or cultic interests just as often as associations based on professional or occupational identity. Nevertheless, because there is some conformity in the ways that professional and non-professional associations were structured, even the charters of religious associations offer valuable evidence for associational life.[160] Most tellingly, this material indicates that *collegia* typically exhibited three features that were characteristic of strong private-order enforcement networks. First, membership in most *collegia* was a privilege and was costly enough that participants were invested in preserving that membership; in practical terms this meant that they were equally invested in protecting their reputations. Second, many *collegia* possessed organized reputation mechanisms for transmitting information about defaulters to other members in the network. Third, members of *collegia* could impose costly and collective sanctions on those who violated important norms and bonds of trust, typically by excluding them from future participation in their organization's economic and social benefits.[161]

Distinctions between members and non-members are important in private-order enforcement networks because members have a vested interest in maintaining a good reputation within a particular organization

---

[157] There is a group of individuals who style themselves *negotiantes vascularii* (*CIL* 6.1065), but these appear to be wholesalers rather than producers (and it remains debatable whether or not they formed an actual *collegium*).

[158] See *CIL* 6.1892, 6.9202, and 6.36771, respectively. Because the latter inscription uses the plural form *conlegia aerariorum* instead of the singular *conlegium aerariorum*, Royden believes that there may have been two *collegia* of bronzesmiths (1988: 186, #261). That seems inconsistent with the remainder of the inscription, which implies that the two individuals named as the dedicators of the monument were co-magistrates. It seems best to postulate either that there is an error in the inscription or that if there were two *collegia* of bronzesmiths, they collaborated very closely with one another.

[159] *CIL* 8.21106.   [160] See, for instance, van Nijf 2002: 326 n. 112 and Meiggs 1973: 314.

[161] I have based this model of strong private-order enforcement heavily on Richman 2004.

when membership is considered to be a privilege. Our evidence from the ancient world suggests that members of Greek and Roman associations created such distinctions by emphasizing the exclusive nature of membership in their organizations. In part, they did so by insisting that candidates for membership meet certain selection criteria, the specifics of which varied from one association to another. Those who belonged to the association of dealers in ivory and citrus-wood at Rome, for example, specified in their charter that only colleagues who worked in the same trades could be admitted to their *collegium*. Likewise, the Athenian Iobacchoi, who formed a cultic association dedicated to the worship of Bacchus in the second century CE, demanded that prospective members be "worthy and suitable" for their company. The charters of these two associations show that members enforced such criteria by subjecting applicants to a vetting process designed to add solemnity to the process of induction. In the association of the dealers in ivory and citrus-wood, that vetting process was in the hands of junior magistrates known as *curatores*. The Iobacchoi, on the other hand, entrusted the initial process of vetting candidates to their priest but stipulated that his decisions were then to be ratified by the vote of the entire membership in a general assembly.[162]

Most Greek and Roman associations, whether structured around professional relationships or not, also imposed fees on their members for the privilege of joining the community. Our evidence on the magnitude of these fees is sparse, but it suggests that membership was costly. In the late second century CE, applicants paid a fee of at least 25 *denarii* to join the Athenian Iobacchoi; this amount represented roughly one-fifth of the annual gross earnings of artisans who were employed by the Roman state in its quarries at Mons Claudianus.[163] Entrance fees were comparable among the worshippers of Diana and Antinous in the Italian town of Lanuvium: there, in the early second century CE, prospective members paid over 100 *sesterces* and an amphora of good wine to enter the association.[164] If the fees charged by professional *collegia* were

---

[162] For the entrance criteria and admission policies of the Iobacchoi, see *IG* II.2 1368, lines 32–41; for those of the ivory and citrus-wood merchants at Rome, see *CIL* 6.33885, lines 4–6. Waltzing 1895–1900, I: 355–7 discusses entrance criteria and admission policies more broadly and cites several other relevant sources.

[163] More specifically, sons of current members paid 25 *denarii* (100 *sesterces*), while others were required to pay twice that amount (*IG* II.2 1368, lines 37–41). For further discussion of entrance fees among associations in general, see Waltzing 1895–1900, I: 450–1. On the wages paid to the workers at Mons Claudianus, see Cuvigny 1996: 139–43.

[164] *CIL* 14.2112, col. I, lines 21–2.

comparable, then their magnitude must have imposed some degree of self-selection on prospective members, thereby increasing the odds that they would be willing to commit themselves over the long term to a particular association, its values, and the value of their own reputations.[165]

Members of *collegia* articulated and reinforced both the boundaries of their associations and the shared privilege of membership with social and ceremonial activities. Regular meetings and banquets were an important part of this process, since the procedures that governed details like seating arrangements and portion sizes served "to express, among many other things, ideas about the identity of a group and about the essential values which govern[ed] its social relationships."[166] More striking were ceremonial occasions that resulted in the creation of formal membership lists (*alba* or *fasti*), which were often displayed in monumental contexts in clubhouses or on statue bases.[167] These lists constituted public pronouncements that the members listed therein "had accepted the codes and values of the *collegium*"[168] and clearly expressed the idea that membership in an association was a privilege that "always distinguished 'ins' from 'outs.'"[169]

Strong private-order enforcement networks rely not only on clearly demarcated membership boundaries but also on mechanisms for disseminating information about the personal reputations of individual members to others. The members of a network circulate much information of this nature as gossip, either during the course of day-to-day business interactions or in the more formal context of an association's regular meetings.[170] Undoubtedly the same was true in the Roman world, in which associations often held regular monthly assemblies in addition to important ceremonial functions such as festivals.[171] Yet information

---

[165] Monson 2006: 233–4 makes this argument about membership fees and other entrance requirements in the context of a discussion of Ptolemaic religious associations. See also McMillan and Woodruff 2001: 2441 on a small fur-traders' association in the early twentieth century. Here, members were required to post bonds that likewise may have served to ensure long-term commitment to transactions within the group.

[166] Van Nijf 2002: 326.

[167] For a short discussion and a list of these texts, see Royden 1988: 17–18. See also van Nijf 2002: 332–3.

[168] Van Nijf 2002: 332–4.   [169] Verboven 2007: 882.

[170] Cf. Bernstein 2001: 1751–2, who notes that efforts on the part of the cotton industry to promote socialization among its members arguably helped to increase the flow of information about personal reputations. Cf. McMillan and Woodruff 2001: 2427. Strahilevitz 2003: 365 n. 31 argues that group size is less important than the existence of mechanisms that help facilitate information flow: what matters most is the "community members' ability to monitor instances of non-cooperation and communicate with fellow members about each member's reputation."

[171] The worshippers of Diana and Antinous at Lanuvium, for example, met once a month to conduct business and at least five times a year to celebrate various special occasions (*CIL* 14.2112, col. 1 lines

transmitted via gossip is susceptible to various kinds of distortion, whether introduced intentionally by the parties who disseminate the information, or by confirmation bias.[172] For that reason, organized mechanisms for sharing information can often be more effective than informal exchange.

There are some indications in our sources that the members of associations in antiquity created mechanisms to centralize information about the reputations of individuals and to regularize the transmission of that information. Where these mechanisms existed, they operated primarily by internalizing dispute resolution between members. In so doing, they ensured that the members of an association as a whole not only learned about potentially serious violations of the values of their community but also could gauge the willingness of individual disputants to submit themselves to arbitration – an act which communicated strong signals about the value they attached to ongoing membership in the association, and hence about their overall trustworthiness.[173] Both concerns are reflected strongly in the statutes of the Athenian Iobacchoi, who insisted that certain disputes among members were to be resolved in general assembly rather than in the public sphere. In this association, members who became involved in a physical altercation with one another were compelled to argue their cases before the assembled membership of the association or face a fine and temporary exclusion from the association's events;[174] at stake was not simply the tranquillity of the association's ceremonial and social gatherings, but rather the integrity of the bonds of trust to which members were expected to adhere. Likewise, in the first century CE, the members of a small association in Roman Egypt drafted a set of statutes specifying that anyone who prosecuted a fellow member in the public courts was liable to a fine.[175] The general ban they imposed on the use of public courts suggests that the members of this association envisioned settling disputes of all

11–13 and col. 2, 11–13). The Iobacchoi likewise met in regular monthly meetings, celebrated special occasions, and convened occasional meetings on short notice to deal with pressing business (*IG* II.2 1368, lines 42–4). The statutes of the ivory and citrus-wood merchants of Rome contained provisions for a number of celebrations (*CIL* 6.33885), and two out of the three extant sets of association statutes from Tebtunis call for monthly banquets (*P. Mich.* V 243 and 244).

[172] See Ogilvie 2011: 362–3 for a discussion of these problems. In her view, members of trust networks in the medieval period were just as likely to transmit inaccurate information as they were to transmit accurate information.

[173] Richman 2006: 395–8. Cf. Bernstein 2001: 1737–9 and 1766–9, who notes that in the American cotton industry, failure to comply with an arbitration ruling results in not only expulsion from the trade society but also swift and extensive publication of this information.

[174] *IG* II.2 1368, lines 84–90.

[175] *P. Mich.* V 243, lines 7–8. The document is dated to the reign of Tiberius. Unfortunately, the precise nature of this association is unknown.

kinds within their own private community, including those arising from economic transactions.[176] In that sense, *collegia* gave additional structure to a long tradition of private dispute settlement and private arbitration in both Greek and Roman practice, in which the whole range of complaints that could launch a civil action could be and often was settled privately.[177]

A funerary inscription hints at the existence of comparable mechanisms in at least one dedicated professional association, the *collegium fabrum tignariorum* (or builders' association) at Rome. The inscription, dedicated to T. Flavius Hilario by his wife and daughter, commemorates the offices he held in the association during the late first and early second centuries CE, one of which entailed serving on a panel of twelve judges who were elected from among the junior and senior magistrates of the association (the *iudices inter electos XII ab ordine*).[178] These judges almost certainly resolved disputes between the members of the association. Although we cannot know precisely what kind of disputes they handled, three considerations suggest that they dealt with matters more substantial than simple procedural arguments generated by the *collegium's* regular social activities, and that their decisions played an important role in the *collegium's* ability to function as a private-order enforcement network. First, the members of this *collegium* derived the name of the panel of judges from the formal name of the civic equestrian judges, which implies that they expected these officials to arbitrate a broad range of disputes.[179] Second, magistrates within a professional *collegium* would have been intimately familiar with the conditions prevailing in the trade and therefore would have been well qualified to render judgments on problems arising from

---

[176] Cf. Monson 2006: 235–6, who notes that some of the Ptolemaic religious associations claimed comparable rights in their statutes by threatening to punish members who took any complaint whatsoever to the authorities before raising it in the association. They threatened even more serious punishment if a member were to reject the association's settlement and then take his complaint before the authorities.

[177] Some forms of arbitration were, in Roman law, subordinate to the legal machinery of the state. This was the case with *arbitrium ex compromisso* and *arbitrium iudicis*, which happened under the authority and nominal supervision of the praetor. *Arbitrium boni viri*, on the other hand – arbitration by a "good man" – remained a strictly private form of dispute settlement. See, in general, Roebuck and de Loynes de Fumichon 2004. On p. 64 they note that "nothing could provide clearer evidence of how commonplace and pervasive *arbitrium boni viri* was in Roman life than that it had its own abbreviation, *ABV*" in the legal sources. See Roebuck 2001 for comparable forms of public and private arbitration in the Greek world through to the end of the Hellenistic period.

[178] *CIL* 14.2630. Hilario seems to have served in this capacity sometime between 99 CE and 103 CE. For further discussion, see the brief comments of Royden 1988: 130–1 and 157–9 as well as those of Meiggs 1973: 319 (who, however, mistakenly identifies Hilario as a member of the builder's association at Ostia rather than the one at Rome).

[179] Royden 1988: 131.

transactions that may have been difficult for the regular machinery of the law to address, such as disputes over quality.[180] Third, comparable boards in modern professional associations frequently handle disputes that arise in the context of their members' professional activities. The Diamond Dealers Club of New York, for example, maintains a body of arbitrators – essentially, private judges – who are elected from among the most well-respected members of the Club. These arbitrators handle all disputes that arise among Club members in the course of business, and members who circumvent the authority of the arbitrators by filing complaints in court instead are penalized with fines and the suspension of their membership. The power of these arbitrators derives principally from the impact that their judgments have on the reputations of individual dealers or diamond cutters: those who are unwilling to abide by their decisions incur reputation penalties, which signal that they are not committed to long-term cooperation with other members of the Club. The arbitration process therefore serves as a centralized mechanism that transmits important information about disputes arising from economic transactions and about individual reputations to others within the network.[181]

Finally, effective private-order enforcement networks permit members to organize collective sanctions against those who refuse to abide by the values of their association. Professional associations in antiquity gave their members at least two means for imposing organized sanctions above and beyond any sanctions individuals applied on a personal level, whether by refusing to engage in business transactions with defaulters or by shaming them during collective gatherings. First, they made it possible for members to deny a defaulter access to some of the association's benefits. Thus, the Athenian Iobacchoi used exclusion from social and religious gatherings to punish members who were found guilty of assault or of other infractions,[182] while the worshippers of Diana and Antinous in Lanuvium refused to contribute to the funerary rights of members who died while delinquent in their dues.[183] Second, the members of an association could employ expulsion as a more serious form of collective sanction. The charter of the ivory and citrus-wood dealers at Rome explicitly mentioned expulsion as a punishment for magistrates who failed to exercise due diligence in admitting new members to the group; whether or not this association

---

[180] The expertise and availability of well-respected insiders who serve as arbitrators is often identified as one of the major advantages of private dispute-resolution procedures that develop within private-order enforcement networks. See Richman 2004: 2341–2 for a short introduction to these issues.

[181] Richman 2006: 395–8.   [182] *IG* II.2 1368, lines 48–53 and 72–95.

[183] *CIL* 14.2112, col. 1, lines 21–3.

employed expulsion in response to other transgressions is unclear. Some *alba* of professional associations, however, do show signs that individuals' names were struck off the list, presumably because the members in question had been ejected from the *collegium*.[184]

Although no explicit evidence demonstrates that misbehavior in economic transactions in particular might elicit dishonor and sanctions of this sort within a professional *collegium*, Pliny the Younger's correspondence with Trajan indicates that expectations about correct behavior in economic matters were important to association members in antiquity even in non-professional groups. In his letter on the prosecution of Christians, Pliny notes that the members of Christian groups swore oaths to one another that they would not only refrain from theft, robbery, and adultery but also from violating economic agreements, whether by reneging on obligations or by withholding deposits.[185] Arguably, comparable expectations were never far from the minds of members of professional associations, and it would be surprising indeed had they not used reputation mechanisms and the various collective sanctions at their disposal when those expectations were violated. In his manual on the interpretation of dreams, Artemidorus of Daldis preserves an interesting anecdote demonstrating that an individual who dishonored himself in some way might face expulsion from an association. In this particular case, a client's dream that he had urinated on his colleagues during a meeting of his *collegium* turned out to portend that he would engage in behavior in his waking life that would render him bereft of honor (*atimos*) in the eyes of his colleagues and that he would be ejected from the group.[186] The anecdote strongly evokes the notion that questionable conduct in an individual's personal or business life could trigger serious sanctions on the part of an association to which he belonged.

Because professional *collegia* were a stronger focus for the sociability of their members than were the guilds and trade corporations of the seventeenth and eighteenth centuries, sanctions of this sort were especially costly, and *collegia* were in turn particularly effective as private-order enforcement networks.[187] By the seventeenth and eighteenth centuries, artisans enjoyed access to an expanded range of venues for sociability; these have been studied most extensively in the case of early modern England, where it was increasingly common for individuals to belong

---

[184] On the procedures involved in expulsion from associations, see Tran 2007.
[185] Plin. *Ep.* 10.96.7.
[186] Artem 4.44. See Tran 2007 for further discussion of expulsion as a sanction in the *collegia*.
[187] For a counterpoint to this claim, see Liu (forthcoming).

simultaneously to several different kinds of clubs, societies, and religious organizations.[188] Comparable developments were underway on the continent, particularly where religious tensions encouraged guilds to abandon spiritual aspects of their communal behavior.[189] One effect of this development was a tendency among artisans to shift their focus away from guilds as the primary nexus of socialization and communal life. By contrast, professional *collegia* remained the major outlet for sociability among artisans and entrepreneurs in antiquity. Wealthier entrepreneurs in the Roman world had more options for sociability, since they had opportunities to make a lateral move into organizations like that of the Seviri Augustales or to forge close links with other associations – we know of several individuals who boasted in their inscriptions of their membership in multiple professional associations, possibly because they were influential enough to be courted by associations eager to cultivate their patronage.[190] Regular members too had other options, particularly in associations organized around neighborhood affiliation or the worship of specific deities. Yet professional associations were appealing to artisans precisely because they provided a social context in which artisans converted the proceeds of their professional work directly into the symbolic capital that conferred status within the *collegium* and the broader civic world.[191] These benefits were presumably particularly attractive to freed slaves or to recent immigrants: for the former, they offered the opportunity to establish a degree of social autonomy, and for the latter they made it possible to establish ties within the local community. Their appeal even to freeborn artisans, however, can be judged by the geographical and social reach of professional associations. Epigraphy from the Latin West shows at least 1,500 professional associations in existence at one time or another, and in the East there were several hundreds (if not thousands) more.[192] Moreover, although most associations probably had memberships on the order of two dozen people, some grew quite large: the *collegiorum fabrorum tignariorum* in Ostia consisted of 350 members in the late first century CE, and a century later the equivalent group in Rome itself had more than 1,300.[193]

---

[188] Clark 2000 is the fundamental study. King 2004 argues that the guilds were still important networks of sociability in Newcastle and Durham but concedes that they were only one of several by the mid-eighteenth century.

[189] De Munck 2009a; cf. de Munck 2009b.   [190] Tran 2006: 102–10.

[191] Verboven 2007; Tran 2006: 89–137.

[192] On the number of professional *collegia* in the Latin West, see Verboven 2007: 874.

[193] Royden 1988: 27 and 127.

No less important is the fact that professional *collegia* were also less likely than early modern guilds to suffer from strong internal hierarchies that could diminish their effectiveness as enforcement networks by eroding their patterns of sociability and strong communal bonds. Although there was considerable variety in the internal structure of early modern guilds, larger organizations often gave regular members no role in selecting their leaders, whom guild officials chose from among a guild's senior and distinguished members. Officers chosen in this way could be sensitive to the desires of regular members, but in many cases the gulf between leaders and members generated starkly divergent priorities between individual constituencies within any given guild, since guild leaders were often more interested in using the political structure of the guild to further their own ambitions than in maintaining a strong communal identity among its members. As a result, some of the collegial aspects of guild life fell by the wayside as guilds became dedicated increasingly narrowly to economic or political agendas.[194] This problem was particularly acute in some London livery companies, which individuals joined solely to secure the political status conferred by the Freedom of the City and often on the basis of hereditary claims rather than profession. In extreme cases, the majority of the members of a livery company had little to no connection with the trade around which the company was ostensibly organized.[195]

Professional *collegia* in the ancient world were certainly not immune to the development of internal hierarchies.[196] Large *collegia* in dense urban environments were perhaps more likely to be stratified than those in small towns, and those in the Roman West (where the Roman state served as a model for internal organization) more so than those in the Greek East.[197] Within stratified *collegia*, wealthy members may have been more interested in their *collegium* as a platform from which to establish ties of patronage to municipal or regional aristocrats than they were in the sociability of the association itself, and they arguably enjoyed more leverage in internal disputes than did members of lower status. They also enjoyed

---

[194] On hierarchies and internal tensions in guilds in France, see S. L. Kaplan 1981, esp. 258–9 and 269–72. On the Netherlands, see de Munck 2009a. On London livery companies (albeit with some qualifications), see Ward 1997: 73–98.

[195] Kahl 1960: 28; Ward 1997: 45–72. On the relative homogeneity of the Cordwainers, see Riello 2006: 143–52.

[196] See Liu (forthcoming) on the kinds of hierarchies and internal cliques that could arise within Roman professional associations.

[197] Royden 1988: 12–17 offers a general discussion of the internal arrangement of Roman guilds, which "followed the model of municipal administrations."

disproportionate influence in their *collegium*'s politics. In Rome, for instance, the *collegium fabrum tignariorum* was stratified no later than the late first century CE, when our inscriptions permit insight into its internal workings. At the top of the power structure sat six senior magistrates, who presided over a council composed of former magistrates and sixty junior officers responsible for managing the *decuriae* into which the membership was divided. Together, these officers appear to have passed decrees on their own authority, and without any obligation to share their deliberations with the members at large.

Yet in at least one important way Roman *collegia* remained relatively responsive to the concerns of regular members even when the power to make most decisions became vested in the upper levels of the group's hierarchy: regular members remained empowered to vote in the *collegium*'s internal elections. One inscription attests to the existence in the *collegium fabrorum tignariorum* of junior officers known as the *nungenti ad subfragia*, who took their name from the public officials entrusted with the ballot boxes in Roman elections. On the basis of their titles, Royden postulates that they helped to tally the votes of the entire membership during elections rather than only those of an inner circle.[198] Because they enjoyed ongoing power to vote for their magistrates, members of this *collegium* and others like it were able to moderate some of the effects of hierarchy: candidates' electability must have depended to some level on the integrity of their individual reputations and on their commitment to the values of the association, and for that reason they ultimately remained accountable to their fellow *collegiati*.

Collegia and the economic performance of the Roman world

I conclude this chapter by considering the broader impact of *collegia* on the performance of the Roman economy. Professional *collegia* had the potential to stimulate intensive growth because, by mitigating transaction costs, they supported a greater degree of specialization than would have been possible otherwise, and thus contributed to the thick market externalities that were crucial to growth in preindustrial economies. In environments lacking access to organizations capable of reducing transaction costs, entrepreneurs are often unwilling to incur the costs necessary to invest in intensive human capital, since coordination problems create a real danger

---

[198] Royden 1988: 131–2, *contra* More 1969: 136–8. The relevant texts are *CIL* 6.30872 and *CIL* 14.2630. Cf. Verboven 2007: 871 on the "one man one vote" principle.

that they will not find customers or employers for their specialized products or services;[199] opportunities for increased specialization and thick
market externalities thus remain unexploited. Precisely because *collegia*
permitted members to address transaction cost problems without creating
integrated firms, which imposed serious financial risks in the seasonal and
uncertain product markets of the Roman world, they encouraged specialization (and thus growth driven by thick markets) by reassuring artisans
that any time and resources they devoted to specialized training were likely
to pay off in the long run.[200]

In more concrete terms, even though the rarity of integrated firms
offered specialist artisans few prospects for direct and stable employment,
collegia facilitated specialists' efforts to establish themselves as independent
producers by limiting some of the attendant risks and costs.[201]
In particular, artisans who applied their skills to transform raw materials
or semi-finished goods belonging to other craftsmen enjoyed low establishment costs. Specialists such as engravers had to carry the costs of their
workspace and any additional labor they required but were able to limit the
costs of their working capital: they had no need for large reserves of raw
materials, and although they were expected to extend credit to the artisans
who sought their services, they themselves were unlikely to be as heavily
indebted to suppliers of goods or services as were artisans who stood at the
apex of subcontracting chains.

Collegia likewise limited costs of establishment for entrepreneurs whose
businesses required them to coordinate the labor of other specialists – not
just because they permitted entrepreneurs like Demetrios of Ephesos to
coordinate production without creating integrated firms but also because
they helped to support credit relationships between their members.
Although credit-based financing of this sort required careful management,
artisans who purchased intermediate goods and services on credit from
their subcontractors were able to defer some of their expenses and pass on
some of the risks of production to their partners.[202]

At the same time, however, the ability of *collegia* to foster both specialization and thick market externalities capable of driving intensive growth
was ultimately limited by these organizations' exclusivity. As we have seen,
that exclusivity was partly a product of a *collegium*'s need to enforce strong
network boundaries in order to ensure both that individual members

---

[199] See above, nn. 8 and 9. [200] Grantham 1999, esp. 218–22.
[201] For a theoretical discussion of the points raised here and in the next paragraph, see Mead 1984:
1096–7.
[202] Cf. Sonenscher 1989: 191–2.

remained invested in their reputations and that accurate information about those reputations could circulate among its membership as a whole.[203] Yet, more significantly, most *collegia* also seem to have excluded women and slaves, who did not gain membership in professional associations with any real frequency.[204] Since members of *collegia* preferred to transact whenever possible with fellow members,[205] women and slaves in particular probably found it difficult to find an outlet for highly specialized skills within established subcontracting networks. And, although they may have gained admission to other kinds of organizations – the apostle Paul, for example, made important professional connections in a synagogue[206] in Corinth, and Apuleius suggests that public baths fostered loose networks of sociability among artisans[207] – these did not substitute fully for the private-enforcement functions provided by organized professional *collegia*. In practice, this meant that numerous inhabitants of a city like Rome were unable to take advantage of a professional *collegium's* ability to mitigate the costs and risks of specialized training, to the extent that they were likely to have been deterred from investing at all in the intensive human capital necessary to produce further thick market externalities.[208] Moreover, since there does not appear to have been a major change in the membership profiles of professional *collegia* during the late Republic or early Empire in this respect, it seems probable that these organizations had exhausted their potential to stimulate growth by the end of the first century CE.

Although these consequences of exclusion are difficult to confirm directly, sources touching on the investment behavior of wealthy Romans offer indirect evidence of their impact on the economy by implying that wealthy slaveholders were reluctant to train their slaves in occupations that demanded participation in subcontracting networks. The risks slaveholders incurred by training slaves as artisans were relatively high in any case, since slave craftsmen faced the same basic challenges as many of their freeborn and freed counterparts; in particular, those established by their masters in autonomous businesses found it necessary to

---

[203] Cf. Carr and Landa 1983; Cooter and Landa 1984.

[204] For a discussion of slave and female *collegiati* with emphasis on the *collegia* of *centonarii*, see Liu 2009: 176–80. But cf. Waltzing 1895–1900, I: 346–7, who suspects that slaves could be found in associations that were less prestigious than most of the occupational associations for which we have membership data.

[205] McMillan and Woodruff 2001: 2454–6; Richman 2004: 2345–6 and 2352.   [206] *Acts* 18.1–4

[207] Apul. *Met.* 9.24.

[208] Cf. Ogilvie 2011 for an extended treatment of how the exclusivity of merchant associations in medieval and early modern Europe may have been detrimental to growth.

manage production schedules in the face of seasonal and uncertain demand and to maintain credit relationships with clients and suppliers without incurring dangerous levels of debt. Those risks were only compounded for owners seeking to train slaves in trades that tended to be incorporated in subcontracting networks, since those slaves were unlikely to make productive use of their skills without access to the networks supported by *collegia*. In these circumstances, wealthy Romans – who had a strong preference for low-risk investment opportunities guaranteeing predictable and regular earnings – may have been more inclined to invest in urban real estate, in industries in which subcontracting was unnecessary, or in industries demanding extensive physical capital (such as baking and fulling), in which their resources gave them a competitive advantage over independent artisans.[209]

These expectations are borne out to some degree by our legal and epigraphic sources, both of which suggest that slaveholders did not often control the labor of slaves trained in highly specialized urban crafts. When Roman jurists mention manufacturing businesses operated by slaves, they refer to enterprises an artisan could manage with the help of one or two assistants and without contracting for the services of other specialists: a smithy and a dye works, for example, are mentioned by Scaevola and Papinian, respectively.[210] Inscriptions from household columbaria suggest that slave or freed artisans who were attached to large households were more likely to have been employed by their owners to meet the internal needs of those households than to have worked in commercial enterprises. Many of the artisans named in these inscriptions performed tasks of considerable utility to an extensive slaveholding household, such as baking, textile production, and clothing manufacture;[211] slave bakers in large households almost certainly produced for internal consumption, and although some of the textiles produced in comparable contexts by dependent artisans may have been marketed by their masters, it remains plausible that many were destined for use within the household itself. The funerary inscriptions of aristocratic households only rarely commemorate slave or freed artisans who practiced trades geared toward market production. Very few goldsmiths and silversmiths are commemorated in the tombs or columbaria of elite Romans who did not belong to the imperial household itself: in her

---

[209] On the investment mentality of wealthy Romans, see Kehoe 1988.
[210] Scaevola, *Dig.* 31.1.88.3; Papinian, *Dig.* 32.1.91.2.
[211] Joshel 1992: 93–5. Cf. Treggiari 1975: 54–5 on Livia's household.

comprehensive study of the economic role of freedmen in Roman society, Joshel could cite only two cases in which workers in precious metals were demonstrably attached to large, private households, as compared to sixteen freed or slave gold- and silversmiths who were affiliated with members of the imperial family.[212] The same is true of artisans who practiced a number of other trades, including those who produced durable goods, those who worked leather, and even those who engaged in fulling or in dyeing.[213]

Our sources offer better evidence that some members of the elite owned slaves or controlled freedmen who specialized in branches of the building trades, but even in these cases it remains possible that most owners of such slaves employed them mostly to meet the needs of their own households. Plutarch claims that Crassus possessed a workforce of over five hundred slave builders and architects,[214] but simultaneously suggests that this was highly unusual, since he implies that Crassus was only able to maintain this workforce because he purchased and renovated properties that were in imminent danger of burning down, when their owners were willing to sell them at substantial discounts. Inscriptions offer evidence of better quality: some show that slaves or freedmen trained in building trades were more likely to be commemorated in ways that imply ongoing connections to aristocratic households than other artisans,[215] and others name builders who had probably been manumitted by Roman senators.[216] It is far from clear, however, that most of these slaves and freedmen worked in commercial rather than domestic contexts. The columbarium of the Statilii Tauri, for example, contains the largest group of household inscriptions dedicated to slave and freed builders outside of the imperial family itself: three of these specialists were described simply as *fabri*, three others as framers (*fabri tignarii*), one worked in marble (*marmorarius*), and one was a bricklayer (*faber structor parietarius*).[217] Although it is tempting to

---

[212] Joshel 1977: 115–16.

[213] E.g., Joshel 1977: 123 (general metalwork), 139 (leatherwork), and 148 (fulling and dyeing). Cf. her remarks in Joshel 1992: 95–6, where she notes that very few of the freed artisans in her sample can be associated with large aristocratic households.

[214] Plut. *Crass.* 2.4.   [215] Joshel 1992: 94–5.

[216] So, for instance, the freedman Quintus Haterius Evagogus, who held office as a *decurio* in the Roman *collegium fabrum tignariorum*, had probably been manumitted by a former slave of the orator Quintus Haterius, who served as a suffect consul in 5 BCE (Joshel 1992: 118–19). Likewise, Titus Flavius Hilario (who, as we saw above, held several offices in the *collegium fabrum tignariorum* from the late 60s CE onward) may have been connected with the household of the emperor Vespasian. See Royden 1988: 150–62 for other examples.

[217] *CIL* 6.6283–6285 (*fabri*), 6.6363–6365 (*fabri tignarii*), 6.6318 (*marmorarius*), 6.6354 (*faber structor parietarius*). For further discussion, see Treggiari 1975: 54 and S. D. Martin 1989: 64.

interpret these inscriptions as evidence that Statilius Taurus and his descendants had invested heavily in one or more commercial building enterprises, it is more plausible that they were employed primarily by Taurus or his descendants to maintain the amphitheater and gardens that the family had built for the enjoyment of the public.[218]

Professional *collegia* clearly provided important benefits to their members for most of their history, and they just as clearly permitted the Roman economy to sustain a level of specialization and intensive human capital that may not otherwise have been achievable. They were, however, unable to drive ongoing growth over the long run, for the simple reason that many inhabitants of Roman cities could not take advantage of what *collegia* had to offer. In that sense, the benefits professional associations offered both to members and to wider economy came with strong strings attached.

---

[218] Treggiari 1975: 54; D'Arms 1981: 155; S. D. Martin 1989: 64–5. Anderson 1997: 78–9 suggests that these specialists engaged in commercial work on behalf of the family as well, but nevertheless believes that they worked primarily to maintain the family's properties.

Manumission and the urban labor market

In the latter half of the first century CE, the knifesmith Lucius Cornelius Atimetus commissioned a funerary altar to perpetuate the memory of his life and career. On its face, the altar bears an inscription: "Lucius Cornelius Atimetus, for himself and for his freedman Lucius Cornelius Epaphra, who is well-deserving; and to his other freedmen and freedwomen and their posterity."[1] More striking are the reliefs on the altar's right and left sides, which provide a rare and valuable glimpse into the dynamics of a Roman artisanal workshop. In the first, two men stand beside a cabinet in which a small collection of the workshop's products is on display (Figure 3.1). In the second, two men are hard at work in the smithy: on the left-hand side, a seated smith holds a work-in-progress on the anvil with his left hand and a small hammer in his right; opposite him, on the right-hand side, stands a striker, poised to deliver a strong blow to the piece in a spot to be indicated by a tap from the smith's hammer (Figure 3.2).[2] Although the identities of the men in the first relief are uncertain – they could represent Atimetus and Epaphra, or perhaps Atimetus and a customer – it seems probable that the second shows Atimetus and Epaphra themselves working at the anvil.[3] The altar thus portrays a small Roman manufacturing firm in which an artisan relied heavily on the labor of a freed slave, who remained affiliated with his master's enterprise even after earning manumission.

By indicating that an artisan like Atimetus was willing to manumit skilled slaves within his own lifetime (*inter vivos*), this altar offers an interesting point of entry into a longstanding debate about the considerations motivating slaveholders to free slaves and the frequency with which they did so.

---

[1] *CIL* 6.16166.

[2] Rome, Vatican Museums, Galleria Lapidaria, inv. 9277. Full discussion and bibliography can be found in Zimmer 1982: 180–2. For further discussion, see Clarke 2003: 121–3 and Kampen 1981: 97–8.

[3] Zimmer prefers to see the two figures in the first relief as Atimetus and Epaphra; Clarke and Kampen, on the other hand, prefer to see this relief as a depiction of Atimetus making a sale to one of his clients. See above for specific references.

Figure 3.1 The altar of Atimetus, sales scene (Photo: Vatican Museum, Galleria Lapidaria/©Photo SCALA, Florence)

Figure 3.2 The altar of Atimetus, workshop scene (Photo: Vatican, Galleria Lapidaria/De Agostini Picture Library/Getty Images)

Scholars have recognized for some time that manumission was an important structural feature of the Roman slave system, largely because slaveholders could use prospective freedom as a powerful incentive to ensure that slaves remained loyal and obedient. Yet, in theory, slaveholders were perfectly capable of extracting that obedience not by manumitting slaves *inter vivos*, but rather by promising to free slaves in their wills. In fact, some slaveholders postponed the gift of manumission even further by obliging slaves to serve their heirs for some time before gaining their freedom. For that reason, and even allowing for other potential motivating factors – some owners freed slaves out of affection or as a reward for exceptional loyalty, while others did so because manumission, like slaveholding itself, could serve as a signal of one's wealth and status – scholars generally argue that slaveholders manumitted slaves *inter vivos* when it was in their immediate economic interests to do so.[4]

In their efforts to understand the economic interests prompting slaveholders to manumit slaves *inter vivos*, scholars have emphasized one of two models. The first is the model developed by Géza Alföldy and Keith Hopkins and defended most recently by Ulrike Roth. In this view, widespread manumission *inter vivos* was an inevitable byproduct of Roman slaveholders' tendency to grant *peculia* to their slaves. A *peculium* was an account consisting of funds or productive capital (including cash, moveable goods, real estate, other slaves, and livestock), which a Roman *paterfamilias* could place under the control of one of his dependents (whether freeborn or slave), all of whom technically possessed no independent property rights of their own. By awarding a *peculium* to one of his slaves, along with the authorization to employ it in commercial transactions (*concessio liberae administrationis*), a Roman *paterfamilias* made it possible for that slave to operate a semi-autonomous business or to participate in the labor market on his or her own account.[5] Because slaves who had been granted economic autonomy by their masters generally retained what was left of their earnings after they had honored any outstanding debts and obligations to their masters, some were able to save enough money to purchase their own freedom. Slaveholders benefited from this arrangement not just because it permitted them to recapitalize the value of aging slaves by purchasing

---

[4] Bradley 1987: 96–9; Wiedemann 1985; Hopkins 1978: 123–32. Mouritsen 2011: 120–205 provides an overview of the complexity of the institution. For further reflections on non-economic motivations for manumission, see Bradley 1987: 81–112 and Zelnick-Abramovitz 2005: 147–53.

[5] So Labeo, *Dig.* 19.2.60.7, who distinguishes between a slave muleteer hired out by his employer and a slave muleteer who sought his own contracts on the basis of a *peculium*.

replacements (while generating steady income in the process) but also because the prospect of manumission by self-purchase motivated slaves to work diligently on their owners' behalf in the interim.[6]

More recently, Henrik Mouritsen has proposed a model stressing that Roman slaveholders conceptualized manumission as merely one stage in an ongoing relationship of dependence between slave and master. In his view, slaveholders rarely manumitted slaves in exchange for payments made on the basis of a *peculium*, but rather employed manumission as a tool for extracting effort from dependent workers both before and after freeing them. Mouritsen suggests that urban slaveholders generally manumitted slaves in the expectation that those slaves, once freed, would continue to serve them in essentially the same capacity, albeit under a somewhat different juridical framework. For that reason, they consciously manumitted only slaves who had already demonstrated considerable loyalty and initiative and from whom they could therefore expect ongoing compliance. More importantly, they freed those slaves who recognized that their former masters' patronage would make available economic and business opportunities from which they would otherwise be excluded after manumission because of their own limited financial resources, and who therefore had more to gain by remaining closely linked to their patrons than they did by forging independent social and economic lives of their own.[7]

In this chapter, I suggest that artisan slaveholders like Atimetus manumitted skilled slaves for somewhat different reasons – to negotiate problems specific to the milieu of urban producers – and that they did so in a very particular way, namely by demanding that their freed slaves deliver specified quantities of skilled labor as repayment for their manumission. Although ancient historians have recognized the potential importance of manumission in exchange for labor obligations in both Greek and Roman practice, those who study Roman manumission in particular have not yet reached a consensus on whether or not manumission in exchange for such obligations (the so-called *operae libertorum*, which were conceptualized as labor services measured in units of a day's worth of work) was a significant aspect of Roman social and economic life. In his classic treatment of the subject, Wolfgang Waldstein argued that the prominence of *operae* in Justinian's *Digest* mirrored their importance in actual social practice and

---

[6] Alföldy 1972: 120–2; Hopkins 1978: 123–32; Roth 2010. Cf. Treggiari 1969: 17. Roth focuses mostly on Junian Latins rather than on formally manumitted freedmen, but her observations about the role of the *peculium* in the manumission process are valid for members of both groups. Mouritsen 2011: 159–80 is more skeptical about the prevalence of this kind of manumission.

[7] Mouritsen 2001; Mouritsen 2011: 206–47.

that Roman slaveholders regularly used manumission in exchange for *operae* as a means of allowing slaves to purchase their freedom on credit instead of for cash.[8] In this view, the legal opinions preserved in the *Digest* should be seen as the product of jurists' efforts to grapple with real-world problems that gave rise to legal disputes, perhaps with some frequency. More recently, Mouritsen has subjected this view to strong criticism. Mouritsen stresses that there is very little evidence for manumission in exchange for *operae* apart from the opinions in the *Digest* and takes this as an indication that slaveholders employed it relatively rarely. He bolsters that argument by suggesting that because the obligations imposed by *operae* were limited to a specified quantity of labor services, they were unlikely to have been appealing to most slaveholders, who preferred to prolong the dependence of former slaves and profit from their labor in other ways – most commonly, by providing financial backing for freedmen who managed businesses of their own.[9]

As I demonstrate in what follows, however, the seasonality and uncertainty of urban demand made manumission in exchange for *operae* a useful tool for artisans, who used it as part of a labor-hoarding strategy designed to meet two potentially contradictory goals: (1) to mitigate financial risks arising from seasonal and uncertain demand by minimizing their fixed outlays on labor; (2) to retain access to the skilled labor they required if they were to profit from favorable market conditions by expanding their output in periods of elevated demand. Yet the fact that they relied upon manumission for this purpose is significant in and of itself: it suggests that the market for skilled labor was tight relative to comparable labor markets in early modern Europe, and that transaction costs were correspondingly high enough to pose problems for artisans who relied on short-term hired help to meet the goals enumerated above. I conclude by suggesting that artisans' use of manumission only exacerbated the sources of market friction that encouraged them to rely upon it in the first place. In that sense, an analysis of manumission from the perspective of urban artisans not only adds considerably to our understanding of manumission in Roman social and economic life but also speaks directly to two key aspects of Roman economic history: the relative level of performance achieved by the Roman economy and the nature of the factors that may have prevented

---

[8] On manumission in exchange for *operae* as an alternative to manumission by self-purchase, see Garnsey 1981: 362–4; Waldstein 1986, esp. 123–30; and, for the Greek context, in which *paramone* could serve the same function, Zelnick-Abramovitz 2005: 219. Cf. Fabre 1981: 317–31, who also believes that manumission in exchange for *operae* may have been relatively common.

[9] Mouritsen 2011: 224–6.

ongoing market expansion and growth in the first and second centuries CE.

Manumission and the rhythms of work in a seasonal and uncertain economy

Roman slaveholders attached considerable importance to the power and authority they wielded over their human property. As Keith Bradley has put it, the ongoing vitality of slavery owed much to the fact that "owning slaves always served to express *potestas* in a society highly sensitive to gradations of status, esteem, and authority."[10] This was undoubtedly just as true for urban artisans and entrepreneurs as it was for the elite, especially in Rome and other heavily urbanized parts of the empire in which chattel slavery had long been prominent.[11]

Yet even though the power and influence slaveholders wielded over their slaves and freedmen were satisfying in and of themselves, there is evidence that Roman slaveholders were nevertheless willing to assess the costs and benefits of slavery from an economic standpoint when making decisions about labor management. The authors of the agronomical treatises, for example, believed that estate owners could enhance their estates' profits by making judicious use of a combination of slave and hired workers. More precisely, they recommended that estate owners maintain relatively small permanent workforces of slaves to tend to ongoing and regular tasks on the farm but that they rely on contract labor for specialized services or additional help during critical periods of the agricultural year (chiefly, during the harvest and vintage). Underpinning that advice was an awareness that slaveholding could be undesirable in some situations, in part because it was not always as cost-effective as other forms of labor.[12]

Given the focus of the advice offered by agronomical authors like Cato, Varro, and Columella, it is plausible that Roman artisans too assessed the perceived costs and benefits of the various labor-management strategies at their disposal and that those who acquired and manumitted slaves did so because they believed that they could better manage their enterprises by

---

[10] Bradley 1994: 10–30; the passage I quote here can be found on p. 30.

[11] Naturally, this point is difficult to substantiate directly, but it seems to be supported indirectly by the tendency of artisans to stress their control over slaves and freedmen in their funerary epigraphy. See Joshel 1992: 79–80.

[12] E.g., Cato, *Agr.* 56–9 and 144-5. For the various ways in which landowners in Italy may have exploited different categories of slave, hired, and tenant labor, see Kehoe 1988; Erdkamp 2005: 81–7; Launaro 2011, esp. 165–83.

relying on the labor of dependent workers than by hiring help. In this section, I suggest that artisans in the Roman world employed manumission as a tool for resolving problems generated by seasonal and uncertain product markets. More precisely, I show that artisans hoarded the labor of freedmen to strike a balance between the need to minimize their fixed costs of production and their desire to expand output in periods of elevated demand.

Artisan employers and short-term wage labor

I begin by establishing the context in which Roman artisans may have been interested in manumitting skilled slaves in exchange for labor obligations. That context can be reconstructed on the basis of comparative evidence from early modern Europe, which demonstrates that seasonal and uncertain product markets tended to limit the demand for regular and permanent labor in the workshops of artisan proprietors. Precisely because the demand for their products and services was seasonal and uncertain, early modern artisans sought to economize as much as possible on their fixed labor costs. Ideally, they did so by recruiting workers as necessary and on short-term contracts in order to adapt their workforces to prevailing conditions of demand; when this was not possible, they instead sought to minimize the costs of hoarded labor.

As I established in Chapter 2, seasonal and uncertain demand discouraged artisans and entrepreneurs in the early modern and ancient worlds alike from incurring the fixed costs necessary to create integrated firms, and instead prompted them to collaborate with specialists in complex subcontracting networks. In addition to limiting the scope of the work most artisans carried out personally, however, seasonal and uncertain demand also clearly limited the size of the workforces most artisans employed in the early modern period, largely because it complicated their efforts to maintain regular production throughout the year.[13] In an economy in which technologies of production remained relatively basic, work was labor-intensive, and labor costs were often an artisan's largest expense,[14] producers were compelled to balance the potential benefits of

---

[13] For a contrary view (albeit with reference to ancient Athens), see Osborne 1995: 34, who argues that although agricultural work entailed fluctuating working rhythms and thus irregular employment, urban production was more regular and thus better suited to permanent workforces of slaves.

[14] See de Vries 1976: 87 and 91 for the costs of various factors of production in the early modern economy in general. Cf. also Sonenscher 1989: 137–8. Earle 1989b: 120–3 provides useful data on the

retaining the flexibility to expand output in periods of elevated demand against the risks and costs of maintaining permanent workforces.

Artisans enjoyed the best prospects for regularizing both their output and their demand for labor when they could expand their customer base by extending its geographical range. In Marseilles during the eighteenth century, for example, shoemakers regularized production by capturing access to sizeable colonial markets.[15] Most, however, lacked the opportunity to regularize their demand for labor in this way and thus found it difficult to resolve the conflict between their need to minimize fixed costs and their desire to recruit the labor necessary to take advantage of seasonal and unpredictable peaks in demand. In practice, they negotiated this conflict in two ways. First, some relied on the spot market: when conditions were good, they hired workers on short-term contracts, and then dismissed those workers when demand tapered off. Second, others hoarded some of the labor they anticipated using during peak moments of annual demand, while structuring contracts in ways that reduced the overall magnitude of their wage accounts.[16]

Most artisans in the early modern period preferred to rely on the spot market – so long, that is, as workers were available on short notice. In the eighteenth century, Adam Smith noted that "in London almost all journeymen artificers [were] liable to be called upon and dismissed by their masters from day to day, and from week to week, in the same manner as day-labourers in other places."[17] Subsequent research has demonstrated that comparable patterns of employment remained characteristic of the London trades well into the nineteenth century.[18] Corporate registers from eighteenth-century Rouen demonstrate that artisans on the continent relied just as heavily on the spot market whenever possible, and in doing so they highlight two important aspects of the early modern urban economy. First, they emphasize that journeymen employed on short-term contracts greatly outnumbered those who remained with the same master artisan for months or years at a time and that their average periods of employment were quite brief. Journeymen locksmiths, wigmakers, and

distribution of assets among artisans in London in the late seventeenth and early eighteenth centuries. Stocks on hand and fixed assets represented on average 20 percent of the wealth of artisans in his sample, most of which consisted of stock in trade. The costs of fixed assets other than working space were relatively minor in most trades. See Burford 1972: 78–80 on the importance of skill relative to physical capital in the ancient world.

[15] Sonenscher 1989: 180–1.   [16] Grantham 1994: 15–16.   [17] Smith 1994: 120 (Bk. I, Ch. X, Pt. I).

[18] See Schwarz 1992: 117–23 for London in the eighteenth century. Stedman Jones 1984: 33–51 argues that these patterns remained essentially unchanged in many London trades well into the nineteenth century (see also 375–8 for his charts of seasonal peaks and troughs in nineteenth century trades).

tailors in Rouen were, respectively, employed for periods of six months, four months, and five weeks on average, but since these averages take into account journeymen hired on long-term contracts as well as those working on a contingent basis, those working on short-term contracts actually spent much less time in any given workshop than the raw averages suggest. Second, the registers also show that the master artisans who employed journeymen formulated their hiring strategies in response to both seasonal fluctuations in demand and the more unpredictable rhythms of work characteristic of bespoke industries. Journeymen wigmakers, for instance, registered for employment in the city in particularly large numbers during January, April, and September, which suggests that employers were particularly interested in recruiting help during these months (no doubt because major holidays generated elevated amounts of business). Likewise, registrations by journeymen tailors peaked modestly after Easter and before the Feast of All Saints. Alongside these seasonal variations in employment patterns, however, there were numerous other irregular fluctuations, produced by the erratic production schedules of individual workshops. On the basis of these observations, Michael Sonenscher concluded that master artisans sought to keep their regular workforces as small as possible and to supplement them as necessary by hiring additional journeymen on short-term contracts – whether by the day, the week, or even the job. "[I]nstead of a permanently employed workforce, most trades depended upon an irregular supply of labour employed for the minimum amount of time."[19]

In the ancient world, some artisans and entrepreneurs took advantage of geographically extended markets to regularize their production in ways that marked the archaeological record: the artisans on Delos who manufactured high-quality bedframes for export to Italy come to mind, as do the manufacturers of Arretine ware in the first centuries BCE and CE, whose goods were distributed in Italy, Gaul, and beyond.[20] Yet enterprises of this nature appear to have been the exception rather than the rule.[21] Most of them probably emerged because of demand generated by intermediary businessmen, who bought products in sizeable quantities in order

---

[19] Sonenscher 1989: 130–73 and esp. 138. For comparable patterns of employment in central Europe, see Ehmer 1997 and Reith 2008. Farr 1997 and 2000, *passim* argues that these features of the eighteenth-century European craft economy were not radically different than those of earlier centuries, when master artisans likewise relied on the spot market to respond to seasonal and uncertain demand.

[20] For a general overview of Arretine ware, see Fülle 1997 and Wallace-Hadrill 2008: 407–21. On the bedframe makers of Delos, see Wallace-Hadrill 2008: 363 and 421–35.

[21] For a more optimistic view of the ability of urban artisans to tap into geographically dispersed markets, see Mayer 2012: 66–74.

to resell them in newly established and distant markets, and who thus created relatively steady work for the artisan producers themselves. When, however, centers of local production emerged to produce goods that had initially been imported over long distances, export-based businesses of this nature tended to lose their extended markets and shrink dramatically, as did the pottery enterprises in Arezzo. Where these kinds of businesses persisted, they tended to do so because of two specific and unusual advantages. First, some artisans manufactured low-value goods in rural contexts, where part-time peasant labor was cheap during slack periods in the agricultural calendar and where raw materials were available locally at little cost.[22] Second, manufacturers of highly prized luxury goods or extremely specialized products, such as medical instruments, had better prospects for striking up long-term relationships with wholesalers operating in extended markets than those who created products that could easily be replicated on the local level.[23]

Without access to geographically extended markets of this sort, however, most urban artisans in the Roman world had to negotiate the same basic conflict as their early modern counterparts – that is, to balance their desire to keep fixed costs to a minimum against their desire to recruit the labor necessary to expand their output when demand was high. This was true in all segments of the market, and especially in segments catering to the demand for bespoke goods. Here, artisans had limited opportunities for regularizing their output over the year, especially if most of their clients were other artisans with erratic production and subcontracting schedules of their own. In these circumstances, artisans faced a real danger that any workers whom they incorporated permanently into their firms would be severely underemployed.

Artisans had more scope for regularizing production when they worked in segments demanding either undifferentiated goods or populuxe goods with only minor variations in form or decoration. Atimetus undoubtedly fell into this category, as demonstrated by the small inventory of knives depicted on his altar (Figure 3.1). Some archaeological material provides further evidence for small inventories maintained by artisan producers. The treasure hoard found at Snettisham in Britain

---

[22] The expansion of pottery production in Roman Gaul can potentially be interpreted on this model (cf. Whittaker 2002). See also Diodorus 5.13.1–2, who suggests that artisans in Puteoli took advantage of their proximity to the iron mines on Elba to manufacture basic or roughed-out pieces in large quantities for export.

[23] The artisan Agathangelos, for example, manufactured surgical equipment that found its way into much of northwestern Europe (Gostenčnik 2002).

arguably represents the stock-on-hand of a silversmith: dated to
the second century CE, it contains not only silver coins (which perhaps
doubled as raw materials) but also several dozen rings, some snake-shaped
bracelets, and a number of unset engraved gemstones.[24] The pieces of
statuary found in the sculptors' workshop at Aphrodisias are equally
instructive. In the case of at least one of the larger statues – a standing
togatus – the sculptors had completed the body of the figure but had only
roughed in the head; seemingly, they had produced this particular piece
for inventory and planned to add details to the statue's head and face once
they secured a buyer.[25] As suggested in Chapter 2, however, inter-annual
fluctuations in the purchasing power of most urban residents created
enough uncertainty for artisans working in these market segments that
they too found it risky to sustain regular output and sizeable
inventories.[26]

Our evidence for the hiring practices of artisans in antiquity suggests
that some, like their early modern counterparts, attempted to navigate
this problem by hiring workers on the spot market as and when necessary.
Apuleius assumed that artisans engaged skilled workers on a more or less
casual basis and structured an episode in his novel, *Metamorphoses*, on the
basis of that premise. Apuleius conceptualizes one of the central characters
in this episode as a man who earns a meager living by doing skilled
work (*fabriles operas*), probably as a carpenter, in a workshop belonging
to another craftsman (an *officinator*).[27] Apuleius clearly imagines that
a skilled worker in this position would have been employed on a short-
term or perhaps even casual basis: the plot is driven by the fact that the
character's pay is computed and doled out daily so that if he does not work
on any given day, he will not have the cash to buy dinner for himself

---

[24] Johns et al. 1997 provide a catalog of the hoard's contents, along with detailed and specific analyses
of the various pieces themselves.

[25] Rockwell 1991: 136–8. As I noted in Chapter 1, however, it is difficult to determine the degree to
which these artisans did or did not work on commission.

[26] The seemingly small sizes of the inventories in these three cases seem to confirm this point.
As depicted on his funerary monument, Atimetus' stock fits easily within a medium-sized standing
cabinet. The workshop of the sculptors at Aphrodisias contained seventeen unfinished sculptures of
varying sizes, five of which were large pieces (Rockwell 1991). It is impossible to tell how many of
these may have been produced as "inventory" and how many had been commissioned.
The Snettisham hoard possessed a value in bullion of about 430 *denarii* (Johns et al. 1997: 75),
including the coins. This was no trifling amount, but neither was it a vast treasure: by way of
comparison, skilled workers who were employed by the state at Mons Claudianus earned the rough
equivalent of 564 *denarii* a year in coin, plus a grain ration (Cuvigny 1996).

[27] Apul. *Met.* 9.5–7. The character is identified as a *faber*, which among other things could mean
a construction worker or a smith, but a pun in the text suggests that in this case we should take it to
mean a carpenter (Hijmans et al. 1995: 80).

and his wife.[28] Since Apuleius' fiction is thought to be rooted in a realistic depiction of social and economic life in the provinces of the Roman Empire,[29] the character's circumstances should be taken as a reflection of an underlying reality, and not as a pure exercise in imagination. The passage thus offers crude but important evidence that some Roman artisans sought to recruit skilled help on a short-term rather than long-term basis, probably to minimize their fixed costs.

The Roman jurists make comparable assumptions about artisans' preferences for short-term hiring in their discussions concerning the building industry. Historians have noted the impact of seasonality on employment within the industry in some detail, stressing that the seasonality of large-scale public building projects affected the job prospects of unskilled laborers.[30] But building projects, both public and private, also required skilled labor, and our sources indicate that Roman building contractors typically recruited skilled workers on an *ad hoc* basis or for specific projects instead of integrating them permanently into their firms. The jurist Venuleius, for instance, assumed that a builder would not possess a dedicated and permanent staff but would instead recruit both laborers and skilled craftsmen once he formed a contract, even if he undoubtedly let out some of the more specialized and technical work piecemeal to independent subcontractors.[31]

Documentary evidence from Roman Egypt likewise suggests that artisans often hired workers on a short-term rather than permanent basis. Here, the key interpretative difficulty is that artisans and their employees were much less likely to document short-term labor contracts than longer agreements. Individuals in the Roman world could create valid and binding contracts with or without employing written records, even when those contracts were extraordinarily complex. Long-term contracts, however, imposed a higher level of obligation on all parties than short-term contracts and were thus more likely to be committed to writing. Oral agreements, on the other hand, were particularly common when contractual terms were simple, straightforward, and binding for short periods of time. In a well-known parable in the Gospel of Matthew, a landowner relies entirely on oral agreements when he recruits day laborers to work in his vineyards, and one imagines that artisans in need of short-term help would have done

---

[28] Cf. the comments of Hijmans et al. 1995: 69.   [29] Millar 1981.
[30] In particular, see Casson 1978 and Brunt 1980. Cf. the comments by Mattingly and Salmon 2001b: 7–8.
[31] Venuleius, *Dig.* 45.1.137.3; Alfenus, *Dig.* 19.2.30.3. For further discussion, see S. D. Martin 1989, esp. 43–72 and 115–16.

likewise.[32] Unsurprisingly, documents recording long-term hires by artisans of slave and free workers thus predominate in the papyri,[33] much as
they predominate in collections of written contracts from later periods,
even when short-term agreements were more typical in practice.[34]

That caveat aside, some of the surviving contracts from Roman Egypt
record short-term labor agreements of the sort that artisans may have
formed to secure temporary help in response to seasonal peaks in demand.
One surviving contract records an agreement between a weaver specializing
in Tarsian fabrics and the father of a boy who agreed to place his son in
the weaver's shop for a period of seven months; in another, a freedman
agreed to work in a shop belonging to an artisan (whose precise specialty
is unfortunately unknown) for five months.[35] To these, we can also add
documents pertaining to shipbuilding, a relatively well-attested activity
in Egypt, even if most of the surviving papyri date from the third century
CE or later. Two of the surviving documents are particularly interesting.
In the first, a contract between a shipwright and a client who had commissioned a boat, the parties inserted language concerning the wages that were
to be paid by the primary contractor to workers involved on the project.
The fact that this provision was included in the contract at all suggests
that the contractor did not maintain a permanent staff, but rather hired
workers as needed to complete specific jobs.[36] The second document
records wage disbursements made over a three-week period to craftsmen
who were employed in a shipyard to help construct a vessel. These

---

[32] For oral contracts in Roman Egypt, see Taubenschlag 1955: 301–3. On verbal contracting by means of *stipulatio* in the building trades, see S. D. Martin 1989: 22–9. Cf. the more general remarks of MacMullen 1974: 65. The parable of the workers in the vineyard can be found at Matthew 20:1–16.

[33] For convenience, I refer to all of these documents as employment contracts. Technically, however, because the contracts that provided for the direct hire of a slave from his or her owner involved an agreement between the slaveholder and a third party, they differed from those that provided for the hire of a free worker, and even from those that provided for the hire of a slave who had been granted a degree of economic independence by his master. Du Plessis 2012: 117–20 and 131–5 discusses legal aspects of different forms of slave hire in the Roman context; Taubenschlag 1955: 367–8 and 371–83 provides discussions and catalogs of the two different types of contracts in Roman Egypt. On the different mechanisms for hiring the services of a slave, see below.

[34] For comments on this problem in the context of a discussion of labor practices in medieval Europe, see Epstein 1991: 65–6 and 114.

[35] *PSI* IV 287 and *P. Mich.* IX 574. Both of these documents, however, are from the fourth century and are therefore admittedly late. For the hiring practices of weavers in Roman Egypt in earlier periods, see Wipszycka 1965: 63–74.

[36] SB XXIV 16254. The text, a translation, and commentary can be found in Sijpesteijn 1996. Because the contract includes provisions concerning the wages to be paid to additional workers, Sijpesteijn believes that the contractor was an employee hired to oversee the project rather than the artisan from whom the ship had been commissioned. This argument is ultimately not compelling, since similar provisions were sometimes a feature of construction contracts at Rome (S. D. Martin 1989: 115–16).

craftsmen included teams of sawyers, who were engaged periodically to cut pieces for the boat's frames and strakes, and shipwrights, who worked on the vessel in numbers that varied consistently over the three-week period.[37] While it is possible that many of these shipwrights worked more or less permanently in the yard, both the daily nature of their wages and the fluctuations in the number of men employed on any given day point to a hiring regime in which the contractor managing the project recruited workers on an as-needed basis.

Scattered references to the participation of slaves in urban labor markets provide additional (albeit indirect) evidence that artisans in the Roman world responded to seasonal and uncertain demand by recruiting short-term help when necessary. They suggest not only that slaveholders hired out skilled slaves, for whom artisans were the most obvious potential employers, but also that much of the work available to these slaves was short term. In both Greek and Roman practice, slaveholders could make the labor of their slaves available to other employers in two ways.[38] First, slaveholders could hire out their slaves personally by entering into a direct contract with a potential employer; contracts of this sort are mentioned frequently by Roman legal authors, and several examples survive on papyrus.[39] Second, slaveholders could authorize their slaves to seek employment on their own account; in all probability, these slaves were expected to pay their masters in exchange for this privilege but were permitted to retain any earnings above and beyond those payments. In Greek-speaking parts of the empire, this practice (which had antecedents in the law of classical Athens) was common enough that Artemidorus of Daldis mentions slaves who hired out their own services in his work on dreams, while documents from Roman Egypt also record slaves who hired out their services.[40] Slaveholders also allowed their slaves to seek out work

---

[37] *P. Flor.* I 69 (translation and commentary in Casson 1990). Also worthy of note is *P. Oxy.* XVI 1893. This document is very late indeed: it is dated 535 CE. Nevertheless, the same basic hiring pattern is visible. The document records a straightforward agreement between a shipwright who had undertaken to build a boat and two other shipwrights whom he hired as assistants. The contractor offered wages at a predetermined rate, but the fact that he did not hire the labor of his assistants for a specified quantity of time suggests that they were retained only for the duration of the project.

[38] For further discussion, see du Plessis 2012: 117–20 and 131–2. Cf. also Brunt 1980: 89.

[39] Numerous passages in the *Digest* reference such agreements between employers and either slaveholders or other individuals who exercised a controlling interest in the slave: 9.4.19.1; 12.6.55; 14.3.11.8 (a *servus vicarius* hired from another slave); 19.2.42–43; 19.2.45.1; 32.1.73.3; 33.2.2. For a recent discussion of the technicalities of these agreements, see du Plessis 2012: 131–5. For contracts of this nature in Roman Egypt, see Taubenschlag 1955: 367–8.

[40] For Athens, see A. H. M. Jones 1956 and, more recently, Cohen 2000: 142 n. 60. For Graeco-Roman Egypt, see Biezunska-Malowist 1965. Artemidorus mentions slaves who hired out their own services and paid a portion of their earnings to their masters at 3.41.

on their own account in the Roman context, where the practice came to be supported by a complex body of law governing a slave's *peculium*.[41] Although the *peculium* remained the property of the *paterfamilias*, in practice he was able to grant his dependents permission to alienate the capital that it contained (*concessio liberae administrationis*), and thus to employ that capital in independent commercial transactions of all kinds – including transactions in which dependents hired out their own services to employers.

Some of the slaves who entered the labor market in these ways clearly possessed technical skills of interest to artisan employers. Ulpian, for example, believed that a builder could recruit workers by borrowing skilled slaves from their owners: he explicitly mentions a plasterer or a worker in stucco and a stonemason.[42] In another interesting passage, the jurist Paul discusses the remedies available to a shopkeeper or artisan who found himself robbed by a slave whom he had rented from the slave's owner to help in his shop.[43] Finally, in an excerpt from his treatment of testamentary trusts (*fideicommissa*), the jurist Scaevola discusses a complicated case in which a testator handed a third of his estate over to trustees on the condition that they would deliver it to his foster son when the boy turned fifteen; in the interim, they were to support his foster son by granting him control of a slave who worked for wages as a shoemaker.[44] Since a shoemaker possessed a specialized set of skills of interest primarily to artisan employers, this particular slave probably earned most of his wages by finding employment in the workshops of other craftsmen.

More importantly, there are reasons to believe that urban slaveholders preferred to allow their slaves to find work on their own account instead of hiring those slaves out personally and that this preference was itself conditioned by the fact that employers – including artisans – tended to recruit these slaves on short-term rather than long-term contracts. This, at any rate, was the pattern in the antebellum United States, for which the evidence is more comprehensive than it is for antiquity. Like slaveholders in the Roman world, many in the Americas either hired out the labor of their slaves personally or permitted them to find employment on their own account in exchange for regular cash remittances.[45] American

---

[41] Kirschenbaum 1987: 31–88 offers a useful and recent overview of the rules governing the *peculium*. Cf. Gamauf 2009 and Aubert 2013.
[42] Ulpian, *Dig.* 13.6.5.7.   [43] Paul, *Dig.* 19.2.45.1.   [44] Scaevola, *Dig.* 36.1.80.12.
[45] For general overviews, see Goldin 1976: 35–47; Higman 1984: 232–47; Johnson 1996: 33–46; J. D. Martin 2004: 17–43; Wade 1964: 28–54. Contracts arranging for the rental of slaves were

slaveholders appear to have been most likely to hire out their slaves personally when they could do so on relatively long-term contracts. Unskilled laborers and domestic servants, for example, were often hired out directly by their owners on a yearly basis in both rural and urban contexts. So too were slave craftsmen, at least in the countryside; in cities they were more frequently hired out on short-term contracts, "probably by the job."[46] Self-hire, however, was more common in urban environments, where it appealed primarily to slaveholders whose slaves worked as casual laborers or as skilled craftsmen. The popularity of self-hire in these contexts was almost certainly a product of "the fluctuating and dispersed demand for that labour in the urban economy," which ensured that most urban employers were interested in hiring laborers and craftsmen only temporarily. In these conditions, slaveholders who insisted on hiring their slaves out personally incurred high transaction costs because of the need to negotiate short-term contracts on a regular basis; they found it more convenient to allow slaves to find jobs on their own and to collect remittances from them than to manage their slaves' contracts directly.[47]

Sparse though it may be, our evidence from antiquity likewise suggests that urban slaveholders seeking employment for their slaves preferred to allow those slaves to find work on their own account, precisely because employers tended to hire them on a short-term or temporary basis. Although the Roman jurists do refer to slaves who had been hired out personally by their owners on long-term agreements, they also imply that this was mostly a rural phenomenon: Paul, for example, mentions a slave blacksmith who was formally attached to an agricultural estate, but who had been hired out by his owner on an annual contract.[48] By contrast, in one of the most explicit comments in our ancient sources about how slaveholders found work for their slaves, Columella strongly suggests that urban slaveholders preferred to allow their slaves to find their own employment, much of which tended to be casual. In a passage in which he criticizes his landowning peers for neglecting the proper management of their rural property, Columella makes the following observation:

---

relatively widespread and uncontroversial. The self-hire of slaves tended to be more controversial, particularly in parts of the antebellum South, where it provoked fears that slaves were exercising too much autonomy. For that reason, it was prohibited in certain times and places. Our evidence, however, suggests that formal prohibitions nevertheless frequently failed to suppress what must have been a common practice.

[46] Goldin 1976: 35–7. Cf. Wade 1964: 39.

[47] Goldin 1976: 38–9; Wade 1964: 38–54; Higman 1984: 244–5. The passage cited is from Higman.

[48] See, e.g., Paul, *Dig.* 33.7.19.1.

But if a wealthy man buys an estate, he sends the oldest and weakest member of his crowd of footmen and litter-bearers into the countryside, though such work requires not only knowledge but also youth and physical strength to match its hardships. On the other hand, if a master of more moderate wealth purchases an estate, he selects one of his slaves who works for hire (*ex mercennariis*) but who, since he no longer pays the daily tribute, cannot be a source of profit; he appoints this man overseer even though the man is ignorant of that which he is to manage.[49]

Two aspects of this passage deserve emphasis. First, Columella's reference to "daily tribute" almost certainly refers to the remittances slaves commonly made to their masters when they had been authorized to find employment for themselves on the basis of a *peculium*. In that sense, it reflects Columella's belief that it was typical for slaveholders of middling wealth to generate income by instructing their slaves to hire themselves out. Second, Columella's assumption that slaves returned these remittances to their masters on a daily basis indicates that the wages earned by these slaves were also computed and paid out daily by employers – including artisans – who hired slaves on short-term contracts.

Manumission and labor hoarding

When read alongside the comparative material from early modern Europe, our scattered evidence for the hiring practices of Roman artisans thus suggests that they faced pressure to minimize their fixed labor costs by recruiting workers on short-term rather than long-term contracts. Importantly, however, the evidence from early modern Europe also suggests that they could only do so easily if the spot market was fluid enough to permit the hire of workers with the requisite skills at relatively short notice. If this were not the case, then Roman artisans may have sought to hoard labor instead.

In the early modern period, labor-hoarding strategies permitted artisans to reduce the costs of permanent workforces by exploiting the fact that they were more tolerant of risk than the journeymen whom they employed, simply because most had access to more resources and better credit. Broadly speaking, in economies characterized by seasonality and

---

[49] Columella, *Rust.* 1.pr.12. There is some dispute over how the word *mercennarius* should be interpreted. Bürge 1990 argues that the term *mercennarius* almost always denotes a slave working for wages. Möller 1993 refutes this view and defends the more common interpretation, namely that *mercennarius* can refer to any wage laborer, free or slave. In any case, Beare 1978 argues convincingly that in this particular case Columella had slaves in mind.

uncertainty, employers who are less risk averse than their employees can economize on wages while securing permanent help (even when employees are likely to be underemployed for part of the year) by creating long-term contracts with two specific features: first, they offer the employee a slightly lower wage than what the employee would otherwise expect to earn on the spot market in any given year; second, they smooth the employee's annual income by distributing his or her wage in more or less even installments throughout the year. In effect, the income-smoothing feature of these contracts compensates the employee for a reduced income by providing insurance against fluctuations in earnings. So long as an employer can prevent an employee from reneging on the agreement during high season, when strong demand and high wages can tempt employees back to the spot market, then contracts of this sort work as a next-best option if the spot market is unreliable.[50] When necessary, urban artisans in the early modern period employed variations of this strategy. In London, for example, employers in trades that demanded high levels of skill were known to hoard workers in the off-season by paying them at half-time rates.[51] Likewise, the fact that "wage-rates varied inversely with the length of periods of employment" in the French trades can be understood as evidence that master artisans hoarded risk-averse workers as a compromise between the need to limit their fixed costs and the desire to expand output in periods of elevated demand.[52]

Slavery and manumission could serve a comparable purpose for craftsmen in the Roman world. Slavery, of course, made it possible for artisans to hoard labor in the strongest way possible, namely by using the property rights and coercive authority they exercised over their slaves to permanently control the labor of their human possessions. By manumitting slaves in exchange for labor obligations, however, they could both hoard labor and economize on the costs of doing so, chiefly by making freed slaves responsible for their own upkeep. Manumission thus appealed to artisans even when they did not have sufficiently large businesses to employ freed slaves as managers or as partners, since they could nevertheless use it as a powerful tool for responding to seasonal and uncertain product markets.

The ability of a slaveholder to impose labor obligations on his or her freed slaves was rooted in the belief that manumission was a gift that

[50] Mukherjee and Ray 1995 and Ray 1998: 515–22 both explore the basic theory in the context of seasonal agriculture in developing economies.
[51] Stedman Jones 1984: 33–4; cf. Schwarz 1992: 117–18.   [52] Sonenscher 1989: 190.

imposed a strong and reciprocal moral obligation on its beneficiary.[53] In both Greek and Roman practice, however, that ability also received considerable institutional support from the law, which ensured that artisans could retain claims on the labor of their former slaves for many years after setting them free. In many local slave systems in the Greek East, slaveholders (including artisans) could impose such obligations on their former slaves by inserting so-called *paramone* clauses into formal manumission agreements. These clauses required freed slaves to make themselves available to receive orders from their former masters for a specified period of time after they had been manumitted. A freed slave's obligation to remain and to serve his or her master could last only a few years, or it could last for the lifetime of the manumittor; it could even be passed on by the manumittor to his or her heirs.[54] In Roman law, slaveholders could not impose such lengthy and unconditional terms of service on their former slaves, but they too could create legal claims to the labor of freedmen by demanding that their former slaves take a contractually binding oath to supply them with a specified quantity of labor, measured in units of a day's worth of work (*operae libertorum*).[55] Although we lack evidence for how many *operae* slaveholders typically imposed on their slaves in exchange for manumission, the jurist Ulpian suggests in one of his opinions that one thousand was not an unbelievable number.[56] Some additional support for his figure is offered by references in our legal sources to the lengthy terms of service imposed by Roman slaveholders on conditionally manumitted slaves, who were often expected to serve the heirs of their masters for several years before finally being released from slavery.[57] While 1,000 days of work represented only three years of service if a freed slave discharged *operae* for his or her patron on a daily basis, in practice artisans who required the labor of a freedman only during periods of peak demand could spread those obligations out over a protracted period of time. If an

[53] Zelnick-Abramovitz 2005: 39–60; Mouritsen 2001: 7–8; Mouritsen 2011: 36–7 and 146–7. Cf. Patterson 1982: 211–19.

[54] Zelnick-Abramovitz 2005: 222–48; Hopkins 1978: 141–58.

[55] The classic studies of freedmen and their obligations are Treggiari 1969: 37–86 (on freedmen in the Republic) and Duff 1958: 36–49 (on freedmen in the early Empire). Gardner 1993: 19–31 offers a recent and accessible treatment of freedmen and the historical development of their obligations to their patrons. Finally, Waldstein 1986 treats *operae libertorum* in considerable detail, while Mouritsen 2011 provides the most up-to-date synthesis of the relationship between Roman patrons and their freedmen (esp. 36–65 and 120–205).

[56] Ulpian, *Dig.* 38.1.15. Cf. the comments of Waldstein 1986: 380–1.

[57] Wiedemann 1985: 169–75.

artisan required a freed slave's labor for only a third of the year, for example, he could rely on that freedman's help for almost a decade.

From the perspective of artisans who grappled with seasonal and uncertain demand, manumission in exchange for labor services was appealing primarily because it permitted them to mitigate some of the fixed costs incurred by hoarding slave labor more easily than by hiring out underemployed slaves during periods of low demand. As noted above, there was clearly a market for the temporary rental or hire of slave workers, and it was certainly possible for artisans to participate in this particular market as suppliers when they themselves had no pressing need for the services of their own slaves. At the same time, however, two considerations suggest that artisans may have found this strategy for offsetting the costs of hoarded labor to be more troublesome than it was worth. First, artisans who hired out their slaves on anything other than a day-by-day basis necessarily would have sacrificed their own ability to use those slaves' labor in response to unpredicted changes in demand. Slaveholders who recalled hired-out slaves to work in their own shops before the terms of an agreement expired would have broken a contract – whether their own or one undertaken by the slave on the basis of his or her *peculium* – and would have been liable to a lawsuit.[58] This limitation would have been especially problematic for artisans who performed most of their work on a bespoke basis, and who could therefore only roughly predict their labor needs in the short term: had they received more orders than anticipated while their slaves were contractually obligated to serve another employer, their own capacity to respond to those orders would have been severely limited.

Second, comparative evidence from later historical periods suggests that the nature of urban product markets made it difficult for most artisans in the Roman world to find suitable employment opportunities for underemployed slaves, particularly when those slaves were skilled craftsmen. Both in British North America and in the antebellum United States, artisans owned skilled slaves whom they hired out to other craftsmen, particularly in the shipbuilding industry.[59] Although the extent of slaveholding among artisans in these contexts can be difficult to establish precisely,[60] artisans appear to have been more reluctant than other

---

[58] Cf. Sen. *Ben.* 7.5.3 on a slaveholder's loss of access to the labor of slaves whom he had hired out.

[59] See Steffen 1984: 41–2 on slave hires between shipbuilders in early nineteenth-century Baltimore. Cf. Johnson 1996: 43. Johnson cites the example of Timothy Cox, a shipbuilder in the Bahamas, who allowed one of his skilled slaves to hire out his own services.

[60] See Steffen 1979 for a discussion of these problems with reference to the artisans of Baltimore at the turn of the eighteenth and nineteenth centuries. Cf. Gillespie 2000: 24 on artisans in Georgia.

employers to invest in slaves of their own, potentially because they could
neither keep those slaves fully employed nor hire them out easily on
temporary contracts when they had no work for them in their own
businesses. Broadly speaking, our evidence implies not only that the
demand for slave labor in urban environments (especially in the antebellum South) was typically more elastic than in the countryside but also that
urban demand for slave labor, wherever its elasticity approached that of the
demand for rural slave labor, was driven not by artisans but by factory
owners with predictable needs for regular help.[61] Walter Scheidel has
recently suggested that low rates of slaveholding among artisans in North
America can be explained best by invoking the "closed" slave system of the
antebellum South, which discouraged frequent manumission and thus
prevented slaveholders from using freedom as an incentive to motivate
effort from slaves in occupations demanding high levels of responsibility
and initiative.[62] This explanation, however, does not seem wholly satisfac-
tory. For one thing, when slaveholders supervised their slaves directly (as
must have been the case in many artisanal workshops in both the ancient
and early modern worlds), it was not necessarily as critical for them to
provide high-powered incentives as it was for those who granted their
slaves more autonomy.[63] Moreover, when slaveholders in North America
found it necessary to offer their slaves incentives, they could use monetary
rewards rather than manumission to motivate slaves who were entrusted
with care-intensive tasks.[64] For these reasons, Goldin's explanation for
slaveholding patterns among artisans in the antebellum South is more
instructive. In her view, the elasticity of demand for urban slave labor
was high relative to that for rural labor because the demand for the goods
produced by urban slaves, particularly luxury items, was itself elastic.[65]
According to this interpretation, the inherent instability of product markets in the cities of the antebellum South discouraged the widespread use

[61] Goldin 1976: 76–122. In particular, see p. 105, where Goldin concludes that the overall rural and
urban elasticities for slave labor were .05 and .86, respectively. This implies that although the urban
demand for slave labor was somewhat inelastic, it was far less so than the demand for slave labor on
plantations. On p. 122, she notes that "Richmond and Savannah, which have lower elasticities, were
cities in which slaves were employed by industry in large holdings and in which there appear to have
been fewer substitutes for slave labor." Hanes 1996: 308–9 oversimplifies this situation somewhat
when he writes that "in the antebellum South, urban shops and factories tended to employ free
workers rather than slaves, except when slave prices were unusually low relative to wages of free
labor."

[62] Scheidel 2008: 112–15.   [63] Higman 1984: 234–5 and 242.

[64] E.g., Whitman 1997: 48–60, who discusses wages and other incentives offered to slaves by industrial
employers in Baltimore.

[65] Goldin 1976: 105.

of dependent labor by urban artisans, because these artisans found it difficult to adapt slave ownership to the pressures generated by seasonal and uncertain demand. Since seasonal fluctuations in demand often affected entire trades (at least in broad outline) rather than just individual workshops, artisans would have found it difficult to find paid jobs for their underemployed slaves at times of the year when underemployment was endemic in a given industry as a whole, and as a result would have been compelled to bear the full costs of maintaining hoarded slave workers. Since there are no compelling reasons to believe that market conditions were drastically different in antiquity, Roman artisans too probably struggled to mitigate the costs of hoarded slave workers when they attempted to do so by hiring them out.[66]

Instead, because freed slaves could be made responsible for their own living expenses, Roman artisans hoping to mitigate the costs of hoarded slave labor could do so more easily by manumitting slaves in exchange for labor obligations, thus reducing the number of dependents making claims on their household budgets.[67] Although many former slaves undoubtedly did continue to live in their former masters' households (particularly when they had been freed by owners of considerable social, political, and economic standing), ongoing co-residence was not an inevitable byproduct of manumission.[68] Freed slaves could just as easily find themselves separated from the physical households of their former masters, whether by their own preferences, or by the desires of their patrons. This was true even in the case of seemingly rigid Greek *paramone* agreements, which ostensibly required manumitted slaves "to remain" (*paramenein*) in the service of their patrons. In some cases, the existence of a *paramone* agreement could imply that a freed slave continued to reside with his or her former master, but in actual practice what mattered most was that the former slave remained available to perform services at his or her patron's behest; co-residence itself was not a requirement.[69]

Our Roman legal sources provide the strongest indications that these cost-saving aspects of manumission appealed to slaveholders. According to several of the comments delivered by Roman jurists, slaves who had been manumitted in exchange for *operae* were expected to discharge their obligations at their own expense, by providing their own food and clothing. While there were exceptions to this rule, they were minimal. Paul and

---

[66] Cf. Brunt 1980: 93–4. [67] Cf. Waldstein 1986: 130; Treggiari 1969: 16.
[68] Fabre 1981: 131–4. Cf. Epictetus' comments on the hardships faced by ex-slaves who left the households of their masters (4.1.35–40).
[69] Westermann 1945: 217; cf. Samuel 1965.

Gaius, for instance, ruled that if freedmen lacked the resources to provide for themselves while performing *operae*, patrons were expected either to provision them personally or to allow them sufficient time off between periods of work to earn their own keep. Patrons also had an obligation to maintain freedmen who were in danger of becoming destitute; those who refused to do so forfeited their claims on any *operae* still owed to them.[70] The fact that the jurists felt the need to reiterate these points suggests that some slaveholders were particularly aggressive in their efforts to cut costs. More importantly, all of these rules were clearly predicated on the assumption that while some freed slaves continued to reside with their former masters, it was more typical for them to support themselves after earning their freedom. In that sense, artisans who manumitted slaves in exchange for *operae* could offset the costs of hoarded labor by passing on to their freedmen many of the financial risks that they otherwise would have incurred by maintaining underemployed workers in periods of low demand.

Just as importantly, artisans who manumitted slaves could retain extensive control over their freedmen's labor, even when those freedmen no longer resided in the household. That control was generated not just by the formal legal frameworks that governed manumission in much of the Roman world but also by the power that artisans could bring to bear against even former slaves. On a formal level, artisans could rely on the legal framework of manumission both to guarantee them an ongoing proprietary interest in the human capital embodied in their former slaves and to ensure that they could deploy their freedmen's labor quickly and at short notice in response to changing demand. In Greek systems of manumission during the Hellenistic and Roman periods, for instance, slaveholders could frame the obligations of a freed slave in a broad and general way: while *paramone* agreements could be specific, they could also simply stipulate that a freed slave was expected "to remain and to obey" whatever orders his master gave. Masters thus enjoyed considerable latitude when it came to determining when and in what contexts they would use a freed slave's labor.[71]

In Roman practice, manumission was not so open-ended, but here too the law preserved both slaveholders' claims over the human capital of their former slaves and their ability to deploy it as and when necessary. In the

---

[70] Paul, quoting Sabinus, *Dig.* 38.1.18; Gaius, *Dig.* 38.1.19; Paul, *Dig.* 38.1.20.pr. On these passages and their apparent conflict with other opinions that seem to suggest a general responsibility on the part of a patron to maintain freedmen who were performing *operae*, see Waldstein 1986: 283–7.

[71] Zelnick-Abramovitz 2005: 246.

first place, the Roman jurists not only recognized a distinction between *operae* consisting of miscellaneous forms of personal service (*operae officiales*) and those consisting of work of a skilled or technical nature (*operae fabriles*) but also consistently maintained that a freed slave who had been trained in a craft was expected to discharge his obligations by performing the latter so long as he continued to practice the trade. Artisans who manumitted skilled slaves in exchange for *operae* were thus able to derive ongoing returns from their investments in their former slaves' skills.[72] More importantly, the law permitted Roman artisans to call upon the services of freedmen who owed them outstanding *operae* as and when they desired. As the jurist Julian put it in the second century CE, the law expected a manumitted slave to discharge his obligations "at the convenience of his patron" (*ex commodo patroni*),[73] presumably even when a freed slave had undertaken contractual commitments to others: not only did Roman law hold as a general principle the view that an individual should honor the oldest of two obligations first when these conflicted with one another, it also stipulated that *operae* were considered overdue the moment a patron demanded their discharge and his freedman failed to deliver them.[74] Although the law did gradually delineate some exceptions to the second of these two principles – for instance, a freed slave who did not live in the same town as his patron was permitted time to travel, which counted toward the balance of his outstanding *operae*, and those who were too ill to work had no legal obligation to respond to patrons who demanded their services despite their poor health – these exceptions remained relatively few in number and did not radically degrade the appeal of *operae libertorum* in the eyes of artisans as an inherently flexible source of labor.[75]

Some artisan slaveholders also retained enough power over their former slaves to enforce their rights without recourse to the law, even when freedmen may have been tempted to renege on their obligations. Although this was important in both Greek and Roman systems of manumission, it was especially significant in Roman contexts, in which a patron's only formal recourse against a recalcitrant freedman was to sue for the value of any *operae* the latter failed to deliver[76] – a potentially serious limitation during times of the year when the demand for skilled labor was at its

---

[72] This was true even if the slave in question learned a craft only after manumission. See Ulpian, *Dig.* 38.1.9; Callistratus, *Dig.* 38.1.38.1; Paul, *Dig.* 38.1.16.pr. See further Waldstein 1986: 223–39 and Gardner 1993: 29.

[73] Julian, *Dig.* 38.1.24; Gaius, *Dig.* 38.1.22.pr.   [74] Ulpian, *Dig.* 19.2.26; Ulpian, *Dig.* 38.1.13.2.

[75] Paul, quoting Proculus, *Dig.* 38.1.20.1; Ulpian, *Dig.* 38.1.15.pr.   [76] E.g., Ulpian, *Dig.* 38.1.2.1.

height, and when freedmen could possibly earn more by working on their
own account than they stood to forfeit if sued by their patrons. Artisans
controlling the labor of freedmen possessed a distinct advantage when they
could use the forms of power at their disposal to ensure that their former
slaves honored their obligations.

The ability to interfere in a freedman's family life was one important
tool for generating compliance. It was not unusual for slaves to form
families with one another, even if these families were not formally recognized by the law.[77] Although slaveholders may have felt some social
pressure to keep slave families together, they enjoyed an almost unlimited
right to split them up by alienating individual slaves at will until at least the
fourth century CE (when imperial legislation possibly limited this
practice).[78] Slaveholders who retained members of a freedman's family in
bondage could therefore bring strong pressures to bear to ensure that
slave's compliance: they could grant or withhold the manumission of
a freedman's spouse or children or even threaten to sell them.[79]

Wealth was another source of power at the disposal of artisan slaveholders seeking to enforce their claims to *operae*, especially since freedmen could find their own ability to accumulate capital constrained by
their labor obligations to their former masters.[80] Some patrons used their
wealth to secure the compliance of their slaves by offering them loans or
access to working capital,[81] while others promised to reward loyal freedmen by writing them into their wills as legatees or heirs.[82] The second of
these two strategies can be detected in the funerary inscriptions, several of
which note explicitly that patron and freedman were both artisans and
that the freedman had received consideration in his patron's will: the
vascularius Marcus Atius Dometius, for instance, was heir to a sixth part
of the estate of his former master, who practiced the same trade.[83] But
even when such inscriptions lack explicit indications of the patron's
profession – as is the case in the inscription commissioned by three

---

[77] On freed slaves and their families in the manumission inscriptions from Delphi, see Tucker 1982:
228–9. For freed slaves and their families in the Greek world in general, see Zelnick-Abramovitz
2005: 163–7. For the Roman context, see Rawson 1966; Rawson 1974; Weaver 1972: 179–95;
Mouritsen 2001: 19–20; Mouritsen 2011: 152–3.

[78] *Cod. Theod.* 2.25.1, with the comments of Harper 2011: 271–3.

[79] E.g., Hopkins 1978: 165–6; Bradley 1987: 57–63; Rawson 1966: 78–82.

[80] Cf. Fabre 1981: 326, who discusses some of the ways in which *operae* could interfere with
a freedman's autonomy.

[81] Cf. Mouritsen 2011: 222.   [82] Champlin 1991: 131–6.

[83] *CIL* 6.37824. In this particular case, however, we cannot be sure that Dometius was manumitted
while Anterotis was still alive. The alternative possibility is that he was manumitted by testament and
made heir in the terms of his former master's will.

freed artisans on behalf of their patron, Lucius Naevius – the fact that freedmen were named as heirs suggests that both patron and freedman had practiced the same craft and that the former had secured the loyalty of his freed slave by promising to reward him in his will.[84]

Finally, some slaveholders could exercise power over former slaves by facilitating or impeding changes in their juridical status even after manumission. This kind of power was easier for Roman slaveholders to apply in the wake of the *lex Aelia Sentia* and the *lex Junia*, both products of the first century CE. Before the creation of this legislation, slaves freed by Roman citizens had generally acquired citizenship themselves when they were manumitted by one of three formal means: by testament, by inclusion in the census, or by a Roman magistrate. Although their patrons retained some residual claims to their property, they were nevertheless able to receive bequests and inheritances and to pass on at least a portion of their estates to their own children. In 4 CE, however, the *lex Aelia Sentia* dramatically restricted formal manumission by imposing new requirements on both master and slave, the most important of which was the stipulation that a slave could not be manumitted formally before the age of thirty. Although slaves could still be manumitted informally, the *lex Junia* imposed important legal disabilities upon them; among other things, informally-manumitted slaves (who became Junian Latins) could neither make a will nor transmit property to their children, but instead forfeited their entire estates to their patrons when they died.[85] While it was possible for Junian Latins to acquire Roman citizenship and to free themselves from these disabilities – for instance, by marrying in the presence of seven Roman citizens and by having a legitimate child within a year or by serving as a member of the *vigiles* – it is not clear that most would have had easy access to the various legal procedures that conferred full citizenship.[86] Instead, because patrons were able to elevate Junian Latins to citizenship by manumitting them formally at a later date (provided that any conditions blocking formal manumission in the first place were no longer an

---

[84] Joshel 1992: 133–4. I discuss this inscription in more detail below.

[85] Lopez Barja de Quiroga 1998: 133–41; Weaver 1990: 275–8; Sirks 1983. The *lex Aelia Sentia* dates to 4 CE. The *lex Iunia*, which established the status of Junian Latins in the law, was almost certainly part of Augustus' legislative program, but its precise date is unknown (Lopez Barja de Quiroga 1998: 137–8).

[86] On the various avenues to full citizenship, see Sirks 1983: 246–8 and Lopez Barja de Quiroga 1998: 145–6. The *anniculi probatio* was probably the most important procedure. Junians who married in the presence of seven Roman citizens and then produced a child who survived the first year could petition for Roman citizenship. Lopez Barja de Quiroga 1998: 155–7 suggests that because concubinage was widespread among ex-slaves, relatively few freedmen took advantage of this procedure.

impediment), many freedmen probably hoped to secure full citizenship with the help of their former masters,[87] who therefore possessed one more tool for securing their freedmen's compliance.[88]

The epitaph of the freed engraver Marcus Canuleius Zosimus provides direct evidence of an artisan patron's ability to manipulate his freedman in this way. Zosimus, who continued to work for his patron as an engraver after manumission, had been freed some time before his death at the age of twenty-eight; since the legally mandated minimum age for formal manumission was thirty at the time, he was probably a Junian freedman. When Zosimus died, his patron commissioned an epitaph on his freedman's behalf, praising Zosimus' honesty and obedience. Although the rhetoric of the inscription evokes typical Roman stereotypes about grateful freedmen and the conduct they were expected to exhibit in their relationships with their patrons,[89] it may also reflect a conscious effort on Zosimus' part to retain his patron's goodwill in the hope of receiving both formal manumission and citizenship in the future.[90]

Finally, although artisans who manumitted slaves in exchange for *operae* risked losing their claims over their freedmen's labor due to circumstances beyond their control, these risks were not prohibitive enough to outweigh the clear advantages of manumitting slaves in exchange for labor obligations. As noted above, Roman artisans could not demand outstanding *operae* from freed slaves whose health prevented them from working. Both Greek and Roman patrons also risked that a freed slave might die before fully discharging his obligations. In practice, however, artisans who retained skilled slaves in bondage contended with these same problems, and – inasmuch as sick slaves could quickly come to be seen as a burden – perhaps bore even greater risk in this respect. Furthermore, while Roman patrons were unable to demand *operae fabriles* from freed slaves who either had ceased to practice a trade or who had attained a social rank in which the practice of a trade was considered unseemly or dishonorable, neither

---

[87] See especially Sirks 1983. Roth 2010, esp. 114–16, argues that slaveholders frequently manumitted slaves informally in exchange for payments, only to exact further payments from them at a later date in exchange for elevating them to Roman citizenship by manumitting them formally.

[88] No ancient text directly states that Junian Latins promised *operae* in exchange for their manumission like other freedmen. Waldstein 1986: 162 argues that they did not, but this is the minority view. Most historians assume that Junians could obligate themselves to *operae* in exchange for manumission in the same way as other freedmen (Sirks 1983: 259–60; Lopez Barja de Quiroga 1998: 144).

[89] On this discourse, see Mouritsen 2011: 57–65.

[90] *CIL* 6.9222. On this inscription, see Joshel 1977: 117, who discusses several difficulties of interpretation. Zosimus' patron may have been an artisan who employed Zosimus in his own workshop, or he could have been a wealthy slaveholder who employed Zosimus as the manager (*institor*) of a business.

eventuality was necessarily probable. Former slaves who possessed craft skills were unlikely to abandon their trades entirely, since in most cases their best prospects for financial security undoubtedly lay in using those skills. Likewise, few freed slaves enjoyed good prospects for achieving a high-enough social rank in the years immediately following their manumission to render the practice of their trades dishonorable. Finally, legislation of the Augustan period absolved male freedmen from their obligations to perform *operae* if they had either two legitimate children of any age who fell under their *potestas*, or one who was at least five years of age.[91] Artisans, however, may have found even this danger manageable. As we have seen, freed slaves tended to remain together with spouses whom they had married informally while both were still slaves; if this was generally the case, then freedmen could not necessarily father legitimate children who fell under their *potestas* until later in life, when they had secured their partners' release from slavery.[92] Moreover, even when a freedman did marry formally shortly after his manumission, a high infant mortality rate was characteristic of Rome and other large cities in the ancient world. While neither absolute nor permanent, an artisan's control over the labor of his former slaves thus stood a good chance of weathering the various eventualities that could potentially undermine it.

Artisans and freed slaves in the Roman funerary inscriptions

Most of the evidence cited above demonstrates that Roman artisans *could* use manumission in exchange for *operae* as a strategy for adapting their workforces to seasonal and uncertain demand but provides little direct confirmation that they normally *did*. For that reason, while my argument so far addresses one component of Mouritsen's claim that *operae* were rare in practice – namely, by establishing a convincing context in which *operae* were useful and appealing to a certain class of slaveholders – it remains susceptible to the second, which stresses that there is almost no direct evidence for manumission in exchange for *operae* once we look beyond the legal sources.

In the remainder of this section, I suggest that the funerary epigraphy produced by or on behalf of artisans at Rome provides substantial if indirect evidence that artisans manumitted slaves in exchange for *operae*

---

[91] Paul, *Dig.* 38.1.37.pr-37.1.   [92] Rawson 1966 and 1974.

as a means of responding to seasonal and uncertain demand. The evidence contained in these inscriptions is hardly straightforward: funerary inscriptions provide only incomplete snapshots of the social worlds in which individuals were embedded at one particular moment, and therefore offer very little explicit information about artisans' employment strategies. That said, three features of the inscriptions commissioned by or on behalf of artisans are ultimately more consistent with the view that artisans manumitted skilled slaves in exchange for *operae* than with other potential models of manumission. First, the inscriptions show that many freed slaves who had been trained as craftsmen had acquired their skills from owners who were artisans themselves; second, they show that artisans did regularly free slaves *inter vivos* and that those slaves were often skilled craftsmen; third, they suggest that freed slaves remained tied to their former masters' workshops in ways that can be understood best if we conclude that they had been freed in exchange for *operae*.

I begin with inscriptions in which it is either clear or at least strongly implied that freed craftsmen had acquired their skills in the workshops of former owners who were artisans themselves. The few inscriptions in which both a freed slave and his patron are identified in terms of their shared occupation make this point most directly. The freedman Marcus Atius Dometius was commemorated in a way emphasizing not only that he had worked in the same trade as his patron Anterotis – they were both *vascularii*, manufacturers of tableware – but also that he had inherited part of his patron's estate:

> Marcus Atius Dometius, *vascularius* on the Sacred Way. A freedman of the *vascularius* Marcus Atius Anterotis, he lived for 62 years and was heir to a sixth part of his patron's estate.[93]

Likewise, the freedman Marcus Sergius Eutychus commemorated his patron in terms suggesting that he had worked alongside his former master in the latter's workshop:

> The wheelwright Marcus Sergius Eutychus, freedman of Marcus, [dedicated this monument] to himself and to his patron, the wheelwright Marcus Sergius Philocalus, freedman of Marcus.[94]

To these we can add a third inscription, which is of interest primarily because it makes explicit what the monument erected by the wheelwright Eutychus implies – namely, that skilled slaves who worked alongside their

---

[93] *CIL* 6.37824.   [94] *CIL* 6.9215.

masters and who were freed might in turn train and manumit slaves of their own:

> Cameria Iarine, freedwoman of Lucius, made this monument for her patron, Lucius Camerius Thraso, freedman of Lucius, and for [Thraso's] patron Lucius Camerius Alexander, freedman of Lucius, and for her own freedman and husband, Lucius Camerius Onesimus, and for all of their posterity. These were tailors of fine clothing along the Vicus Tuscus.[95]

The key detail in this particular inscription is Iarine's claim that she herself, along with all three of the men mentioned by name, was a tailor who worked along the Vicus Tuscus, a major commercial street that fed into the Roman Forum from the south. The monument conveys the impression that artisans trained and manumitted skilled slaves over multiple generations of ownership – a phenomenon Sandra Joshel has referred to as "freedmanship."[96]

Inscriptions like these, in which freed slaves and their patrons both unambiguously bear the same occupational title, are unfortunately rare. More typical are inscriptions in which an occupational title is assigned only to a former slave or to a patron, but in which a working relationship between the two can nevertheless be inferred. These inscriptions are quite numerous and, as we shall see in Chapter 4, they account for a large proportion of the inscriptions from Rome in which at least one individual is identified as an artisan or shopkeeper. The monument commissioned by the freedman Lucius Novius Apollonius offers a representative example; here the patron is identified explicitly as an artisan:

> To the Sacred Shades. To the swordsmith, Lucius Novius Felix, freedman of Lucius. His freedman Apollonius [made this] for his well-deserving patron.[97]

Even though inscriptions of this type do not conclusively demonstrate that the patron and freedman in question had worked alongside one another on the shop floor,[98] two observations offer good grounds for believing that this must have been true in many cases. First, Sandra Joshel has noted an important pattern in the inscriptional record: when slaves and freedmen are attested in the inscriptions primarily as practitioners of occupations geared toward production for the market rather than toward

---

[95] *CIL* 6.37826.   [96] Joshel 1977, esp. 619–33.   [97] *CIL* 6.9442.
[98] For discussions of the various kinds of relationships that could be reflected in these inscriptions, see Joshel 1977: 106; Treggiari 1969: 91–106; and Mouritsen 2011: 206–47.

service in domestic contexts, few are commemorated in ways suggesting connections with large households. While this pattern may partly be a product of how slaves or freedmen attached to large households were commemorated – there is no guarantee, for instance, that the occupations of slaves or freedmen interred in family *columbaria* were typically noted by their commemorators – it may also indicate that most of the artisan freedmen named in occupational inscriptions were manumitted by artisans rather than by wealthy slaveholders who did not practice specific trades.[99] Second, many of these inscriptions suggest that patrons transmitted property to their freedman for reasons most readily comprehensible if we assume that patron and freedman practiced the same occupation. Some inscriptions make the transmission of property explicit, as does the inscription on the tomb commissioned by the freedmen of Lucius Naevius Helenus, which indicates both that they were skilled craftsmen and that their patron had named them joint heirs:

> Lucius Naevius Eleutherius and Naevius Narcissus and Lucius Naevius Thesmus, heirs to their patron Lucius Naevius Helenus, in accordance with his will, made this monument for him and for themselves and their freedmen and freedwomen and their posterity. [They are] makers of bronze tableware (*aerarii vascularii*). This monument and tomb shall pass to their heir.[100]

Other inscriptions commissioned by freed slaves on behalf of patrons make no obvious mention of inheritance, but because Roman custom stressed that commemoration was the responsibility of the estate's primary heir, it seems safe to infer that many of the freed craftsmen who set up monuments on behalf of their patrons did so because they had succeeded to a major share of their patrons' property. While some patrons may have named freed slaves as heirs because they had no living descendants, others probably did so because they had trained their slaves in their own trades before freeing them and felt that their business assets (and liabilities) would be more useful to these freedmen than to their spouses or children, to whom they awarded legacies instead.[101]

Strictly speaking, the inscriptions examined so far show only that slaves who had been trained as craftsmen were often manumitted by masters who

---

[99] Joshel 1977: 123, 165, 200; Joshel 1992: 98–112. Goldsmiths are a notable exception to her observation that slaves who practiced commercially valuable skills are rarely attested in the inscriptions. Cf. Higman 1984: 234–5, who notes that artisan slaves in the British Caribbean were likely to be owned by craftsmen rather than by other types of slaveholders.

[100] *CIL* 6.9138.   [101] I develop these points in more detail in Chapter 4.

worked as artisans themselves and not that they had been freed *inter vivos* rather than by the terms of their owners' testaments. Yet, even though many of the inscriptions dedicated by freed slaves to their former masters cannot tell us when and under what circumstances those slaves had been manumitted, others clearly refer to skilled slaves who had been freed during their owners' lifetimes, thus raising the possibility that many of the other skilled freedmen named in the funerary inscriptions had been manumitted *inter vivos*. The inscription dedicated to Publius Avillius Menandrus, for example, suggests not only that Menandrus himself was a tailor but also that he had manumitted several skilled slaves during his own lifetime. Menandrus was commemorated by four of his freed slaves, all of whom worked as tailors in the exclusive Cermalus Minusculus district of the Palatine.[102] Although Menandrus' former slaves did not identify him explicitly as a tailor, the fact that they served as his commemorators suggests that he had named them as his heirs, probably in the expectation that they would inherit his tailoring business. More importantly, Menandrus' former slaves had quite possibly been freed *inter vivos*, since the inscription suggests that at least one of them had died before the dedication of the monument, and thus probably also before Menandrus' death. The inscription commissioned by Veturia Flora offers a clearer example of a case in which an artisan slaveholder manumitted skilled slaves *inter vivos*. A dyer and a former slave, Veturia Flora commissioned a monument on behalf of herself and three men, all of whom she named individually in the inscription and identified as dyers who worked near the Marian monuments in Rome. The three men named in the inscription include her husband (and fellow-freedman, or *conlibertus*) Decimus Veturius Nicephorus; their patron, Decimus Veturius Diogenes (himself a former slave); and a freedman named Decimus Veturius Philargurus, whom Flora had owned jointly with either her husband or her patron and whom she had clearly manumitted *inter vivos*. Significantly, Flora noted explicitly that her patron Diogenes was still alive when she commissioned the inscription, which indicates that she and Nicephorus had both been manumitted *inter vivos*.[103]

---

[102] *CIL* 6.33920.
[103] *CIL* 6.37820 = *ILLRP* 809. Here, I follow the emendation proposed by G. Barbieri (see the *apparatus criticus* attached to *ILLRP* 809). Rather than reading *purpuraria Marianeis*, which we should interpret to mean that Flora was a dyer somewhere near the Marian monuments, Barbieri reads *purpurari a Marianeis*, which would mean instead that all of the individuals whom Flora names on the stone practiced the same trade. Barbieri's emendation is preferable on grammatical grounds and for that reason should be accepted (Fabre 1981: 339 n. 201).

Figure 3.3 The funerary monument of C. Iulius Helius. Musei Capitolini (Photo: Zeno Colantoni, courtesy Musei Capitolini, Centrale Montemartini)

Inscriptions of the so-called *se vivo / sibi* type provide additional indirect evidence that artisans in the city of Rome not only manumitted skilled slaves *inter vivos* but also did so with some regularity. This category consists of inscriptions commissioned by individuals who sought primarily to commemorate themselves, but who also instructed the engraver to name other individuals with whom they shared significant relationships. Artisans were responsible for commissioning several of the inscriptions of this type that have been found in Rome itself. Many chose to include a variation of the phrase *libertis libertabusque poteriisque eorum* ("on behalf of his freedmen and his freedwomen and their posterity"), which could indicate that they had freed slaves within their own lifetimes. Yet, more tellingly, most explicitly named one or more former slaves, whom they had clearly manumitted *inter vivos*. The monument purchased by the shoemaker C. Iulius Helius offers a representative example (Figure 3.3). Beneath a bust of Helius himself, the monument bears the following inscription:

C. Iulius Helius, shoemaker near the Fontinalis Gate, made this for himself, and for his daughter Iulia Flacilla, and for his freedman C. Iulius Onesimus, and for his freedwomen and their posterity.[104]

Here, there can be no doubt that Helius had freed Onesimus within his own lifetime, even if the precise circumstances of Onesimus' manumission remain unclear. More telling, of course, is Atimetus' funerary altar, which not only reveals that Atimetus had manumitted his former slave Epaphra *inter vivos* but also demonstrates that Epaphra was a skilled craftsman in his own right, who continued to work for his patron after being freed. By making this last detail explicit, Atimetus' altar strongly suggests that the freed slaves who were named on the *se vivo / sibi* inscriptions of other artisans were likewise craftsmen who had learned their skills in the workshops of their former owners and who continued to work for their patrons after manumission.

One last circumstantial detail suggests that the artisans who named former slaves in their *se vivo / sibi* inscriptions had employed those slaves in their own workshops – the notable gender imbalance among the freed slaves named on these monuments. Not only do freedmen outnumber freedwomen by a significant margin in terms of total numbers in this small sample, they also outnumber freedwomen on each individual inscription save one. The most extreme imbalance is found in the inscription commissioned by the cloak-maker Q. Caecilius Spendo, who had the names of seventeen freedmen and one freedwoman engraved on his monument. A comparable imbalance is found in the inscription commissioned by A. Fulvius Dorotheus, who, as a *vascularius*, specialized in manufacturing metal tableware. Although damage to his monument has partly destroyed the names of some of the Dorotheus' freedmen, he may have manumitted as many as nineteen slaves *inter vivos*. Of these, six were female and at least ten male, and the three others whose names are still partially extant were probably male as well. Although the other artisans who commissioned surviving *se vivo / sibi* inscriptions at Rome named fewer freed slaves on their monuments than did Spendo and Dorotheus – the numbers range from one to five – all of them manumitted more men than women.[105]

Because gender adversely affected both the ability of slaveholders to enforce claims to *operae* and their willingness to provide women with

---

[104] *CIL* 6.33914. The others are 6.5638 b, 6.9208 b, 6.9375, 6.9625, 6.9865, 6.33906, 6.33919, and 6.37820. In one case (6.9625) the author is a surveyor (*mensor aedificorum*), but the authors of the other inscriptions appear to be artisan shopkeepers.

[105] Q. Caecilius Spendo: *CIL* 6.9865. A. Fulvius Dorotheus: *CIL* 6.33919.

specialized training in craft skills, the predominance of freedmen over freedwomen in the *se vivo / sibi* inscriptions commissioned by artisans may indicate that most of these freed slaves had been trained as skilled workers. First, from the time of the Augustan marriage legislation onward, a male patron who consented to the marriage of his freedwoman could not claim any outstanding *operae* from her while she remained married.[106] Technically, the wording of the law left the door open for patrons who had not consented to the marriages of their freedwomen to press their claims for *operae*, but in practice these claims may have been difficult to enforce: because patrons could not actually prevent their freed slaves from marrying,[107] in many cases it must have been necessary for them to attempt to prove in court (and well after the fact) that they had not consented to the marriage. Female patrons did not suffer from this restriction, but male artisans who chose to manumit slaves in exchange for *operae* as part of a response strategy to uncertainties in their product markets may have preferentially manumitted male rather than female slaves to safeguard their rights, even if they had trained female slaves in their own crafts.[108] Second, women in general (both slave and freeborn) did not enjoy the same level of access to formal craft training as men, and when they did work as skilled artisans, they did so in a relatively narrow range of industries: although slaves of both sexes often worked as domestic servants, female slaves and freedwomen are both attested in far fewer trades than men, who worked in a much broader range of crafts, whether as free workers or as slaves.[109] For that reason, we can perhaps best explain the overrepresentation of men among the freed slaves in the *se vivo / sibi* inscriptions by postulating that most were skilled craftsmen: had most been domestic servants, we would expect to see a more balanced sex ratio in the names of the freed slaves that artisans inscribed on their monuments.

Finally, in addition to suggesting that many freed artisans learned their trades from owners who were themselves craftsmen and that artisans regularly freed such slaves *inter vivos*, the funerary inscriptions also suggest that Roman artisans who manumitted skilled slaves during their own

---

[106] Hermogenian, *Dig.* 38.1.48.pr; for further discussion, see now Perry 2014: 80–2.

[107] Paul, *Dig.* 37.14.6.4.

[108] A similar imbalance in sex ratio characterizes inscriptions in which male and female *colliberti* who practiced a common craft chose to commemorate themselves collectively – e.g., *CIL* 6.9398 (eight men and two women, all of whom may have been *ferarii*); 6.9435 (four men and one woman who worked as *gemarii*); 6.9933 (five men and two women who worked as *thurarii*). Only in a few trades do concentrations of women seem normal. See, e.g., *CIL* 6.9846, which commemorates four women who appear to have been dyers or purple-sellers.

[109] For further discussion of this point, see Chapter 4.

lifetimes did so in exchange for *operae*. The key detail supporting this interpretation is the fact that those artisans who commissioned inscriptions of the *se vivo* / *sibi* type emphasized the locations of their workshops alongside their occupational titles and their relationships with their former slaves. Sandra Joshel has suggested that this particular emphasis reflects individual artisans' desire to depict themselves not only as independent proprietors but also as successful enough to employ the labor of dependent workers. For that reason, she suggests, the freedmen named in these inscriptions should be seen as skilled craftsmen who continued to work in the enterprises of their patrons in some capacity after manumission.[110] Some of these freed slaves may very well have worked as workshop foremen, both before and after their manumission, supervising production while their patrons specialized in marketing or sales. In these cases, an artisan's decision to manumit such a slave can be explained best in terms of Mouritsen's model: patrons used manumission to create incentives for slaves to whom they assigned important responsibilities and retained access to the labor of those slaves once manumitted not by exacting formal labor obligations, but rather by offering them ongoing stakes in their businesses, possibly in the form of a limited partnership. At the same time, however, it seems probable that only a minority of the freedmen who were manumitted by artisans worked as supervisory staff in the workshops of their former masters and that most engaged in skilled work on the shop floor. This seems to have been true for Epaphra, who – judging from the reliefs on Atimetus' altar – continued to work as a craftsman in his former owner's shop. It was also undoubtedly true of most of the slaves freed by artisans who, like Q. Caecilius Spendo and A. Fulvius Dorotheus, controlled large dependent workforces, since only a few of these could have been entrusted with managerial responsibilities. Manumission in exchange for *operae* offers the most plausible model for understanding not only how these freed slaves who continued to work for their patrons as skilled craftsmen secured their manumission but also the nature of the ongoing relationship between former master and former slave. Even though artisans could not necessarily offer many of these slaves managerial positions or partnerships as a way of retaining their loyalty, and even though slaves who worked alongside their owners on the shop floor were unlikely to amass enough funds in their *peculia* to purchase their own freedom, the uncertainty of urban product markets in the Roman world provided strong incentives for artisans to negotiate terms of manumission in exchange for *operae* with

[110] Joshel 1992: 144–5.

individual slaves – who, in turn, could offer labor services as a way of purchasing "manumission on credit" from their masters.[111]

One valuable piece of legal evidence dovetails nicely with these conclusions by indicating that artisan slaveholders not only manumitted slaves in exchange for *operae* with some regularity but also did so precisely because the nature of urban product markets made it risky for them to maintain permanent workforces. That evidence consists of an observation made by the jurist Julian in his analysis of the *lex Aelia Sentia* of 4 CE – which, among other things, stipulated that patrons who possessed claims to the *operae* of freed slaves were not to make a profit by selling those services to others, but instead were to use the *operae* of their freedmen personally.[112] In a discussion of these rules, Julian noted some important exceptions:

> A patron who hires out the *operae* of his freedman is not immediately to be perceived as making a profit from him. Rather, this should be inferred from the kind of *operae* and from the character of the patron and his freedman . . . doctors often produce as freedmen slaves who are skilled in this same craft, whose *operae* they cannot otherwise continually use except by hiring them out. And the same things can be said in the case of other craftsmen (*in ceteris artificibus*). But he who can use the *operae* of his freedman and prefers to get a price for them by hiring his freedman out is to be understood as making a profit from the freedman's *operae*.[113]

Importantly, Julian believed that his analysis reflected actual social practice, in particular the tendency of artisans to manumit skilled slaves in exchange for *operae* with some regularity (*plerumque*). No less significant is Julian's rationale for excluding artisans from the general rule that patrons were not to hire out the *operae* of their freedmen, which again seems based on his observations of actual practice. In his view, artisans were entitled to hire out the *operae* of skilled freedmen specifically because they could not make regular or continuous use of those services personally. While Julian unfortunately does not elaborate on why artisans could only use the *operae* of skilled freedmen on an intermittent basis, the seasonal and uncertain demand that characterized urban product markets in antiquity explains this phenomenon: artisans called in the *operae* of their freedmen only

---

[111] Waldstein 1986, esp. 123–30. Waldstein attributes the phrase "manumission on credit" (Freilassung auf Kredit) to Franz Wieacker (127 n. 30).

[112] See Waldstein 1986: 161–85 for a general discussion of the *lex Aelia Sentia* and its implications for the rights of freedmen.

[113] Julian, *Dig.* 38.1.25.pr – 2. The translation is adapted from that of Alan Watson in the University of Pennsylvania's edition of the *Digest of Justinian* (Philadelphia: University of Pennsylvania Press, 1985).

when windfall orders or seasonal peaks in the demand for their products increased their own demand for labor. In that sense, Julian's observations align closely with the patterns that can be inferred from the funerary inscriptions and serve as strong evidence that Roman artisans relied heavily upon manumission in exchange for *operae* as a means of responding to the seasonality and uncertainty of urban product markets.

Manumission, transaction costs, and urban labor markets

As my argument so far has demonstrated, an analysis of the economic environment in which artisans made decisions about labor management offers fresh insight into the practice of manumission in the ancient world. In particular, it shows that manumission in exchange for labor obligations exercised considerable appeal for artisans and other urban entrepreneurs, who could use it to meet two seemingly irreconcilable goals – to reduce their fixed costs as a means of buffering themselves against the risks generated by seasonal and uncertain demand, while simultaneously retaining control over the skilled labor they needed to expand their output during favorable market conditions. In that sense, it adds a new layer to our understanding of why and in what circumstances slaveholders set their slaves free.

At the same time, however, that analysis also raises an important question about the relationship between the structure of Roman labor markets and the two basic strategies of labor management available to Roman artisans: one based on using the spot market to hire short term help when necessary and the other based on using manumission in exchange for labor obligations to minimize the costs of hoarding servile workforces. Julian certainly believed that Roman artisans regularly relied upon the second, and since the patterns of manumission visible in our inscriptions support his belief, it is plausible that most, in fact, preferred to hoard the labor of freedmen rather than to hire short-term help on the spot market. That preference is potentially significant: because artisans in the early modern context relied on strategies emphasizing labor hoarding when skilled workers were difficult to hire on short notice (as they were in certain highly skilled trades, such as goldsmithing), it indicates that labor markets in antiquity were, in general, subject to high transaction costs.[114]

---

[114] For the view that widespread chattel slavery was often a response to high transaction (or turnover) costs, see Hanes 1996 and Scheidel 2008. Cf. Bezís-Selfa 2004: 105–9, who argues that ironworkers in British North America often preferred to acquire slave forgemen for comparable reasons.

In what follows, I add further support for this claim by arguing that markets for skilled labor in the Roman world were relatively tight, that transaction costs were correspondingly high, and that Roman artisans who depended on skilled help could better adapt their workforces to fluctuations in demand by hoarding the labor of freedmen than by relying on the spot market. The apparent popularity of slavery and manumission in Rome's artisan economy thus reinforces the view that market structures in the Roman world remained underdeveloped relative to those of later historical periods, even in the comparatively thick metropolitan markets of Rome itself. I conclude by suggesting that the tendency of artisans to hoard the labor of servile workers also limited possibilities for ongoing and intensive growth during the early Empire: by interfering with the expansion of middling income groups that may have fueled further consumption, it curtailed the development of the thick market externalities responsible for driving both increased specialization and intensive growth in Europe's later preindustrial history.

Manumission and labor markets in the Roman world: a transaction cost perspective

Given the importance of *potestas* in Roman social identity, it is of course possible that artisans owned and manumitted slaves partly because slaveholding itself communicated important messages about an individual's status. On this view, widespread manumission on the part of Roman artisans can be seen as an epiphenomenon of their desire to own slaves: manumission in exchange for *operae* permitted artisans to make claims about their status without incurring the full weight of the costs associated with slaveholding. This possibility cannot be tested directly given the state of our evidence, but Kyle Harper's recent analysis of slave prices in late antiquity suggests that the desire to broadcast messages about status may not have been strong enough to provoke extensive patterns of slaveholding and manumission among artisans. Harper concludes that slave prices in antiquity more likely than not reflected the capacity of slaves to perform productive labor rather than their value as prestige goods alone and speculates that the same may have been true in the early Empire.[115] If this view is correct, then it provides a strong warrant for believing that Roman artisans acquired slaves primarily as economic assets, even if they derived additional forms of satisfaction from owning human property.

[115] Harper 2010: 233–4 and 238.

That said, we can rule out the most obvious potential explanation for why artisans may have seen a specific economic benefit to owning slaves – namely, that they were able to economize on their labor costs when they used slavery and manumission rather than the spot market to adapt their output to changing levels of demand. Control of slaves or freedmen imposed costs upon slaveholders, which included not just the expenses they incurred to feed and maintain their slaves but also costs of other kinds: opportunity costs generated by the value of the capital vested in their slaves and freedmen, which they could have put to an alternative use; costs produced by depreciation in the value of that capital as slaves aged; and costs reflecting the risk that a slave or freedman would die, escape, or otherwise evade work.[116] When these costs are modeled, they suggest that artisans who relied primarily on labor-management strategies based on slavery and manumission paid a steep premium to do so.

Three variables are essential for understanding the relative costs of the strategies artisans could employ to manage their workforces: the price of skilled slaves, the costs of slave maintenance, and the skilled wage rate. The first two can be approximated on the basis of information provided by Columella and Cato. Columella claims that a slave trained as a vinedresser cost between 6,000 and 8,000 *sesterces* in the first century CE,[117] and Cato offers recommended rations for slaves that ranged from roughly 400–700 kg of wheat-equivalent (yielding maintenance costs of between 353 and 618 *sesterces* in Columella's day).[118] The skilled wage is more difficult to estimate, since no reliable figures from Italy in the early Empire have survived.[119] Two stray references in our sources, however, imply unskilled wage rates of 3 and 4 *sesterces* in the first centuries BCE and CE, respectively; if we assume that skilled workers could earn double that amount, then a wage rate of 8 *sesterces* per day seems plausible.[120]

If we adopt the midpoints of the ranges proffered above as approximations of the market prices and maintenance costs of skilled slaves, then

---

[116] I adapt this analytical framework from Whitman 1997: 54–5.   [117] Columella, *Rust.* 3.3.8.

[118] Cato, *Agr.* 56–9, with the comments of Scheidel 2005: 12–13. Wheat prices in central Italy probably ranged between 4 and 8 *sesterces* per *modius* (6.8 kg) in the first century CE (but see Rathbone 2009: 308 for the difficulties involved in assessing those figures); here, I assume an average price of 6 *sesterces*.

[119] Contrary to what is sometimes believed, Cato does not refer to a daily wage rate at *Agr.* 21.5, but rather to the total cost of hiring a skilled worker for tasks that may have taken longer than a day.

[120] Cicero suggests that unskilled workers in Rome could earn 3 HS per day in the 70s BCE (*QRosc.* 28), and a stray graffito from Pompeii indicates that a wage paid to a day laborer may have consisted of a denarius (4 HS) plus rations (*CIL* 4.6877). Both pieces of evidence are subject to problems of interpretation; for more details, see Scheidel 2010: 444 (with n. 56) and 445. Finally, see Rathbone 2009: 314–16 on skill premiums in Roman Egypt.

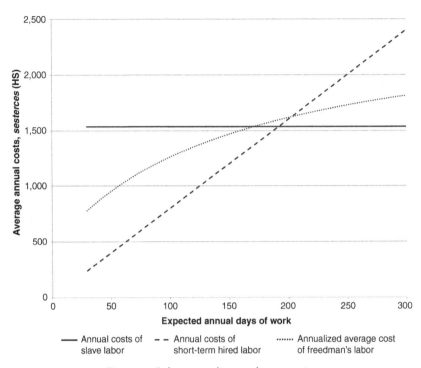

Figure 3.4 Labor costs: direct and opportunity.

these estimates can generate a series of cost curves (Figure 3.4) relating the costs of three particular labor-management solutions to the amount of skilled help an artisan required each year from a particular worker (measured in units of a day's work).[121] The first curve, representing the wages artisans could expect to pay on the spot market, is the most straightforward of the three; in this particular case, the costs depicted by the curve are the product of the typical daily wage rate and the number of days per year that an artisan anticipated employing a given worker. The second curve represents the overall annual costs of labor incurred by an artisan who retained a slave in bondage permanently; it models the costs of maintenance, the costs of depreciation and potential loss, and the opportunity costs of the capital embodied in the slave. Because these were essentially fixed costs,

---

[121] Note, however, Scheidel's warning (2005: 13) that Cato's figures for maintenance probably reflect a "minimalist" assessment of what was necessary. By taking the midpoint of Cato's range, my model may therefore underestimate the overall costs of slave labor.

borne regardless of how often an artisan was able to employ his slave, this particular curve is a flat line.[122] Finally, the third curve depicts the average annual costs incurred by an artisan who acquired a skilled slave with the intention of manumitting him after several years' worth of service in exchange for a specified number of *operae*. For modeling purposes, I make two assumptions: first, that artisans typically kept their slaves in bondage for five years; second, that they freed slaves in exchange for a number of *operae* that not only reflected the slave's current market value but also imposed a premium in exchange for freedom. I also average costs that were, in reality, distributed unevenly over a lengthy period of time. So long as his slave remained in bondage, an artisan opting for this strategy would have borne the same costs as one who relied on slave labor. In subsequent years, however, those costs would have been smaller, since the artisan would have saved on maintenance expenses (albeit while still incurring some opportunity costs reflecting the value of the capital he had originally invested in the slave).[123]

Together, these curves strongly imply that it was considerably more costly over the long run for artisans to rely on labor-hoarding strategies based on slavery and manumission than it was for them to hire workers as necessary on the spot market, unless they could guarantee a particular worker employment for approximately 200 days a year – at which point it became more cost-effective to rely on slaves. The comparative evidence from early modern Europe, however, suggests that most artisans were unable to keep all but a few workers employed for longer than three to four months. In that range, the savings of Roman artisans who relied on the spot market would have been considerable – very roughly, on the order of 390–490 *sesterces* per year, depending on how much additional help they required.[124]

---

[122] Here, $C_s = M + V_s (r + l + i)$, where C_s represents the total annual costs of slave labor, M the annual costs of housing and feeding a slave, V_s the slave's initial market value, r the rate at which a slave's market value declined as he or she aged, l the probability that a slave would die or run away, and i the interest rate used to calculate the opportunity costs of capital. I assume that depreciation costs were 6 percent of the slave's maximum capital value (following Whitman 1997: 54–5). I have calculated the risk of mortality at 1.4 percent per year between the ages of 15 and 30 on the basis of the level 3 female model life table in Saller 1994: 24. I have arbitrarily assigned roughly the same value for the risk of flight, for a total effective "risk of loss" of 3 percent of the slave's maximum capital value. Finally, I have calculated the opportunity cost of capital by assuming that artisans could lend out money at interest at a 6 percent rate of return.

[123] For a full exposition of the relevant calculation, see Appendix A.

[124] These figures represent the difference between the cost curves for freedmen's labor and hired labor at 120 and 90 expected days of work, respectively.

Although Roman slaveholders were unable to calculate their margins so precisely, the model above nevertheless emphasizes trade-offs they themselves would have recognized on some level, even if they did not express them in monetary terms.[125] The market price of a slave (and the corresponding value it added to one's estate) was known to decrease over time, and the risk of flight was ever-present.[126] Even the concept of opportunity costs has some value in this context, since artisans did have valuable and important alternative outlets for their capital: not only do members of their social milieu appear to have lent money at interest with some frequency, they could also use their wealth to enhance their status within their professional associations.[127] Even so, if we discount the opportunity costs of capital and assume that artisan slaveholders were sensitive only to the more explicit costs of depreciation and potential loss, the model still indicates that it was costlier for an artisan to hoard the labor of freedmen than it was to hire additional workers on the spot market: the typical savings generated by the spot market in this model are 42 *sesterces* per year for artisans who could keep a worker employed for 120 days per year and 148 for those who had only enough work to employ a worker for ninety days (Figure 3.5).

Because the model shows that artisans effectively paid a substantial premium when they hoarded the labor of skilled freedmen, factors other than the relative costs of labor itself must be invoked to explain any economic considerations prompting artisans to prefer manumission-based strategies of adaptation to those relying on the spot market. Transaction costs are an obvious potential factor. Although this hypothesis is difficult to test directly because transaction costs themselves are difficult to measure in any precise way, two indirect considerations strongly suggest that transaction costs affecting markets for skilled labor in the Roman world were high relative to those in seventeenth- and eighteenth-century Europe: first, the skilled labor markets in the Roman world were tight compared to those of later historical periods; second, institutions and organizations that could have mitigated transaction costs arising from those tight markets were not as

---

[125] For a discussion of how Roman slaveholders reckoned the contributions of their human property to the overall value of their estates, see, e.g., Minaud 2005: 143–9.

[126] Scheidel 1996c and 2005 both offer comments about the impact of a slave's age on his or her market value. Bradley 1994: 118–29 discusses runaway slaves and the anxieties slaveholders experienced because of the possibility that their slaves would flee.

[127] Verboven 2007 discusses the various ways in which artisans converted wealth into symbolic capital within their associations. On the likelihood that artisans and other "middling" Romans lent out money, see Veyne 2000: 1187–94.

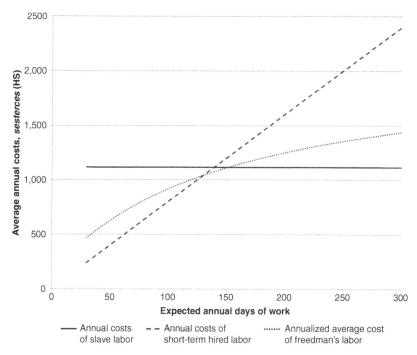

Figure 3.5 Labor costs: direct only.

highly developed in the Roman world as they were in later historical periods.[128]

Broadly speaking, labor markets are tight when the ratio of employers to employees skews in favor of the latter, and qualified employees are correspondingly scarce. A tight labor market will tend to drive up the transaction costs incurred by an employer in two ways: first, it will complicate an employer's efforts to locate suitable employees on short notice, thus increasing search costs; second, it will increase an employee's bargaining power (especially in periods of elevated demand) and will thus generate high enforcement costs – whether by tempting employees to hold up production opportunistically in the hope of securing higher

---

[128] For a recent and much more optimistic assessment of labor markets in the Roman world, see Temin 2013: 114–38. In my view, Temin overstresses the ability of individuals to select jobs and relocate in response to market conditions, as my following discussion of both apprenticeship and institutions should make clear. He also blurs the distinctions between slave (or former slave) and free workers – distinctions which, as I have argued above, were in practice quite significant.

wages or by encouraging them to renege on agreements altogether in order to seek more profitable contracts elsewhere.[129]

Scheidel has argued that Roman labor markets in general were relatively tight in the middle and late Republic but that they thickened notably in the wake of the Augustan transition. In his view, the tight markets of the Republic were generated both by the heavy political and military commitments of the citizenry, which interfered with their ability to engage in regular employment, and by state-sponsored colonization programs that relocated tens of thousands of Romans and Italians to the provinces. By contrast, the Augustan transition not only brought about the end of large-scale colonization programs but also eliminated the key factors that impeded regular employment: Augustus' decision to replace the militia-based army with a professional military force reduced the citizenry's military commitments, and changes in political culture during the early Empire likewise prompted a gradual and long-term reduction in their political commitments.[130]

It is far from clear, however, that these changes thickened all segments of the labor market equally. More plausibly, they primarily affected markets for unskilled or semi-skilled labor by encouraging rural workers to migrate to large cities, whether seasonally or permanently. Many of these arrived with only limited experience or training in skills that were relevant to urban production, and they therefore expanded the reserves of low-skilled urban inhabitants seeking casual labor or finding self-employment as peddlers or hawkers, which – in Rome as in other preindustrial cities – were already large.[131] To the extent that women entered the labor market or migrated seasonally for this purpose (as, perhaps, did those who worked in the textile industries in Patrae), they too probably joined its unskilled or semi-skilled segments: since women were less likely to acquire training in craft skills than men, they gravitated toward lines of work that drew on domestic skills.[132] Finally, slaves may have entered the labor market in large numbers after receiving permission from their owners to undertake work on their own account; while some were clearly skilled, most probably sought employment primarily as casual laborers, as Columella's critique about slaveholding landowners implies. Like the labor markets typical of large

---

[129] See Hanes 1996: 310, who makes this point in a discussion about slavery in British North America.

[130] Scheidel 2008: 115–26 discusses both changes over time in the political and military commitments of the citizenry and the potential impact exerted by those changes on patterns of slaveholding. For complementary data on diachronic developments in slave prices, see Scheidel 2005.

[131] Holleran 2011 and Holleran 2012: 216–31.

[132] On women's access to technical skills, see Chapter 4; for the women of Patrae, see Chapter 1.

cities in early modern Europe, those in ancient cities were thus populated increasingly densely in the early Empire by unskilled and semi-skilled workers who undoubtedly found themselves chronically underemployed.[133]

On this view, skilled segments of the labor market did not benefit greatly from the more general trend toward thicker markets after the Augustan transition and remained tight. Circumstantial information about wage premiums in our sources supports that view by implying that these segments remained tight compared both to other labor market segments in antiquity and to skilled labor markets in the seventeenth and eighteenth centuries. Our best data about skill premiums reflect conditions in Roman Egypt, where skilled workers in the third century CE could command wages two to three times higher than unskilled rural laborers, especially in cities. Comparable premiums are reflected in Diocletian's price edict, even if the relationship between the maximum prices established in the edict and real-world wages remains difficult to untangle.[134] Finally, although our evidence provides no real data for wages in Roman Italy during the early Empire, it does suggest that training in a skill was likely to increase the value of a slave twofold, if not more. The jurist Paul assumed that a slaveholder would double his slave's market value by training him in a skill like smithing or carpentry,[135] and Columella's estimate for the cost of a skilled vinedresser – as we have seen, between 6,000 and 8,000 *sesterces* – indicates that Paul may have underestimated the value of such skills.[136] Judging from the comparative data, the skill premiums visible in these sources fall into the very upper range of what was typical for wages in northwestern Europe during the late medieval and early modern periods and for slave prices in the antebellum South.[137] Since skill premiums often reflect the efficiency of training regimes, the high premiums in our Roman sources are consistent with Saller's conclusion that inhabitants of the Roman Empire did not invest as heavily in human capital as did individuals in later historical periods.[138] They therefore show that skilled labor in the Roman world was scarce and that the skilled segments of the market were correspondingly tight relative to those of early modern European economies.

---

[133] For conditions in early modern Europe, see Stedman Jones 1984: 52–66; Schwarz 1992: 117–18.

[134] Rathbone 2009, esp. 314–21.   [135] Paul, *Dig.* 17.1.26.8.   [136] Columella, *Rust.* 3.3.8.

[137] For wages, see van Zanden 2009, esp. 126–31. For slave prices, see Fogel 1989: 68. If Scheidel 2005: 6 is right to take 2000 HS as the most representative price of an unskilled slave in the early Roman Empire, then training enhanced the value of slaves more strongly in antiquity than it did in the antebellum South, where blacksmiths and carpenters typically possessed market values 55 percent and 45 percent higher than those of unskilled slaves.

[138] See, most recently, Saller 2012, esp. 75–7 and 82–5.

That point is confirmed by what we can infer about the opportunity costs of apprenticeship in antiquity, which were high enough relative to typical household incomes to exclude many freeborn young men from opportunities to acquire skills. Conventional models of apprenticeship tend to underestimate the value of an apprentice's labor in the early stages of a training program, both to his instructor and to his parents. Briefly put, these models posit that the value of an apprentice's labor was insufficient for him to compensate his instructor for training costs until he had acquired the skills necessary to perform skilled tasks within the workshop; an apprentice was therefore a net liability to a master artisan for months or even years during the early phases of his apprenticeship.[139] More recent assessments of apprenticeship confirm some aspects of these conventional models, chiefly by stressing that the experiential and progressive learning typical of apprenticeship occurred only gradually and over a protracted period of time. In the early stages, apprentices were typically assigned menial chores by their masters, who expected their pupils to learn primarily by observing senior members of the workshop. Gradually, apprentices earned the opportunity to put what they had observed into practice and to refine their skills through a process of trial and error, mediated by the feedback of their instructors.[140] At the same time, however, new assessments of apprenticeship also emphasize that this process served partly to ensure that master artisans could recoup their costs progressively throughout the apprenticeship, rather than only once the apprentice became capable of performing skilled work. Because the work performed even by unskilled junior apprentices had economic value, especially for master artisans who operated enterprises on a scale that produced enough "busy work" to make retaining unskilled help worthwhile, master artisans could ensure that they were compensated for their training costs by providing instruction only in successive stages, punctuated by periods of work by their apprentices.[141] Crucially – and precisely because the labor of junior apprentices did have economic value – parents and guardians incurred opportunity costs when they apprenticed young men in their charge to artisans or entrepreneurs. These can be conceptualized as the value to their own households of the labor they sacrificed when they placed their sons under the control of others.[142]

---

[139] For the basic theory, see Smits and Stromback 2001: 68–93, and esp. 72–7. Epstein 1998: 688–93 discusses the theory in relation to apprenticeship in early modern Europe.

[140] De Munck and Soly 2007: 13–16 give an overview of training rhythms in the early modern context, while Lancy 2012 provides a comparable overview from an anthropological perspective.

[141] Wallis 2008, esp. 845–51.   [142] Minns and Wallis 2013: 344.

From this perspective, an apprenticeship represented a genuine investment on the part of the apprentice or his parents.[143] Precisely how substantial it was in any given case depended on various factors: whether instructors typically charged additional premiums for training; whether they covered their apprentices' living expenses or provided a small stipend; and whether an apprentice's household could make do without his labor or potential earnings.[144] In the Roman world, where real incomes were low relative to those of early modern Europe,[145] the last of these factors was significant enough to price many boys out of the apprenticeship market unless they received some form of financial compensation for their labor. Because most household heads were unable to sustain their families at even a bare-bones subsistence level on their wages alone, the earning potential of sons – who, as adolescents, could earn a third or more of an adult's wage in exchange for unskilled labor – was a crucial bridge for a household between deprivation and a modest level of comfort.[146] In other words, the opportunity costs of apprenticeship were high enough from the perspective of a young man's parents that many were more willing than their early modern counterparts to forego training for their sons to boost the household's income in the present.

A small collection of apprenticeship documents from Roman Egypt provides most of our information about the terms of apprenticeship agreements in the Roman world.[147] These documents indicate that artisans in Roman Egypt typically did compensate their apprentices (or their apprentice's parents or owners) for their labor but not at a rate commensurate with the incomes that those apprentices could have produced for their households by working for wages.[148] They therefore suggest that

---

[143] For a contrary view, see Saller 2007: 109 and 2012: 76–7.   [144] Wallis 2008: 835–6.

[145] See Chapter 1 for a detailed exposition of this view.

[146] Here, I follow Scheidel's estimate (2010: 434–5) that an adolescent male in Roman Egypt could generate roughly 100 *drachmai* per year of additional revenue for his household.

[147] Bergamasco 1995 offers a comprehensive overview of the existing documents. See also Freu 2011, Laes 2011: 191–5, Bradley 1991: 103–24, and Westermann 1914.

[148] Some apprentices received compensation from the beginning of their contracts. In those cases in which the apprenticeships were for brief terms (i.e., on the order of a year or two), we should probably imagine that the apprentices in question had already received some relevant training within the context of a family enterprise (Bradley 1991: 111; see, e.g., *P. Oxy.* II 322, *P. Fouad.* I 37). On the other hand, when the apprenticeships were for long terms (e.g., *PSI* X 1110, three years; *P. Oxy.* XIV 1647, four years; *P. Oxy.* XXXI 2586, five years; *P. Oxy.* XLI 2977, five years), the apprentices may have been untrained. In all of these cases, however, the apprentices seem to have been compensated at a rate below the market value of their labor. The rate paid to the short-term apprentices in *P. Oxy.* II 322 and *P. Fouad.* I 37, both of whom may have had some training already, was 4 *drachmai* per month, which is well below what adolescents may have been able to earn for unskilled work (see above, n. 147), let alone semi-skilled or skilled work (a point to which I return in

apprenticeship remained out of reach for most young men in the Roman world. In 183 CE, for example, a resident of Oxyrhynchus named Ischyrion apprenticed a minor in his charge, Thoonis, to the weaver Heraclas for a period of five years. The terms of the agreement specified that Ischyrion was to remain responsible for Thoonis' living expenses throughout the period of the apprenticeship but that Heraclas would compensate his apprentice on a progressive scale. Heraclas agreed to provide Thoonis with a new tunic each year (the quality and value of which would increase over the lifetime of the contract) and to supplement this with a stipend beginning midway through the third year of the apprenticeship. The stipend itself was to consist of 12 *drachmai* per month for the last few months of the third year, 16 *drachmai* per month during the fourth year, and 24 *drachmai* per month in the contract's fifth and final year.[149] Under these terms, Ischyrion incurred opportunity costs on the order of 100 *drachmai* per year in the first two and a half years of the contract – that is, the value of the income that Thoonis could have earned from paid work.[150] Moreover, his opportunity costs would have remained high even during the second half of the contract: while Heraclas agreed to offer progressively higher wages during years four and five, by that stage Thoonis would have been skilled enough to earn more on the open market than Heraclas was willing to pay.[151] Ischyrion's decision to have Thoonis trained as a weaver thus demanded a hefty investment on his part. While Ischyrion was clearly willing and able to absorb the costs of that investment, the same would not necessarily have been true of household heads who struggled to maintain families on an income of between 200 and 300 *drachmai* per year and who were dissuaded from arranging apprenticeships

---

Chapter 4). In three of the four long-term contracts listed above, apprentices were likewise compensated for the full lengths of their terms at a rate below what unskilled workers were probably able to earn in a year, sometimes dramatically so, as in *P. Oxy.* XLI 2977 (which should be read in conjunction with Scheidel's estimates for the earning potential of unskilled workers in the two main periods of price stability in Roman Egypt, on which see Scheidel 2010: 428–35). The one exception occurs in *P. Oxy.* XXXI 2586, in which the apprentice was compensated at a rate below the market value of his (unskilled) labor in the first two years of the contract, at a rate perhaps approximating what he could have earned for unskilled work in year three and at a rate that finally exceeded what he could have earned as an unskilled worker in years four and five (but which still probably fell below the typical rate for skilled work).

[149] *P. Oxy.* IV, 725.   [150] On Thoonis' probable earning potential, see above, n. 147.

[151] The near-contemporary payment *entolae* from Mons Claudianus provide evidence that skilled workers were paid at one of three monthly cash rates – 28, 37, or 47 *drachmai* – plus food. The rate a worker received seems to have varied primarily on the basis of his age, which suggests that the two lower figures may have been the rates paid to junior and senior apprentices (Cuvigny 1996: 140–1). Even the lowest of these rates exceeded Thoonis' wage in the final year of his contract, especially once the additional wages-in-kind of the workers at Mons Claudianus are taken into account.

for their sons precisely because they needed those sons to generate cash income instead.[152]

The transaction costs generated by these tight markets for skilled labor in antiquity were further exacerbated by the comparative underdevelopment of institutions and organizations capable of mitigating them. Guilds and journeymen's associations were, respectively, the organizations and institutions that structured urban production in the seventeenth and eighteenth centuries most heavily. Both were critical to the efforts of artisans to adapt their workforces to seasonal and uncertain demand: by controlling key transaction costs in the labor market, they enabled most artisans to hire workers as necessary on the spot market rather than to hoard underemployed labor in periods of low demand. More importantly, they did so to a degree that analogous institutions and organizations in the Roman world were unable to match.

Guilds affected the nature of labor markets in early modern Europe chiefly by imposing institutional constraints on individual artisans' ability to work on their own account rather than as employees in the enterprises of other craftsmen. In that sense, they helped mitigate transaction costs for artisans who relied on the spot market by artificially thickening the labor market in any given trade. There was naturally extensive variation among early modern guilds, both on the level of internal organization and in the ways they were integrated into the social, political, and economic fabric of European cities.[153] That said, many possessed formal regulatory powers over their respective trades by virtue of concessions granted by royal or municipal authorities – powers which they then exercised by formulating and enforcing corporate statutes. While these statutes possessed their own local and trade-specific idiosyncrasies, most guilds sought to protect their members' interests by stipulating that only master artisans belonging to the guild were entitled to manufacture and sell the products of their trade.[154] Not only did such statutes technically prohibit artisans who were not masters from operating workshops of their own,[155] they also sometimes prohibited those artisans from undertaking subcontracted work: in 1763, for instance, the master glaziers of Paris ruled that journeymen were not to

---

[152] As per Scheidel 2010: 427–36, an income of between 200 and 300 *drachmai* per year would have met something on the order of only 70–80 percent of a family's bare-bones subsistence needs.
[153] See, for example, the comments of Edgren 2006: 43–5 and Pfister 2008: 32–6.
[154] See Chapter 2 for a more detailed discussion of the differences between early modern guilds and ancient *collegia*.
[155] S. L. Kaplan 1996: 296–301 (with specific reference to the bakers of Paris). Cf. Farr 1988: 17 and 61 and Sewell 1980: 27–8.

accept subcontracted work, precisely because extensive subcontracting within the trade threatened master glaziers' ability to secure additional skilled help during high season.[156] Some guilds were more successful than others at enforcing such restrictions, but it is clear that when they did retain enough influence to protect their interests they actively prosecuted offenders.[157]

Guilds reinforced this effect on the labor market by imposing barriers on artisans who hoped to acquire the rank of master. Because master artisans in any given guild were often reluctant to create excessive intra-guild competition, they were typically unwilling to broaden their membership more than was strictly necessary. As a result, barriers against entry into guilds could be high, particularly for artisans who did not already possess strong ties of patronage. In addition to imposing admission fees – some of which were extremely costly – guilds also often required applicants for the rank of master to produce masterpieces at their own expense.[158] Some also stipulated that applicants must have served an apprenticeship or a period of journeywork in the city in which they were applying for mastership or even that they had completed several years of work as itinerant journeymen.[159] Although some historians have argued that such policies did not necessarily limit journeymen's prospects for attaining the rank of master as much as is sometimes thought,[160] most still support the conventional view that apprentices and journeymen

---

[156] Sonenscher 1989: 24–5.

[157] E.g., S. L. Kaplan 1979: 26–7; Berlin 1997, esp. 79–83; Edgren 2006: 51–2. Cf. Berlin 2008: 325–38, who argues that the London livery companies lost their formal regulatory powers much later than is commonly assumed.

[158] On admission fees, see S. L. Kaplan 1996: 275–8; Sewell 1980: 118; Farr 1988: 20–3; Heimmermann 1994: 362–6. In Paris, they could range from 500 to 1,500 *livres* for men who had not served an apprenticeship in the city; these sums were far from insignificant for journeymen who grossed only a few hundred *livres* per year. Although admission fees in Paris may have been higher than was the case elsewhere, evidence from Bordeaux shows that even in smaller French cities they still typically amounted to well over 100 *livres*. Moreover, informal expenses in the form of bribes and gratuities could increase these costs by anywhere from 25 to 100 percent. Altogether, these expenses could easily exceed the amount of capital that would establish an artisan in an independent business.

[159] S. L. Kaplan 1996: 271–5; Farr 1988: 20–3; Ehmer 1997: 186; Heimmermann 1994: 349–95.

[160] On the basis of age distributions reconstructed from a handful of corporate records and hospital registers, Sonenscher 1989: 99–104 suggests that most French artisans eventually became masters: itinerant journeymen in eighteenth-century France were overwhelmingly young compared to the general population (more than half were younger than twenty-five), and this may indicate that as craftsmen aged they were increasingly likely to establish themselves as independent producers in their own right. As he acknowledges, however, it is impossible to know how many journeymen abandoned the trades altogether or established themselves beyond corporate control in small towns or unincorporated suburbs. Moreover, settled journeymen, who tended to be older than their itinerant colleagues, are probably underrepresented in these data sources (see, e.g., Garrioch and Sonenscher 1986 for a discussion of settled journeymen in Paris).

found it increasingly difficult during the seventeenth and eighteenth centuries to become master artisans in their own right and instead spent their careers working for wages. This conventional view draws considerable support from the dramatic surge in the number of bakers who were admitted as master artisans in Paris in 1776, after the royal government reformed the guild's admission policies and fees.[161]

Organizations of journeymen also served to reduce transaction costs, albeit in different ways. They did so primarily by encouraging the development of labor markets in given trades that exhibited considerable integration not just locally but also regionally. In their earliest form, journeymen's associations had functioned primarily as local mutual aid and devotional societies. From these roots, however, they gradually evolved into influential regional or even national organizations that not only gave itinerant journeymen some ability to resist collectively the corporate power of master artisans but also provided economic and psychological support for their members.[162] At a basic level, journeymen's associations functioned as communication networks capable of circulating information on local labor market conditions over wide geographical areas and provided structure to the movement of itinerant journeymen between different cities.[163] As journeymen increasingly sought to use their organizations to control labor placement, however, these associations also began to play an important role in the circulation of skilled workers within local labor markets. Often, the inns or pubs in which itinerant journeymen of a given trade congregated in any given city became important hubs for the exchange of labor. The favorable terms of credit available to journeymen in these establishments ensured that the supply of skilled workers remained physically concentrated, and this concentration itself ensured that new arrivals to the city could easily integrate themselves into the local labor market.[164]

While journeymen organized themselves primarily to contest master artisans' control of the labor market, master artisans did benefit from

---

[161] S. L. Kaplan 1996: 278–83. See also Sewell 1980: 1–32.

[162] In France, the brotherhoods of *compagnonnage* are the most well-known journeymen's organizations (Farr 1988: 65–75 and Truant 1994). On associations of itinerant journeymen in England and the Holy Roman Empire, see Leeson 1979 and Ehmer 1997: 188–91, respectively.

[163] The eighteenth-century glazier Jacques-Louis Ménétra received a number of job offers through such a network; see Roche's commentary in Ménétra 1986: 288.

[164] Farr 1988: 65–7; Ehmer 1997: 188–91; Sonenscher 1989: 169–72; Leeson 1979: 122–47; Schwarz 1992: 119–21.

some of the mechanisms created by the journeymen's associations.[165] Generally speaking, any form of organization that decreased an employer's effort in locating potential employees and negotiating employment contracts could effectively reduce his transaction costs.[166] By physically concentrating a labor force drawn from a geographically extensive catchment area in specific inns and taverns, journeymen's associations made it relatively easy for early modern employers to locate skilled labor on short notice.[167] These institutions were effective enough that when trade corporations or state authorities periodically sought to regulate labor placement, they frequently appropriated and formalized the structures that journeymen had already developed. In eighteenth-century Rouen, for example, the job registers that were created by several of the trade guilds simply added a layer of guild oversight on top of a pre-existing informal network centered upon the inns frequented by journeymen.[168] Likewise, when the state sought to regulate tax collection and the policing of journeymen in the Holy Roman Empire during the eighteenth century, it co-opted and regulated journeymen institutions that had long been in place.[169]

Artisans in the ancient Roman world, on the other hand, lived and worked in an economic environment that possessed neither institutions capable of artificially thickening local labor markets nor organizations that reduced artisans' transaction costs by concentrating local labor markets and integrating them over geographically-extensive areas. Because *collegia* and other professional associations functioned primarily as private organizations in the early Empire, they possessed none of the formal and institutional regulatory powers that permitted the members of early modern guilds to limit opportunities for other craftsmen to take up work on their own account. Instead, to the extent that artisans in the Roman world attempted to prevent others from setting up their own shops, they did so by exercising personal leverage over specific individuals, and not always successfully. Our documentary evidence from Roman Egypt, for example,

---

[165] Edgren 2006: 48–52 notes that guilds in Sweden in fact devoted considerable time to managing the interplay between their regulations and those of journeymen's associations in an effort to regulate the labor market more broadly.

[166] Acheson 2002: 28–31.   [167] Schwarz 1992: 189–90. Cf. Clark 1983: 229–30.

[168] Sonenscher 1989: 161 and 171–2. Sonenscher does note that these mechanisms affected some employers differently than others. Artisans who regularly employed large numbers of workers may have found official placement mechanisms somewhat limiting, since these mechanisms made it possible for artisans who produced on a smaller scale to compete with them for labor more effectively.

[169] Ehmer 1997: 177–8 and 192–4.

shows that proprietors who leased out their workshops to other craftsmen sometimes stipulated that their lessees were not to open shops of their own in the same neighborhood after the lease had expired. Clearly, whether or not an artisan could insert a clause of this nature into a contract depended entirely on his bargaining power relative to that of his lessee.[170] Patrons of skilled freedmen, on the other hand, sometimes attempted to restrict competition by ordering their former slaves not to establish businesses of their own. In such cases, however, the Roman jurists ruled that they had no right to impose such constraints on their former slaves.[171]

The absence of institutional barriers preventing independent production meant that skilled craftsmen in antiquity had more opportunity to establish themselves as entrepreneurs in their own right than those in early modern cities; the boundary between wage laborers and independent producers was thus more permeable in antiquity than in many early modern contexts (at least for those with access to cash, credit, and – in industries that depended on subcontracting – membership in a *collegium*), and the market in skilled labor comparatively tight from the perspective of employers.[172] This was true not just in the case of freeborn craftsmen but also for freedmen or slaves who remained closely tied to patrons or masters. Nothing legally prevented wealthy urban slaveholders from establishing skilled slaves as workshop managers or as semi-autonomous proprietors of their own *peculium*-based enterprises. Such slaves would have competed with free employers to hire skilled workers on the market or to take on apprentices, just as some slaves who worked on their own account in the antebellum South competed with white artisans to hire the labor of other slaves.[173] Cicero, for example, mentions the case of a slave named Cillo, who took on construction projects as an independent contractor; Cillo controlled a workforce consisting not only of other slaves who belonged to his master but also of apprentices.[174]

---

[170] *BGU* IV 1117.

[171] E.g., Scaevola, *Dig.* 38.1.45. Varus, *Dig.* 38.1.26.pr, discusses an interesting case in which a doctor, because he could not actually prevent his freedmen from establishing practices of their own, did his best to limit their ability to compete with him for patients by calling in their *operae* when they were likely to attract clients of their own.

[172] According to Acheson 1982: 326–7 and 1994: 155, skilled woodworkers in Cuanajo, Mexico produce precisely this effect on the labor market by seeking to establish shops of their own. As a consequence, employers not only find it more difficult to recruit and retain skilled labor but they also find that they must devote more time to supervising those employees that they are capable of hiring, who tend to be less skilled than desirable.

[173] Goldin 1976: 39 cites city ordinances that were designed to regulate or forbid this practice. Cf. Wade 1964: 49, who discusses the case of Charles Ball. Permitted by his master to hire out his own time, Ball was employed by another slave who worked as an agricultural contractor.

[174] Cic. *QFr.* 3.1.3. Three interpretative problems complicate our understanding of this particular passage. First, some scholars have suggested that Cillo was not necessarily a slave (see S. D. Martin

Nor did the Roman world possess organizations capable of mitigating transaction costs to the same extent as the journeymen's associations that integrated labor markets on a regional level in early modern Europe.[175] Organizations and informal practices that provided structure for labor markets on the local level certainly did exist. A Roman city's forum or *agora*, for example, served as an obvious meeting place for employers and potential employees.[176] Likewise, other locations, such as the meeting places or *scholae* that served as the headquarters of professional associations, easily could have served as hubs for labor markets in individual, specialized trades.[177] Professional associations themselves may have enabled artisans to rely on their personal networks to recruit some skilled help as and when necessary; like landowners in late antiquity, who often relied on recommendations from their peers when making hiring decisions, artisans who belonged to a common association possibly referred potential employees to one another.[178] This was perhaps most true of those who controlled dependent labor: some evidence suggests that artisans hired out the *operae* of their own freedmen to other employers, and those who owned skilled slaves may likewise have been willing to loan or hire them out.[179] Yet to the

---

1989: 55 and especially n. 51, in which she provides the relevant bibliography). That he was in fact a slave remains the most probable conclusion.

    Second, there is some ambiguity concerning the relationship between Cillo and the slaves who worked under his direction. Cicero calls these slaves *conservi*, and while this word often refers to several slaves who were owned by one master, Roman authors also used it in reference to *servi vicarii*, "under-slaves" who "belonged" to a slave who had been granted a *peculium* or separate account by his master (Erman 1896: 407 n. 2; cf. Staerman 1976: 111, who likewise assumes that the *conservi* in question were *vicarii* belonging to Cillo). Assuming that Cillo was himself a slave, he therefore either managed a business on behalf of his master with the help of his master's other slaves or ran a semi-autonomous business with the help of slaves who were treated in a *de facto* sense as his own property.

    Third, while the apprentices could have been slaves placed with Cillo by other owners, or even free children, they too could have been *servi vicarii* who belonged to Cillo himself. Cf. Plut. *Cat. Mai.* 21.7, who reports that Cato the Elder provided the necessary capital for his slaves to purchase *servi vicarii*, whom they trained and later sold at a profit.

[175] Holleran (forthcoming) discusses mechanisms of job placement in Rome in more detail.

[176] See Treggiari 1980: 51 and n. 9. She refers to three main passages. Unfortunately, two reflect conditions in the middle to late Republic: Plaut. *Pseud.* 804–9, in which cooks gather in the Forum to sell their services; Plaut. *Curc.* 482–3, which refers either to a casual labor exchange in the Vicus Tuscus or to a known area for prostitution. The third is Matt. 20:1–16, in which casual agricultural labor is recruited in the local *agora*.

[177] Mayer 2012: 92–9 provides a recent discussion of the prominent locations that the *scholae* of *collegia* enjoyed in some Roman cityscapes.

[178] Grey 2004: 30–7 discusses the importance of letters of recommendation in the rural context.

[179] As I have noted above, Ulpian, *Dig.* 13.6.5.7, mentions slave plasterers and slave stonemasons who were loaned out for use. Likewise, Marcian, *Dig.* 19.5.25, raises the possibility that slaveholders exchanged the labor of their underemployed slaves with one another rather than letting them out for hire.

extent that these labor-placement mechanisms remained primarily local, they could not always supply local artisans with necessary labor. Broadly speaking, they functioned well in response to idiosyncratic fluctuations in demand – for instance, to serendipitous or windfall orders – rather than during generalized and seasonal surges in demand, when artisans who controlled dependent workers were reluctant to hire them out to others.

Skilled workers undoubtedly were mobile in the ancient world, but whereas journeymen in early modern Europe could rely on networks organized by fellow journeymen both for news about local job markets and for help integrating themselves into new environments, itinerant craftsmen in antiquity depended more heavily on personal and haphazard contacts.[180] According to the author of *Acts*, for example, Paul found employment as a leatherworker when he visited Corinth primarily because he met two other recent arrivals, Aquila and his wife Priscilla, who practiced the same trade. Significantly, Paul met the couple serendipitously, while visiting a local synagogue.[181] One can imagine that migrants to other Roman cities formed comparable relationships by exploiting the possibilities of chain migration – that is, by forging relationships in associations of other migrants who hailed from their home communities.[182] Although contacts of this sort must have been useful, they were imperfect substitutes for more organized networks of communication and migration beyond the purely local level. Without organizations more comparable to journeymen's associations, craftsmen in the Roman world would not have had ready access to up-to-date information about labor market conditions in nearby cities and would not have been able to travel in response to unanticipated or periodic changes in labor market conditions elsewhere as easily as could those in later historical periods. Contacts based on chain migration were also poor substitutes for the kinds of organized support structures – easy access to credit and the like – that gave early modern journeymen some assurance of being able to provide for themselves wherever they landed, and not just in cities that housed immigrant communities from their home regions.

Thanks to the combined impact of tight markets and comparatively underdeveloped institutions and organizations, entrepreneurs in the Roman world were confronted by transaction costs that were high from a comparative historical perspective – high enough that they had the

---

[180] Noy 2000: 89–90 and 113–14 compiles some of the evidence testifying to migration on the part of skilled workers to Rome itself, and at p. 89 makes brief mention of some of the information problems that could affect such migration.
[181] *Acts* 18:1–4.   [182] On these associations and their functions in Roman cities, see Verboven 2011.

potential to affect an artisan's ability to recruit workers as necessary on the spot market. Those least affected were artisans who could recruit unskilled or semi-skilled workers, since the low-skilled segments of the labor market were in all probability overstocked, especially from the Augustan period onward. Builders belong to this category, but so do fullers, since some stages in their process – soaping and rinsing in particular – depended largely on brute labor rather than skill.[183] For that reason, fullers could hire relatively untrained workers in the expectation that they would pick up the basics on the job. Some of the large fulleries in Ostia and Rome were equipped with multiple treading stalls, each of which would have been manned by an unskilled worker, and since these facilities lack housing for resident slave workforces, much of the necessary labor was probably provided by casual employees whom the proprietor could recruit and let go as necessary.[184] Even weavers could employ some unskilled or semi-skilled labor, since they often required the help of assistants to manage their warps and to take care of other sundry tasks in the shop.[185] More broadly, the more artisans focused on producing low-end consumer goods for customers who valued low prices rather than quality products, the more they could probably make do with unskilled help.[186] Because unskilled labor was abundant, artisans in this group could find workers with relative ease, even in conditions of elevated demand, and workers themselves lacked the leverage to apply pressure to their employers by holding up production; the costs of search and enforcement were therefore low, and artisans could recruit workers as necessary on short-term contracts to adapt their output to prevailing market conditions.

Most artisans, however, depended more heavily on skilled labor than they did on unskilled or semi-skilled help. This was most true of artisans who manufactured bespoke goods, since the emphasis clients placed on product quality made it necessary for artisans to employ highly skilled help, especially when they worked on valuable raw materials or semi-finished goods that belonged to clients or to other artisans.[187] Yet even those who produced relatively simple and standardized objects often required the

---

[183] Flohr 2011; Flohr 2013: 96–121 and 242–87.
[184] On the layout of these fulleries, see Flohr 2013: 72–84.
[185] Wipszycka 1965: 63–4; Freu 2011: 37–8.
[186] Schwarz 1992: 179–207 discusses both the different grades of skill among the workforce of early modern London, and the degree to which some trades were able to rely on unskilled or semi-skilled help.
[187] Styles 1995: 116 makes an analogous point about subcontracting in the urban market of early modern London. See S. D. Martin 2001 for comments on the risks incurred by Roman artisans who worked on precious materials, and for comments on the liabilities they could incur if something

assistance of skilled workers with training and experience in the production processes specific to their trades. The funerary altar commissioned by Atimetus illustrates that point nicely. The altar's right face depicts the freedman Epaphra assisting Atimetus as a striker (Figure 3.2) – a role that could not be performed adequately by an unskilled or semi-skilled assistant. Instead, a good striker needed to have essentially the same knowledge of the process as the smith himself if they were to operate together efficiently as a team.[188]

For artisans who, like Atimetus, depended on skilled help, high transaction costs in the market for skilled labor were much more problematic. Simply put, these costs meant that artisans were not necessarily able to find additional help on relatively short notice if they wished to expand their output to take advantage of favorable market conditions without incurring additional fixed costs. Some sense of the frustration produced by this conundrum is captured in a letter from Hermoplis in Roman Egypt, which reflects comparable transaction cost problems that could arise in estate-based textile production. The letter is part of a larger archive documenting the personal and professional affairs of the *strategos* Apollonios and his family. In the letter, Apollonios' mother Eudaimonis describes a seasonal bottleneck in the local supply of labor. Charged with overseeing textile production on Apollonios' estate, Eudaimonis found that the estate's slavewomen could not keep pace with the required level of output and sought to hire slaves from other nearby estates to supplement her own workforce. Ultimately, however, she failed, seemingly because her neighbors were facing a high-enough seasonal demand for labor of their own that they would not hire out their slaves even at premium rates. As Eudaimonis put it, "I cannot find women to work with us, for they are all working for their own mistresses. For our people went round the whole town offering more pay."[189]

---

went wrong, which in and of themselves provided strong incentives for recruiting appropriately skilled help.

[188] See Watson 2000: 33–4, albeit with reference to more recent periods.

[189] *C. Pap. Jud.* II 442. In the past, this document has been interpreted differently: the second clause has been translated as "for our townsfolk went round the town demanding more pay," and the women to whom Eudaimonis refers have correspondingly been identified as free wage workers striking for better terms of employment. See van Minnen 1987: 62 n. 109 for the relevant bibliography; Aubert 2001: 107 is the most recent writer to defend this view. The better explanation is that the women in question were slaves, as suggested by the statement that they were working with their mistresses and that Eudaimonis was unable to persuade the slaveholders to hire out their slaves despite the promise of high wages (van Minnen 1987: 62–3; cf. the editorial comments of Tcherikover and Fuks in *C. Pap. Jud*, vol. 2., 245–6).

Obviously, the situation described by Eudaimonis in her letter does not offer a precise parallel for conditions in larger urban labor markets. Nor does it necessarily reflect conditions that were typical in Hermoplis itself, since it was written near the end of the Jewish revolt of 115–117 CE, which may have affected the local economy in unknown ways. Those caveats aside, however, the problems encountered by Eudaimonis would have been uncomfortably familiar to urban artisans in antiquity who hoped to respond to elevated levels of demand by recruiting additional help on the spot market. Without access to organizations designed to ensure an adequate supply of skilled labor in high season, many Roman artisans may have found themselves, like Eudaimonis, unable to secure the extra help they required without paying exorbitant wages, even if they invested considerable time and effort in contacting members of their personal networks.

It is conditions of precisely this nature that provide a context for understanding why artisans in the Roman world may have sought whenever possible to use manumission in exchange for *operae* as a means of hoarding the labor of skilled workers. Because so much of their work was time sensitive – especially in bespoke segments of the market, where clients who could not be accommodated were likely to move on to another supplier – artisans found it necessary to exploit fleeting opportunities as and when they arose.[190] Tight markets for skilled labor, however, meant that artisans simply could not count on recruiting skilled help when they required it, particularly given the comparatively underdeveloped state of institutions and organizations that may have otherwise served to mitigate transaction costs. By contrast, labor-hoarding strategies based on the manumission of slaves in exchange for labor obligations offered a reliable alternative to the spot market, even if slaves and freedmen were more expensive to employ in the long run. Through the selective use of manumission, an artisan could limit his fixed costs, perhaps by gradually manumitting slaves who had served him for several years and acquiring new slaves as his business expanded. At the same time, he assured himself continued access to skilled labor that he could deploy as and when he required it, and – thanks to the power that most slaveholders continued to wield over their former slaves even after manumission – he could generally expect his freedmen to honor their obligations. The nature of urban labor markets in the Roman world therefore goes far toward explaining the apparent popularity of manumission among artisans in antiquity and

---

[190] Sonenscher 1989: 138–9.

toward establishing the intrinsic value of *operae* for at least certain kinds of Roman slaveholders.

Manumission, markets, and constraints on intensive growth

The preceding analysis shows that the labor-hoarding strategies devised by artisans in antiquity can serve as a proxy for the overall level of integration attained by the Roman economy in the early Empire. Artisans manumitted slaves not simply to respond to seasonal and uncertain demand but also because skilled labor markets were tight enough in comparative perspective that it was difficult for them to respond to changing demand by hiring short-term help on the spot market. The fact that artisans in Rome itself manumitted slaves in exchange for *operae* with some regularity indicates that labor markets in the ancient world simply did not reach a level of performance commensurate with that achieved by comparable markets in the early modern period – even in the empire's Italian heartland, where those markets must have been thicker and better-developed than elsewhere.

The tendency of artisans to hoard labor, however, not only reflected the nature of urban product and labor markets but also potentially affected them in ways that were inimical to sustained growth in productivity. Their impact was likely twofold: not only did they inhibit the expansion of demand by limiting the purchasing power of numerous skilled freedmen but they also indirectly perpetuated the Roman world's tight markets for skilled labor.

In the first place, artisans who hoarded the labor of freedmen directly obstructed the development of thick market externalities that could foster growth by limiting the extent of the market for basic services and for undifferentiated or populuxe goods in Roman cities. This was a direct consequence of the nature of manumission in exchange for labor obligations. Manumission altered a slave's status so fundamentally – above all, by making it possible for them to produce freeborn children – that many undoubtedly leapt at the chance to secure it, even when doing so meant undertaking extensive labor obligations to their former masters.[191] Those obligations, however, imposed a steep cost: they depressed the ability of freed slaves to generate income or to accumulate capital for several years after they were freed, since much of their productivity continued to be appropriated by their former masters – especially, one imagines,

---

[191] Bradley 1987, esp. 81–2 and 139–43.

during times of the year when demand was high and when opportunities for freed slaves to find remunerative work were most abundant. As a consequence, freed craftsmen had less access to disposable income than their freeborn counterparts so long as they still owed a portion of their labor to their patrons and were thus less capable of purchasing goods or services beyond those required for immediate subsistence. Unless slaveholding artisans themselves increased their own consumption of goods and services in direct proportion to the benefits they gained by exploiting the labor of their freedmen, neither consumer demand nor further opportunities for growth deriving from thick markets and increased specialization were likely to have expanded as much as they might have had the profits of urban production been distributed more equitably.

Second, and more importantly, the tendency of artisans to hoard freedmen's labor also possibly limited prospects for growth by curtailing opportunities for training among the freeborn. On one level, artisans may have been less inclined to accept apprentices when they relied heavily on the labor of slaves and freedmen. Although apprentices and freedmen hardly occupied the same niche in the economy of a given workshop – most freedmen had mastered advanced skills before being manumitted, whereas apprentices usually had not yet acquired extensive proficiency – many freedmen undoubtedly passed through a period of training at the hands of their masters while still enslaved. During that process, slaveholding artisans presumably had little need for the services of freeborn apprentices and may have been reluctant to undertake the responsibility of training one unless they felt impelled to do so because of family ties or other social obligations, particularly since apprentices were more likely than slaves to become direct competitors in the immediate future.[192] On another level, the preference artisans exhibited for hoarded labor may have discouraged household heads from seeking training for their sons by reducing the perceived likelihood that those sons would be able to find work easily, especially given the apparent absence in the Roman world of organizations capable of circulating information about labor market conditions over a wide geographical area.[193] This concern was most pressing for heads of households that hovered on the brink of material comfort, and who were

---

[192] See especially Epstein 1998: 688–93. Cf. Lancy 2012.
[193] On the basic coordination problem created by intensive specialization, see Chapter 2. On the importance of institutions capable of integrating markets over long distances, see Grantham 1999: 199–201 and 217–22. Grantham is interested chiefly in product markets, but the same logic holds in the case of labor markets.

therefore likely to be averse to risk even if they were nominally capable of absorbing the high opportunity costs associated with apprenticeship; the possibility that their investments in the human capital of their sons would not yield commensurate returns tipped the balance in favor of foregoing training in the first place. Those with better access to resources would have been more willing to invest in apprenticeships for their children, especially when they had sufficient capital and connections to ease those sons into careers as independent producers in their own right. Yet since household heads of the former category were almost certainly more numerous than those of the latter, it seems probable that many chose not to secure training for their sons even when they had the means, and in so doing perpetuated the scarcity of skilled labor typical of the economy as a whole.

By affecting opportunities for training among the freeborn in these ways, the labor-hoarding strategies of artisans arguably pushed the labor markets of the Roman world toward a low-skill equilibrium trap with no clear exit. Because these strategies decreased incentives on the part of household heads of marginal prosperity to invest in the skills of their sons, they worked to reinforce the scarcity of skilled labor responsible for the high transaction costs that prompted artisans to adopt them in the first place. An escape route from this self-reinforcing cycle could only be opened up by the factors so important to de Vries' model of growth in the long eighteenth century – namely, changes in household consumption patterns that were capable not only of producing market conditions that supported increased returns to specialization but also of sending the necessary signals to individuals that they were likely to realize those returns by investing in training. As we shall see in Chapter 4, however, such changes do not appear to have taken place in antiquity.

The artisan household and the Roman economy

The funerary monument erected in memory of Mecia Dynata offers a rare and valuable snapshot of a family that was embedded firmly in Rome's artisanal economy. The distinguishing feature of the monument is its lengthy (if highly abbreviated) inscription, consisting of two main clauses. The first informs the reader that the monument was commissioned on behalf of Dynata by the members of her natal family and in accordance with the terms of her will:

> To the Sacred Shades. To Mecia Dynata, daughter of Lucius. In accordance with her will and because of a gift specified in one of its clauses [the following people dedicated the monument]: her father Lucius Ermagoras, son of Lucius; her mother Mecia Flora, a wool-comber; her brother Lucius Mecius Rusticus, son of Lucius, a wool-worker in the quarter [of the goddess] Fors Fortuna.

The second clause details several pieces of property that Dynata bequeathed to her parents and to her brother.[1]

Dynata's inscription is notable primarily because it illustrates the complexity of the household strategies that artisans and entrepreneurs at Rome were capable of crafting for themselves and for other members of their households. By providing information about the occupations pursued by Dynata's family members, it suggests that members of artisan households in Rome could and did take advantage of a wide range of economic opportunities that presented themselves in the urban market. Dynata's father unfortunately chose not to name his own occupation in the inscription, but her mother and brother both seem to have pursued careers of their

---

[1] *CIL* 6.9493. This is a vexed inscription, primarily because its extensive abbreviations can produce variant readings. Here, I largely follow Mommsen's editorial notes. The first clause, which I have translated above, is the least problematic. It reads as follows: "Dis Man(ibus) / Meciae L(uci) f(iliae) Dynat(a)e / ex testam(ento) et dona(tione) t(estamenti) c(ausa) / L(ucius) Mecius L(uci) f(ilius) Ermagoras / pater Mecia Flora mater / tonstrix L(ucius) Mecius L(uci) f(ilius) Rusticus / frater lanarius ad vic(um) Fort(is) / Fortun(ae)."

own: her mother Flora worked as a wool-comber (possibly in a business based in the household itself), and her brother Rusticus not only identified himself as a wool worker but also laid claim to a shop address somewhere in the vicinity of the temple of Fors Fortuna – a detail implying that he was an independent artisan in his own right. Beyond providing insight into occupations of members of Dynata's family, the inscription also demonstrates that members of households in this particular socioeconomic stratum were capable of using complex legal instruments to manage or even reconfigure their property rights and the formal relationships that bound them together, all while maintaining strong reciprocal ties. The key detail is that Dynata possessed substantial property of her own, which she distributed to her family members according to the terms of a relatively complex will. While her use of a will to allocate property is interesting in and of itself, more significant is the fact that she held property in her own right at all. Since her father was still alive at the time of her death, one would expect that she would have fallen under his *potestas*, in which case she would have possessed no property rights of her own; that she instead appears to have been legally independent (*sui iuris*) and capable of owning property therefore indicates that she had been freed from the *potestas* of her father. Her father may have transferred her formally into the power of a husband by arranging for her to marry *in manu*, and her husband may have subsequently died, leaving her legally independent. Alternatively, her father may have legally emancipated her so that she could benefit personally from the terms of a will – probably the will of a wealthy husband, who bequeathed to her the assets that are cataloged in the second clause of the inscription, and which she herself then distributed to the members of her own natal family.[2] Since marriage *in manu* was mostly obsolete by the late Republic, the latter possibility is more likely, and in that sense the inscription reveals a high degree of legal literacy and sophistication in Rome's working population.[3]

By offering clues about the occupations of Dynata's family members and about the sophistication of the legal strategies they employed, Dynata's inscription evokes questions concerning the nature of the relationships between work, the household, and the family in Rome's artisan economy.

---

[2] Gardner 1998: 104–13 discusses potential motives for emancipation, including the desire to permit a child to benefit from the terms of a will.

[3] By the late Republic, marriage *in manu* seems to have given way mostly to marriage *sine manu*, in which a wife remained in the *potestas* of her own father (or grandfather) until she became *sui iuris* upon his death. For brief remarks on the chronology of this development, see Treggiari 1991: 32–6 and Dixon 1992: 41–4.

It also evokes questions about the extent to which artisans manipulated those relationships in navigating the seasonal and uncertain demand characteristic of urban product markets in antiquity and, by extension, about the aggregate impact exerted by individual artisans' household strategies on the Roman world's urban economies. The information communicated by the inscription therefore intersects nicely with recent trends in the historiography of the Roman family, which has increasingly focused on the strategies implemented by the members of individual households and on how those strategies affected the performance of the Roman economy as a whole. In particular, recent contributors to this historiography have stressed two main points. First, they have noted that households in antiquity – which tended to be conceptualized by Romans themselves as "nuclear family plus" households consisting primarily of parents, their children, and their slaves, and which functioned primarily as units of coresidence and economic cooperation – could be adaptable structures and that their members could tailor their strategies of economic production and inheritance to meet the specific demographic and economic needs of the group.[4] Second, they have also stressed that the strategies of individuals, although highly adaptable, were nevertheless constrained by various asymmetries of authority and gender that structured their relationships with other household members and created strong expectations about their roles and behavior.[5]

While this work has certainly not neglected the households of working people in the Roman world's urban environments, much of it has tended to focus primarily on the strategies of individuals from elite or peasant households. Only recently have Roman historians begun to focus explicitly on the complicated question of how household members made decisions about allocating their time and labor in urban environments.[6] For that reason, and in spite of the current trends in the historiography, we are still in the early stages of exploring both the household strategies pursued by members of the Roman world's urban population and the potential effects that those strategies wrought on the economy as a whole. To cite just the most obvious example, the inscription of Mecia Dynata strongly implies that her brother Rusticus ran a business of his own – a detail that runs counter to the common view that artisans often employed their sons

---

[4] The fundamental study in this respect remains Saller 1994, which concentrates chiefly on strategies of property transmission. On strategies of labor allocation, see Erdkamp 2005: 55–105 on peasant households and Groen-Vallinga 2013, who discusses women's work in urban contexts by drawing on the adaptive family economy model proposed by Wall 1986.

[5] See especially Saller 2003 and 2007.   [6] E.g., Saller 2003; Groen-Vallinga 2013; Holleran 2013.

personally (a problem to which I return in much more detail below). In this chapter, I therefore seek to refine our knowledge of household strategies among urban working populations by addressing these issues more explicitly. I do so by concentrating on the roles played within artisan households by two key members of the "nuclear family plus" model of the household: sons and wives. As we shall see, the roles assigned to sons in the family economy reflect artisans' efforts to respond to the challenges created by the Roman world's seasonal and uncertain product markets. Wives, on the other hand, found their roles shaped strongly by preferences rooted in strong ideologies of gender, which had profound implications for the Roman world's ability to sustain intensive economic growth after the end of the late Republic.

Roman artisans and their sons

When Richard Wall proposed his model of the adaptive family economy, stressing simply that families could be expected to "attempt to maximize their economic well-being by diversifying the employments of family members," he broke away from an earlier strand of scholarship that conceptualized the household not just as a unit of consumption and production but also as one in which household members devoted much of their labor to a single and dominant productive enterprise – whether the cultivation of a farm or the operation of a manufacturing or retail business.[7] According to this older "family economy" model of the household, the head of a household employed its other members directly whenever possible. The family enterprise therefore gave the household much of its coherence – so much so that if individual members could not be employed within the household, they tended to leave it.[8] As applied to urban households, this model systematized a long-held view that artisans and other urban entrepreneurs naturally relied heavily on the labor of family members, especially sons.[9]

Following in Wall's footsteps, other historians of early modern Europe have shown that it was not necessarily typical for artisans and businessmen to employ their own sons. Instead, fathers were more likely to establish their sons in careers outside of the household, whether in their own line of work or in a different trade. For sons, the typical career trajectory involved an apprenticeship in the workshop of one or more artisans, followed by a

[7] Wall 1986, esp. 265. [8] E.g., see Medick 1976, esp. 297; Tilly and Scott 1987, esp. 21–2.
[9] Ehmer 2001: 189.

period in which they worked for wages as journeymen (often in multiple establishments), and finally by establishment as master artisans in their own right, often with the help of resources they inherited from their own families or acquired through marriage. Much of the evidence supporting this view is indirect but compelling. Several studies, for example, show that family continuity was often weak among the members of any given guild or trade corporation. In spite of the fact that the membership profiles of guilds and trade corporations differed tremendously from one geographical and chronological context to the next, sons of established masters in a given trade rarely constituted a majority of newly admitted members; in most cases, they were outnumbered by the sons of artisans who belonged to other corporations. Other historians emphasize that artisans were much more likely to rely on the labor of apprentices and journeymen recruited from outside the household itself than on the labor of their own family members, even when their sons were trained in the same trade they practiced themselves.[10]

These revised views of artisan households in the early modern period have not yet been taken up in detail by ancient historians, who remain influenced by the older "family economy" approach. The work of Roger Bagnall and Bruce Frier is a case in point. In their groundbreaking study of the census returns from Roman Egypt, Bagnall and Frier drew a parallel between the economic structure of the households recorded in their evidence and the structure of households based on the "family economy" model by observing that "'inherited' professions are not uncommon in premodern societies; the household is conceived as a single economic unit, with sons succeeding to their fathers."[11]

As Bagnall and Frier noted, however, the Egyptian census records do not necessarily support the view that sons in Roman Egypt typically worked alongside and succeeded to their fathers. There are a number of census documents recording households in which co-resident adult males (typically fathers and sons) shared the same occupation, but these must be read alongside other documents showing that adult sons could just as easily remain in their natal households even though they did not practice the

---

[10] For a recent survey of the literature, see Farr 2000: 244–51. For more detailed discussion, see Ehmer 1984 and 2001; Sonenscher 1989: 99–243; Cerutti 1991. Finally, see Knotter 1994: 40–3 for a more general criticism of the utility of the "family economy" as a concept for understanding the organization of preindustrial craft production.

[11] Bagnall and Frier 1994: 73. Dixon 2001a: 124 likewise assumes that the transmission of occupational skills (and ultimately of workshops) from father to son was the norm in the Roman world. Cf. the view of Finley 1999: 19, originally written in the 1970s, and Tran 2013: 161–4.

same trades as their fathers. Bagnall and Frier ultimately concluded that their sample was too small to permit easy generalizations about which kind of household organization was more common than the other.[12] Additionally, there is no guarantee that co-resident males worked alongside one another even when they worked in the same trade, since one can easily imagine that sons in such households spent some or even much of their time working for wages in the shops of other artisans (and perhaps even engaging in seasonal migration to do so).

Inscriptions from the Latin West present comparable problems of interpretation. The inscriptions of professional associations point to a degree of family continuity in particular trades, since fathers and sons sometimes appear together in membership lists, and honorific inscriptions permit historians to trace the careers of multiple members of the same family who became magistrates of individual *collegia*.[13] Family continuity in a given trade, however, is not the same thing as family continuity in a business, and since most members of professional associations were likely men who ran their own enterprises, those fathers and sons who held contemporaneous memberships in the same association were arguably proprietors of separate workshops rather than co-workers.[14] Moreover, some funerary inscriptions either demonstrate or strongly imply that sons did not find employment in the business or workshops of their fathers. While the funerary monument dedicated to Mecia Flora offers one example, the inscription commissioned by the freedman Lucius Maelius Thamyrus is more explicit: it demonstrates that although Thamyrus himself earned his living as an artisan who manufactured metal tableware

---

[12] Bagnall and Frier 1994: 72–3. Their most striking example (*BGU* I 115 i) documents a large household that was composed of twenty closely related kin (the declarant, his wife, their children and grandchildren, and the children of the declarant's deceased brother) along with seven other peripheral kin (mostly spouses). Although the declarant and one of his sons shared an occupation (in this case, weaving), one of his other sons was a goldsmith. The sons of his deceased brother were, respectively, a cloth-beater, a goldsmith, and a laborer. While we cannot rule out the possibility that there were close business relationships between the two weavers and the two goldsmiths, the overall picture is one of heterogeneity: clearly, neither of the two nuclear family units that belonged to this household formed a discrete family enterprise. Other interesting documents include a case in which a father and his co-resident son worked, respectively, as a scribe and a doctor (*P. Giss.* 43), and a case in which one of two brothers who lived together worked as a doctor, while the other worked as a turner (*P. Hamb.* I 60).

[13] Burford 1972: 162–3; Meiggs 1973: 323; Tran 2006: 474–8. But cf. Joshel 1977: 410–11 and 623–4, who catalogs a number of inscriptions in which family members practiced different occupations.

[14] The diary of Jacques-Louis Ménétra offers the best comparandum from the early modern period: he, his father, and at least one of his uncles were all glaziers and members of the glaziers' corporation in Paris; they also ran workshops of their own. (Ménétra 1986, esp. 168–9.)

(a *vascularius*), his son pursued a career as a scribe in the offices of the curule aediles and quaestors.[15]

When read against recent work on fathers and sons in early modern Europe, these ambiguities in our evidence encourage us to revisit the question of whether or not artisans in the Roman world regularly employed their own sons, especially if the answer has relevance for our understanding of the Roman economy's structure. In what follows, I begin by exploring two lines of evidence that bear indirectly on this question. The first consists of the many references to apprenticeship that appear in our legal, literary, and epigraphic sources and the second of Roman funerary inscriptions commissioned by or on behalf of artisans. Together, these lines of evidence indicate that artisans and retailers in the Roman world employed their own sons infrequently, and that they generally sought instead to establish those sons in careers of their own. I then consider the factors responsible for this pattern, as well as its implications for our understanding of the Roman economy more broadly. Here, I show that the rarity with which fathers employed their own sons can be understood primarily as a product of the seasonal and uncertain demand typical in urban product markets. Unless fathers possessed especially valuable business-related capital that gave them an incentive to transmit their enterprises to their sons, seasonal and uncertain demand tended to limit their own need for regular and permanent help and to encourage them to diversify their households' sources of income. Finally, I suggest that this pattern builds upon some of the conclusions advanced in previous chapters about market integration in the Roman Empire, namely by confirming that product and labor markets remained thin relative to those of early modern Europe even if artisans clearly did have an interest in ensuring that their sons were productively employed.

Artisans, sons, and apprenticeship

Embedded in our ancient sources is a considerable amount of information on the importance of apprenticeship as a means for transmitting craft skills from one generation to the next. By itself, this information cannot tell us whether or not it was more common for fathers to arrange apprenticeships for their sons in other workshops than to train them personally, particularly since our sources say little about sons who were trained at home. That said, this information remains significant because

---

[15] *CIL* 6.1818.

the early modern evidence suggests that apprenticeship can serve as a proxy indicator for the willingness of artisans and other entrepreneurs to establish sons in careers of their own. Artisans in the early modern period apprenticed their sons to other craftsmen with some frequency, whether to men who practiced different trades or to those who specialized in the same craft as they did themselves. Those who apprenticed their sons to craftsmen in different trades did so in the expectation of launching their sons on independent careers. Likewise, although some fathers who apprenticed their sons to craftsmen in their own trades undoubtedly intended to employ those sons personally once their training was complete, these seem to have been in the minority; instead, even fathers who apprenticed their sons to other artisans in the same trade often hoped that those sons would establish themselves as independent entrepreneurs or wage earners in their own right.[16] As I suggest in the following paragraphs, the ancient evidence for apprenticeship, though far from comprehensive, is at least consistent with the early modern pattern. Not only was apprenticeship widespread, it was also used to secure training for sons by fathers who operated their own enterprises, and who therefore could have trained their sons personally – perhaps as the first step in preparing those sons for careers of their own.

The strongest indication that apprenticeship was a familiar institution in the Roman world is the mention of apprentices or apprenticeship in several different categories of evidence.[17] A handful of opinions preserved in the *Digest* indicates that apprenticeship was common enough to attract attention from the Roman jurists, who were interested in the legal problems that arose when apprentices were mistreated or represented their instructors in transactions with clients.[18] Some of these opinions clearly reflect cases in which slaveholders contracted with artisans to have slaves instructed in a particular craft, but others just as clearly refer to freeborn apprentices. The

---

[16] This, at any rate, seems to be the implication of a low degree of continuity in most trades (see the scholarship cited above, n. 10). Here, I necessarily simplify for the purposes of generalization what was, in reality, a social process that exhibited a wide range of variation from place to place, time to time, and profession to profession. De Munck and Soly 2007: 18–20 offer a recent overview of the kinds of factors that were relevant when artisans made decisions about the careers of their sons; as they note, much additional research will be necessary to flesh out our understanding of general patterns. For a recent contribution to this debate, see Harding 2009, who notes not only that fathers rarely trained their own sons in most trades in medieval and early modern London, but also that they rarely passed down their businesses to their sons.

[17] The most accessible introduction to the evidence remains Bradley 1991. See now Tran 2013: 147–85, who offers particularly strong coverage of the epigraphic evidence from the Latin West.

[18] For brief discussions of the most important pieces of legal evidence, see Bradley 1991: 113 and Du Plessis 2012: 57–60 and 67–70.

most famous of these is Julian's discussion of the remedies available to a
father whose son had been blinded in one eye when the shoemaker to
whom he had been apprenticed punished him by striking him with a last,[19]
but Ulpian too may have had freeborn apprentices in mind when discussing a (possibly hypothetical) case in which a fuller left his business in the
hands of several apprentices while he himself went abroad.[20]

Periodic references to apprenticeship also exist in the texts of literary
authors from the first two centuries CE, who – like the Roman jurists –
appear to take for granted the notion that both slaves and freeborn boys
were often apprenticed to artisans. Cicero mentions several apprentices
who worked alongside the building contractor Cillo, whom he had hired to
work on his brother's estate near Arpinum, albeit in a context which
suggests that they were slaves.[21] Vitruvius, on the other hand, believed
that freeborn Romans regularly learned architecture (if poorly) as apprentices in the Augustan period; such, at any rate, seems to be the thrust of his
complaint that architects no longer followed the example of the ancients,
who transmitted their knowledge only to their sons or other close relatives.[22] Apprenticeship also appears in works of fiction or satire: in
Petronius' *Satyricon*, the freedman Echion, an artisan specializing in woo-
len textiles (a *centonarius*), contemplates having his son trained as a lawyer,
an auctioneer, or a barber, and Lucian of Samosata based a significant part
of one of his satires on his own brief career as a stonemason's apprentice in
his uncle's workshop.[23]

Finally, several dozen pieces of documentary evidence also refer directly
to apprentices or apprenticeship. Some funerary inscriptions from the
Latin West were commissioned by or on behalf of young men who had
served apprenticeships in the workshops of artisans and entrepreneurs;
some died before completing their training, while others outlived and then
memorialized their instructors.[24] More interesting are the apprenticeship
documents from Roman Egypt. About forty documents produced between
the first and third centuries CE survive; they include not only notices of
apprenticeship filed with municipal authorities for tax purposes but also
actual apprenticeship agreements.[25] As Christel Freu has pointed out, the
sheer number of surviving apprenticeship documents is itself impressive:

---

[19] Julian, quoted by Ulpian at *Dig.* 9.2.5.3 (and cf. his remarks at *Dig.* 19.2.13.4).
[20] Ulpian, *Dig.* 14.3.5.10.   [21] Cic., *QFr.* 3.1.3.   [22] Vitr., *De arch.* 6.pr.6.
[23] Petron. *Sat.* 46 and Luc. *Somn.* 1–4.
[24] Tran 2011: 128–9 presents some particularly clear examples. Cf. Tran 2013: 169–70.
[25] For a general overview, see Bradley 1991: 107–12 and Freu 2011. Bergamasco 1995 offers more in-
depth discussion.

by comparison, only about a hundred marriage contracts survive from the same period.[26] While this could simply be an accident of preservation, it may just as easily indicate that young men (and the occasional young woman) who learned craft skills normally did so as apprentices, and not in their parents' workshops.

The demographic realities of urban living ensured that many freeborn young men would have needed to acquire craft skills through apprenticeship if they acquired them at all, for the simple reason that approximately one-third of freeborn boys in the Roman world may not have had living fathers by the time they became old enough to start learning a trade in earnest.[27] A number of the Egyptian documents drive that point home by demonstrating that a young man's mother or guardian was often compelled to arrange his apprenticeship, presumably because his father had died.[28] That said, several pieces of evidence imply that fathers consciously chose to place their sons as apprentices in the workshops of others, even though they may have been capable of training them personally. Petronius' characterization of the fictional Echion is an obvious example, but Julian's discussion of the apprentice blinded by his instructor possibly fits this pattern too: at the very least, it is clear that the boy's father arranged the apprenticeship,[29] perhaps hoping to establish his son in an independent career. Lucian's account of his own brief apprenticeship is equally illuminating. The story is so heavily layered with sophisticated literary allusions that it is impossible to disentangle fiction or embellishment from genuine autobiographical details, but Lucian seems to have been interested in constructing a plausible depiction of family life in an artisanal or entrepreneurial household. For that reason, his portrayal of his father's approach to the question of Lucian's own career speaks to an outlook that was probably common among households of this type.[30] Two aspects of that portrayal deserve emphasis. First, Lucian depicts his father's deliberations not as something exceptional, but rather as a typical

---

[26] Freu 2011: 29 n. 12.

[27] See Saller 1994: 52, table 3.1.e, which suggests that only 63 percent of young men had a living father when they reached the age of fifteen.

[28] See the data compiled by Bergamasco 1995: 162–7, in which it is clear that some of the freeborn apprentices in the Egyptian documents were under the care of their mothers or of male relatives other than their fathers when they were bound to instructors.

[29] In fact, the central issue in the case is what kind of legal action a father could bring against the artisan to whom he had apprenticed his son.

[30] On the literary quality of Lucian's autobiographical writings, see Humble and Sidwell 2006. C. Jones 1986: 9–10 argues that the details of the account are at least plausible in spite of the account's artifice.

family event, which featured considerable discussion between his father and various family members and friends about what occupation would be most suitable for his son. Second, Lucian attributes to his father a clear belief that apprenticeship was an important first step toward establishing Lucian in an independent career that would provide the household as a whole with additional income.[31]

Unfortunately, neither Julian nor Lucian specifies whether the fathers who feature in their accounts operated their own enterprises. It is therefore not clear that we can read these anecdotes as reflections of strategies that were typical among artisans or entrepreneurs who had the option to train and employ their sons personally. Other pieces of evidence can partially dispel that ambiguity by demonstrating that artisans too may have placed their sons as apprentices in other workshops with some regularity. Echion's deliberations about his son's future are especially interesting, since they imply that it was not unusual for a successful artisan to consider having his son trained by another and in a different profession.[32] No less valuable are several Egyptian apprenticeship documents reflecting the arrangements made by three weavers in Oxyrhynchus on behalf of their sons or other relatives. As we saw in Chapter 2, the weaver Pausiris had at least three sons, all of whom he apprenticed to fellow weavers in Oxyrhynchus during the first century CE; he also accepted the nephew of one of these weavers as an apprentice of his own.[33] Likewise, Pausiris' contemporary Tryphon son of Dionysios helped his mother arrange an apprenticeship for his younger brother in another weaver's workshop, in 36 CE, and secured apprenticeships for his own two sons in the enterprises of colleagues some years later, in 54 CE and in 66 CE.[34] Although these documents say little about the intentions of these men, it is not unreasonable to believe that they, just like Lucian's father and the fictional Echion, saw apprenticeship as a necessary step in their efforts to secure employment for young men in their charge outside of their own households.[35]

---

[31] Luc. *Somn.* 1–2.   [32] Petron. *Sat.* 46, with the comments of Mayer 2012: 32–3.

[33] The apprenticeships of Pausiris' three sons are documented in *P. Mich.* III 170, *P. Wisc.* I 4, and *P. Mich.* III 172; for his agreement to accept the weaver Epinikos' nephew as an apprentice, see *P. Mich.* III 171.

[34] The apprenticeship contracts of Tryphon's brother Onnophris and his younger son Thoonis are documented in *P. Oxy.* II 322 and *P. Oxy.* II 275, respectively. The apprenticeship of his elder son is known from a tax receipt, *P. Oxy.* II 310.

[35] I deal with this point in much more detail below.

The Roman occupational inscriptions and patterns of inheritance
in artisan households

Although the qualitative evidence for apprenticeship in the Roman world shows that artisan fathers certainly did not feel compelled to train or employ their sons personally, on its own it cannot reveal whether it was more typical for sons to strike out in independent careers or to remain in the family workshop (or even to return to the family workshop after serving an apprenticeship elsewhere). Only quantitative evidence can be used to address these issues satisfactorily, and ultimately only the funerary inscriptions from Rome offer a sizeable-enough body of data to permit quantification, in spite of the limitations of the inscriptions as sources of evidence.

The surviving funerary inscriptions from Rome can provide a crude sense of the familial and household strategies typical among Roman artisans, albeit in a roundabout way – by generating insight into patterns of succession and inheritance in urban households. Broadly speaking, Romans not only expected that a deceased's formal heirs would assume the primary obligation for performing the *sacra* or funerary rites on his or her behalf but also conceptualized the act of commemoration both as an opportunity to display their own *pietas* and as an important element of the *sacra* themselves. For that reason, even though the individuals who commissioned the tens of thousands of funerary inscriptions found within Rome itself did so for a complex cluster of reasons in which sentiment and affection obviously mattered,[36] they were often motivated just as strongly by cultural and legal expectations concerning succession. Several scholars have accordingly concluded that we can reconstruct approximate patterns of succession in Roman households by analyzing the patterns of commemoration visible in these inscriptions – that is, by assessing how frequently the deceased were commemorated by individuals belonging to one of several different categories of kin and non-kin relations.[37]

Because the decisions household heads made about succession were influenced by numerous individual factors – legal, cultural, economic, and personal – those decisions need not always have been closely linked with other decisions they made about their sons' careers. On the other hand, since it is difficult to imagine factors that would have prompted men who employed their sons in their own enterprises to name individuals other than those sons as primary heirs, we can anticipate that there was a

---

[36] Good introductions to the various social expectations mediating commemoration can be found in Joshel 1992: 16–24, in Bodel 2001b: 30–9, and in Saller 2001.
[37] Saller and Shaw 1984, esp. 126–8. Cf. Meyer 1990: 76–8.

correlation between the household strategies they pursued during their lifetimes and the dispositions they made in their final testaments. In the following pages, I explore that correlation by analyzing patterns of commemoration in those Roman funerary inscriptions in which at least one individual is identified by his or her occupation. As I demonstrate, these inscriptions provide indirect evidence that Roman entrepreneurs – particularly artisans and retailers – generally chose to establish their sons in independent careers rather than to employ them in their own businesses. They do so primarily by demonstrating that artisans and retailers were unlikely to appoint their sons as their heirs. This is true even if the freeborn are underrepresented in the inscriptions relative to freed slaves, who were perhaps more likely to subscribe to the "epigraphic habit" and to commission inscriptions than the freeborn, but less likely to leave behind grown sons when they died. As a group, the artisans in the sample were commemorated by their sons so infrequently that the patterns in the inscriptions can be explained more convincingly as the product of conscious strategies of succession than as the result of the uneven representation of freeborn and freed artisans or of demographic factors affecting the lives of freedmen. Those strategies can in turn be interpreted as an indication that artisans and retailers normally did not employ their sons personally and that they consequently had some incentive to appoint others – chiefly wives or former slaves – as their primary heirs.

Although more than 200,000 funerary inscriptions have survived from Rome of the late Republic and early Empire, only about 1,200 are inscriptions in which individuals identified either themselves or those whom they commemorated by citing specific occupational titles.[38] Furthermore, of these so-called occupational inscriptions, only a minority provides information about the social networks of independent entrepreneurs or artisans (whether freeborn or freed). Many refer instead to slaves or freedmen who remained associated with large aristocratic households and who were ultimately laid to rest within *columbaria* maintained by their owners or patrons.[39] These inscriptions were often commissioned by other members of the slave *familiae* to which the men and women they commemorate belonged, and while they therefore offer valuable information about social relationships in large, slaveholding households, they say little about social conditions in other sub-elite strata of the urban population: the rhythms of

---

[38] These are conventionally referred to as the occupational inscriptions. Joshel 1992 offers the most comprehensive discussion of these inscriptions as a group (but cf. Joshel 1977).

[39] See Joshel 1992: 94–8 for a discussion of the social contexts of commemoration.

patronage and manumission in large households produced patterns of family life among their slave and freed members that differed significantly from those experienced both by the freeborn and by slaves and freedmen attached to small artisan households.[40] At the same time, few occupational inscriptions reveal more than the briefest details about the social relationships of the deceased even when they do refer to freeborn entrepreneurs or former slaves who had established businesses of their own. Some, for example, record only the deceased's name and occupation, without revealing any information about the identity of his or her commemorators, while others list the names of two or more individuals, but neither distinguish between commemorator and deceased nor provide concrete information about the nature of the social relationships tying those individuals together.

Given these limitations, I have chosen to analyze patterns of commemoration and succession among Roman entrepreneurs by concentrating on a sample of 208 inscriptions.[41] Each of these inscriptions provides a straightforward (if selective) snapshot of the social world in which at least one individual identified by his or her occupation was embedded. Some of these inscriptions present evidence for more than a single dyadic social relationship. These include ante-mortem inscriptions, which individuals typically commissioned not just for themselves but also for other family members and for dependents entitled to share their tombs. They also include inscriptions commissioned by more than one commemorator, like the inscription dedicated to Caius Fufius Zmaragdus:

> To Caius Fufius Zmaragdus, pearl-seller on the Sacred Way. [Erected under] the guidance of Fufia Galla, his wife, and of Atimetus and Abascantus, his freedmen. [They also dedicated this monument] to their freedmen and freedwomen and to their posterity.[42]

Most, however, are very simple inscriptions in which the commemorator stated his or her own name along with the name of the person being memorialized and either claimed an occupational title personally or assigned one to the deceased. The inscription commissioned by Marcus Sergius Eutychus for his patron is a true outlier in the sense that Eutychus paid to have both his own occupation and that of his patron engraved on the stone: "Marcus Sergius Eutychus the wheelwright, freedman of

---

[40] See Weaver 1972 on the *familia Caesaris* and the degree to which the social status and opportunities available to many of these slaves differed drastically from those available to slaves outside the imperial *familia*.

[41] A full list of the inscriptions in the sample can be found in Appendix B.   [42] *CIL* 6.9547.

Marcus, [set this monument up] for himself and for his patron, Marcus Sergius Philocalus the wheelwright, freedman of Marcus."[43]

I have followed the procedure employed by Richard Saller and Brent Shaw in their analysis of Roman family relations during the early Empire. Saller and Shaw approached several large samples of funerary inscriptions by tabulating the various kinds of interpersonal relationships memorialized in each inscription.[44] The inscription commissioned by Marcus Sergius Eutychus, for instance, would yield a single entry in the "freedman-to-patron" column in their table when subjected to this methodology, whereas the one commissioned jointly by Fufia Galla, Atimetus, and Abascantus would produce both a "wife-to-husband" and a "freedman-to-patron" entry. Although there are weaknesses in this approach – among other things, it can distort our view of family structure by overemphasizing selected dyadic relationships in any given household at the expense of extended family structures – the main advantage it offers is the ability to compare the commemorative pattern produced by the occupational inscriptions with the patterns Saller and Shaw extracted from their own samples.[45]

In Table 4.1, I present the preliminary results of this analysis. The first panel displays the commemorative pattern produced by the occupational inscriptions. For comparative purposes, the other panels display the patterns produced by the inscriptions belonging to two of the samples studied by Saller and Shaw: those produced by members of the lower orders at Rome and those produced by members of the senatorial and equestrian orders.[46] As this table indicates, commemorations from sons to fathers are no more common in the occupational inscriptions than in the inscriptions of the Roman lower orders in general. More importantly, they are decidedly less common within the occupational inscriptions than they are in the inscriptions of the senatorial and equestrian orders. This point is significant, since if we can legitimately assume that members of the senatorial and equestrian orders tried to ensure that sons in particular would have had access to the wealth and connections necessary to maintain their social status, we would expect to see sons serving often as heirs within this particular social group.[47] Their inscriptions therefore offer a good baseline

---

[43] *CIL* 6.9215.   [44] Saller and Shaw 1984: 130–3.
[45] D. Martin 1996 offers the most in-depth critique of this particular methodology.
[46] The data for the senatorial and equestrian order can be found at Saller and Shaw 1984: 147, columns 3 and 4.
[47] Cf. Saller and Shaw 1984: 138. They note that "[A]mong the wealthy the transmission of property from the deceased to his or her descendants was a central factor in shaping family life," and attribute the relatively large number of son-to-father and daughter-to-father commemorations among the senatorial and equestrian orders to this factor.

Table 4.1 *Commemorative patterns*

Dedication		Occupational inscriptions		Rome: senators & equites		Rome: lower orders	
From	To	N	%	N	%	N	%
Husband	Wife	66	(36)	10	(16)	48	(26)
Wife	Husband	45	(25)	5	(8)	31	(17)
Total: conjugal family		111	(61)	15	(24)	79	(42)
Parents	Son	4	(2)	6	(10)	24	(13)
Parents	Daughter	0	(0)	1	(2)	6	(3)
Father	Son	14	(8)	7	(11)	9	(5)
Father	Daughter	10	(5)	3	(5)	6	(3)
Mother	Son	1	(1)	6	(10)	11	(6)
Mother	Daughter	2	(1)	0	(0)	6	(3)
Total: descending nuclear family		31	(17)	23	(37)	62	(33)
Son	Father	10	(5)	7	(11)	6	(3)
Son	Mother	4	(2)	2	(3)	13	(7)
Daughter	Father	6	(3)	11	(17)	2	(1)
Daughter	Mother	3	(2)	2	(3)	5	(3)
Total: ascending nuclear family		23	(13)	22	(35)	26	(14)
Brother	Brother	13	(7)	1	(2)	12	(6)
Brother	Sister	3	(2)	0	(0)	1	(1)
Sister	Brother	2	(1)	2	(3)	3	(2)

Table 4.1 (*cont.*)

Dedication		Occupational inscriptions		Rome: senators & equites		Rome: lower orders	
From	To	N	%	N	%	N	%
Sister	Sister	0	(0)	0	(0)	3	(2)
Total: siblings		18	(10)	3	(5)	19	(10)
Total: nuclear family		183	(100)	63	(100)	186	(100)
Extended family		4	1	4	5	11	5
Heredes		2	1	4	5	1	0
Amici		35	12	8	10	5	2
Patron	Freedman	21	7	0	0	6	3
Master	Slave	1	0	0	0	3	1
Freedman	Patron	40	14	3	4	25	11
Slave	Master	2	1	0	0	0	0
Total: servile		64	22	3	4	34	14
Total: relationships		288		82		237	

Notes:
(a) The data for the panels labeled "Rome: senators and equites" and "Rome: lower orders" are taken from Saller and Shaw 1984.
(b) The figures without parentheses in the percentile columns are the proportions of all relationships in the panel represented by a particular category of relationship; those enclosed in parentheses are the proportions of nuclear family relationships represented by each particular category.

value for the frequency of son-to-father commemorations we might expect to see in a social group in which son-to-father succession was important. The comparative rarity of these kinds of commemorations in the occupational inscriptions thus offers preliminary grounds for believing that household heads in the social group from which these inscriptions originated were not often succeeded directly by their sons.

Yet even though fathers do not seem to have been succeeded by their sons in this social group as often as in senatorial and equestrian families, the social and economic factors that produced this pattern are far from self-evident. While it is tempting to suggest that artisan fathers rarely appointed sons as their heirs simply because they rarely employed them in their own businesses, two considerations raise the possibility that the small number of son-to-father commemorations in this sample was instead the product of demographic factors rooted in slavery and manumission, which may have exerted an undue influence on the epigraphic record. First, most Roman historians believe that freed slaves subscribed more heavily to the "epigraphic habit" than the freeborn and are therefore overrepresented in Rome's funerary epigraphy. Advocates of this position generally stress that the kind of funerary display responsible for most of our inscriptions was fashionable among the freeborn only briefly during the late Republic and early Empire and chiefly among the municipal elite, but that freed slaves – who saw commemoration as a way to celebrate both their freedom and their ability to form families of their own – adopted the practice on a much larger scale. In this view, roughly 75 percent of the individuals known to us from Roman funerary inscriptions are likely to have been former slaves, even though freed slaves almost certainly made up a much smaller proportion of the city's actual population than this figure implies.[48] Second, freed slaves as a group may have been less likely than the freeborn to form stable families and thus less likely to produce freeborn children while they were still young enough to survive until those children reached an age at which they could commemorate their parents. This was particularly true after the creation of the *lex Aelia Sentia* in 4 CE. Among other things, this legislation restricted the ability of slaveholders to manumit their slaves formally unless both master and slave met certain conditions, one of which stipulated that the slave was to be at least thirty years of age; to the extent that this provision encouraged slaveholders to keep slaves in

---

[48] In particular, see Mouritsen 2005. As noted by Mouritsen 2011: 120–3, how much of Rome's population consisted of freed slaves is largely a matter of guesswork. For recent estimates that place the number of freedmen in Rome itself in the range of 50,000–100,000 (as compared to a free population of roughly 500,000–800,000), see Morley 2013: 39–43 and Hermann-Otto 2013: 72–3.

bondage longer than they may have in other cases, it meant that former slaves may have started families of their own at a later age than was typical among the freeborn. Together, these factors could explain many of the characteristics of the commemorative pattern visible in the occupational inscriptions.

In fact, certain features of the occupational inscriptions can initially be interpreted as evidence that freed slaves who suffered from limitations on their ability to form families are more heavily represented in this sample than they are in the inscriptions of the Roman lower orders in general. In their original analysis of the Roman funerary inscriptions, Saller and Shaw invoked both the prevalence of former slaves in the urban population and the impact of manumission on their ability to form families as potential explanations for the relative scarcity of commemorations among specific members of the nuclear family in the epigraphy of the Roman lower orders: between children and parents, between parents and children, and between siblings.[49] With the exception of commemorations from sons to fathers – which occur with roughly the same frequency in both samples – commemorations among members of the nuclear family in each of these categories are less common in the occupational inscriptions than they are in the inscriptions of the lower orders. These differences would hardly be surprising had the population responsible for the occupational inscriptions skewed more heavily in favor of freedmen than did the populations responsible for other samples, or had freedmen in the sample been especially unlikely to leave behind grown children when they died.

Ultimately, however, it is difficult to assess these different hypotheses in any direct way, because it is often impossible to differentiate precisely between former slaves and the freeborn in any given sample of inscriptions reflecting Rome's non-elite population. As a result, while we can generate crude estimates concerning the proportion of freed slaves in any epigraphically attested population, those estimates remain too provisional to permit us to detect all but the most obvious variations across different samples. Only a minority of those who commissioned inscriptions either employed formal indications of freed or freeborn status in their nomenclature or signaled clearly in other ways that they were freed slaves – by, for example, making explicit references to their former masters or to their fellow freedmen.[50] Moreover, although historians have argued that certain

---

[49] Saller and Shaw 1984: 138.

[50] Taylor 1962 offers the classic discussion of the use of formal status markers in the epigraphic material. Cf. Huttunen 1974 and Joshel 1992: 37–46.

features of personal nomenclature are more likely than not to indicate that an individual was a former slave rather than a freeborn citizen, those features are at best only suggestive, not determinative. It is often thought, for instance, that most individuals who bore Greek rather than Latin *cognomina* were former slaves.[51] Yet, while it seems indisputable that Greek *cognomina* are more common than Latin *cognomina* among securely identified freedmen in several epigraphic samples, parents did continue to give freeborn children Greek names, sometimes in significant numbers. For that very reason, Greek *cognomina* may not be as reliable as indicators of freed status as is sometimes maintained.[52] Likewise, when presented with cases in which spouses shared the same *nomen*, historians have often concluded that both were former slaves who had been freed by the same master. This is certainly one way of explaining why spouses shared the same *nomen*, but it is not at all apparent that this should be the preferred explanation in any given case, since in the sample drawn from the occupational inscriptions alone, almost all of the few men who can be identified securely as freeborn Roman citizens were married to women who bore the same *nomen* as they did themselves. The inscription commissioned on behalf of Mecia Dynata provides a convenient example: not only did Dynata's parents share the same *nomen* (Mecius / Mecia), her father was also freeborn and indicated as much in the inscription.[53] One can imagine a number of different scenarios capable of producing this kind of homonymy, including both simple coincidence or a tendency on the part of men to marry relatives, but one that deserves emphasis is the possibility that men in this particular social stratum often manumitted and married their own slaves, who necessarily would have assumed their husbands' names when they were freed. The framers of the *lex Aelia Sentia* clearly believed that men regularly chose to marry their slaves, since they specifically exempted slaveholders who freed slaves in order to marry them from some of the provisions of the law that otherwise would have constrained their ability to manumit slaves formally.[54] That belief clearly reflected social realities to some extent, since several of the occupational inscriptions

---

[51] Solin 1971 is fundamental in this respect; see esp. 123–4. Mouritsen 2011: 123–6 offers a more recent defense of this position, along with more extensive citations.

[52] Huttunen 1974: 148–9 and n. 59, and 194–7; Bruun 2013: 21–5, 34–5.

[53] *CIL* 6.9493. For other good examples in the occupational inscriptions, see 6.8455 (the caster Publius Calvius Iustus and his wife, Calvia Asclepias); 6.9573 (the doctor Tiberius Claudius Leitus and his wife Claudia Glaphyra); 6.10000 (the perfume-dealer Gaius Iulius Clementus and his wife Iulia Prisca).

[54] Gai. *Inst.* 1.18–19. After the *lex Aelia Sentia* of 4 CE, formal manumission was generally restricted to slaves who were older than thirty.

explicitly identify couples in which the wife had been manumitted by her husband.[55]

Although these uncertainties prevent us from accurately assessing how slavery and manumission affected the commemorative patterns in the occupational inscriptions, those patterns – far from simply reflecting the potential demographic challenges encountered by freed slaves – can provide evidence that many Roman entrepreneurs consciously chose not to appoint their sons as their heirs. First, although it is true that commemorations among certain members of the nuclear family are unusually rare in the occupational inscriptions, there are grounds for concluding that this feature of the commemorative pattern exists not so much because these inscriptions skew heavily in favor of former slaves, but rather because they skew heavily in favor of adult men. Men, for instance, were much more likely than women to claim an occupational title, or to be assigned one by others, especially in those inscriptions that do not refer to slaves or former slaves who remained attached to large, aristocratic households.[56] Likewise, boys who died in or before their early teens were less likely to be given an occupational title by those who commemorated them than were those who died later in life. Although some boys in their early teens certainly do appear in our inscriptions as trained artisans, most would not have completed their apprenticeships until they were a few years older.[57] For these reasons, the occupational inscriptions inevitably fail to report certain kinds of commemorative relationships that are more prominent in the inscriptions of other social groups – those between mothers and daughters, those between parents and young children of both sexes, those between sisters – and skew instead in favor of relationships featuring adult men identified in terms of their occupation, both as commemorators and as the recipients of dedications.

Table 4.2 presents the data in a way designed to compensate for these biases, and in so doing it confirms that the demographic profile of the population represented by the occupational inscriptions does not necessarily differ dramatically from the profile of the population represented in the inscriptions of the lower orders analyzed by Saller and Shaw. In this table, I have included only those commemorative links documented in occupational inscriptions which commemorate men to whom the dedicators assigned an occupational title. It therefore emphasizes those

---

[55] E.g., *CIL* 6. 9590; 6.9567; 6.9569; 6.9609; 6.9975; 6.33880; 6.33882.

[56] Joshel 1992: 69, table 3.1; her data show that most of the women who were assigned an occupational title in the inscriptions were attached to large households as domestic servants.

[57] Bradley 1991: 114–15; Laes 2011: 189–95; Tran 2013: 150–9.

Table 4.2 *Commemorations to adult males*

Commemorator	Occupational inscriptions			Rome: senators & equites			Rome: lower orders		
	N	%		N	%		N	%	
Wife	41	35	(63)	5	11	(19)	31	30	(57)
Son	9	8	(14)	7	16	(27)	6	6	(11)
Daughter	6	5	(9)	11	24	(42)	2	2	(4)
Brother	7	6	(11)	1	2	(4)	12	11	(22)
Sister	2	2	(3)	2	4	(8)	3	3	(6)
Total nuclear	65		(100)	26		(100)	54		(100)
Extended	2	2		4	9		11	10	
Heredes	2	2		4	9		1	1	
Amici	18	15		8	18		5	5	
Patron	4	3		0	0		6	6	
Master	0	0		0	0		3	3	
Freedman	26	23		3	7		25	24	
Total relationships	117			45			105		

Notes:
(a) The data for the panels labeled "Rome: senators and equites" and "Rome: lower orders" are taken from Saller and Shaw 1984.
(b) The figures without parentheses in the percentile columns are the proportions of all relationships in the panel represented by a particular category of relationship; those enclosed in parentheses are the proportions of nuclear family relationships represented by each particular category.

relationships that are most likely to reflect instances in which the commemorator(s) succeeded to the estates of individual entrepreneurs. Alongside those figures, I also present corresponding subsets of the data gathered by Saller and Shaw, representing both the inscriptions of the lower orders and the senatorial and equestrian inscriptions. It is important to note here that there is only an approximate correspondence in this table between the data drawn from the occupational inscriptions and the data excerpted from the analysis of Saller and Shaw, because the tables provided by Saller and Shaw do not break down commemorative links outside the nuclear family by gender. As a result, their data for these categories undoubtedly includes commemorations that were dedicated to women rather than to men. Even with that caveat, however, Table 4.2 shows that the commemorative patterns generated by the occupational inscriptions and by the inscriptions of the lower orders do not differ from one another as dramatically as initially seemed to be the case. In particular, although differences between the two patterns remain when the data are configured in this way, commemorations from children to their fathers now appear to have been somewhat more common in the occupational inscriptions than they are in the inscriptions of the lower orders. This would hardly be the case had the population represented by the occupational inscriptions been dominated more heavily than other populations by former slaves, who may have been less likely than were the freeborn to be survived by adult children.

Second, a closer look at the occupational inscriptions reveals that men practicing certain occupations were far more likely than others to be commemorated by their own children. As we shall see, this pattern seems difficult to explain on demographic grounds alone, and it therefore suggests that household heads belonging to the social group reflected in these inscriptions made conscious choices about which family members would succeed to their estates. Although our data are too sparse to yield meaningful patterns of commemoration when broken down by individual occupations, they can be partially disaggregated to reflect patterns of commemoration in broad occupational categories. In Table 4.3, I summarize those inscriptions in which children both commemorated their fathers and assigned them occupational titles and group them into three principal categories on the basis of economic conditions common to individual trades or professions. The first category includes artisans and retailers. Men practicing these occupations did not necessarily possess trade-specific capital assets of high value but did often hold a substantial amount of their assets in the form of credit that they had extended to clients; they also frequently carried substantial liabilities in the form of debts that they had incurred to their own suppliers. The second includes men who provided skilled or professional services; while they too extended considerable credit to their clients, they were much less likely than artisans and retailers to be heavily indebted to suppliers. In the third category are bankers, merchants, and wholesalers. Even though many of these were no less reliant on debt and credit than were artisans and retailers, on average they may have been more wealthy than men in the latter category and therefore better able to bequeath estates of considerable value to their

Table 4.3 *Commemorations to adult males in the occupational inscriptions, by occupational category*

Commemorator	Artisans and retailers			Skilled and professional services			Bankers, merchants, wholesalers		
	N	%		N	%		N	%	
Wife	24	40	(80)	9	27	(53)	8	31	(44)
Son	1	2	(3)	4	12	(24)	4	15	(22)
Daughter	1	2	(3)	1	3	(6)	4	15	(22)
Brother	2	3	(7)	3	9	(18)	2	8	(11)
Sister	2	3	(7)	0	0	(0)	0	0	(0)
Total nuclear			(100)			(100)			(100)
Extended	0	0		1	3		1	4	
Heredes	1	2		1	3		0	0	
Amici	11	19		7	21		2	8	
Patron	4	7		0	0		0	0	
Master	0	0		0	0		0	0	
Freedman	14	23		7	21		5	19	
Total relationships	60			33			26		

Notes:
(a) The figures without parentheses in the percentile columns are the proportions of all relationships in the panel represented by a particular category of relationship; those enclosed in parentheses are the proportions of nuclear family relationships represented by each particular category.

heirs.[58] As Table 4.3 reveals, most of the fathers commemorated by their children practiced occupations belonging to the second and third of these three categories. Of the nine fathers who were commemorated by their

[58] See Earle 1989b: 112–23, who offers a useful framework for conceptualizing the assets and liabilities held by businessmen of different kinds in London during the late seventeenth and early eighteenth century.

sons, four were merchants or wholesalers,[59] four provided professional services (two were educators, one was a professional philosopher, and the fourth a doctor),[60] and only one – an armorer or weaponsmith (*armamentarius*) – worked as an artisan.[61] Moreover, although inscriptions in which daughters commemorated their fathers are fewer in number, these too conform to the same general pattern: while one father commemorated by his daughter operated what was probably a retail business devoted to the sale of papyrus or writing tablets,[62] the rest worked in occupations that fell into the second and third categories enumerated above.[63]

Since it is difficult to identify the formal legal status of most individuals in the occupational inscriptions, we cannot exclude the possibility that men who worked as artisans and retailers were simply more likely to have been freed slaves than those in other occupations. On this view, the pattern displayed in Table 4.3 would reflect nothing more than the impact exerted by slavery and manumission on their ability to leave behind adult children when they died. Yet, at the same time, it is important to stress that the limited information we possess about the legal statuses of the individuals in this sample does not provide much support for this interpretation because it does not reveal any kind of direct relationship between legal status and occupation that could have produced dramatic differences in family formation among men who worked in different kinds of professions. Table 4.4 makes this point by tabulating the legal status of adult men in the sample who were assigned occupational titles by their commemorators. As should be clear from the table itself, our data, when organized in this way, provide no real grounds for believing that former slaves were more numerous among artisans and retailers than in the other occupational groups. In fact, men who can be securely identified as freeborn represent a slightly larger proportion of the individuals in this group than is the case in the other two occupational categories, while the proportion who can be identified as former slaves is lower among artisans and retailers than it is

---

[59] *CIL* 6.9661, 6.9669, and 6.9674 are all dedicated to men identified as *negotiatores*; 6.33887 commemorates a dealer in swine and sheep (*negotiator suariae et pecuariae*).

[60] The educators (*grammatici*) are commemorated in *CIL* 6.9445 and 6.9448; the philosopher in *CIL* 6.9785; the doctor in *CIL* 6.9606.

[61] *CIL* 6.37778. For another possible case of son-to-father commemoration that may point to the inheritance of a business, however, see *CIL* 6.9659, in which a freeborn *negotiator* commemorates his father, his mother, and his brother.

[62] He is identified as a *chartarius* (*CIL* 6.9255).

[63] These include the professional philosopher mentioned above in n. 60, who was commemorated jointly by his daughter and his son; two bankers, or *argentarii* (*CIL* 6.9156, 6.9159); and two *negotiatores* (CIL 6.9661 and 6.9674).

Table 4.4 *Juridical status of males commemorated with occupational title,*
by occupational category

	Artisans and retailers		Skilled and professional services		Bankers, merchants, wholesalers	
Juridical status	N	%	N	%	N	%
Freeborn (*ingenuus*)	4	8	1	5	1	4
Freed slave (*libertus*)	13	24	7	35	6	22
Free, status otherwise unknown (*incertus*)	36	68	12	60	20	74
Totals	53		20		27	

among bankers, merchants, and wholesalers (although it is somewhat higher among artisans and retailers than it is among practitioners of skilled or professional services).

More importantly, by differentiating between occupational categories in this way, Table 4.3 emphasizes that artisans and retailers were commemorated by their sons so infrequently that this pattern is difficult to explain by invoking demographic factors alone. Tables 4.5 and 4.6 reinforce that point by modeling the proportion of freeborn fathers belonging to Rome's upper and lower orders that would have been survived by sons old enough to serve as their heirs and commemorators when they died. These tables are based on Richard Saller's simulation of the kinship networks in which individuals were embedded at different moments during their life courses; together, they show that men belonging to the senatorial and equestrian orders were only about 25 percent more likely to leave behind sons over the age of fourteen than were freeborn men in other social strata[64] – a difference largely

---

[64] These tables suggest that roughly 28 percent of freeborn men in the lower orders were survived by a son over the age of fourteen when they died, whereas 35 percent of those in the senatorial and equestrian orders left behind a son of the same age. In Tables 4.5 and 4.6, Q(x) and L(x) represent, respectively, an individual's probability of dying before reaching the next age bracket and the notional number of individuals from a putative birth cohort of 100,000 people still alive at a given age *x*. I draw these figures from Saller 1994: 24, table 2.1, *Level Three Female* (for Table 4.5) and *Level Six Female* (for Table 4.6). I take the values for the columns labeled *Proportion with living sons* and *Son's mean age* from Saller 1994: 52–3 (tables 3.1.e and f) and 64–5 (tables 3.3.e and 3.3.f). For a discussion of the assumptions and data behind these mortality figures, see Saller 1994: 12–25. Debate about typical mortality profiles in antiquity is ongoing and intense. Kron 2012 offers a recent and revisionist perspective; Scheidel 2012b surveys recent developments in the field and proposes that the framework employed by Saller remains sound enough, even if it could stand some modification.

Table 4.5 *Deceased fathers with surviving sons, freeborn lower orders*

Father's age	Q(x)	L(x)	Proportion with living sons	Son's mean age	Fathers deceased, no son older than 14	Fathers deceased, sons older than 14
25	0.08565	42,231			3,617	
30	0.09654	38,614	0.16	0.9	3,728	
35	0.10541	34,886	0.51	2.7	3,677	
40	0.11227	31,208	0.65	5.4	3,503	
45	0.11967	27,705	0.67	8.8	3,316	
50	0.15285	24,389	0.69	12.4	3,728	
55	0.19116	20,661	0.69	16	1,224	2,725
60	0.27149	16,712	0.68	19.5	1,452	3,085
65	0.34835	12,175	0.65	23.7	1,588	2,653
70	0.47131	7,934	0.62	28.4	1,421	2,318
				Totals:	27,254	10,781 (28.34%)

Notes:
Q(x) represents an individual's probability of dying before reaching the next age bracket;
L(x) represents the notional number of individuals from a putative birth cohort of 100,000
people still alive at a given age *x*.

attributable to the fact that men from senatorial and equestrian families both enjoyed slightly better life expectancies than average and also tended to marry for the first time at younger ages than men in other social groups.[65] By contrast, when read in conjunction with Table 4.2, Table 4.3 shows that men in the "artisans and retailers" group were far less likely to be

[65] For the model on which this claim is based, see Saller 1994: 12–69. For men, Saller adopts twenty-five and thirty as the average age at first marriage among the "senatorial" and "ordinary" strata of the population, respectively. These ages themselves are founded on a comprehensive analysis of the funerary inscriptions: by tabulating the ages at which men began to be commemorated more often by members of their conjugal families than by members of their natal families, Saller is able to derive approximate values for the ages at which men first married. (Lelis et al. 2003 argue that average ages at first marriage were in fact much lower in the Roman world, but their views have not been widely accepted; see Scheidel 2007b for an overview of the current debate.) Coupled with certain assumptions about mortality, these figures permit Saller to project model kinship universes for individuals in various age categories and provide hypothetical values for three important variables: mean numbers of living kin, mean ages of living kin, and the proportion of individuals in any given age cohort who possessed living kin of different categories.

Table 4.6 *Deceased fathers with surviving sons, senatorial and equestrian orders*

Father's age	Q(x)	L(x)	Proportion with living sons	Son's mean age	Fathers deceased, no son older than 14	Fathers deceased, son older than 14
25	0.06551	53,037	0.15	1	3,474	
30	0.07393	49,563	0.49	3.1	3,664	
35	0.08112	45,899	0.58	6.2	3,724	
40	0.08725	42,175	0.59	10.3	3,679	
45	0.09462	38,496	0.58	14.9	1,530	2,113
50	0.12200	34,853	0.57	19.8	1,828	2,424
55	0.15472	30,601	0.55	24.7	2,130	2,604
60	0.22153	25,867	0.52	29.7	2,750	2,980
65	0.29119	20,137	0.5	34.6	2,932	2,932
70	0.40306	14,273	0.47	39.5	3,049	2,704
				Totals:	28,760	15,757 (35.40%)

Notes:
Q(x) represents an individual's probability of dying before reaching the next age bracket; L(x) represents the notional number of individuals from a putative birth cohort of 100,000 people still alive at a given age *x*.

commemorated by their sons than were those belonging to the senatorial and equestrian orders: whereas commemorations from sons to their fathers represent 27 percent of commemorations to men from members of their nuclear families in the latter group, they represent only 3 percent of commemorations to men from members of their nuclear families in the former (a ninefold variance). Demographic factors arising from slavery and manumission can only account for this variance if we make two critical and highly pessimistic assumptions: first, that more than 85 percent of the men in the "artisans and retailers" category were freedmen; second, that virtually none of these freedmen was able to produce children old enough to commemorate him when he died. If either of these assumptions were relaxed, then these factors would only account for at most two-thirds of the actual variance visible in the inscriptions. Moreover, under what could plausibly be characterized as a more realistic set of assumptions – that roughly 75 percent of the artisans and retailers commemorated in the inscriptions were former slaves and that perhaps a quarter of these were able to marry at a young-enough age to produce freeborn and legitimate children at roughly the same rate as freeborn entrepreneurs – demographic factors would only account for about a third of the observed variance.[66]

Succession in artisan households

As rough as these figures are, they suggest that artisans and retailers intentionally passed over their sons as heirs, particularly when the rate at which artisans were commemorated by their sons is compared to the rates at which other men in Rome's working population or men in Rome's senatorial and equestrian orders were commemorated by theirs. Yet although the occupational inscriptions provide convincing evidence that Roman artisans and retailers did not normally name their sons as heirs, they unfortunately offer no direct insight into why this was the case. Nor, for that matter, do any of the other kinds of evidence that occasionally offer information about the business and family strategies of Roman entrepreneurs. For that reason, any explanation for this pattern will necessarily be speculative.

[66] The most straightforward way to model these various scenarios is to begin by treating all of the deceased tallied in the sixth and seventh columns of Table 4.5 (that is, the 27,254 who did not leave behind sons over the age of fourteen when they died, and the 10,781 who did) as the freeborn minority in a larger cohort consisting of a majority of freedmen. The size (n) of this mixed cohort can then be defined as $(27{,}254 + 10{,}781)/(1-l_r)$, where l_r is the proportion of freedmen (*liberti*) in the cohort. The total number of individuals in this enlarged cohort who could expect to leave behind a son older than fourteen when they died can then be expressed as

$$s' = 10781 + s\, l_r\, nf$$

where s is the proportion of freeborn fathers who left behind sons over the age of fourteen when they died (28.34 percent, or 0.2834), and f is the proportion of the freedmen in the cohort who married at roughly the same age as their freeborn counterparts. The result, s', can then be expressed as a fraction of the overall enlarged cohort if it is divided by n.

If we assume a population in which 85 percent of the members were former slaves ($l_r = 0.85$), none of whom were likely to marry at the same age and reproduce at the same rate as the freeborn ($f = 0$), then the model produces an enlarged cohort of 253,567 individuals (n), 10,781 (or 4.3 percent) of whom would have left behind sons over the age of fourteen. These circumstances would come close to accounting for the ninefold variance between the rates at which fathers were commemorated by sons in the "senatorial and equestrian orders" group and the "artisans and retailers" group, respectively (i.e., 35.4 percent is greater than 4.3 percent by a factor of roughly 8.4). If, however, we assume a population in which 75 percent of the members were former slaves ($l_r = 0.85$), and as few as a quarter of those were able to marry at the same age as the freeborn ($f = 0.25$), then the model produces an enlarged cohort of 152,140 individuals, 18,865 of whom (12.4 percent) would have left behind sons over the age of fourteen. With these as the default parameters, members of the senatorial and equestrian orders would have been only about three times as likely to leave behind sons over the age of fourteen as those belonging to the "artisan and retailers" group – well short of the ninefold variance documented in Tables 4.2 and 4.3.

That said, because a father's occupation seems to have strongly affected whether or not he chose to name his son as his heir, there are good reasons to suspect that Roman entrepreneurs based their decisions about succession and inheritance on the degree to which they did or did not integrate those sons into their own businesses. In the remainder of this section, I pursue this possibility in more detail by arguing that the rarity of son-to-father commemorations in the inscriptions of artisans and retailers can be read as indirect evidence that entrepreneurs in these trades were unlikely to employ their sons in their own businesses. More specifically, I suggest that because artisans and retailers were particularly likely to find themselves deeply embedded in networks of credit, on which the viability of their businesses often depended, they had strong incentives to appoint as legal heirs individuals who were capable of sustaining both their enterprises and their credit networks, even if in practice they distributed much of their assets to other beneficiaries in the form of legacies. The fact that they rarely appointed their sons as their heirs may therefore indicate that they tended to establish those sons in independent careers rather than to employ them personally and that their sons were typically not as capable of assuming control of their businesses as were other potential heirs. Those other potential heirs included freedmen and also wives, who could certainly manage a business on their own if they also retained access to the labor of skilled slaves or freedmen.

I begin by noting that historians of both the ancient and early modern worlds sometimes suggest that sons born to fathers with few material and financial assets were especially likely to leave their natal households, and often the communities in which they were raised. According to this argument, because sons in such households had only limited prospects for receiving a substantial inheritance, they often chose to pursue better opportunities elsewhere, and in many cases severed connections with their natal households in the process.[67] Since artisans and retailers in antiquity – like those in the early modern period – may have accumulated less wealth, on average, than men who pursued other occupations, it is tempting to invoke family fragmentation generated by this kind of process to explain why the rate of son-to-father succession among retailers and artisans in Rome was so much lower than it was among men belonging to other occupational categories.[68] Yet there are reasons to doubt that this model

---

[67] E.g., Tilly and Scott 1987: 21–2; Saller and Shaw 1984: 138.
[68] On the ability of artisans and other kinds of businessmen to accumulate wealth in early modern London, see Earle 1989b: 106–42 and Schwarz 1992: 57–73.

offers a convincing explanation of the commemorative pattern we see in the inscriptions of Roman artisans and retailers. For one thing, many of the artisans and retailers commemorated in the occupational inscriptions owned one or more slaves; that fact alone implies that most of the men named in these inscriptions belonged to the wealthier strata of the working population and that they were consequently capable of transmitting inheritances of at least some substance to potential heirs.[69] Additionally, even poorer households in Rome itself were probably less likely than those in smaller regional centers to fragment in ways that would have prompted sons to move away from their home towns, because the metropolis offered more economic opportunities than did other cities and towns in Italy and in the Mediterranean more broadly.[70] For both of these reasons, even sons who established households of their own in Rome were more likely than not to maintain close contact with their families and to remain available to serve as heirs. Together, these observations suggest that we should look for an explanation for the scarcity of son-to-father commemorations among artisans and retailers by identifying factors specific to these kinds of businesses that were capable of prompting men in these trades to name individuals other than their sons as heirs.

The extent to which artisans and retailers relied on credit offers just such an explanation, since entrepreneurs in these trades depended heavily on credit as both debtors and creditors, and thus had strong incentives to ensure that their heirs were capable of sustaining their credit networks. Credit was a ubiquitous feature of the Roman urban economy, and artisans and retailers in particular were probably embedded deeply in complicated networks of obligations. By way of comparison, in the early modern period artisans and retailers not only extended substantial amounts of credit to clients but also depended heavily themselves on credit advanced to them by their suppliers

---

[69] The economic status of the individuals who were commemorated in the funerary inscriptions has occasionally been a matter of debate. Some scholars have argued that inscribed tombstones were expensive enough to be beyond the reach of a sizeable fraction of the urban population and that epitaphs in general are consequently products of a relatively wealthy segment of society (e.g., Hopkins 1966: 247). More recently, historians have inclined toward the view that commemoration was available to a broader cross-section of the urban population than is sometimes acknowledged. Elaborate monuments were of course costly, but modest tombstones were considerably cheaper and could perhaps be purchased for a hundred *sesterces* or less. Associations – both professional and otherwise – also helped to defray the costs of funerals for individual members. For these reasons, it seems plausible that "[t]he bulk of our tombstone data offers evidence of social relationships of those Romans between the elite and the very poor" (Saller and Shaw 1984: 127–8), albeit possibly with some bias toward wealthier individuals. Cf. Joshel 1992: 19–20.

[70] In that sense, urban environments were ideally suited to the kind of adaptive household strategies envisioned by Wall 1986 and de Vries 2008.

and subcontractors. Broadly speaking, many early modern artisans and retailers tended to carry trade-specific liabilities amounting to roughly one-quarter of the value of their gross assets at any given time, and likewise held one-third or more of their own assets in the form of credit that they had extended to their own clients.[71] Although our evidence does not permit us to assess the portfolios of typical Roman artisans and retailers in a comparable amount of detail, there is no reason to believe that they were any less dependent than their early modern counterparts on relationships of credit. As I have noted in other chapters, there are indications in our sources that artisans and retailers in antiquity relied heavily on credit and that the magnitude of both their trade-related debts and their accounts receivable did not differ dramatically in magnitude from what was typical in later periods. This is certainly the implication of the jurists' commentary on the *actio tributoria*, which provided a remedy to creditors of businesses operated by slaves by allowing them to demand that a slave's owner liquidate the *peculium* of a slave who became insolvent.[72] Part of what set the *actio tributoria* apart from the *actio de peculio* was the fact that a successful claimant who sued under the former procedure was required to guarantee that if other creditors launched similar lawsuits against the slave (whose *peculium* may have been entirely depleted by the initial action), he would grant them *pro rata* payments from his own settlement.[73] In that sense, it reflects an awareness on the part of the *praetor* who framed it that a slave-run business was likely to have multiple creditors and leaves little doubt that slaves who operated businesses regularly incurred substantial trade-related debts to numerous different parties. Ulpian's commentary also indicates that slaves often held equally substantial assets in the form of credit that they had extended to regular customers: Ulpian notes that sums owed to a slave by his customers were to be counted among his assets (and credited to his *peculium* by his owner) if his creditors pressed for liquidation.[74] A case discussed by

---

[71] Earle 1989b: 112–37 offers the most detailed discussion of the assets and liabilities held by London artisans and businessmen in the early modern period; see especially 118–22 and the tables on 119 and 121. For studies of credit relationships and small business proprietors in slightly later periods, see Kent 1994 (eighteenth- and nineteenth-century England) and Young 1995 (Scotland in the nineteenth century). On the importance of credit relationships in the early economy more broadly, Muldrew 1998 remains fundamental; for a more focused study of credit in early modern commerce, see Smail 2005.

[72] For a brief overview of the *actio tributoria* and its relationship to related remedies like the *actio de peculio*, see Aubert 2013. Chiusi 1993 offers a much more exhaustive discussion of this procedure.

[73] Ulpian, *Dig.* 14.4.5.19. By contrast, if a successful claimant who sued on the basis of the *actio de peculio* exhausted the slave's *peculium*, other creditors could find themselves with no remedy (see now Aubert 2013: 198).

[74] Ulpian, *Dig.* 14.4.5.12.

the jurist Papinian complements Ulpian's observations by showing that both the debts and credits generated by such a business could easily be substantial enough to become the focus of a legal dispute among the heirs and other beneficiaries of an estate: Papinian seems to have been asked to deliver a ruling on whether or not a legacy consisting of a purple-seller's shop and its slave managers included not just the capital set aside to buy additional stock but also the outstanding debts and the accounts receivable associated with the operation of the business.[75] Finally, it is worth noting that although much of the legal evidence pertains to slave-run businesses, free artisans were no less likely to depend on credit, and snippets of evidence do refer to them as providers of shop credit and as consumers of credit provided to them by their own suppliers.[76]

Just as importantly, because the Romans practiced a system of universal succession, artisans and retailers had distinct incentives to appoint heirs capable of carrying on their enterprises, even if in doing so they found it necessary to disinherit their sons formally (which did not, of course, preclude them from awarding those sons generous legacies). The principle of universal succession meant that an individual's legal heirs acquired not only his or her assets but also his or her liabilities. As a result, the heirs of an artisan or retailer effectively succeeded to a complex cluster of obligations and claims linking them to the former clients and suppliers of the testator, both of whom potentially numbered in the dozens.[77] In these circumstances, heirs who could sustain the businesses of the deceased were not just more likely than those who could not to preserve the estate's full value, they were also less likely to perceive succession to the estate and its liabilities as a burden that they might reject. First, heirs who could keep an enterprise viable would have been better equipped than others to manage the difficult process of both honoring the testator's business obligations and realizing the full value of the assets held as accounts receivable. They could secure flexible terms of payment from the testator's creditors, who might have been more interested in maintaining an ongoing business relationship with

---

[75] Papinian, *Dig.* 32.1.91.2.

[76] Plaut. *Aul.* 505–519 and Sen. *Ben.* 7.21, though widely separated in time, both refer to artisans and shopkeepers offering credit to customers; Artem. 4.1 refers to an artisan who became insolvent because of outstanding debts to his creditors, who were possibly suppliers.

[77] Kent 1994: 52 provides figures for the number of unpaid accounts on the books of ten artisans who went insolvent in early nineteenth-century Britain. As he notes, "the number of customers with unpaid accounts could vary considerably, as could the value of the unpaid portion, but both were likely to be substantial." The most extreme case he presents is that of a chairmaker, W. Launcer. When Launcer went bankrupt in 1837, he had 202 account customers, 60 of whom had not paid their bills.

a testator's successors than in pressing for an immediate settlement of their outstanding claims. They also arguably enjoyed better prospects for calling in debts of their own than did heirs who could not maintain the business, simply because they could threaten to withdraw further shop credit from clients who did not make regular payments against their accounts. Second, heirs capable of sustaining a business were likely to see the need to manage the testator's credit network not as a burden but as an opportunity to appropriate that network for their own purposes. After all, those who succeeded in doing so could greatly enhance their own businesses' prospects, particularly if they had not yet been able to build extensive networks of their own. This would have been true especially in the case of heirs who had not yet been able to gain entry into a professional *collegium*, in which members cultivated reputation-based relationships not only with suppliers and subcontractors but also with potential clients seeking to let out work of their own. Testators could therefore feel confident that heirs capable of carrying on the business would be satisfied with portions of the inheritance that ultimately may not have consisted of much more than claims to outstanding accounts receivable once an estate's debts were cleared.[78]

For artisans and retailers who chose not to appoint sons as their primary heirs, wives and freed slaves were the most obvious alternatives. Both had at least some of the skills necessary to maintain an artisan's or retailer's business, and both potentially had their own incentives for accepting inheritances that may have been burdened not just by outstanding accounts payable and receivable but also by legacies allocated to other beneficiaries (such as the testator's children). As far as the skills necessary to sustain a business were concerned, slaves and freedmen often found themselves in a strong position, because many had been acquired and trained by masters intent on employing them directly in their enterprises;[79] they were therefore well qualified to step into new roles as proprietors of ongoing concerns, provided they were given access to the necessary capital. Wives were somewhat disadvantaged in this respect, since – as I argue in more detail in Chapter 4– they often had few opportunities to acquire technical skills pertaining to the production side of artisanal businesses. Nonetheless, in practical terms, many women did help manage their husbands' businesses and could keep an inherited concern viable if their

---

[78] The only real limitation that constrained the testator in these cases was the *lex Falcidia* of 40 BCE. This legislation limited the amount of legacies a testator could award by specifying that the designated heir of an estate was entitled to a quarter of its value after funeral expenses, debts, and the value of any manumitted slaves were deducted. See Buckland 1921: 338–9.

[79] See Chapter 3 for an extended treatment of this issue.

husbands assigned them either ownership of skilled slaves or control over the outstanding labor services (*operae*) of skilled freedmen.[80] Wives and freedmen in this position were also especially likely to see the opportunity to gain access to a testator's credit networks as a net benefit, even if they were required to pay out substantial legacies in addition to discharging the testator's debts. This was so because both women and freed slaves could otherwise find it difficult to create networks of their own. Freed slaves were not always able to expand their own businesses quickly, especially when they had been required to discharge *operae* on behalf of their patrons for several years after their manumission. Women, on the other hand, found it difficult to secure membership in professional associations, and thus access to the networking opportunities such membership conferred; any links with clients and suppliers they inherited from their husbands therefore would have been particularly valuable.[81]

From this perspective, it is significant that the low incidence of son-to-father commemorations in inscriptions dedicated to artisans and retailers is complemented by relatively high numbers of commemorations from wives to husbands and from freedmen to patrons. This pattern is most noticeable in the case of wife-to-husband commemorations, which are particularly prominent among dedications to male artisans and retailers – they constitute 40 percent of this sample but no more than 30 percent in the samples drawn from the epigraphy of other occupational groups listed in Table 4.3. Freedmen too are more visible as commemorators in inscriptions dedicated to artisans and retailers than they are in other inscriptions. At 23 percent, the rate at which freedmen commemorated male patrons who were artisans or retailers is at least two to three percentage points higher than the rate at which freedmen commemorated patrons who pursued other occupations, and it would probably be higher than the rate at which they commemorated patrons in the lower orders in general (Table 4.2) if we could fully compensate for gender and age biases in the data provided by Saller and Shaw. These figures suggest that when artisans and retailers chose to pass over sons as formal heirs, they did in fact turn to wives and freedmen. This is readily comprehensible if we conclude not only that wives and freedmen were capable of sustaining businesses that

---

[80] The *operae* of skilled freedmen – that is, *operae fabriles* – were considered an asset that could be transmitted by a testator to his or her heir or legatee (see, e.g., Ulpian, *Dig.* 38.1.6 and 38.1.15), just as they could be hired out or assigned by a patron to a third party (e.g., Julian, *Dig.* 38.1.25.pr-2).

[81] Although it was not uncommon for women to be co-opted as patrons by members of Roman professional *collegia* (see, most recently, Hemelrijk 2008), they rarely seem to have been members of professional associations in their own right (cf. Meiggs 1973: 319).

they inherited from entrepreneurs in these trades but also that artisans and retailers typically chose to establish their sons in independent careers rather than to employ them in their own enterprises.

Urban demand and artisans' familial strategies

Although the occupational inscriptions show that artisans and retailers in the Roman world rarely employed their own sons, they offer little to no direct evidence about the considerations motivating this behavior, nor about how those considerations were influenced by the broader economic environment in which artisans and retailers were embedded. In the following paragraphs, I explore these issues in more detail. As I show, there are reasons to believe that the decisions artisans and retailers made about their sons were driven primarily by the seasonal and uncertain demand characteristic of urban product markets in the Roman world. Because the nature of that demand ensured that their own requirements for regular and permanent help were often limited, most artisans could not keep sons productively employed in their own enterprises and saw advantages in diversifying their household income streams by encouraging their sons to work outside of the home – whether by working for wages or (ideally) by establishing themselves in workshops of their own.

As we have seen, seasonal and uncertain demand strongly affected artisans' efforts to organize their businesses and manage their labor forces. There are thus strong *a priori* reasons for suspecting that it had an equally profound impact on their efforts to plan their sons' futures. Studies of artisans and their familial strategies in the early modern period provide support for this view, not only because they indicate that seasonal and uncertain demand did affect the familial strategies of artisans in some specific contexts but also because there are reasons to believe that the impact of such demand was more pervasive than is sometimes recognized. In a provocative study of familial strategies among Viennese artisans in the nineteenth century, for example, Josef Ehmer broke from what was then the dominant view that artisans regularly employed their own sons. Instead, he argued that artisans in German-speaking regions of Europe did not normally integrate their sons into their own enterprises during this period and that they had been even less likely to do so in the preceding century. Ehmer offered a twofold explanation for the patterns he detected in the evidence. First, he sided with several other scholars who argued that the infrequency with which sons worked in and succeeded to the enterprises of their fathers prior to the nineteenth century should be explained primarily as a product of guild structures. On this view, the "collective social relations" fostered by trade corporations shaped the structure of artisan families more strongly than did individual familial or economic strategies. Since corporate expectations and regulations governed training, employment, and establishment as a master artisan, they often effectively prevented fathers from simply handing their enterprises over to their sons. For that reason, most artisans arranged apprenticeships for their sons, who spent several years working as journeymen in the workshops of other craftsmen once they had completed their training, before finally establishing themselves as proprietors in their own right. Because corporate regulations no longer factored strongly in the nineteenth century, however, Ehmer turned to a second factor to explain the fact that fathers were only somewhat more likely to employ sons in this period than they had been in preceding centuries – namely, to the seasonal and uncertain demand that characterized most segments of the urban product market. In Ehmer's view, the nature of demand for their products and services ensured that most nineteenth-century artisans had only a limited need for regular and permanent help and encouraged them to meet most of their own labor requirements by employing apprentices and journeymen rather than their own sons.[82]

Although Ehmer felt that seasonal and uncertain demand could explain artisans' reluctance to employ their own sons only as guilds lost their authority in the nineteenth century, it seems more probable that guild regulations had only formalized or amplified patterns of behavior that would have been produced in any case by the impact of seasonal and uncertain demand on artisans' requirements for regular, permanent help. This interpretation accounts not only for the essential continuity of artisans' familial strategies in central Europe after guild regulations ceased to be a primary factor in their formulation but also for the fact that artisans were not necessarily more likely to employ their own sons in contexts in which guild regulations did not limit their ability to transmit enterprises to their sons. As I have noted, the reluctance of artisans to employ their own sons seems to have been a widespread phenomenon in early modern Europe, even though the regulations of some guilds may have favored a degree of father-to-son continuity, and even where guild authority may have been weaker at certain times than elsewhere, as it was in eighteenth-century England.[83] The ancient Roman pattern is significant here too:

---

[82] Ehmer 1984. Cf. Knotter 1994: 40–3, who echoes many of these points.

[83] De Munck and Soly 2007: 19 offer some general comments on variations in guild regulations concerning the kin of master artisans. As they note, Rosser 1997: 17 has made the intriguing suggestion that efforts on the part of guilds to encourage father-to-son continuity in some medieval cities may in fact indicate that such continuity was not the norm.

since *collegia* in the early Empire were private associations with no formal regulatory functions, Roman artisans' reluctance to employ their own sons was clearly not a product of corporate regulations.

The factors that did encourage a minority of early modern artisans to integrate sons into their own enterprises only emphasize the extent to which seasonal and uncertain demand shaped the strategies of most others. Inelastic demand was one such factor: artisans who manufactured products for which demand was relatively inelastic typically possessed a stable-enough need for permanent help that they could keep their sons productively employed. The fact that bakers appear to have been more likely than other artisans to employ their own sons can be explained at least partly in these terms – not only did the difficult working hours make dependent, live-in employees useful (since work in most bakeries began in the very early hours of the morning), the demand for bread was also inelastic enough that bakers had a constant need for predictable amounts of labor.[84]

The nature and extent of the capital artisans had at their disposal were also factors that could encourage them to integrate sons into their own businesses. On one level, this may have been true simply because artisans who enjoyed financial security felt less pressure than others to ensure that their sons remained productively employed (or, in other words, they were less risk-averse than colleagues who possessed fewer financial resources). More important, however, were the positive incentives for family continuity that came into play when significant amounts of capital were at stake. Both artisans and their sons in these situations had a vested interest in ensuring that sons inherited their fathers' enterprises: sons because they would enjoy more long-term social and financial success by assuming control of healthy and well-capitalized businesses than by establishing enterprises of their own; fathers because they could better preserve the value of estates rich in business-related assets by bequeathing them intact to sons who were capable of employing those assets. Fathers operating businesses on this scale were therefore more likely than not to groom sons as their successors and to do so in part by employing them personally.[85]

Guild regulations too could mitigate problems arising from seasonal and uncertain demand in ways that encouraged fathers to employ their sons. In his analysis of the chimney-sweeping trade in eighteenth- and nineteenth-century Vienna, Ehmer argues that a small number of families were able to

[84] Ehmer 1984: 207 (on bakers in Vienna); S. L. Kaplan 1996: 291–3 (on bakers in Paris).

[85] Ehmer 1984: 206–7 makes this argument about innkeepers in particular in Vienna. Cf. Baker 2009: 171–8, who notes that family continuity was higher in London trades devoted to the manufacture of scientific materials than it was in other lines of work, partly due to the affluence of these trades.

artificially constrain the supply of chimney-sweeping services, both by securing an enforceable monopoly for their corporation and by limiting membership in that corporation to a maximum of eighteen master artisans. In this environment of limited competition, demand regularly exceeded supply, and strategies emphasizing family continuity were far less risky than otherwise would have been the case; as a result, masters of the corporation sought to ensure that their sons would succeed to their positions.[86] The evolution of the Parisian printing industry in the seventeenth and early eighteenth centuries offers a comparable example from early modern France. Royal legislation limited the number of print-shops in Paris to thirty-six during the late seventeenth century and stipulated that each of those shops was to contain at least four presses; it therefore not only constrained the supply of printing services but also encouraged the owners of printing shops to invest heavily in physical capital. These developments seem to have been matched by (and possibly prompted) a renewed emphasis on family continuity among members of the printers' corporation, reflected in changes in the corporate statutes discouraging printers from accepting apprentices – which, in practice, ensured that most new members of the corporation in the seventeenth and eighteenth centuries were the sons or sons-in-law of other master printers.[87]

Given these considerations, it is reasonable to hypothesize that seasonal and uncertain demand was the primary factor driving the reluctance of artisans and retailers in the Roman world to employ their own sons. Circumstances undoubtedly differed for artisans working in industries that generated relatively stable demand, or possessing sufficient capital that they had an incentive to ensure their sons could inherit and operate their businesses. For most, however, seasonal and uncertain demand made it preferable to find work outside the household for sons, who – after their apprenticeships ended – may have spent several years working as small-scale subcontractors or moving from shop to shop on short-term contracts, before finally establishing workshops of their own. This was true both in the case of fathers who operated enterprises hovering on the margins of viability, as well as those operating relatively successful businesses, albeit for different reasons. Although seasonal and uncertain demand may have ensured that individuals in neither category had a stable-enough need for regular, permanent help to keep their sons productively employed, for those struggling to stay in business, the decision to establish a son in an independent career could provide badly needed insurance against hard times by diversifying their

---

[86] Ehmer 2001: 194–6.   [87] Sonenscher 1989: 14–19.

households' income streams. On the other hand, while proprietors of successful businesses could also benefit from such diversification, in general they would have been less vulnerable to the severe budget pressures that drove poorer artisans to find alternative sources of employment for their children. Even so, the interplay between the life cycle of an entrepreneur's business and the seasonal and uncertain character of urban demand meant that his own labor requirements did not always align well with labor supplied by members of his family. Many entrepreneurs, for instance, may have been confronted with the opportunity to expand their businesses before their sons were old enough to contribute to their enterprises in any meaningful way. In these circumstances, they developed strategies for recruiting additional permanent and temporary help from beyond the family itself, provided that the structure of local and regional labor markets or their access to the labor of slaves and freedmen allowed them to do so in a straightforward way.[88] Those who succeeded in crafting such strategies could then find it difficult to integrate the labor of sons into their workshops when those sons finally matured, unless that moment coincided with a major change in their ability to enlist the help of others – as would have been the case, for instance, had an apprentice or long-term journeyman in the shop moved on in search of other opportunities.[89] In these circumstances, many probably encouraged their sons to work elsewhere rather than disrupt the rhythms of their own workshops, unless they felt a strong desire to groom their sons as their successors.

Although our ancient evidence is not comprehensive enough to permit an examination of the finer details of this hypothesis, it is nevertheless broadly consistent with the view that fathers with substantial capital assets were more likely to groom their sons to succeed them than were most other artisans and retailers, who found their efforts to keep those sons employed productively complicated by seasonal and uncertain demand. The commemorative patterns generated by the occupational inscriptions offer support for this view, if only indirectly, since they suggest that at least some of the men commemorated by their sons were likely to have been wealthier or better-capitalized than most artisans, and thus potentially more interested

---

[88] Ehmer 1984: 205–6 makes this point in the context of the Viennese trades in the eighteenth and nineteenth centuries.

[89] Cerutti 1991: 114–16 notes that Turin tailors often took on apprentices or journeymen slightly before their own sons departed to take up apprenticeships of their own. The precise cause of this pattern remains unclear, since Cerutti notes that the labor of apprentices and journeymen otherwise does not seem to have been a substitute for the labor of children. For that reason, it is possible that the pattern indicates that most tailors became successful enough in their own businesses to employ others at roughly the same time that their own sons entered early adolescence.

in ensuring that their sons could inherit their businesses. The wholesalers (*negotiatores*) and the doctor commemorated by their sons arguably fit this model. So too, perhaps, does the arms manufacturer, who also may have enjoyed more stable demand than did most artisans.[90] The frequency with which daughters commemorated men in these kinds of occupations, though initially surprising, also makes sense if the entrepreneurs who practiced them were wealthier than most artisans and retailers, and thus interested in ensuring that their children succeeded to a major share of their estates. By contrast, the low rate of son-to-father succession among artisans and retailers themselves reflects the fact that men in these trades were less likely to possess enough business-specific capital to have strong incentives for ensuring that their sons succeeded them, even though many either owned skilled slaves or controlled the *operae* of freedmen – especially if the demand for their products and services made it difficult to keep those sons employed regularly.

In spite of the interpretative problems it poses, Lucian's satirical account of his own apprenticeship is also consistent with this model of the considerations that encouraged artisans and retailers to establish their sons in independent careers. Not only does it suggest that the modest amounts of physical capital required in many trades factored into a father's deliberations, it also evokes concerns that were probably widespread among artisans in an economic environment subject to seasonal and uncertain demand. Lucian is more explicit about the first of these considerations than the second, and he portrays the affordability of the equipment necessary to embark on a career as a sculptor as one of the deciding factors in his father's decision to secure an apprenticeship for him in that trade. While he claims that his father was anxious to find him a career "suitable for a man of free birth," he also stresses that his father was careful to weigh the balance between the startup costs associated with potential trades and the standards of living each could produce: he hoped to find a trade for Lucian "requiring easily accessible equipment, and bringing in an adequate income." At the same time, Lucian hints that the seasonal and uncertain nature of demand in urban product markets made his father unwilling or unable to employ him productively at home. He does so by claiming that his father's interest in ensuring that he could generate income from employment outside the

---

[90] Not only were military implements themselves relatively standard in form, they were also presumably in consistently high demand in Roman culture. In ancient Athens, comparable factors may have likewise made it possible for individuals to invest in workforces consisting of large numbers of slaves who were dedicated to the manufacture of weapons and shields (e.g., Aeschin. 1.97; Dem. 27.9; Lys. 12.19).

household itself reflected his father's desire to diversify the household's income stream. As he phrases it, "if I were to learn one of your ordinary crafts, I would straightaway earn a living from it and not be a drain on my family at such an age, and before long my father would be enjoying a share of my earnings."[91] Implicit in this statement is the notion that Lucian's labor had only limited value within the context of his father's household, even if our ability to parse that notion is limited by Lucian's decision not to reveal his father's occupation. Yet, because Lucian's family was embedded in an artisanal milieu – his maternal grandfather and uncles were all stonemasons[92] – it is not implausible to believe that his father ran his own business but found it difficult to integrate him into that business thanks to the pervasive impact of seasonal and uncertain demand on his own need for regular, permanent help.

Comparable points can be made about the apprenticeships the Egyptian weavers Pausiris, Epinikos, and Tryphon son of Dionysios arranged for their sons or wards, in spite of the fact that historians have tended to interpret them from the perspective that weavers in Roman Egypt sought regularly to integrate sons into their own businesses. That interpretation owes much to the fact that Tryphon's grandfather, Tryphon son of Didymos, is known to have headed a household that included his three adult sons, each of whom had also been trained as a weaver.[93] Because the four men lived together, historians typically conclude that they worked in a common family enterprise and adopt this view as a general model for understanding the organization of weaving businesses in Roman Egypt. In this model, fathers and sons both had strong incentives to ensure the continuity of individual family businesses: fathers had an interest in retaining access to the labor of their sons, and sons themselves were motivated to remain in the family workshop by the prospect of eventually inheriting the assets of their fathers. Advocates of this position then explain the apparent tendency of weavers to apprentice their sons or wards to other artisans by suggesting that men like Pausiris, Epinikos, and the younger Tryphon relied on formal apprenticeships to complement or round out the training they provided to their sons within their own workshops. On this view, sons apprenticed by their fathers to other artisans working in the same trade not only had the opportunity to learn techniques in which their fathers may not have been well versed, or to gain experience in the

---

[91] Luc. *Somn.* 1. Translations adapted from Costa 2006. On comparable motivations underlying the strategies of peasant farmers in both classical Greece and contemporary contexts, see Gallant 1991: 34–59 and Ellis 1993: 82–98.

[92] Luc. *Somn.* 7.   [93] *P. Oxy.* II 314.

manufacture of specific articles their instructors were known for producing, but also experienced firsthand what it was like to be subjected to the
standards of discipline expected by an employer to whom they were not
closely related.[94]

Yet even if we accept the view that the elder Tryphon employed his sons
in a family business, it is not clear that this conclusion should serve as a
general model for the strategies employed by other weavers in Roman
Egypt. Instead, the apprenticeships arranged by Pausiris, Epinikos, and the
younger Tryphon are potentially more compatible with the model I
proposed above – namely, a model in which artisans used apprenticeship
as a tool for establishing sons in their own careers – both because the
limited amounts of capital they employed gave them little incentive to
ensure that sons inherited their enterprises and because the seasonal and
uncertain demand for their products limited their own requirements for
regular, permanent help.

First, the nature and extent of the capital normally employed by weavers
in their trades did not normally create strong incentives for them to pass their
businesses on to their sons. Some weavers were undoubtedly successful
enough that they accumulated substantial amounts of business-related capital, but such cases were not the norm. Most weavers would have accumulated assets on a scale more in keeping with what seems to have been typical
among artisans in general, especially given the affordability of the equipment
used in this trade.[95] Weavers in this category would not have faced strong
incentives to integrate their sons into their own enterprises, particularly if
seasonal and uncertain demand posed problems insofar as their own needs
for regular, permanent help were concerned. They may even have seen the
affordability of physical capital in this trade as an inducement to help their
sons establish themselves as independent weavers in their own right, much in
the same way that the affordability of a sculptor's toolkit encouraged
Lucian's father to establish him in that trade.[96]

---

[94] Wipszycka 1965: 61 and 63–5; Biscottini 1966: 65–6; Bergamasco 1995: 150–2; Freu 2011: 30–1. In the
editorial comments for *P. Wisc.* I 4, Sijpesteijn makes the suggestion that Pausiris and Epinikos
specialized in different branches of the weaving trade. Ruffing 2008 may add further support to that
hypothesis by compiling the evidence for horizontal specialization in the textile trades (see 113–14 for
an overview).

[95] Wipszycka 1965: 48–54 discusses the tools used in the weaving trade and concludes that they were
generally inexpensive (a loom was sold in 54 CE for 20 *drachmai*, or about 75 kg wheat-equivalent).

[96] Also relevant in this context is a dialogue written by Lucian, in which the characters – a blacksmith's
widow and her daughter – are able to support themselves for only seven months after the widow sells
the anvil and tools of her husband (Luc. *DMeretr.* 6). This too suggests that equipment in many
trades was not prohibitively expensive. In trades like baking and fulling, which required more in the
way of physical plant, it was more difficult for fathers to establish sons in independent careers, and

Second, artisans who had a regular-enough demand for skilled help that they could employ their relatives personally may have been unwilling to incur the opportunity costs necessary to apprentice those relatives to others in the late stages of their training. As we saw above, the opportunity costs many parents incurred when arranging apprenticeships for young men were substantially higher than ancient historians have recognized, since the income adolescents could generate by undertaking even unskilled work instead of serving apprenticeships was substantial enough to make a notable difference in the standards of living enjoyed by other household members. For Pausiris, Epinikos, and Tryphon, who apprenticed their relatives to others after investing time and energy in training them person-ally,[97] the opportunity costs would have been steeper yet, especially if they needed the labor of those relatives within their own workshops. By apprenticing them to other artisans in these circumstances, they would have foregone access to skilled labor that they presumably would have needed to replace if they did not wish to absorb a loss in overall productiv-ity, and replacing that labor would have been costly in and of itself. In theory, these men could have recruited substitutes for their relatives at a reduced rate by accepting apprentices of their own, provided that those apprentices already had a basic level of training. In practice, however, it was difficult to arrange matters so precisely, and the timing of Pausiris' one known decision to enlist an apprentice does not correlate in any obvious way with his decisions to place his own sons in the workshops of other artisans.[98] Nor could fathers substitute the labor of younger children for the labor of sons they apprenticed to others, since in most cases younger children would have needed to invest further time in observation and practice before becoming capable of matching the skills of their older

---

they may have aimed instead to pass down their own businesses to their sons. (For the nature of the equipment required by fullers, see now Flohr 2013: 121–48.) In other respects, workspace was liable to be one of the major expenses for a craftsman attempting to establish a business. In smaller centers these costs were not excessive. In 18 BCE, for example, Evangelus son of Archoneus made an advance payment on a goldsmith's shop in Roman Egypt and received possession when he paid the remaining balance of 300 *drachmai* (*BGU* IV 1127). The document once recorded the amount of the advance payment, but this figure is now unfortunately lost. Because it is unlikely to have exceeded the remaining balance, however, the shop sold for no more than 600 *drachmai* – roughly 1,970 kg of wheat-equivalent at 9 *drachmai* per *artaba* (Rathbone 1997: 217 and Duncan-Jones 1990: 143–55). The sale price of a pottery in 324 CE was comparable in magnitude: 15 talents or roughly 900 kg of wheat-equivalent at 300 *drachmai* per *artaba* (*PSI* IV 300; see Bagnall and Worp 1980: 16 for the date of the sale, and Bagnall 1985: 64 for the price of wheat). In a city like Rome, however, rents were likely to be high in general.

[97] See especially Biscottini 1966: 65–6 and Bergamasco 1995: 151. Cf. Bradley 1991: 111.

[98] Epinikos and Pausiris apprenticed their relatives to one another in 58 and 62 CE, respectively. Pausiris had apprenticed his other two sons in 49 and 53 CE (*P. Mich.* III 170–172, *P. Wisc.* I 4).

siblings.[99] And, although artisans like Pausiris could have hired skilled help during a son's apprenticeship, the wages they would have had to offer to attract such help would have been high – certainly much higher than the value of the small subsidies they received from the artisans to whom they had apprenticed their children, which often amounted to no more than a monthly sum of 4 or 5 *drachmai*, plus an additional allowance for clothing.[100]

Third, although artisans seeking to establish sons in independent careers likewise incurred opportunity costs when they apprenticed those sons to others (albeit chiefly in the form of foregone income, rather than in the form of diminished productivity in their own shops), they were arguably likely to see these costs as an important and justifiable investment in their sons' future prospects than were artisans hoping to employ their sons personally. This was so because apprenticeship was, from the perspective of a young man, an opportunity not just to learn skills but also to establish his own networks of personal and business contacts. Throughout their terms, apprentices had multiple opportunities to forge connections with suppliers, subcontractors, and clients: in early stages, they could find themselves visiting clients or suppliers to make deliveries or take possession of raw materials and intermediate goods; in advanced stages, they could be entrusted with the responsibility of managing the shop itself.[101] Connections of this sort, though not without value for young men intending to return to their fathers' workshops, were absolutely critical for those hoping to establish themselves in careers of their own when their apprenticeships ended.

Fourth, and finally, some incidental details revealed by the apprenticeship agreements of Pausiris, Epinikos, and the younger Tryphon are consistent with the view that they hesitated to employ their own relatives

---

[99] *Contra* Biscottini 1966: 66.

[100] For further discussion of the typical terms of these agreements, see below. Tryphon's younger brother was compensated at a rate of 4 *drachmai* per month in 36 CE (*P. Oxy.* II 322); his son at the rate of 5 *drachmai* per month in 66 CE (supplemented by an additional lump-sum payment of 12 *drachmai* for clothing). By contrast, and judging from the payment *entolae* from Mons Claudianus, the going rate for skilled labor at this particular moment in time was perhaps on the order of 50–60 *drachmai* per month if employers hired workers on long-term contracts or 3–4 *drachmai* per day when employers relied on the spot market (see Chapter 2 for more details).

[101] On the contacts that an apprentice could forge while making deliveries, see Lane 1996: 76–7 (and in particular her observation that William Masters "remarked in his memoirs that in this way he had come to know many watchmakers, journeymen and customers in the community, and these acquaintances had helped him as an adult workman"). Ulpian, on the other hand (*Dig.* 14.3.5.10), imagines that a fuller in the ancient world might leave his apprentices to manage the shop and deal with his clients while he himself went on a journey. Cf. Wallis 2008: 845, who notes that master artisans almost necessarily revealed "their client, credit, and supplier networks" to their apprentices.

because seasonal and uncertain demand made it difficult for them to guarantee those sons regular employment. They do so only indirectly, by suggesting that weavers in Roman Egypt were reluctant to shoulder the financial risks they would incur when they expanded their permanent workforces. The clearest sign of that reluctance is the terms on which they accepted skilled or semi-skilled apprentices who had already received some training in the profession from their own fathers: those terms reveal that instructors who accepted the sons of colleagues as apprentices were willing to do so only because they negotiated apprenticeship agreements designed to minimize their own additional costs. When, for example, the weaver Abaros agreed to take on Tryphon's younger brother Onnophris as an apprentice, he did so on the understanding that Onnophris' mother would remain responsible for most of the boy's living expenses and that his own costs would amount only to a monthly stipend of 4 *drachmai* (supplemented, perhaps, by a clothing allowance).[102] At an effective rate of 48 *drachmai* per year – equivalent to what a weaver would have needed to pay every month to maintain a regular employee – Onnophris' labor was a bargain from Abaros' perspective and would not have increased his fixed costs to the extent that unanticipated fluctuations in demand were likely to drive him into financial ruin. Likewise, when the weaver Ptolemaios accepted Tryphon's son Thoonis as an apprentice some thirty years later, he did so on comparable terms: he agreed to pay a stipend of 5 *drachmai* per month, along with a one-time clothing allowance of 12 *drachmai*, on the understanding that Tryphon would provide for the boy's remaining needs.[103] Lastly, although it is structured differently, the contract recording Pausiris' decision to apprentice his son Dioskos to the weaver Apollonios also seems weighted in favor of the instructor, if not quite so strongly. In this case, Apollonios assumed primary responsibility for Dioskos' daily maintenance, while Pausiris agreed to offset his costs by paying him a lump sum of 14 *drachmai* for clothing and providing a monthly food allowance of 5 *drachmai*.[104] If we assume that Dioskos' living expenses fell within the range of 75–100 *drachmai* per year,[105] then Apollonios' own financial exposure remained minimal. The fixed costs assumed by the instructors in all these cases, while not insignificant, were still exceptionally low compared to what they would have been required to pay in wages had

---

[102] *P. Oxy.* II 322. The document is unfortunately damaged precisely where a stipulation about a clothing allowance may have fallen.

[103] *P. Oxy.* II 275.   [104] *P. Wisc.* I 4.

[105] I base this figure on Scheidel's estimate that the bare-bones living expenses of an adult male in Roman Egypt at this time were roughly 112 *drachmai* per year (Scheidel 2010: 434).

they recruited semi-skilled or skilled help for only a fraction of the year, and low even when compared to the costs of housing and feeding one of their own family members. The fact that they accepted apprentices only under these conditions signals a strong aversion to risk, which can itself be interpreted as a product of the pressures that seasonal and uncertain demand exerted on artisans in the Roman world and on their own willingness to maintain permanent workforces. If this interpretation is correct, then it seems safe to conclude that the same factors undoubtedly influenced the tendency of artisans to establish their sons in careers of their own rather than to employ them personally. Doing so permitted artisans not only to limit their own fixed costs but also to generate insurance against risk by gaining access to additional revenue streams for their households once their sons had acquired the skills necessary to find gainful employment.

Artisans, sons, and the market structure of the Roman world

In the preceding discussion, I emphasized important points of similarity between the familial strategies crafted by artisans in the Roman world and those in early modern Europe in the hope of clarifying our understanding of the former. In both historical contexts, seasonal and uncertain demand was a daily reality for most entrepreneurs in urban environments. For artisans in particular, the nature of urban demand was a key factor motivating them to establish their sons in independent careers rather than to employ them in their own businesses.

Presented in this way, however, my argument risks obscuring changes in the dynamics of artisans' household strategies between 1650 and 1850 (the long eighteenth century), which – while seemingly small – nevertheless reflect a profound point of contrast between the structure of the early modern economy and the structure of the Roman economy. In the final pages of this section, I draw attention both to those changes and to the ways in which they differentiated the dynamics of artisans' household strategies in the early modern period from those in the Roman world. In the process, I offer some thoughts about the significance of these differences for our understanding of the Roman economy more broadly. As I suggest in what follows, detectable differences between the familial strategies of artisans in these two periods confirm that the product and labor markets of the Roman world, though sophisticated in some ways, remained thin relative to those of northwestern Europe during the long eighteenth century. First, our evidence for apprenticeship in antiquity indicates that Roman artisans found it more difficult to arrange apprentice-ships for their sons than did their early modern counterparts, and thus implies that the market for this kind of labor was not as fluid as in later periods, perhaps because most artisans themselves had little demand for apprentices. Second, from the late seventeenth century onward, the devel-opment of increasingly thick demand for goods and commodities in the lower and middle segments of the urban market encouraged artisans in different industries to integrate their sons more firmly into their own enterprises, albeit in ways that depended on their own individual fortunes. The fact that Roman artisans rarely integrated their sons into their enter-prises therefore signals indirectly that the urban populations of the Roman world did not generate enough demand for goods and services to thicken product markets in a comparable way, despite the sizeable aggregate purchasing power these populations commanded in large cities like Rome. In both cases, the strategies Roman artisans devised to arrange for their sons' futures therefore further support the arguments I have advanced in previous chapters about the performance and structure of the Roman economy during the late Republic and early Empire.

By stressing the importance of family connections in his account of his own brief apprenticeship, Lucian emphasizes a point made implicitly in the documents from Roman Egypt – namely, that artisans in the Roman world relied heavily on relationships of trust based in strong social ties when they sought apprenticeships for their sons, whether by apprenticing those sons to colleagues in professional associations, or by placing them in the care of relatives.[106] Lucian himself, of course, was apprenticed to his maternal uncle, but he further emphasizes the importance of strong social ties when he depicts his father's deliberations about his future as a long and pro-tracted process in which his father discussed the issue with several close friends and family members. Finally, Lucian's uncle too had probably learned his trade with the help of relationships anchored in family ties or professional associations, since he shared that trade with his own father and brother.[107]

If this reliance on strong social ties can be taken to reflect a general pattern in the Roman world, then it suggests that the market for appren-tices was less fluid in antiquity than it was in parts of early modern Europe during the seventeenth and eighteenth centuries. Recent research on the

---

[106] On the importance of relationships of trust in apprenticeship agreements, cf. Venticinque 2010 and esp. 288–92.
[107] Luc. *Somn.* 1–4 and 7.

market for apprentices in London has stressed that strong networks were much less important to a young man's ability to secure an apprenticeship in early modern England than historians had previously believed. Rather, apprenticeship opportunities in London were remarkably open, and young men from the provinces who had no clear connections to the London market were able to find positions with seemingly little difficulty. To the extent that personal ties played a role in the process, apprentices or their parents relied primarily on acquaintances to pass on information about prospective job opportunities.[108]

Although it is not yet clear why London's apprenticeship market was so fluid, one potential explanation is that slow growth in the metropolitan consumer market provoked a complementary growth in artisans' own demand for the labor of apprentices. If so, then the seeming importance of strong ties to prospective apprentices in the Roman world may be a symptom of product markets that were not so favorable to artisans as those in the early modern period. On this view, Roman artisans may have been reluctant to accept apprentices in the absence of strong personal ties based on family connections or anchored in *collegia*.

Differences in the frequency with which artisans in the ancient and early modern contexts employed their sons also point to product markets that remained thin in all segments in antiquity. Although many artisans in the early modern period chose not to employ their own sons, there was nevertheless an increasing tendency among certain groups of urban producers to integrate sons into their own enterprises. That trend was partly a consequence of the thickening product markets in which they were embedded. In particular, the growing demand for relatively affordable manufactured goods among members of urban working and middle classes made it possible for some artisans to produce longer runs of undifferentiated products than had been feasible in the past. Those pursuing this strategy developed enterprises that were more heavily capitalized than most: even though they continued to subcontract for some services and intermediate goods, they nevertheless chose to invest in the space and working capital necessary to coordinate production on a relatively large scale. Because those who succeeded had strong incentives to transmit their businesses intact to their sons, they were increasingly inclined to integrate their sons into those enterprises.[109]

At the same time, the growing demand for undifferentiated goods provoked poorer artisans to make heavy use of the labor of their sons as

---

[108] Leunig et al. 2011.   [109] Ehmer 2001: 191–3.

well, albeit for different reasons. Thickening markets led to an expansion of specific kinds of subcontracting networks that developed to supply low-cost semi-finished goods and component parts to emerging capital-intensive enterprises. Subcontracting networks of this type differed from those common in segments of the market catering to the demand for quality or high-end populuxe goods, in which artisans had long economized on fixed costs by subcontracting for specialized skills or extra capacity as necessary. Instead, subcontracting networks in low-end segments of the market permitted coordinating artisans to economize on costs by breaking the production process down into a series of low-skilled or semi-skilled steps that could be performed by subcontractors in their own homes. In these circumstances, craftsmen who accepted work as subcontractors enlisted the help of family members – including sons – to boost their output: the necessary steps were simple enough that subcontractors could train wives and children quickly and on the job, and family labor was much less expensive to enlist in this context than was the help of semi-skilled or even unskilled workers recruited from outside of the household.[110]

Here, the evidence presented by the occupational inscriptions converges with our evidence for industrial organization in the Roman world to support the claim that all product market segments remained thin during the late Republic and early Empire. Subcontracting networks designed to minimize production costs through the exploitation of unskilled labor do not appear in our sources, and while this may simply reflect gaps in our evidence, it could also indicate that demand in low-end segments of the market did not become stable enough to support such networks. The commemorative pattern in the occupational inscriptions, however, supports the latter interpretation. The frequency of son-to-father commemorations in the occupational inscriptions offers only a crude index of the extent to which fathers integrated sons into their own enterprises in the Roman world, but it nevertheless implies that they did so rarely – more rarely, perhaps, than their early modern counterparts. Additionally, since the inscriptions probably reflect a prosperous slice of Rome's artisan population, the rarity of son-to-father commemorations suggests that artisans in this group did not use that prosperity to increase the capital assets of their businesses sufficiently to motivate them to bequeath their enterprises to their sons. That observation can be understood best as evidence that there was little development in the depth of the Roman world's product markets during the early Empire. To understand fully why

---

[110] Ehmer 1984: 203; Schwarz 1992: 179–207 and esp. 206–7; Riello 2006: 172–6.

that was the case, however, it is necessary to invoke the nature of household consumption goals in antiquity – a topic best explored by examining the role of women in artisan households.

Wives in artisan households

Historians of the Roman world are increasingly sensitive to the fact that women worked hard to enhance the well-being of their family members, whether by handling tasks necessary to keep a household running smoothly or by contributing directly to the family income. In particular, historians have focused much of their recent research on determining how often and in what ways women engaged in work designed to generate income, despite various social constraints that could limit their economic opportunities. This research has demonstrated that while freeborn women in particular could enjoy extensive property rights and considerable freedom of action, they nevertheless faced more limitations on their ability to market their labor or engage in production in their own right than men, thanks largely to constraints that were themselves the product of a strongly gendered ideology of work. This ideology stressed not only that women ideally belonged within the home rather than in public but also that certain kinds of work were more suitable for women than others – principally, those that drew on traditional domestic skills. It operated chiefly by curtailing freeborn women's ability to acquire specialized skills or training, especially outside of the home: although the apprenticeship documents from Roman Egypt suggest that both male and female slaves were often apprenticed to craftsmen by their owners (particularly to weavers), free-born girls were far less likely to be apprenticed to artisans than freeborn boys. Moreover, even enslaved women who were apprenticed to artisans by their masters were trained in a narrow range of trades, and probably less frequently than male slaves.[111]

Although this recent research has done much to clarify our understanding of the economic roles women could adopt when they chose to allocate time to income-generating work, it has devoted less attention to two important and interrelated problems. The first is the nature of the considerations that shaped women's choices about how to allocate their time. Many, of course, had no real choice at all. Those who were unmarried and

---

[111] For the most recent general surveys, see Saller 2003 and 2007. For conditions in the urban economy, see Treggiari 1979; Kampen 1981, esp. 107–29; Joshel 1992, esp. 141 n. 25; Groen-Vallinga 2013; Holleran 2013. For women in agriculture, see Scheidel 1995 and 1996a; Erdkamp 2005: 87–94.

had no family members to support them needed to earn money just to keep body and soul together. Married women too could find themselves compelled to work to ensure that their households were able to make ends meet, like the wife of the impoverished craftsman in Apuleius' *Metamorphoses*, who spins wool in order to supplement the meager day-wages brought home by her husband. Given the nature of our evidence, however, it is more difficult to identify how women made decisions concerning work when they belonged to households with better access to resources, and when they therefore faced genuine choices about how they would allocate their time and labor. The second is the relationship between women's choices and the overall performance of the economy. Here, Richard Saller has established the basic groundwork by arguing that growth was constrained by women's poor access to training.[112] This was undoubtedly true, but inasmuch as growth was possible in other contexts in which women were disadvantaged in comparable ways, Saller's argument can potentially be pressed further.

De Vries' recent study of work and the household in early modern Europe provides a framework capable of generating insight into both problems. De Vries has emphasized that household consumption goals played a crucial role in shaping decisions about how women in particular would allocate their time between two broad categories of work – work designed to generate income and work designed to address the internal needs of the household.[113] De Vries draws heavily on the work of Gary Becker, who modeled the household as an organization in which members produce goods (so-called Z-commodities) to satisfy their consumption goals by combining two different kinds of inputs: (1) goods and services purchased on the market and (2) tasks performed within the household itself, many of which add value to (or extract utility from) inputs in the first category. The model therefore implies that members of a household must decide how much of their time to allocate to income-generating activities in order to purchase desired goods and services, and how much to allocate to the household tasks that are necessary to exploit them fully.[114] In de Vries' elaboration of this model, the specific consumption goals targeted by individual household members profoundly affect how they weigh the relative merits of devoting time to one type of work versus the other. In particular, if they believe both that tasks performed within the household are critical to their well-being and that they cannot find acceptable

---

[112] Saller 2003, 2007, and 2012.   [113] De Vries 2008, and esp. 25–37.
[114] Becker 1991, esp. 20–9.

substitutes for them by purchasing goods and services on the market, then they will be reluctant to reallocate time from household tasks to income-generating work. Conversely, if household members adopt goals prioritizing the consumption of purchased goods and services, they will allocate more of their time to work directed at the market in order to fund their purchases. Crucially, if consumption goals of this sort become widespread, the aggregate impact of countless individual decisions to allocate time to income-generating work can transform both labor and product markets, thus giving rise to the kind of thick market externalities so vital to per capita growth in preindustrial contexts.[115]

For de Vries, Europe's long eighteenth century (1650–1850) stands out because of the intensity with which household members realigned their consumption goals and women reallocated their time – and because of how that behavior affected the performance of the early modern economy. In this period, members of working- and middle-class households began to place increasingly less emphasis on consumption goals in which leisure time was important to their overall satisfaction. In their place, they adopted new goals prioritizing the consumption of both comestibles (such as tea, coffee, and sugar) and certain kinds of manufactured goods (like clothing, furniture, and tableware). Because these goods needed to be acquired on the market, the spread of new consumption goals triggered changes in the way household members (especially women) allocated their time. Since household tasks were often coded as women's responsibility, and since men enjoyed a competitive advantage in the labor market thanks to better access to training, women had devoted much of their time to household tasks before 1650. As households began to place more emphasis on the consumption of marketed goods and services, however, women reallocated much of that time to income-generating work and, in the process, transformed labor and product markets in ways that provoked a period of sustained, if gentle, growth.[116]

De Vries' analysis suggests that we cannot fully understand how women allocated their time in artisanal and entrepreneurial households in the Roman world without first attempting to identify the consumption goals prioritized by the members of such households, since these would have been pivotal in determining how individuals split their time between income-generating work and household tasks. In what follows, I therefore

---

[115] De Vries 2008: 71–2. Cf. Grantham 1999, who focuses on thick market externalities generated by improvements in the technologies and infrastructure of trade and communication rather than on those created by changes in individual consumption preferences.

[116] De Vries 2008: 1–185.

pursue this problem in detail. I suggest that members of households at all ranges of the socioeconomic spectrum prioritized consumption goals that could be met only if they allocated the time of some of their members – in particular, women – to tasks designed to meet the internal needs of the household itself. On the level of the individual household, this meant that wives especially had strong incentives to allocate their time to these kinds of tasks rather than to income-generating work and that they consequently did not seek to buffer their households against the risks of the urban market by enhancing or diversifying their household's incomes as aggressively as they otherwise might have. Furthermore, I suggest that this behavior also had significant consequences for the overall performance of the Roman economy: because women in antiquity did not allocate as much of their time to work that enhanced the purchasing power of their households as did women in Europe during the long eighteenth century, demand in urban product markets remained highly seasonal and uncertain, and opportunities for sustained productivity growth in the economy as a whole remained limited.

Household consumption goals in the Roman world

Due to the paucity of our evidence, the consumption goals of Roman households are difficult to elucidate. Ancient historians do not possess anything comparable to the probate records that generate insight into changes in consumption habits in Europe's long eighteenth century.[117] Any approach to Roman consumption goals must therefore be indirect and must contend with sources that are colored by idealized and prescriptive representations of women and their roles in the family economy. That said, a careful reading of these sources suggests that the consumption goals of sub-aristocratic households in antiquity were shaped more strongly than those of the early modern working and middle classes by the belief that a wife contributed best to her household's well-being when she allocated much of her time to household tasks rather than to work meant to generate extra income.

That belief is expressed consistently in the literary and legal sources of the late Republic and early Empire, which stress two aspects of a wife's ideal role in the household. First, she was to act as the household's *custos* – its guardian or steward. In this capacity, she was expected to manage the

---

[117] On what probate inventories can tell us, see de Vries 2008: 125–6, who cites the relevant bibliography for France, England, and New England in the early modern period.

household's material and human assets by monitoring its stores and super-vising its slaves.[118] Second, she was to produce essential goods such as clothing for the household's own consumption. Augustus famously boasted that he wore only clothing produced by the women of his house-hold,[119] and while we might be tempted to dismiss the idea that this boast accurately reflected general aristocratic *mores*, to some extent it did align with wider social attitudes. Some scholars have argued that women in wealthy households continued to maintain looms in public areas of the house, and even if these looms served mostly symbolic purposes, they nevertheless reflect the ongoing cultural relevance of the Roman matronly ideal.[120] Nor should we necessarily assume that those looms were in fact mostly symbolic: even if we reject the view that women in wealthy house-holds produced all (or even most) of the textiles required by their family members and domestic slaves, the jurist Pomponius took for granted the possibility that a wife might nevertheless supervise the production of some clothing within the home, whether it was intended for use by herself, by her husband, or by other members of the household.[121]

Although the literary and legal evidence reflects a predominantly elite perspective, comparable beliefs about a wife's role in the family economy are communicated by sculptural reliefs and funerary inscriptions that capture the views of a broader cross-section of Roman society. These sources emphasize the importance of the goods and services women produced for household consumption, while overlooking the potential value of their income-generating work. Natalie Kampen, for example, has stressed that visual depictions of working women in Roman art differ in a critical way from those of working men: while the latter offer realistic depictions of male subjects that are designed to highlight the social and economic value of their work, the former are instead allegorical and use work to evoke well-known myths. Kampen notes that there are some exceptions to this general pattern – most notably, the realistic depictions of female vendors and retailers on several reliefs – but argues that exceptions were rare precisely because a woman's income-generating work detracted from, rather than enhanced, her status, even in an artisanal and entrepreneurial social milieu.[122] Funerary

---

[118] On the role of the Roman wife as *custos* of her household, see Pearce 1974 and Saller 2003: 190. Among our Roman authors, Columella offers the most extensive commentary on gender roles in his discussion of the duties of the *vilicus'* wife: see *Rust.* 12.pr-3.

[119] Suet. *Aug.* 73.1.

[120] On the complex relationship of these ideologies to actual social practice, see Dixon 2001b, esp. 117–25. On wool-working as a symbol of idealized feminine behavior, see Lovén 1998 and 2007: 230–3.

[121] Pomponius, *Dig.* 24.1.31.pr.   [122] Kampen 1982, esp. 72–3.

inscriptions likewise emphasize the work performed by women within the household. It is true that some women were given occupational titles in their funerary inscriptions, which indicate that they (or their commemorators) valued the various kinds of income-generating work they performed, but our evidence shows that they were commemorated more often in ways that emphasized their roles as wives and mothers. Undoubtedly, these modes of representation were conventional, especially when they stressed the matronly virtues of the deceased, such as their fidelity or devotion to their children.[123] It is nevertheless significant that our inscriptions emphasize the contributions women made to their domestic economies by producing goods and services for household consumption, both by spinning or weaving – tasks that are evoked visually on tombstones, albeit more frequently in the East than in the West – and by undertaking work that was associated with a wife's role as *custos*.[124] Each of these aspects of a wife's role is captured in the well-known epitaph of a woman known only as Claudia, which stresses that "she took care of the household and wove wool (*domum servavit lanam fecit*)."[125]

The critical question is whether or not the beliefs expressed in these sources corresponded in any way to actual consumption preferences and social practices. The evidence cannot support a definitive answer, but if typical social practice did diverge notably from the ideal expressed in these sources, then we might expect to find some trace of that fact in our evidence. The early modern material, for example, shows how consumption preferences that conflicted with traditional gender ideologies could affect practice in detectable ways. First, changing consumption preferences affected the way in which women from working- and middle-class families were represented in certain sources. In the Netherlands during the seventeenth century, visual artists began to depict women working outside of the home in realistic and unproblematic ways, even though moralizing literary texts continued to stress that a wife should devote herself to work within the household. This development reflected new valuations of work that stressed industriousness and diligence as virtues for men and women alike: although gender ideologies still encouraged wives to apply their industriousness and diligence within the household, individuals became more capable of appreciating women's ability to contribute directly to a household's income as they adopted consumption preferences assigning increased importance to the value of goods and services purchased on the

---

[123] Dixon 2001b: 115.
[124] On regional differences in visual depictions of women and spinning, see Cottica 2003.
[125] *CIL* 6.15346 (=*ILS* 8.403).

market rather than produced within the home.[126] Second, these changing preferences also enhanced opportunities for women to acquire craft and business skills within their own households, even though their access to formal apprenticeships remained limited. By drawing on records produced by the London livery companies, Amy Louise Erickson has recently estimated that, at a bare minimum, at least 15 percent of the members of most London livery companies in the seventeenth and eighteenth centuries worked alongside their wives. Crucially, most of the wives in these partnerships had sufficient training that they could not only maintain an enterprise after the death of their husbands but also train apprentices.[127] As a result, "there was a wide band of couples in the middle [of the socioeconomic spectrum] who were not only more likely to work in the same business but whose prosperity was probably built on the very fact of their running a joint establishment."[128] In Erickson's view, most of these women acquired their skills in enterprises belonging to their spouses or parents: as changing consumption goals motivated households to allocate more resources to income-generating work, individuals came to realize that women could better help their families meet their new goals if they could acquire training that enhanced their ability to contribute directly to a household business.[129]

In stark contrast, however, the meager and indirect evidence for social practices among sub-aristocratic families in antiquity reveals little interest in women's potential to enhance the purchasing power of their households. Instead, it suggests strongly that consumption goals at this level of society conformed to the idealized view that women were to spend their time providing key goods and services to other members of their households. Artemidorus' dream interpretations are a case in point. Given Artemidorus' belief that he could provide a correct interpretation only by accounting for the dreamer's personal characteristics – things like age, sex, wealth, and occupation[130] – his interpretations that touch upon women's roles within the domestic economy ought to reflect preferences and social practices of individuals from a broad cross-section of society. For that reason, it is significant that these interpretations focus instead on themes that evoke only the literary image of women, and thus seem incompatible with a model in which consumption preferences

---

[126] Schmidt 2011.   [127] Erickson 2008: 286–92.   [128] Erickson 2008: 278–86 and esp. 285.
[129] A point strongly implied by Erickson 2008: 269, even if she does not articulate it in quite these terms.
[130] See Harris-McCoy 2012: 15–18 on Artemidorus' belief that dreams could only be properly interpreted if the diviner took the individual's personal circumstances into account.

prompted women in antiquity to allocate large amounts of time to income-generating work.[131]

First, several of Artemidorus' interpretations imply that wives and daughters were not expected to contribute directly to their households' incomes in the same way as sons. Artemidorus refers to a son's ability to generate income in his analyses of dreams in which a client ate his or her child, in whole or in part. A dream in which the client ate only the body part from which the child earned a livelihood meant that the dreamer would profit from his or her child's professional success. The examples Artemidorus uses to illustrate the point all seem to feature sons: one concerns a parent who eats the feet of a child who runs races; another, a parent who eats the hands of a child who works as an artisan; a third, a parent who eats the shoulders of a child who wrestles.[132] Conversely, when he offers interpretations predicting that women will bring material benefits to their households, Artemidorus assumes that they will do so by providing access to property rather than by generating income: a daughter by becoming rich in her own right, possibly because of an advantageous marriage;[133] a wife by bringing her husband a large dowry or by using her personal wealth to pay off his debts.[134] Only in one interpretation does Artemidorus describe a wife generating income for the household through her own labor – and that is in the context of a problematic case in which a client had been selling the sexual services of his spouse.[135] More common are interpretations indicating that daughters in particular, because they required dowries, were conceptualized as drains on the household's resources: Artemidorus observes that money-lenders and daughters were interchangeable as symbols in dreams because, like a money-lender, "a daughter too necessarily makes demands, and after she has been raised (with much attention), she takes her portion and leaves."[136]

Second, several of Artemidorus' interpretations rest on the belief that a wife's most important function was to serve her household as a conscientious *oikouros* – the Greek equivalent of the Latin *custos* – by tending to the welfare

---

[131] For a comparable approach to the depiction of women in Artemidorus, see Knapp 2011: 53–96.

[132] Artem. 1.70.

[133] More specifically, Artemidorus 1.78 remarks that it is good for a poor man who has a rich daughter to dream of having sexual intercourse with her, "for, deriving benefits from her in many ways, he will rejoice in her."

[134] Examples of dreams portending that the dreamer would find a wealthy wife can be found at 2.31 and 2.32. See 1.79 for Artemidorus' interpretation of a dream in which the dreamer received oral sex from his wife or lover; in his view, if the dreamer had a wife who was wealthier than he was himself, the dream meant that she would "pay off many debts on behalf of her husband."

[135] Artem. 5.2.   [136] Artem. 3.41; cf. 1.15 and 1.78.

of its members and the security of its stores and property. A dream in which a client was beheaded, for instance, could be interpreted as a sign that he was about to suffer the loss of the person who cared for his property. That person could be a slave or a friend, but Artemidorus also explicitly mentions the dreamer's wife.[137] Just as interesting are Artemidorus' interpretations of dreams that offered clients contemplating marriage insight into the character of prospective wives. Artemidorus framed many of these specifically in order to answer questions about whether or not a woman would prove to be a good *oikouros*. The most straightforward interpretations concern dreams portending a successful marriage, in which a client's wife would prove to be not just faithful or pious but also good at managing the household; these include dreams in which the client saw either the goddess Athena or other significant symbols, such as watchdogs, swallows, and keys.[138] More complicated are interpretations of dreams in which a client fought in the arena as a gladiator. Here, Artemidorus stresses that the nature of a man's prospective wife could be deduced either from the nature of his opponent or from the weapons that he himself carried in the dream. In most cases, this kind of dream portended that a man's wife would possess some notable flaw alongside any potential virtues: a man who dreamt of fighting a *secutor*, for instance, would marry a woman who, although attractive and rich, would prove to be materialistic, prone to insulting her husband, and "the source of many evils." From Artemidorus' perspective, only one variant of the gladiator dream portended an unambiguously positive marriage, and it is telling that his interpretation stresses his belief that the prospective wife would serve her husband well as his *oikouros*.[139]

Evidence concerning women's roles in household businesses likewise shows that consumption goals in Roman antiquity motivated individuals to prioritize the tasks women performed in the household more strongly than was the case in seventeenth and eighteenth century Europe, and to do so at the expense of women's ability to generate income. They do so primarily by implying that Roman women had fewer opportunities to acquire training in craft or business skills within their own households than their early modern counterparts. Greek and Latin literature of the Roman period assumes that wives and daughters did not participate directly in

---

[137] For household management as the typical work of a wife, see 1.78. Artemidorus' comments on what serving as an *oikouros* entailed can be found at 1.35 and 2.27.

[138] Artem. 2.11 (watchdogs, which signify good housekeeping on the part of both a man's wife and his slaves), 2.35 (Athena), 2.66 (in which the client sees a swallow, which also signifies that his wife will be both musically inclined and Greek), and 3.54 (keys).

[139] Artem. 2.32.

family businesses and thus did not acquire comprehensive training in the relevant skills. In his *Metamorphoses*, for instance, Apuleius imagines that the married daughter of a murdered miller might auction off the assets she inherited from her father after he died, including his slaves and animals; it is tempting to read this as an indication that, in Apuleius' view, a daughter who had grown up in the household of an artisan would not have had the skills necessary to exploit her father's business on her own.[140] Lucian's *Dialogues of the Courtesans* makes the same point concerning a wife. One of the episodes in this collection of stories revolves around the efforts of a woman named Crobyle and her daughter to cope with the death of Crobyle's husband, a prosperous blacksmith. Crobyle initially responds to her husband's death by selling his equipment to raise money to meet her household's expenses. Like Apuleius, Lucian thus implies that women belonging to artisan households would generally not have acquired the skills necessary to run such businesses themselves.[141] In that sense, these anecdotes seem to lend support to Keith Bradley's suggestion, founded on his analysis of the Egyptian apprenticeship documents, "that daughters in artisanal families, like their counterparts in upper-class society at Rome, may not normally have been trained for work other than that of a tradi-tional, domestic sort, but were instead prepared only for marriage and childbearing in the seclusive manner typical of women's life in antiquity as a whole."[142]

Scaevola's discussion of a partially preserved Roman will shows that actual social practices did not conflict dramatically with the assumptions embedded within these anecdotes and that many women lacked access to the skills necessary to operate certain kinds of artisanal enterprises on their own. According to Scaevola, a female testator had specified in her will that ownership of her ironworking shop, along with its equipment, was to be granted jointly to her slave Pamphilus (who was to be freed) and to a man named Lucius Eutychus, so that the two of these men together could carry on the business. Complications arose because Lucius Eutychus predeceased the testator, who did not update the terms of her will. When an unnamed coheir took possession of the workshop, he attempted to exclude the newly manumitted Pamphilus from a share in its ownership, apparently on the grounds that Eutychus' death would prevent Pamphilus from maintaining the business as the testator had desired. For our purposes, the most significant detail is the belief of all concerned that Eutychus himself was vital to the ongoing health of the business. Given the importance accorded

---

[140] Apul. *Met.* 9.31.   [141] Luc. *DMeretr.* 6.1.   [142] Bradley 1991: 108.

to him, both in the terms of the will and in the dispute that unfolded after
the testator's death, it seems that Eutychus had been closely involved in
operating the business while the testator was still alive. If so, then the will
may reflect a case in which a woman who had acquired a workshop, its
equipment, and its slaves from a male relative lacked the comprehensive
training necessary to operate all aspects of the enterprise herself and was
forced to enlist the help of someone possessing the requisite skills so that
she could continue to exploit those assets.[143]

Finally, even evidence that reflects artisanal or entrepreneurial milieus
more directly than do the literary and legal sources implies that women in
Roman households were less likely to acquire comprehensive training in
family businesses than those in early modern Europe. That evidence does
show that some women, at least, could benefit from training within their
own households. A well-known anecdote in the New Testament mentions a
husband and wife, Aquila and Priscilla, who worked together as tent-makers
in Corinth.[144] As we saw in Chapter 3, women in Rome sometimes claimed
the same occupational titles that they assigned to men whom they commemorated in funerary inscriptions, thus implying that they too had benefitted
from dedicated training.[145] Other inscriptions imply that a woman contributed to a household business in ways that permitted her to develop business
or technical skills, even if they do not state so outright. When Pompeia
Memphis commemorated her husband, a goldsmith, she did not claim an
occupational title explicitly. Nevertheless, the fact that she manumitted a
skilled slave in her own right shows that she herself possessed the skills
necessary to carry on the business after her husband's death:[146]

> Pompeia Memphis made this for herself and
> for her husband Cnaeus Pompeius Iucundus,
> the goldsmith, who lived for 35 years,
> and for her freedman Cnaeus Pompeius Fructus,
> the goldsmith, who lived for 40 years, and for her freedmen
> and freedwomen and their posterity.

That said, there are reasons to believe that these examples represent
exceptions rather than the rule and that women in the Roman world were

---

[143] Scaevola, *Dig.* 31.1.88.3.   [144] Acts 18:2–3.
[145] In addition to the inscriptions of Veturia Flora and Cameria Iarine (both of which I discuss in
Chapter 3), *CIL* 6.6939 and 6.9211 each name what seem to have been husbands and wives who
worked as manufacturers of gold leaf (Treggiari 1979: 66–7; but cf. 76, where Treggiari suggests that
such women may have specialized in the retail side of the business). On these and on similar
inscriptions, some of which show groups of male and female *colliberti*, cf. Joshel 1992: 138–44.
[146] *CIL* 6.37781.

on the whole less likely to enjoy access to training within the household than those in early modern Europe. The juridical status of women like Pompeia Memphis is one reason to doubt that freeborn women in particular generally acquired training within the household: the fact that Memphis shared a *nomen* (Pompeia / Pompeius) with her husband suggests that they were both former slaves who had been freed by the same master (Cn. Pompeius), or that Memphis had once belonged to her husband. Veturia Flora and Cameria Iarine, who (as we saw in Chapter 3) commissioned comparable inscriptions, were likewise both freedwomen, as were most of the other women given occupational titles in Roman funerary inscriptions.[147] While this detail could simply indicate that freeborn women were less likely to be represented as workers than freedwomen, for whom occupation perhaps functioned as a strong source of social identity,[148] it does raise the possibility that women with the skills to participate heavily in household enterprises owed those skills to their status as former slaves. As I have noted in passing, some slaveholders invested in the skills of slave women in their power to better exploit their labor, even though gender ideologies continued to affect beliefs concerning what kinds of work were appropriate for female slaves;[149] this is consistent with the fact that most women commemorated with reference to their occupation were not only former slaves but also worked in a narrow range of crafts (primarily in the textile industry).[150]

The scarcity in the funerary inscriptions of skilled slaves manumitted by women is a second reason to believe that women in the Roman world often lacked the comprehensive skills necessary to operate family enterprises as proprietors when their husbands or fathers died. Apart from the inscriptions commissioned by Veturia Flora, Cameria Iarine, and Pompeia Memphis, only a few were dedicated by or for skilled freed slaves whose nomenclature demonstrates that they had been freed by female owners. In a world in which women married for the first time at younger ages than men,[151] and in which fathers tended to establish their sons in careers of their own, the wives of artisans were likely to outlive

---

[147] Kampen 1981: 125–7; cf. Joshel, cited in n. III above.

[148] Dixon 2001b: 115. On the importance of occupation as a source of identity for freed slaves in particular, see Joshel 1992: 128–45, and esp. 144–5.

[149] For the impact of ideologies on slaveholders' exploitation of female labor, see Saller 2003, esp. 189–97 and 199–200.

[150] Joshel 1992: 141 n. 25 provides a breakdown of the statuses and occupations of the thirty-three female artisans.

[151] In addition to the secondary scholarship cited in n. 65, see also Bagnall and Frier 1994: III–34 on marriage patterns and average ages at first marriage in Roman Egypt.

their husbands and inherit their husbands' businesses. Had those women
who inherited their husbands' enterprises typically possessed the skills
necessary to operate them personally, then we might expect to see
evidence that they – like other artisans – manumitted skilled slaves
regularly in an effort to adapt their workforces to the pressures generated
by seasonal and uncertain product markets.[152] The fact that the skilled
freedmen named in our inscriptions were only rarely manumitted by
women thus suggests that women were not often able to assume control
of family enterprises without help and that they either sold off the assets
they inherited from male relatives (like Crobyle in Lucian's *Dialogues of
the Courtesans*, or the miller's daughter in Apuleius' *Metamorphoses*) or
retained slaves in permanent bondage to control the skilled labor necessary to sustain a business (like the female testator mentioned above, who
relied not just on the help of Eutychus to operate her ironworking shop
but also on the help of her slave Pamphilus).

It is even possible to read some inscriptions that record the manumission
of skilled slaves by women as evidence that those women lacked the full
range of skills necessary to operate a given business and thus depended
heavily on the assistance of male partners. The inscription commemorating
the freed slaves of a woman named Babbia and a man named Quintus
Plotius is a case in point:

> Babbia Asia, freedwoman of Babbia (Living)
> Gaius Babbius Regillus, freedman of Babbia (Living)
> Quintus Plotius Nicephor, freedman of Quintus (Deceased)
> Quintus Plotius Anteros, freedman of Quintus (Living)
> Quintus Plotius Felix, freedman of Quintus (Living)
> Jewelers on the Sacred Way.[153]

The inscription suggests that the owners of these slaves, Babbia and
Quintus Plotius, were spouses or partners who had pooled their slaves
together to exploit a shared business. Although it is possible that Babbia
was fully trained as a jeweler, it is equally possible that she – like the female
testator who enlisted the help of Eutychus – entered into a relationship
with Quintus Plotius partly because she herself lacked the technical skills
necessary to keep an inherited business afloat and needed the support of a
new partner or husband to do so. An inscription commemorating a group
of freed ironworkers (eight men and two women) lends itself to a comparable interpretation. The precise relationships articulated in this inscription

---

[152] See above, Chapter 3.   [153] *CIL* 6.9435.

are difficult to untangle, but most of the named individuals seem to have belonged at one point to one or both of two slaveholders, a woman named Fannia and a man named Titus Titius, each of whom had owned two of the ten former slaves personally and five in common with the other.[154] Like Babbia, Fannia was perhaps a spouse or partner in a business in which her male partner handled most of the technical aspects of craft production, while she devoted her time principally to household tasks or to the management of other aspects of the business. If so, then these inscriptions reinforce the impression that household consumption goals in the Roman world prompted individuals to assign more value to tasks that a wife performed as *custos* or *oikouros* than was the case in the early modern context, where preferences inclined more heavily toward a wife's ability to generate income.

Women, work, and the economy of the Roman world

Two implications follow from the conclusion that household members at all levels of the socioeconomic spectrum in the ancient world held consumption goals emphasizing the value of tasks performed by women within the household. First, whenever possible women in the Roman world probably responded to those goals by allocating more of their time toward household tasks than did their early modern counterparts and less toward income-generating work. Second, to the extent that this was true, the ways women allocated their time affected the capacity of their households to purchase goods and services – and, by extension, the depth of the Roman world's market structure. In what follows, I develop this line of argumentation in more detail. I begin by suggesting that what little evidence we possess concerning household strategies in the Roman world is consistent with the view that women in artisanal and entrepreneurial families preferred to allocate their time to household tasks. Naturally, some women devoted more time than others to income-generating work, whether by working on their own account or by contributing their labor to the enterprises of their husbands. How much time they allocated to this work depended upon the household's overall financial well-being and a woman's own particular skills, but generally they did not engage in this kind of work as extensively as did women in the early modern context. Next, I tease out the significance of this conclusion for our understanding

---

[154] *CIL* 6.9398. A tenth member of the group, identified as Fannia Calliste, freedwoman of Gaius, may have been manumitted by one of the other nine freed slaves.

of the Roman economy more broadly. As we shall see, women's decisions about how to allocate their time inhibited the development of thicker and more stable product markets in those segments of the urban economy that were crucial to sustained economic growth in northwestern Europe during the long eighteenth century. In that sense, the strategies adopted by members of artisan households are entirely consonant with a view of Roman economic history in which growth in per capita output was already beginning to stagnate in the early Empire.

From a theoretical standpoint, the consumption goals that predominated in antiquity ought to have encouraged women to shift most of their time from income-generating work to household tasks whenever their households' overall incomes exceeded a basic threshold that permitted members to acquire those purchased goods and services deemed necessary for their collective well-being. At that point, women could deploy their time and labor more productively by allocating it to household tasks than by seeking to produce additional income, since the marginal utility of any income a wife could generate decreased as the household became more prosperous, while that of the work performed within the household grew. In part, this was because the limited avenues of training open to women meant that any income they could generate was often modest and was thus less useful to prosperous households than to poorer ones. At the same time, the household tasks performed by women in their roles as *custodes* or *oikouroi* complemented goods and services purchased on the market in the sense that improved access to the latter created more demand for the former. For that reason, as the collective income of a household's members increased, so too did their need for members to devote time to the kinds of household-focused tasks that were especially valued in antiquity – that is, not just tasks like preparing meals or producing clothing for the household's own consumption (although these undoubtedly remained important) but also tasks like managing the household's stores, revenues, and expenses, and supervising its slaves.[155]

In practical terms, this meant that wives were least likely to allocate their time to income-generating work when they belonged to households headed by prosperous artisans or entrepreneurs. As long as the tasks women typically performed within the home remained important to the consumption goals held by household members at this social level, a wife

---

[155] De Vries 2008: 199–201. Cf. Bourke 1994: 173–9, who examines some of these issues in a nineteenth-century context, in which working- and middle-class households had reoriented their goals away from an emphasis on purchased goods and services and toward an emphasis on time devoted to various kinds of household tasks.

could, in a very real sense, contribute more effectively to the overall well-being of her family by devoting most of her time to household tasks than she could by seeking paid work. Exceptions undoubtedly occurred, especially when a wife possessed skills or a well-capitalized business that increased the value of her labor on the market – as perhaps was true both in the case of Mecia Dynata's mother, Flora, who worked as a wool-comber even though she seems to have belonged to a relatively prosperous household, and in the case of the freedwoman Nostia Daphne, who pursued an independent career as a hairdresser after her manumission, even though she had probably married a former slave with valuable skills of his own, the goldsmith Marcus Nerius Quadratus.[156] Even so, one suspects that prosperous households in which wives devoted most of their time to household tasks were common features of the urban landscape during the late Republic and early Empire. Lucian's story about Crobyle begins from the assumption that a wife would not normally have engaged in income-generating work, possibly because she typically would have allocated much of her time to work within the household instead.[157] Apuleius likewise grounds several details in his story about the hard-working miller in *Metamorphoses* on the same assumption. Although he caricatures the miller's wife as an adulteress and murderer, he nevertheless implies that a successful artisan would have expected his wife to spend most of her time performing tasks that fell within the brief of a *custos* or *oikouros*: not only does the miller expect his wife to prepare meals,[158] he also relies upon her to manage the household's assets, including its animals and slaves.[159]

At the other end of the spectrum, women were most likely to allocate their time heavily to income-generating work when they belonged to households in which their husbands either earned most of their income from wage labor or ran enterprises that hovered on the margins of viability. The productivity of any time a wife in this position might choose to devote to household tasks would have been relatively low, since her household would not have been complex enough to generate extensive demand for time allocated to preparing meals and so on, let alone extensive demand for time allocated to supervising its material assets and slaves.[160] At the same time, because households of this type were much more vulnerable to financial hardship than those headed by successful artisans or businessmen, the extra income a wife could generate for her family at this social level had considerable utility,

---

[156] *CIL* 6.37469. [157] Luc. *DMeretr.* 6.1. [158] Apul. *Met.* 9.26. [159] Apul. *Met.* 9.15.

[160] Or, to put it another way, the utility of cash income was higher in households with lower money earnings, since purchased goods and household labor are ultimately complements in the production of Z-commodities, and the former make the latter more productive (de Vries 2008: 200).

since it could tip the balance in many cases between deprivation and modest material comfort.[161] This was true despite the fact that most women in this position would have found it necessary to engage in work that was unlikely to generate appreciable levels of income in its own right. Because husbands at this socioeconomic level either did not operate enterprises of their own or operated enterprises that were not successful enough to require a wife's help, most of these women were compelled to find work elsewhere when they chose to allocate their time to generating income. Some would have worked for wages, perhaps in households seeking temporary domestic help of a sort that was not always easily supplied by resident slaves (such as wet-nursing).[162] Others turned to entrepreneurial occupations that demanded little capital or formal training: as street hawkers, for instance, they could market basic services like fortune-telling or sell inexpensive goods that they had purchased, scavenged, or manufactured themselves.[163] A majority, perhaps, undertook various kinds of work on contract. As we have seen, literary authors saw spinning as the prototypical work performed by women to generate income, and while some women engaged in spinning purely on speculation in the hope of selling the yarn at a later date, others clearly did so on commission.[164] Likewise, in a comment concerning some of the legal obligations created by a *peculium* arrangement, the jurist Gaius implies that married women in particular undertook tailoring jobs under contract. According to Gaius, a woman still under the legal authority of her father who engaged in paid work by sewing, mending clothes, or practicing some other "common craft" was liable to lawsuits directed against her *peculium* on the basis of the action on loan and deposit, whether her father knew of her business activities or not.[165] His emphasis on the action on loan and deposit suggests that he had in mind women who drew on skills acquired in the household to engage in basic entrepreneurial activities in their own right rather than women working for wages, since it evokes situations in which women temporarily took possession of property belonging to clients for the duration of a contract.[166] No less interesting is Gaius' belief that a father may

---

[161] Cf. Allen 2009: 339.

[162] Dio Chrys. *Or.* 7.114 refers to wet-nursing as an occupation that was appropriate for free women in need of work.

[163] Holleran 2012: 194–231 and 2013: 321–5.

[164] *P. Oxy.* XXXI 2593 presents a case in which Apollonia, the author of the letter, engaged the services of at least one other person on contract to help her spin wool. Apul. *Met.* 9.5 provides the prototypical example of a woman spinning wool to make ends meet; see below.

[165] Gaius, *Dig.* 15.1.27.pr.

[166] Du Plessis 2012: 55–67 provides a detailed discussion of the legal responsibilities of workers who accepted possession of a client's property for modification or repair.

not have known of his daughter's activities, since it raises the possibility that Gaius was thinking specifically of married women who worked to supplement the incomes of their marital households, even though they legally remained under the *potestas* of their fathers.

Decisions about how to allocate their time were more complex for women in households occupying intermediate positions in the economic spectrum, because households at this level often straddled the income threshold at which women began to reallocate time from income-generating to household work. Yet here too women probably allocated as much of their time as possible to household tasks (unless they possessed skills with which they could earn high incomes in the labor market), even though they undoubtedly made sensitive reallocations of their time in response to changes in their households' income flows. By way of comparison, during the Victorian period, when consumption goals emphasized the importance of household tasks more heavily than they had during the eighteenth century, working-class women in London often sought paid work only when seasonal or idiosyncratic fluctuations in the overall demand for labor created prolonged periods of underemployment for their husbands.[167] Otherwise, they devoted much of their time to tasks meant to manage and control household expenses, whether by hunting down and bargaining for cheaply priced foodstuffs or by producing basic goods like clothing to meet the household's immediate needs.[168] Given the value placed by individuals in antiquity on a woman's role as *custos* or *oikouros*, this behavior would have been entirely at home in the Roman world. It may, in fact, have been the kind of behavior that Apuleius had in mind when crafting his story in *Metamorphoses* about the poor carpenter and his wife. Here, Apuleius depicts a husband who seems to be employed irregularly, and wife who complains that she must therefore spin wool to ensure that the household can afford basic necessities like lamp oil; possibly, he believed that wives would not normally have engaged extensively in paid work even in relatively poor households had their husbands been able to generate stable incomes.[169]

Women belonging to households in the middle ranges of the spectrum did have an advantage over those belonging to households at either end, because many may have married men who operated their own enterprises and who owned or rented premises in which the boundary between residential and working space was rather porous. In these circumstances, the boundary between income-generating work and household tasks was likewise porous, and as a result women could combine the two kinds of

---

[167] Stedman Jones 1984: 84.   [168] Bourke 1994: 178–9.   [169] Apul. *Met.* 9.5.

work or reallocate time between them as necessary. In Pompeii, for example, commercial work was situated predominantly in *tabernae* that frequently served both as residential and productive spaces. Although *tabernae* often included small back rooms or mezzanines used as sleeping or cooking areas, these dedicated residential spaces were small. Instead, the main feature of most *tabernae* was a wide-fronted rectilinear room opening onto the street, in which most household members undoubtedly spent the bulk of their time during any given day. In practical terms, this meant that many of the tasks a woman might perform as the household's *custos* or *oikouros* – even tasks like fetching water or preparing food for her husband and the workshop's slaves or freedmen – contributed in a direct if immeasurable way to the productivity of those who devoted most of their time to income-generating work. Conditions may have been different in some of the larger workshops built into converted atrium houses in Pompeii, which permitted more differentiation between working and living space. They may likewise have been different in the dense urban environment of Rome, where many *tabernae* not only were small compared to those in Pompeii but also did not double as residential units – a fact which implies that artisans in Rome were more likely than those in Pompeii to rent separate working and living premises. At least in the case of workshops built into atrium-style houses, however, it remained possible for all members of the household to contribute to a family business as necessary.[170]

Yet because women in the Roman world had limited access to comprehensive training even within their own households, most who did combine income-generating work with household tasks in this way probably did so either by engaging in ancillary tasks – fetching water, preparing food, cleaning the work area – or by assuming responsibility for aspects of their husbands' businesses that were extensions of the household tasks normally thought to be the province of a *custos* or *oikouros*.[171] Elizabeth Musgrave provides a sense of the possibilities in her study of the building industries in eighteenth-century Brittany, in which she suggests that wives who worked alongside their husbands in this context often did so by purchasing raw materials, selling finished goods, and taking care of sundry administrative chores.[172] These were jobs that were wholly compatible with those typically assigned to a wife in her role as keeper of the household in the ancient world. The Roman jurists in fact recognized that women in

---

[170] On the commercial architecture of workshops in Pompeii and the ways in which they differed from those at Rome and Ostia, see Flohr 2013: 266–73 (who emphasizes fulleries).

[171] Saller 2003: 194 (following Treggiari 1979: 76 and Kampen 1981: 125–6).

[172] Musgrave 1993. For comparable patterns of women's work in early modern Rome, cf. Groppi 2002.

artisan households might handle tasks of this sort: Ulpian, in his wider discussion of the legal issues in play when individuals appointed others as agents (*institores*), stresses that women were (from the point of view of the law) fully capable of acting on behalf of someone else in this capacity,[173] and (more pointedly) the jurist Gaius notes that children, both boys and girls, were often left in charge of shopfronts – an observation which, even if it does not refer to wives specifically, nevertheless points explicitly to some division of labor within artisan families.[174] Some of our iconographic evidence is also perfectly compatible with this model, like the well-known relief from Rome, dating from the second century CE, depicting the interior of a butcher's shop (Figure 4.1). The butcher is shown hard at work on the right-hand side of the panel, while on the left is a seated woman, holding what appears to be a writing tablet. No other clues concerning her identity are offered. Natalie Kampen has suggested that she is a scribe, but she could just as easily represent the butcher's wife, balancing his accounts.[175] The paintings on the façade of the so-called shop of Verecundus in Pompeii may likewise reflect this division of labor. Beneath a complex tableau depicting the deity Venus Pompeiana on the right pier of the doorway, a smaller panel portrays felt-makers working under the supervision of Verecundus himself, who holds up a sample piece of finished cloth for display. On the left pier, dominated by an image of the god Mercury standing in front of a temple, another small panel depicts a woman sitting behind a table and displaying one of the several finished articles in the shop to a male customer. Although the panel does not identify the woman, most scholars believe that the image represents Verecundus' wife.[176] If this interpretation is correct, then it offers an important window into the dynamics of at least one artisanal household, in which husband and wife divided the production and sales aspects of the business between themselves.

While these assistive roles were far from unimportant – at the very least, women who assumed responsibility for managing sales or for overseeing a business' accounts freed their husbands to specialize more intensively in the technical aspects of production – the extent to which wives undertook them does establish a clear and important contrast between the kinds of work undertaken by wives in Roman antiquity and the kinds performed by women belonging to middle-class households in seventeenth- and

---

[173] Ulpian, *Dig.* 14.3.7.1.   [174] Gaius, *Dig.* 14.3.8.
[175] Kampen 1981: 118. The relief itself is Inv. ZV 44, Skulpturensammlung, Staatliche Kunstsammlungen, Dresden.
[176] Clarke 2003: 105–12 and esp. 109. Cf. Holleran 2013: 316.

Figure 4.1 Roman relief of butcher's shop (Photo: bpk Berlin/Staatliche
Kunstsammlungen, Dresden/Elke Estel/Art Resource, NY)

eighteenth-century Europe. As we have seen, women in early modern
London who worked alongside their husbands were more likely than
those in the ancient world to acquire the training necessary to participate
in all aspects of a given business. To that, one might add that women in
London's middle-class households who did not work alongside their husbands nevertheless worked regularly for wages or operated businesses of
their own.[177] Together, these observations all indicate that most women in
early modern England allocated significant amounts of their time to work
that was directed explicitly toward the market – so much so, in fact, that
middle-class families in London appear to have hired servants specifically
so that women belonging to households headed by artisans or by retailers
could free themselves from the need to devote time to household tasks and
could instead specialize in income-generating work.[178] Recent studies of
women and work in the Dutch Republic during the seventeenth and
eighteenth centuries suggest that the same was true in continental
Europe as well.[179] In that sense, women in the Roman world had less in

---

[177] So Erickson 2008, esp. 278–82 and 294, who builds on the earlier work of Earle 1989a by showing
that women in middle-class households not only worked for wages but also frequently operated
businesses of their own.
[178] Kent 1989: 119–20.   [179] Van Nederveen Meerkerk 2012: 328–30 and 335–7.

common with women who belonged to working- or middle-class households in the seventeenth and eighteenth centuries than they did with those who belonged to such households in the nineteenth century, when a new cluster of consumption goals encouraged women to withdraw their labor from the market to concentrate on domestic work.[180]

Precisely because the household consumption goals dominant in the Roman world encouraged women to allocate their time to household tasks whenever it was possible for them to do so, those goals (along with the behavior they provoked) profoundly affected economic life in antiquity, in at least two ways. First, because they encouraged women to shift time away from income-producing work once their households had achieved a level of income considered suitable to their needs, the purchasing power of individual households was not as high as otherwise may have been the case. By extension, members of artisan households possibly remained more vulnerable to the risks typical of ancient urban environments – namely, the risk that food prices would rise because of a poor harvest and that demand in product and labor markets would be low enough in any given year to erode the household's income – than they would have had women in such households allocated more of their time to income-generating work. Second, the apparent stability of these consumption preferences over time forestalled changes in consumer behavior of the kind that generated real and sustained growth in the long eighteenth century by thickening early modern product markets and provoking increasing returns to specialization.

The recent work on real wages in the Roman world makes it possible to be more precise about the ongoing vulnerability of most households to sudden shocks. As we have seen, unskilled workers generated incomes that were insufficient to permit them to support families at a bare-bones subsistence level, let alone maintain a more comfortable level of consumption.[181] Members of households headed by artisans fared better,

---

[180] On women's withdrawal of their labor from the market in the nineteenth century, see Bourke 1994 and de Vries 2008: 186–237.

[181] Scheidel 2010: 427–36; Allen 2009: 337–43. Scheidel's results suggest that unskilled workers in Roman Egypt probably earned about 40 percent of what they required to maintain a family at a "respectable" level of household consumption, and perhaps only about 70–80 percent of what they needed to support families at subsistence level. Allen's results indicate that unskilled workers may have been somewhat better off in the late third century, but not by much: based on the wages and prices recorded in Diocletian's edict on maximum prices, Allen suggests that unskilled workers earned enough to support a family at subsistence level with a little left over to spare, but still only half of what they would have needed to purchase a "respectable" consumption basket for a family. Cf. Rathbone 2009: 314 on the purchasing power of unskilled workers at Rome.

since skilled workers could earn perhaps twice as much in a given year as unskilled laborers;[182] at that level of income, the members of a typical artisan household were able to purchase a basket of consumption goods ranging in value from roughly 150 percent to 200 percent or more of the cost of basic subsistence.[183] Yet even at this level, skilled workers in the Roman world were worse off in real terms than unskilled laborers in the more economically advanced areas of northwestern Europe during the long eighteenth century. For that reason, members of Roman households headed by skilled workers could find themselves hard pressed if business proved to be slower than anticipated or if the price of wheat was unusually high, particularly since expenses on bread may have represented anywhere from 25 percent to 50 percent of the typical family budget even at this level of the social spectrum. Depending on her skills, a wife could generate additional protection against these dangers by earning perhaps as much as an unskilled male worker, provided that she devoted the bulk of her time to paid work.[184] In so doing, she would have raised the overall purchasing power enjoyed by the members of her household to something in the range of 200 percent to 300 percent of the costs of subsistence − a standard of living comparable to what a laborer in early modern London could provide for his family on the basis of his labor alone, if he had regular work. Given the nature of the consumption preferences revealed in our ancient sources, however, it seems unlikely that women belonging to artisan households contributed to the family income at this level, even if they allocated more time to income-generating work while their children were still too young to contribute to household income than they did during later stages of their lives.[185] The value individuals attached to the household tasks provided by women in their roles as *custos* or *oikouros* therefore came at the price of ongoing susceptibility to the vagaries of the urban market.

---

[182] See esp. Rathbone 2009: 312–17.

[183] As I suggested in Chapter 1, this is roughly the same standard of living that would have been enjoyed by members of the urban cohorts in Rome.

[184] It is important to note, however, that even this estimate may be too high. Van Nederveen Meerkerk 2008: 254–9 shows that women in Zwolle in the late seventeenth century (or, at least, those belonging to households that required some poor relief) tended to generate between 12 percent and 34 percent of the household's income. Cf. de Vries 2008: 107–10, who suggests that the combined contribution of women and children to household income in early modern Europe tended to range between 25 percent and 50 percent depending on the respective ages of the household head and any children.

[185] On the relationship between the labor of women and children, see Bourke 1994: 173–7. Cf. Groen-Vallinga 2013: 297 and Holleran 2013: 321 on women's work and the life cycle of Roman households.

More significantly, because the consumption preferences prompting women to allocate their time to household tasks do not appear to have undergone any notable changes during antiquity, they also curtailed the potential for ongoing per capita growth in the economy of the Roman world after the Augustan transition. Here, it is important to revisit the example of the long eighteenth century, which suggests that sustained growth in an advanced premodern economy like that of the Roman Empire required significant changes in the consumption preferences influencing how household members allocated their time between income-generating and household tasks. In de Vries' model of economic change, growth in the consumer market was driven by the incremental efforts of working- and middle-class families to allocate more time – especially the time of women – to income-generating work, so that they could purchase the goods and services that were increasingly important to their consumption goals. In turn, the expansion of the consumer market produced thick market externalities capable of stimulating more intensive specialization and, by extension, growth: by lowering overall transaction costs, thicker markets enhanced the potential rewards of specializing for market production in ways that motivated entrepreneurs to invest more heavily in such specialization; by specializing more intensively, entrepreneurs in turn became more dependent on the market in order to secure basic goods and services that they no longer produced personally, and hence thickened markets even further. For de Vries, the story of the European economy in the long eighteenth century is therefore a story about how women, in response to new household consumption goals, allocated their time in ways that enhanced household purchasing power, thickened markets, and stimulated a burst of specialization and growth, all in the absence of major technological innovations capable of reducing either the costs of production or the costs of transport.[186]

In the Roman world, where consumption goals consistently emphasized the value of the tasks performed by a wife in her role as *custos* or *oikouros*, household members had less incentive than those in the early modern period to reallocate women's time in ways designed to enhance their own purchasing power. As a consequence, there was little scope for the kind of thick market externalities generated by changes in consumption preferences that were so vital to the expansion of the early modern economy in its late stages. In that sense, the ongoing vitality of consumption preferences emphasizing the value of women's work within the

---

[186] For the most concise statement of this view, see de Vries 2008: 71–2.

household both supports those models of Roman economic history that postulate gradual stagnation in growth soon after the Augustan transition and also offers a partial explanation for that stagnation. Briefly put, while the work of George Grantham suggests that improvements in the technologies and infrastructure of trade offered the most straightforward path toward thick market externalities capable of generating growth in the preindustrial world, the two most decisive developments in these domains in the Roman world took place in the middle and late Republic. The first was the sustained series of conquests that permitted the Romans to weld the Mediterranean together into an increasingly coherent political and economic space; the second was the development and crystallization of the long-distance trade routes that bound Rome itself to grain-producing centers in North Africa and in Egypt and that enhanced the overall connectivity of intermediate points in the process. On this view, the basic processes capable of generating the kind of growth envisioned by Grantham had mostly played themselves out by the first century CE at the latest, and growth would have slowed or even stopped in the absence of some other factor that was capable of driving thick market externalities.[187] Significant changes in household consumption goals could have driven further growth by enhancing the desire of individuals to consume purchased goods and services while simultaneously giving them the purchasing power necessary to satisfy that desire. As I have argued here, however, such changes do not seem to have taken place.

Finally, I conclude this chapter by noting that the decisions household members made about how to allocate the time of women exacerbated the structural challenges confronting Roman artisans and entrepreneurs on the shop floor during the late Republic and early Empire. In the long eighteenth century, the segments of the market that changed most dramatically in response to new consumption habits and to women's efforts to reallocate their time were precisely those that catered to members of the working and middle classes. Here, however haltingly, the seasonality and uncertainties long characteristic of urban product markets began to yield to more stable mass demand. In the Roman world, in which households of comparable socioeconomic brackets did not place such a high value on the consumption of goods and services purchased on the market, comparable changes in the basic character of urban demand did not take place, and markets for a range of products targeted at consumers of modest income therefore

---

[187] This, essentially, is the scenario postulated by Scheidel 2009: 67–70.

remained vulnerable to seasonal and uncertain demand. When artisans and entrepreneurs turned to professional dream interpreters like Artemidorus to divine whether or not they would have work, they were thus expressing anxieties that remained widespread and persistent in the Roman world for much of its history.

Epilogue

Marcus Vergilius Eurysaces – baker, contractor, public servant – was a fortunate man. In part, of course, his success seems to have depended on lucrative contracts from the state. Yet, at the same time, he also worked in a trade in which demand for his products was relatively consistent. In the dense and built environment of Rome, where much of the populace lived in small, rented rooms in multi-story apartment buildings, the local bakery with its attached mill was a vital feature of the urban landscape. For a fee, bakers like Eurysaces processed the grain that urban residents who qualified for the dole received every month and converted it into bread, and they purchased additional grain in order to make bread for sale on a daily basis. Because bread was a staple food in the early Empire, its demand was relatively inelastic, and a baker like Eurysaces could count on brisk business most days of the year.

By contrast, and as I have argued throughout this book, most artisans who lived and worked in the cities of the Roman Empire during the Late Republic and Early Empire were not so lucky. Instead, they contended with product markets that were fundamentally unstable thanks to the impact of seasonal and uncertain demand. This was just as true of those artisans who manufactured high-end goods for the bespoke market as it was for those who produced either simple, undifferentiated goods or populuxe wares, even if the precise causes of seasonality and uncertainty differed by market segment. From the point of view of artisans who manufactured bespoke high-end goods, seasonal changes in demand were caused primarily by the movement of wealthy residents and visitors in and out of Rome over the course of the year in accordance with a well-established social, political, and economic calendar (and, likewise, in and out of other large cities in response to comparable phenomena). Whereas the political and judicial life of Rome peaked during the winter and spring, summer brought with it the harvest, the malarial season, and the vintage, in that order. Wealthy residents left the heat and dangers of the city behind during these months, retreating to their summer villas for relaxation or to working estates in order to supervise the critical phases of the agricultural calendar personally. Visitors stayed home largely for the same reason. As a consequence business was best for artisans who manufactured high-end goods during the winter and early spring. Even during these times of the year, however, demand always remained uncertain, largely because artisans in these market segments catered to clients who prided themselves on their refinement, expressed through competitive display, and who therefore purchased goods on a bespoke basis and to their own specifications. From the point of view of urban producers, the whims of these clients must have seemed highly unpredictable.

The sources of seasonality and uncertainty were slightly different for those artisans who manufactured undifferentiated or populuxe goods, but no less pressing. Some of the seasonality experienced by artisans in these segments was certainly produced by seasonal travel and migration, but it tended to be travel and migration motivated almost exclusively by economic factors: at the peak of the agricultural season, rural and urban inhabitants alike often took up temporary work as harvest hands in the countryside, while during other months of the year they either returned home or temporarily migrated to cities in search of employment within the urban market. In that sense, the busy season of the year for artisans who produced undifferentiated or populuxe goods was not radically different from the busy season in the market's upper ranges. Yet seasonality at this level of the market was further compounded by fluctuations in the purchasing power of most non-elite urban residents. On the one hand, cyclical changes in the price of grain cut into the disposable income of many urban inhabitants during the early spring, when grain prices tended to reach their annual peak. On the other, seasonal changes in the weather profoundly affected the level of low-skill employment available within urban environments. Because building slowed dramatically during the depths of winter, work for laborers in the construction industry became scarce. So too did work for the stevedores, porters, bargemen, and animal handlers responsible for unloading ships at Ostia and Puteoli and for transferring cargoes to Rome itself, since maritime traffic fell off precipitously during the winter months. Both of these seasonal rhythms must have had a serious impact on poorer urban residents' ability to earn enough for basic goods and services. That problem was only compounded by the main source of uncertainty confronting producers at this level of the market – namely, unpredictable intra- and inter-annual fluctuations in the price of foodstuffs, which could quickly erode the purchasing power of the average city-dweller. These fluctuations never fully stabilized even in Rome, where the state took care to monitor the food supply.

Eurysaces, because he was lucky enough to work in a trade with stable demand, had the luxury of maintaining a relatively consistent level of output over the course of any given year, and thus could both maintain a regular workforce and invest some capital in his business without fear of excessive financial risk. In this sense too he and artisans like him were exceptionally privileged, for my second major argument suggests that most artisans faced substantial risks when they assumed the fixed costs necessary to maintain consistent output and regular workforces over the course of the year. Because the consumption habits of wealthy clients were highly particularized, artisans who produced goods for the bespoke segments of the market naturally ran the risk that any employees whom they sought to maintain year round would be underemployed for stretches of the year, especially if those employees possessed specialized skills that were not always necessary for any given commission. Artisans who manufactured products for the populuxe and undifferentiated segments of the market, on the other hand, theoretically enjoyed more scope for smoothing production over the year, since they could manufacture to stock, as did the knifemaker Atimetus. Yet here too there were risks, since an unanticipated harvest failure could easily leave an artisan with stock that he would be unable to move quickly. All of these problems were only exacerbated by the heavy reliance of most urban artisans on credit: all seem to have depended on credit extended to them by their suppliers, and many (particularly in upper segments of the market) extended credit in turn to their clients. In these circumstances, artisans had to monitor their cash flows carefully. If they found themselves short of cash on hand, whether because wealthy clients were slow in paying their bills or because they themselves were unable to dispose of ready-made inventory in the populuxe or undifferentiated segments of the market, they could easily find themselves on the receiving end of a lawsuit launched by one of their creditors, and confronted by the danger of insolvency.

I have argued that these risks gave most artisans strong incentives to minimize their fixed costs and devise strategies emphasizing flexible rather than regular output. This they could accomplish by operating small and specialized enterprises and by either contracting with other artisans for intermediate goods and services or recruiting additional help as circumstances warranted. Yet this strategy in and of itself entailed some risks. Broadly speaking, the market in skilled labor was tight in the Roman world. In part, this was true because the Roman world did not give rise to organizations like the journeymen's associations of medieval and early modern Europe, which facilitated the circulation of information and workers on a regional level. Yet it was also true because average household incomes in the Roman world were low enough that many household heads were unwilling to incur the opportunity costs necessary to have their sons trained in a craft, and instead encouraged them to supplement the household income by seeking unskilled but paid work as soon as they were old enough to do so. These tight market conditions translated inevitably to high transaction costs, since skilled workers were scarce and in demand during high season in particular. Unless artisans could break down their production processes into relatively unskilled tasks, they could therefore find it difficult to secure the help or the services required during high season to successfully operate small and specialized businesses.

In these circumstances, artisans were most likely to navigate the urban economies of the Roman world successfully if they could take advantage of certain kinds of social relationships in order to circumvent some of the challenges produced by high transaction costs. Those who required the occasional services of skilled specialists found it much easier to coordinate production if they joined a professional association, since these organizations in general supported strong private-order enforcement mechanisms based on the politics of reputation and communal sanctions. In that sense, they operated as governance structures that permitted artisans to coordinate production in subcontracting networks rather than in integrated firms, which imposed high fixed costs (and risks) on their proprietors. On the other hand, artisans who had a semi-regular demand for skilled help within their own workshops found that they could adapt slavery to their needs by manumitting skilled slaves while imposing upon them an obligation to perform a specified quantity of work, measured in days – the so-called *operae libertorum*. Because artisans could call in the labor of freed slaves at their convenience and at the freedman's own expense and because they generally enjoyed enough social and economic power over their freedmen to enforce compliance with these terms, they found manumission an effective tool for structuring flexible workforces. The practice of manumission in Rome's artisan economy, much like the nature of professional associations, can therefore only be fully understood if we view it in relation to the seasonal and uncertain demand typical of urban product markets and in relation to the challenges that these product markets posed for artisans.

Finally, I have argued that an understanding of the strategies adopted by artisans in the Roman world elucidates both the overall performance of the

Roman economy and the potential of that economy to generate sustained growth in productivity after Rome's conquest of the Mediterranean world was complete. The key intellectual developments here are (1) George Grantham's arguments concerning the relationship between thick market externalities and increasing returns to specialization and (2) Jan de Vries' insight that endogenous changes in consumption preferences can trigger these forces by encouraging individuals to become more engaged with market structures – both as consumers of goods and services and as suppliers of income-generating labor. The basic idea holds that the aggregate behavior of individuals can thicken market structures if consumption preferences emphasizing the desirability of purchased goods and services become wide-spread enough that households supply more labor to the market (generally, the labor of women) in order to fund elevated levels of consumption. Those thickened markets signal to entrepreneurs that intensive specialization will yield dividends, and increasing specialization in turn feeds back into even thicker market structures.

These models provide a useful vantage point from which to examine growth in the Roman world, largely because artisans' strategies suggest that there were impediments to thick markets in antiquity. By reducing transaction costs typical of subcontracting arrangements, *collegia* supported higher degrees of specialization than may have been possible in other circumstances, but the exclusivity of these structures seems to have limited the social benefits of that specialization. The reliance of artisans on the labor of freedmen – a relationship that was, ultimately, highly exploitative – constrained the growth of middling income groups that were capable of generating additional consumption, as did the high opportunity costs of apprenticeship. Finally, although artisans typically sought to maximize the productivity of their sons' labor – namely, by establishing them in independent careers rather than by employing them personally when they could not guarantee those sons regular work – different priorities structured the way in which they deployed the labor of their wives. Broadly speaking, household consumption goals in the Roman world emphasized the value of tasks performed by women both within and for the household. There is no evidence that these goals changed in ways that would have prompted household members in antiquity to reallocate women's labor to income-generating work in order to fund additional consumption once their basic needs had been met. From that perspective, sustained growth in productivity was unlikely to have taken place in the Roman world once the consequences of Rome's conquests in the second and first centuries BCE had played themselves out.

The annualized costs of freed slaves' operae

Algebraically, we can use the following equation to express the annualized costs incurred by an artisan who hoarded the labor of a freedman whom he had manumitted in exchange for *operae*:

$$C_f = \frac{n_s C_s + n_f C_o}{n_s + n_f}$$

In this equation, n_s and n_f represent the number of years of work an artisan extracted from a skilled worker – first while that worker was a slave and then while that worker was a freedman; C_s represents the annual cost of slave labor and C_o the average annual cost of a freedman's *operae*.

The average annual cost of a freedman's *operae* (C_o) can be conceptualized as a sum of three other individual costs. The first is a cost reflecting the rate at which an artisan used up the *operae* of his freed slave, equivalent to the slave's putative market value at manumission (V_m) divided by the number of years during which an artisan could expect to use his *operae* (n_f). The second is a cost reflecting the possibility that a freedman would abscond, become ill, or otherwise prove unable to honor his obligations, and which is equivalent to the product of the slave's value at manumission and the annual risk of loss (l). The third is the opportunity cost an artisan incurred by manumitting a slave in exchange for *operae* instead of selling the slave in order to put the slave's capital value to work in its next best economic function (e.g., by lending it out at interest). This cost is the product of the slave's market value at manumission and the interest rate (i).

$$C_o = \frac{V_m}{n_f} + V_m l + V_m i$$

In practice, the number of years over which an artisan spread out the *operae* of a freed slave (n_f) depended on the frequency with which he was likely to call upon the freedman's services:

$$n_f = \frac{O}{d}$$

Here, O represents the total number of *operae* that an artisan demanded from a slave in exchange for manumission, while d once again represents the number of *operae* (or, in other words, how many days of work) that he was likely to require in a given year. The average annual cost of *operae* can therefore be expressed as a function of the number of *operae* used by an artisan in any given year as follows:

$$C_o = \frac{V_m d}{O} + V_m l + V_m i$$

I estimate the number of *operae* an artisan extracted from a slave in exchange for manumission by assuming that he took into account both the slave's market value at manumission and the wage rate for skilled labor (w) and computed an appropriate number of *operae* after allowing for a manumission premium, which can be conceptualized as a discount (δ) on the effective wage rate:

$$O = \frac{V_m}{w(1 - \delta)}$$

After the appropriate substitutions are made, the average annual costs of a freedman's *operae* can be reduced to

$$C_o = dw(1 - \delta) + V_m l + V_m i$$

The total annualized costs incurred by an artisan who hoarded the labor of a slave whom he manumitted in exchange for *operae* can therefore also be written as a function of the average number of *operae* he called in during any given year (d):

$$C_f = \frac{n_s C_s + V_m + \frac{V_m^2(l+i)}{dw(1-\delta)}}{n_s + \frac{V_m}{dw(1-\delta)}}$$

The annual cost of slave labor and the value of the slave at the moment of manumission can both be broken down further:

$$C_s = M + V_s(r + l + i)$$
$$V_m = V_s(1 - n_s r)$$

In the preceding two equations, M represents the annual costs necessary to feed and house a slave; r is the rate at which the slave's market value depreciated from its high point as the slave aged; and V_s is the slave's initial market value.

Occupational inscriptions from CIL 6 used in succession study

2226	9239	9550	9669	9843	9999c
5638	9255	9552	9670	9847	10000
5638	9283	9553	9672	9851	10001
6192	9375	9554	9674	9855	10006
7601	9387	9559	9675	9864	33833
7882	9390	9567	9677	9865	33835
8455	9394	9569	9678	9868	33846
9104	9402	9571	9679	9884	33870
9136	9404	9572	9682	9886	33880
9138	9405	9573	9683	9889	33882
9140	9407	9580	9706	9895	33886
9141	9408	9583	9707	9897	33887
9142	9418	9584	9709	9902	33889
9143	9429	9585	9710	9905	33904
9152	9433	9586	9711	9910	33906
9156	9434	9587	9713	9931	33914
9159	9435	9590	9720	9933	33918
9160	9442	9604	9784	9950	33920
9164	9445	9605	9785	9952	33921
9166	9448	9606	9792	9953	33923
9177	9454	9609	9793	9956	37778
9178	9475	9616	9794	9958	37781
9179	9477	9618	9795	9961	37784a
9182	9478	9623	9801	9967	37798
9183	9489	9624	9802	9969	37806
9207	9492	9625	9806	9970	37807
9208b	9493	9630	9810	9971	37811a
9209	9494	9648	9817	9973	37813

9211	9499	9650	9819	9975	37814
9214	9528a	9659	9821	9977	37820
9215	9528b	9661	9822	9992	37822
9221	9533	9663	9823	9993	37824
9222	9544	9664	9824	9995	37826
9225	9546	9665	9827	9997	
9227	9547	9668	9841	9998	

Bibliography

Acheson, J. M. (1982) "Limitations on firm size in a Tarascan pueblo," *Human Organization* 41: 323–9.

(1994) "Transaction costs and business strategies in a Mexican Indian pueblo," in *Anthropology and Institutional Economics*, ed. J. M. Acheson. New York: 143–65.

(2002) "Transaction cost economics: accomplishments, problems, and possibilities," in *Theory in Economic Anthropology*, ed. J. Ensminger. Walnut Creek: 27–58.

Aldrete, G. S., and Mattingly, D. J. (1999) "Feeding the city: the organization, operation, and scale of the supply system for Rome," in *Life, Death, and Entertainment in the Roman Empire*, ed. D. S. Potter and D. J. Mattingly. Ann Arbor: 171–204.

Alföldy, G. (1972) "Die Freilassung von Sklaven und die Struktur der Sklaverei in der römischen Kaiserzeit," *RSA* 2: 97–129.

Allen, R. C. (2009) "How prosperous were the Romans?: evidence from Diocletian's price edict (AD 301)," in Bowman and Wilson (eds.), 327–45.

Anderson, J. C., Jr. (1997) *Roman Architecture and Society*. Baltimore.

Arnaoutoglou, I. (2002) "Roman law and *collegia* in Asia Minor," *RIDA* 49: 27–44.

(2005) "Collegia in the province of Egypt in the first century AD," *Ancient Society* 35: 197–216.

Aubert, J.-J. (1994) *Business Managers in Ancient Rome: A Social and Economic Study of Institores, 200 B.C.–A.D. 250*. Leiden.

(2001) "The fourth factor: managing non-agricultural production in the Roman world," in Mattingly and Salmon (eds.), 90–112.

(2013) "'Dumtaxat de peculio': what's in a peculium or the extent of the principal's liability," in *New Frontiers: Law and Society in the Roman World*, ed. P. Du Plessis. Edinburgh: 192–206.

Bablitz, L. E. (2007) *Actors and Audience in the Roman Courtroom*. Oxon.

Bagnall, R. S. (1985) *Currency and Inflation in Fourth-Century Egypt*. Chico.

(1993) *Egypt in Late Antiquity*. Princeton.

Bagnall, R. S., and Frier, B. W. (1994) *The Demography of Roman Egypt*. Cambridge.

Bagnall, R. S., and Worp, K. A. (1980) "Notes on Byzantine documents, IV," *BASP* 17: 5–18.

Baker, A. S. (2009) "The business of life: the socioeconomics of the 'scientific' instrument trade in early modern London," in Eliassen and Szende (eds.), 169–91.

Baker, G., Gibbons, R., and Murphy, K. (2002) "Relational contracts and the theory of the firm," *The Quarterly Journal of Economics* 117/1: 39–84.

Balsdon, J. P. V. D. (1969) *Life and Leisure in Ancient Rome*. New York.

Bang, P. F. (2008) *The Roman Bazaar: A Comparative Study of Trade and Markets in a Tributary Empire*. Cambridge.

  (2009) "The ancient economy and new institutional economics," *JRS* 99: 194–206.

Barzel, Y. (2005) "Organizational forms and measurement costs," *Journal of Institutional and Theoretical Economics (JITE)/Zeitschrift für die gesamte Staatswissenschaft* 161/3: 357–73.

Beare, R. (1978) "Were bailiffs ever free born?," *CQ* 28: 398–401.

Becker, G. S. (1991) *A Treatise on the Family*. Enlarged edn. Cambridge.

Becker, G. S., and Murphy, K. (1992) "The division of labor, coordination costs, and knowledge," *The Quarterly Journal of Economics* 107/4: 1137–60.

Bergamasco, M. (1995) "Le διδασκαλικαί nella ricerca attuale," *Aegyptus* 75: 95–167.

Berlin, M. (1997) "'Broken all in pieces': artisans and the regulation of workmanship in early modern London," in Crossick (ed.), 75–91.

  (2008) "Guilds in decline? London livery companies and the rise of a liberal economy, 1600–1800," in Epstein and Prak (eds.), 316–42.

Bernstein, L. (2001) "Private commercial law in the cotton industry: creating cooperation through rules, norms, and institutions," *Michigan Law Review* 99: 1724–90.

Bezís-Selfa, J. (2004) *Forging America: Ironworkers, Adventurers, and the Industrious Revolution*. Ithaca.

Biezunska-Malowist, I. (1965) "Les esclaves payant l'ΑΠΟΦΟΡΑ dans l'Égypte gréco-romaine," *JJP* XV: 65–72.

Birk, S. (2012) "Carving sarcophagi: Roman sculptural workshops and their organisation," in *Ateliers and Artisans in Roman Art and Archaeology*, ed. T. M. Kristensen and B. Poulsen. Portsmouth, RI: 13–37.

Biscottini, M. V. (1966) "L'archivio di Tryphon, tessitore di Oxyrhynchos," *Aegyptus* 46: 60–90 and 186–292.

Bodel, J. (ed.) (2001a) *Epigraphic Evidence: Ancient History from Inscriptions*. London and New York.

  (2001b) "Epigraphy and the ancient historian," in Bodel (ed.), 1–56.

Bourke, J. (1994) "Housewifery in working-class England 1860–1914," *Past and Present* 143/1: 167–97.

Bowman, A. K. (1986) *Egypt after the Pharaohs, 332 B.C.–A.D. 642*. Oxford.

Bowman, A. K., and Wilson, A. (eds.) (2009) *Quantifying the Roman Economy: Methods and Problems*. Oxford.

Bradley, K. R. (1987) *Slaves and Masters in the Roman Empire: A Study in Social Control*. Oxford.

(1991) *Discovering the Roman Family*. New York and Oxford.

(1994) *Slavery and Society at Rome*. Cambridge.

Brewer, J., and Porter, R. (eds.) (1993) *Consumption and the World of Goods*. London.

Broekaert, W. (2011) "Partners in business. Roman merchants and the potential advantages of being a *collegiatus*," *Ancient Society* 41: 221–56.

Brunt, P. A. (1950) "Pay and superannuation in the Roman army," *Papers of the British School at Rome* XVIII: 50–71.

(1980) "Free labour and public works at Rome," *JRS* 70: 81–100.

(1988) *The Fall of the Roman Republic and Related Essays*. Oxford.

Bruun, C. (2013) "Greek or Latin? The owner's choice of names for *vernae* in Rome," in *Roman Slavery and Roman Material Culture*, ed. M. George. Toronto: 19–42.

Bryant, K. (1990) *The Economic Organization of the Household*. Cambridge.

Buckland, W. W. (1908) *The Roman Law of Slavery: The Condition of the Slave in Private Law from Augustus to Julian*. Cambridge.

(1921) *A Textbook of Roman Law from Augustus to Justinian*. Cambridge.

Burford, A. (1972) *Craftsmen in Greek and Roman Society*. Ithaca.

Bürge, A. (1990) "Der *mercennarius* und die Lohnarbeit," *ZRG* 107: 80–136.

Campbell, R. (1747) *The London Tradesman*. London.

Carandini, Andrea. (1981) "*Sviluppo e crisi delle manifatture rurali e urbane*," in Giardina and Schiavone (eds.), 249–60.

Carr, J., and Landa, J. (1983) "The economics of symbols, clan names, and religion," *The Journal of Legal Studies* 12/1: 135–56.

Carrié, Jean-Michel. (2002) "Les associations professionnelles à l'époque tardive: entre munus et convivialité," in *Humana Sapit: études d'antiquité tardive offertes à Lellia Cracco Ruggini*, ed. G. Clark. Turnhout: 309–32.

Casson, L. (1974) *Travel in the Ancient World*. Toronto.

(1978) "Unemployment, the building trade and Suetonius, *Vesp.* 18," *BASP* 15: 43–51.

(1990) "Documentary evidence for Graeco-Roman shipbuilding (P.Flor. I 69)," *BASP* 27: 15–19.

Cerutti, S. (1991) "Group strategies and trade strategies: the Turin tailor's guild in the late seventeenth and early eighteenth centuries," in *Domestic Strategies: Work and Family in France and Italy 1600–1800*, ed. S. Wolf. Cambridge: 102–47.

Champlin, E. (1991) *Final Judgments: Duty and Emotion in Roman Wills, 200 B.C.-A.D. 250*. Berkeley.

Chartres, J. A. (1985) "The marketing of agricultural produce," in *The Agrarian History of England and Wales, 1640–1750*, vol. V.II, ed. J. Thirsk. London: 406–502.

Chiusi, T. (1993) *Contributo allo studio dell'editto 'de tributoria actione'*. Rome.

Clark, P. (1983) *The English Alehouse: A Social History, 1200–1830*. London.

(2000) *British Clubs and Societies 1580–1800: The Origins of an Associational World*. Oxford.

Clarke, J. R. (2003) *Art in the Lives of Ordinary Romans: Visual Representation and Non-Elite Viewers in Italy, 100 B.C. – A.D. 315*. Berkeley.

Clifford, H. (2004) *Silver in London: The Parker and Wakelin Partnership 1760–1776*. New Haven.

Coase, R. (1937) "The nature of the firm," *Economica* 4: 386–405.

(1960) "The problem of social cost," *Journal of Law and Economics* 3: 1–44.

(1988) "The nature of the firm: influence," *Journal of Law, Economics, & Organization* 4/1: 33–47.

Cohen, D. J. (1991) *Law, Sexuality, and Society: The Enforcement of Morals in Classical Athens*. Cambridge.

Cohen, E. E. (2000) *The Athenian Nation*. Princeton.

Coleman, R. R. (1965). "A Roman terracotta figurine of the Ephesian Artemis in the McDaniel collection," *Harvard Studies in Classical Philology* 70: 111–15.

Collyer, J. (1761) *The Parent's and Guardian's Directory, and the Youth's Guide, in the Choice of a Profession or Trade*. London.

Cooter, R. D., and Landa, J. T. (1984) "Personal versus impersonal trade: the size of trading groups and contract law," *International Review of Law and Economics* 4: 15–22.

Coquery, N. (1997) "The aristocratic hôtel and its artisans in eighteenth-century Paris: the market ruled by court society," in Crossick (ed.), 92–115.

Costa, C. D. N. (trans.) (2006) *Lucian: Selected Dialogues*. Oxford.

Cottica, D. (2003) "Spinning in the Roman world: from everyday craft to metaphor of destiny," in Gillis and Nosch (eds.), 220–8.

Crook, J. A. (1967) *Law and Life of Rome*. Ithaca.

Crossick, G. (ed.) (1997) *The Artisan and the European Town, 1500–1900*. Aldershot.

Cuvigny, H. (1996) "The amount of wages paid to the quarry-workers at Mons Claudianus," *JRS* 86: 139–45.

D'Arms, J. H. (1970) *Romans on the Bay of Naples. A Social and Cultural Study of the Villas and Their Owners from 150 B.C. to A.D. 400*. Cambridge.

(1981) *Commerce and Social Standing in Ancient Rome*. Cambridge.

DeLaine, J. (2000) "Building the eternal city: the construction industry of imperial Rome," in *Ancient Rome: The Archaeology of the Eternal City*, ed. J. Coulston and H. Dodge. Oxford: 119–41.

(2001) "Bricks and mortar: exploring the economics of building techniques at Rome and Ostia," in Mattingly and Salmon (eds.), 230–68.

(2003) "The builders of Roman Ostia: organisation, status and society," in *Proceedings of the First International Congress on Construction History, Madrid, 20th–24th January 2003*, ed. S. Huerta et al. Madrid: 723–32.

De Ligt, L. (1993) *Fairs and Markets in the Roman Empire: Economic and Social Aspects of Periodic Trade in a Pre-Industrial Society*. Amsterdam.

(2000) "Governmental attitudes towards markets and *collegia*," in *Mercati permanenti e mercati periodici nel mondo romano: atti degli Incontri capresi di storia dell'economia antica, Capri 13–15 ottobre 1997*, ed. E. Lo Cascio. Bari: 237–52.

De Munck, B. (2009a) "From religious devotion to commercial ambition?," in *From Quinten Metsijs to Peter Paul Rubens: Masterpieces from the Royal Museum Reunited in the Cathedral*, ed. R. Fabri and N. van Hout. Antwerp and Schoten: 21–31.

(2009b) "Fiscalizing solidarity (from below). Poor relief in Antwerp guilds: between community building and public service," in *Serving the Urban Community: The Rise of Public Finance in the Low Countries*, ed. M. van der Heijden et al. Amsterdam: 168–93.

De Munck, B., and Soly, H. (2007) "'Learning on the shop floor' in historical perspective," in *Learning on the Shop Floor: Historical Perspectives on Apprenticeship*, ed. B. de Munck, S. L. Kaplan, and H. Soly. New York and Oxford: 3–34.

De Vries, J. (1976) *The Economy of Europe in an Age of Crisis, 1600–1750*. Cambridge.

(1993) "Between purchasing power and the world of goods: understanding the household economy in early modern Europe," in Brewer and Porter (eds.), 85–132.

(1994) "The industrial revolution and the industrious revolution," *The Journal of Economic History* 54: 249–70.

(2008) *The Industrious Revolution: Consumer Behavior and the Household Economy, 1650 to the Present*. Cambridge.

De Zulueta, F. (1945) *The Roman Law of Sale*. Oxford.

Dillon, M. (1997) *Pilgrims and Pilgrimage in Ancient Greece*. London.

Dixon, S. (1992) *The Roman Family*. Baltimore.

(2001a) "Familia Veturia: towards a lower-class economic prosopography," in *Childhood, Class, and Kin in the Roman World*, ed. S. Dixon. London and New York: 115–27.

(2001b) *Reading Roman Women: Sources, Genres and Real Life*. London.

Drexhage, H., Konen, H., and Ruffing, K. (2002) *Die Wirtschaft des römischen Reiches (1. – 3. Jahrhundert): Eine Einführung*. Berlin.

Drinkwater, J. F. (1982) "The wool textile industry in Gallia Belgica and the Secundinii of Igel," *Textile History* 13: 111–28.

Du Plessis, P. J. (2012) *Letting and Hiring in Roman Legal Thought: 27BCE-284 CE*. Leiden.

Duff, A. M. (1958) *Freedmen in the Early Roman Empire*. Cambridge.

Duncan-Jones, R. (1982) *The Economy of the Roman Empire: Quantitative Studies*. 2nd edn. Cambridge.

(1990) *Structure and Scale in the Roman Economy*. Cambridge.

Dyson, S. L. (1992) *Community and Society in Roman Italy*. Baltimore.

Earle, P. (1989a) "The female labour market in the late seventeenth and early eighteenth centuries," *The Economic History Review* 42/3: 328–53.

(1989b) *The Making of the English Middle Class: Business, Society, and Family Life in London, 1660–1730*. Berkeley.

Edgren, L. (2006) "What did a guild do? Swedish guilds in the eighteenth and early nineteenth century," in *Guilds and Association in Europe, 900–1900*, ed. I. A. Gadd and P. Wallis. London: 43–56.

Ehmer, J. (1984) "The artisan family in nineteenth-century Austria: embourgeo-isement of the petite bourgeoisie?," in *Shopkeepers and Master Artisans in Nineteenth-Century Europe*, ed. G. Crossick and H. Haupt. London and New York: 195–218.

(1997) "Worlds of mobility: migration patterns of Viennese artisans in the eighteenth century," in Crossick (ed.), 172–99.

(2001) "Family and business among master artisans and entrepreneurs: the case of 19th-century Vienna," *History of the Family* 6: 187–202.

Eliassen, F.-E., and Szende, K. (eds.) (2009) *Generations in Towns: Succession and Success in Pre-Industrial Urban Societies*. Newcastle.

Ellis, F. (1993) *Peasant Economics: Farm Households and Agrarian Development*. 2nd edn. Cambridge.

Elsner, J. (1992) "Pausanias: a Greek pilgrim in the Roman world," *Past & Present* 135: 3–29.

Ensminger, J. (1992) *Making a Market: The Institutional Transformation of an African Society*. Cambridge.

Epstein, S. A. (1991) *Wage Labor and Guilds in Medieval Europe*. Chapel Hill.

Epstein, S. R. (1998) "Craft guilds, apprenticeship, and technological change in preindustrial Europe," *The Journal of Economic History* 58/3: 684–713.

Epstein, S. R., and Prak, M. (eds.) (2008) *Guilds, Innovation, and the European Economy, 1400–1800*. Cambridge.

Erdkamp, P. (1999) "Agriculture, underemployment, and the cost of rural labour in the Roman world," *CQ* 49: 556–72.

(2005) *The Grain Market in the Roman Empire: A Social, Political and Economic Study*. Cambridge.

(2008) "Mobility and migration in Italy in the second century BC," in *People, Land and Politics. Demographic Developments and the Transformation of Roman Italy, 300 BC–AD 14*, ed. L. de Ligt and S. Northwood. Leiden: 417–49.

(2012) "Urbanism," in Scheidel (ed.), 241–65.

(ed.) (2013a) *The Cambridge Companion to Ancient Rome*. Cambridge.

(2013b) "The food supply of the capital," in Erdkamp (ed.), 262–77.

Erickson, A. L. (2008) "Married women's occupations in eighteenth-century London," *Continuity and Change* 23/2: 267–307.

Erman, H. (1896) *Servus vicarius: l'esclave de l'esclave romain*. Lausanne.

Fabre, G. (1981) *Libertus: recherches sur les rapports patron-affranchi à la fin de la République romaine*. Rome.

Fairchilds, C. (1993) "The production and marketing of populuxe goods in eighteenth-century Paris," in Brewer and Porter (eds.), 228–48.

Farr, J. R. (1988) *Hands of Honor: Artisans and Their World in Dijon, 1550–1650*. Ithaca.

(1997) "On the shop floor: guilds, artisans, and the European market economy, 1350–1750," *The Journal of Early Modern History* 1: 24–54.

(2000) *Artisans in Europe, 1300–1914*. Cambridge.

Farrell, H. (2005) "Trust and political economy: institutions and the sources of interfirm cooperation," *Comparative Political Studies* 38: 459–83.

Finley, M. I. (1999) *The Ancient Economy*. Updated edn. Berkeley.

Flambard, J. M. (1987) "Éléments pour une approche financière de la mort dans les classes populaires," in *La Mort, les morts et l'au-delà dans le mond romain: Actes du colloque de Caen, 20–22 Novembre 1985*, ed. F. Hinard. Caen: 209–44.

Flohr, M. (2007) "Nec quicquam ingenuum habere potest officina? Spatial contexts of urban production at Pompeii, AD 79," *BABesch* 82: 129–48.

(2011) "Exploring the limits of skilled craftsmanship: the fullonicae of Roman Italy," in Monteix and Tran (eds.), 87–100.

(2013) *The World of the Fullo: Work, Economy, and Society in Roman Italy*. Oxford.

Fogel, R. W. (1989) *Without Consent or Contract: The Rise and Fall of American Slavery*. New York.

Frank, T. (1920) *An Economic Survey of Ancient Rome to the End of the Republic*. Baltimore.

(1940) *An Economic Survey of Ancient Rome*. Baltimore.

Frayn, J. M. (1979) *Subsistence Farming in Roman Italy*. London.

Freu, C. (2011). "Apprendre et exercer un métier dans l'Égypte romaine (Ier – VIe siècles ap. J.-C.)," in Monteix and Tran (eds.), 27–40.

Frier, B. W., and Kehoe, D. P. (2007) "Law and economic institutions," in Scheidel, Morris, and Saller (eds.), 113–43.

Fülle, G. (1997) "The internal organization of the Arretine *terra sigillata* industry: problems of evidence and interpretation," *JRS* 87: 111–55.

Gabrielsen, V. (2007) "Brotherhoods of faith and provident planning: the non-public associations of the Greek world," *Mediterranean Historical Review* 22: 183–210.

Gallant, T. W. (1991) *Risk and Survival in Ancient Greece: Reconstructing the Rural Domestic Economy*. Stanford.

Gamauf, R. (2009) "Slaves doing business: the role of Roman law in the economy of a Roman household," *European Review of History* 16: 331–46.

Gardner, J. F. (1993) *Being a Roman Citizen*. London.

(1998) *Family and Familia in Roman Law and Life*. Oxford.

Garnsey, P. (1981) "Independent freedmen and the economy of Roman Italy under the Principate," *Klio* 63: 359–71.

(1988) *Famine and Food Supply in the Graco-Roman World: Responses to Risk and Crisis*. Cambridge.

(1998) *Cities, Peasants and Food in Classical Antiquity*, ed. W. Scheidel. Cambridge.

Garrioch, D. (1986) *Neighbourhood and Community in Paris, 1740–1790*. Cambridge.

Garrioch, D., and Sonenscher, M. (1986) "Compagnonnages, confraternities, and associations of journeymen in eighteenth-century Paris," *European History Quarterly* 16: 25–45.

Geertz, C. (1978) "The bazaar economy: information and search in peasant marketing," *American Economic Review* 68: 28–32.

Geertz, C., Geertz, H., and Rosen, L. (1979) *Meaning and Order in Moroccan Society: Three Essays in Cultural Analysis*. Cambridge.

Giardina, A., and Schiavone, A. (eds.) (1981) *Merci, mercati, e scambi nel Mediterraneo.* Rome.

Gibbons, R. (2005) "Four formal(izable) theories of the firm?," *Journal of Economic Behavior & Organization* 58: 200–45.

Gil, R., and Hartmann, W. R. (2009) "Airing your dirty laundry: vertical integration, reputational capital, and social networks," *Journal of Law, Economics & Organization* 27: 219–44.

Gillespie, M. (2000) *Free Labor in an Unfree World: White Artisans in Slaveholding Georgia, 1789–1860.* Athens.

Gillis, C., and Nosch, M.-L. B. (eds.) (2007) *Ancient Textiles. Production, Craft and Society.* Oxford.

Goldin, C. D. (1976) *Urban Slavery in the American South, 1820–1860: A Quantitative History.* Chicago.

Goldsmith, R. W. (1984) "An estimate of the size and structure of the national product of the early Roman Empire," *Review of Income and Wealth* 30: 263–88.

González, J. (1986) "The Lex Irnitana: a new copy of the Flavian municipal law," *JRS* 76: 147–243.

Gostenčnik, K. (2002) "Agathangelus the bronzesmith: the British finds in their continental context," *Britannia* 33: 227–56.

Graham, S. (2006) *Ex Figlinis: The Network Dynamics of the Tiber Valley Brick Industry in the Hinterland of Rome.* Oxford.

Grantham, G. (1994) "Economic history and the history of labour markets," in *Labour Market Evolution: The Economic History of Market Integration, Wage Flexibility, and the Employment Relation*, ed. G. Grantham and M. MacKinnon. London: 1–24.

(1999) "Contra Ricardo: on the macroeconomics of pre-industrial economies," *European Review of Economic History* 3: 199–232.

Green, D. R. (1995) *From Artisans to Paupers: Economic Change and Poverty in London, 1790–1870.* Aldershot.

Greene, K. (1986) *The Archaeology of the Roman Economy.* Berkeley.

Greif, A. (2006) *Institutions and the Path to the Modern Economy: Lessons from Medieval Trade.* Cambridge.

Grey, C. (2004) "Letters of recommendation and the circulation of rural laborers in the late Roman west," in *Travel, Communication and Geography in Late Antiquity: Sacred and Profane*, ed. L. Ellis and F. L. Kidner. Aldershot: 25–40.

(2011) *Constructing Communities in the Late Roman Countryside.* Cambridge.

Groen-Vallinga, M. (2013) "Desperate housewives? The adaptive family economy and female participation in the Roman urban labour market," in Hemelrijk and Woolf (eds.), 295–312.

Groppi, A. (2002) "A matter of fact rather than principle: women, work and property in papal Rome (eighteenth-nineteenth centuries)," *Journal of Modern Italian Studies* 7: 37–55.

Gummerus, H. (1916) "Industrie und Handel. (Bei den Römern)," *RE* 9: 1439–535.

Hall, P. G. (1962) *The Industries of London since 1861.* London.

Hanes, C. (1996) "Turnover cost and the distribution of slave labor in Anglo-America," *JEH* 56: 307–29.

Harding, V. (2009) "Sons, apprentices and successors: the transmission of skills and work opportunities in late medieval and early modern London," in Eliassen and Szende (eds.), 153–68.

Harland, P. (2003) *Associations, Synagogues, and Congregations: Claiming a Place in Ancient Mediterranean Society.* Minneapolis.

Harper, K. (2010) "Slave prices in late antiquity (and in the very long term)," *Historia* 59/2: 206–38.

(2011) *Slavery in the Late Roman World, AD 275–425.* Cambridge.

Harris-McCoy, D. (2012) *Artemidorus' Oneirocritica. Text, Translation and Commentary.* Oxford.

Harrison, G. W. M. (2001) "Martial on *sportula* and the Saturnalia," *Mouseion* 1: 295–312.

Hawkins, C. (2012) "Manufacturing," in Scheidel (ed.), 175–94.

Heimmermann, D. J. (1994) *Work and Corporate Life in Old Regime France: The Leather Artisans of Bordeaux (1740–1791).* PhD Dissertation, Marquette University.

Hemelrijk, E. (2008) "Patronesses and 'mothers' of Roman *collegia*," *ClAnt* 27/1: 115–62.

Hemelrijk, E., and Woolf, G. (eds.) (2013) *Women and the Roman City in the Latin West.* Leiden.

Hermann-Otto, E. (2013) "Slaves and freedmen," in Erdkamp (ed.), 60–76.

Higman, B. W. (1984) *Slave Populations of the British Caribbean, 1807–1834.* Baltimore.

Hijmans, B. L., Jr., et al. (eds.) (1995) *Apuleius Madaurensis Metaphorphoses: Book IX Text, Introduction and Commentary.* Groningen.

Hodgson, G. (1999) *Evolution and Institutions: On Evolutionary Economics and the Evolution of Economics.* Cheltenham and Northampton.

Holleran, C. (2011) "Migration and the urban economy of Rome," in *Demography and the Graeco-Roman World: New Insights and Approaches*, ed. C. Holleran and A. Pudsey. Cambridge: 155–80.

(2012) *Shopping in Ancient Rome: The Retail Trade in the Late Republic and the Principate.* Oxford.

(2013) "Women and retail in Roman Italy," in Hemelrijk and Woolf (eds.), 313–30.

(Forthcoming) "Getting a job: finding work in the city of Rome," in Verboven and Laes (eds.).

Hollis, A. S. (1977) *Commentary on Ovid, Ars Amatoria, Book I.* Oxford.

Hopkins, K. (1966) "On the probable age structure of the Roman population," *Population Studies* 20: 245–64.

(1978) *Conquerors and Slaves.* Cambridge.

(1995–1996) "Rome, taxes, rents and trade," *Kodai* 6/7: 41–75.

Horden, P., and Purcell, N. (2000) *The Corrupting Sea: A Study of Mediterranean History.* Malden.

Humble, N., and Sidwell, K. (2006) "Dreams of glory: Lucian as autobiographer," in *The Limits of Ancient Biography*, ed. B. McGing and J. Mossman. Swansea: 213–26.

Huttunen, P. (1974) *The Social Strata in the Imperial City of Rome*. Oulu.

Johns, C., et al. (1997) *The Snettisham Roman Jeweller's Hoard*. London.

Johnson, H. (1996) *The Bahamas from Slavery to Servitude, 1783–1933*. Gainesville.

Johnston, D. (1999) *Roman Law in Context*. Cambridge.

Jones, A. H. M. (1956) "Slavery in the ancient world," *Economic History Review* 9: 185–99.

(1960) *Studies in Roman Government and Law*. Oxford.

Jones, C. P. (1986) *Culture and Society in Lucian*. Cambridge.

Jongman, W. (2007) "The early Roman Empire: consumption," in Scheidel, Morris, and Saller (eds.), 592–618.

Jongman, W., and Kleijwegt, M. (eds.) (2002). *After the Past: Essays in Ancient History in Honour of H.W. Pleket*. Leiden.

Joshel, S. R. (1977) *The Occupations and Economic Roles of Freedmen in the Early Roman Empire: A Study in Roman Social and Economic Patterns*. PhD Dissertation, Rutgers.

(1992) *Work, Identity, and Legal Status at Rome: A Study of the Occupational Inscriptions*. Norman.

Kahl, W. F. (1960) *The Development of London Livery Companies*. Boston.

Kampen, N. (1981) *Image and Status: Roman Working Women in Ostia*. Berlin.

(1982) "Social status and gender in Roman art: the case of the saleswoman," in *Feminism and Art History: Questioning the Litany*, ed. N. Broude and M. D. Garrard. New York: 63–77.

Kaplan, M. (1992) *Les hommes et la terre à Byzance du VIe au XIe siècle: propriété et exploitation du sol*. Paris.

Kaplan, S. L. (1979) "Réflexions sur la police du monde du travail, 1700–1815," *Revue Historique* 261: 17–77.

(1981) "The luxury guilds in Paris in the XVIIIth century," *Francia* 9: 256–98.

(1996) *The Bakers of Paris and the Bread Question, 1700–1775*. Durham.

Kehoe, D. P. (1988) "Allocation of risk and investment on the estates of Pliny the Younger," *Chiron* 18: 15–42.

Kent, D. A. (1989) "Ubiquitous but invisible: female domestic servants in mid-eighteenth century London," *History Workshop Journal* 28/1: 111–28.

(1994) "Small businessmen and their credit transactions," *Business History* 36/2: 47–64.

Kessler, D., and Temin, P. (2008) "Money and prices in the early Roman Empire," in *The Monetary Systems of the Greeks and Romans*, ed. W. Harris. Oxford: 137–59.

Kim, S. (1989) "Labor specialization and the extent of the market," *Journal of Political Economy* 97/3: 692–705.

King, R. (2004) "The sociability of the trade guilds of Newcastle and Durham, 1660–1750: the urban renaissance revisited," in *Creating and Consuming Culture in North-East England, 1660–1830*, ed. H. Berry and J. Gregory. Aldershot: 57–71.

Kirkham, P. (1988) *The London Furniture Trade, 1700–1870*. London.

Kirschenbaum, A. (1987) *Sons, Slaves and Freedmen in Roman Commerce*. Jerusalem.

Kleijwegt, M. (2002) "Textile manufacturing for a religious market. Artemis and Diana as tycoons of industry," in Jongman and Kleijwegt (eds.), 81–134.

Klein, B. (1996) "Why hold-ups occur: the self-enforcing range of contractual relationships," *Economic Inquiry* XXXIV: 444–63.

Kloppenborg, J. S. (1996) "*Collegia* and *thiasoi*: issues in function, taxonomy, and membership," in *Voluntary Associations in the Graeco-Roman World*, ed. J. S. Kloppenborg and S. G. Wilson. London: 16–30.

Knapp, R. (2011) *Invisible Romans*. Cambridge.

Knotter, A. (1994) "Problems of the family economy: peasant economy, domestic production and labour markets in pre-industrial Europe," in *Economic and Social History in the Netherlands: Family Strategies and Changing Labour Relations*, ed. M. Baud et al. Amsterdam: 19–60.

Kooijmans, L. (1995) "Risk and reputation: on the mentality of merchants in the early modern period," in *Entrepreneurs and Entrepreneurship in Early Modern Times: Merchants and Industrialists within the Orbit of the Dutch Staple Market*, ed. C. Lesger and L. Noordegraaf. The Hague: 25–34.

Kron, G. (2012) "Nutrition, hygiene, and mortality. Setting parameters for Roman health and life expectancy consistent with our comparative evidence," in *L'impatto della "Peste Antonina,"* ed. E. Lo Cascio. Bari: 193–252.

Kudlien, F. (1970) "Medical education in classical antiquity," in *The History of Medical Education*, ed. C. D. O'Malley. Berkeley: 3–37.

Laes, C. (2011) *Children in the Roman Empire: Outsiders Within*. Cambridge.

Lamb, H. H. (1995) *Climate, History and the Modern World*. 2nd edn. London.

Lancaster, L. (1998) "Building Trajan's markets," *AJA* 102: 283–308.

Lancy, D. F. (2012) "'First you must master pain': the nature and purpose of apprenticeship," *Anthropology of Work Review* 33/2: 113–26.

Lane, J. (1996) *Apprenticeship in England, 1600–1914*. London.

Launaro, A. (2011) *Peasants and Slaves: The Rural Population of Roman Italy (200 BC to AD 100)*. Cambridge.

Leary, T. J. (1996) *Martial Book XIV: The Apophoreta*. London.

Leeson, R. A. (1979) *Travelling Brothers: The Six Centuries' Road from Craft Fellowship to Trade Unionism*. London.

Lelis, A. A., Percy, W. A., and Verstraete, B. C. (2003) *The Age of Marriage in Ancient Rome*. Lewiston.

Leunig, T., Minns, C., and Wallis, P. (2011) "Networks in the premodern economy: the market for London apprenticeships, 1600–1749," *The Journal of Economic History* 71/2: 413–43.

Lintott, A. W. (1993) *Imperium Romanum: Politics and Administration*. London.

Lio, M. (1998) "Uncertainty, insurance, and division of labor," *Review of Development Economics* 2/1: 76–86.

Lis, C., and Soly, H. (2008) "Subcontracting in guild-based export trades, thirteenth-eighteenth centuries," in Epstein and Prak (eds.), 81–113.

Liu, J. (2005) "Local governments and *collegia*: a new appraisal of the evidence," in *A Tall Order: Writing the Social History of the Ancient World*, ed. J. Aubert and Z. Várhelyi. München and Leipzig: 285–316.

(2009) *Collegia Centonariorum: The Guilds of Textile Dealers in the Roman West*. Leiden.

(Forthcoming) "Group membership, trust networks, and social capital: a critical analysis," in Verboven and Laes (eds.).

Lo Cascio, E. (2006) "The role of the state in the Roman economy: making use of the new institutional economics," in *Ancient Economies, Modern Methodologies: Archaeology, Comparative History, Models and Institutions*, ed. P. F. Bang, M. Ikeguchi, and H. G. Ziche. Bari: 215–34.

Lo Cascio, E., and Melanima, P. (2009). "GDP in pre-modern agrarian economies (1–1820 AD). A revision of the estimates," *Rivista di storia economica* 25: 391–420.

Loane, H. J. (1938) *Industry and Commerce of the City of Rome (50 B.C.–200 A.D.)*. Baltimore.

Lopez Barja de Quiroga, P. (1998) "Junian Latins: status and number," *Athenaeum* 86: 133–63.

Lovén, L. (1998) "« Lanam fecit »: woolworking and female virtue," in *Aspects of Women in Antiquity*, ed. L. Lovén and A. Strömberg. Jonsered: 85–95.

(2007) "Wool work as a gender symbol in ancient Rome. Roman textiles and ancient sources," in Gillis and Nosch (eds.), 229–36.

Lucassen, J. (1987) *Migrant Labour in Europe 1600–1900: The Drift to the North Sea*. London.

MacMullen, R. (1974) *Roman Social Relations: 50 B.C. to A.D. 284*. New Haven.

Maddison, A. (2007) *Contours of the World Economy, 1–2030 AD: Essays in Macro-Economic History*. Oxford.

Manning, J. G., and Morris, I. (eds.) (2005a) *The Ancient Economy: Evidence and Models*. Stanford.

(2005b) "Introduction," in Manning and Morris (eds.), 1–44.

Martin, D. (1996) "The construction of the ancient family: methodological considerations," *JRS* 86: 40–60.

Martin, J. D. (2004) *Divided Mastery: Slave Hiring in the American South*. Cambridge.

Martin, S. D. (1986) "A reconsideration of probatio operis," *ZRG* CIII: 321–37.

(1989) *The Roman Jurists and the Organization of Private Building in the Late Republic and Early Empire*. Brussels.

(2001) "*Imperitia*: the responsibility of skilled workers in classical Roman law," *AJPh* 122: 107–29.

Mattingly, D. J. (1996) "First fruit? The olive in the Roman world," in *Human Landscapes in Classical Antiquity: Environment and Culture*, ed. J. Salmon and G. Shipley. London: 213–53.

Mattingly, D. J., and Salmon, J. (eds.) (2001a) *Economies Beyond Agriculture in the Classical World*. London.

(2001b) "The productive past: economies beyond agriculture," in Mattingly and Salmon (eds.), 3–14.

Mattusch, C. C. (1996) *Classical Bronzes: The Art and Craft of Greek and Roman Statuary*. Ithaca.

Mayer, E. (2012) *The Ancient Middle Classes*. Cambridge, MA.

Mayeske, B. (1972) *Bakeries, Bakers, and Bread at Pompeii: A Study in Social and Economic History*. PhD Dissertation, University of Maryland.

McMillan, J., and Woodruff, C. (2001) "Private order under dysfunctional public order," *Michigan Law Review* 98: 2421–58.

Mead, D. C. (1984) "Of contracts and subcontracts: small firms in vertically dis-integrated production/distribution systems in LDCs," *World Development* 12: 1095–106.

Medick, H. (1976) "The proto-industrial family economy: the structural function of household and family during the transition from peasant society to industrial capitalism," *Social History* 1: 291–315.

Mees, A. W. (2002) *Organisationsformen römischer Töpfer-Manufakturen am Beispiel von Arezzo und Rheinzabern: unter Berücksichtigung von Papyri, Inschriften und Rechtsquellen*. Mainz.

Meiggs, R. (1973) *Roman Ostia*. 2nd edn. Oxford.

Ménétra, J.-L. (1986) *Journal of My Life*. A. Goldhammer (trans.), with introduction and commentary by D. Roche, and foreword by R. Darnton. New York.

Meyer, E. (1990) "Explaining the epigraphic habit in Roman Empire: the evidence of epitaphs," *JRS* 80: 74–96.

Millar, F. (1977) *The Emperor in the Roman World (31 BC–AD 337)*. Ithaca.

(1981) "The world of the *Golden Ass*," *JRS* 71: 63–75.

Millett, P. (1991) *Lending and Borrowing in Ancient Athens*. Cambridge.

Minaud, G. (2005) *La comptabilité à Rome: Essai d'histoire économique sur la pensée comptable commerciale et privée dans le monde antique romain*. Lausanne.

Minns, C., and Wallis, P. (2013) "The price of human capital in a pre-industrial economy: premiums and apprenticeship contracts in 18th century England," *Explorations in Economic History* 50/3: 335–50.

Möller, C. (1993) "Die *mercennarii* in der römischen Arbeitswelt," *ZSS* 110: 296–330.

Mols, S. T. A. M. (1999) *Wooden Furniture in Herculaneum: Form, Technique and Function*. Amsterdam: Gieben.

Monson, A. (2006) "The ethics and economics of Ptolemaic religious associations," *Ancient Society* 36: 221–38.

Monteix, N., and Tran, N. (2011) *Les savoirs professionnels des gens de métier: études sur le monde du travail dans les sociétés urbaines de l'empire romain*. Naples.

More, J. H. (1969) "*The fabri tignarii of Rome*." PhD Dissertation, Harvard University.

Morel, J.-P. (1981) "La produzione della ceramica campana," in Giardina and Schiavone (eds.), 81–97.

(2007) "Early Rome and Italy," in Scheidel, Morris, and Saller (eds.), 487–510.

Morley, N. (1996) *Metropolis and Hinterland: The City of Rome and the Italian Economy, 200 B.C.–A.D. 200*. Cambridge.

(2007) *Trade in Classical Antiquity*. Cambridge.

(2013) "Population size and social structure," in Erdkamp (ed.), 29–44.

Morris, I. (2002) "Hard surfaces," in *Money, Labour and Land*, ed. P. Cartledge, E. E. Cohen, and L. Foxhall. Abingdon: 8–43.

Mouritsen, H. (2001) "Roman freedmen and the urban economy: Pompeii in the first century AD," in *Pompei tra Sorrento e Sarno*, ed. F. Senatore. Rome: 1–27.

(2005) "Freedmen and decurions: epitaphs and social history in imperial Italy," *JRS* 95: 38–63.

(2011) *The Freedman in the Roman World*. Cambridge.

Muhkerjee, A., and Ray, D. (1995) "Labour tying," *Journal of Development Economics* 47/2: 207–39.

Muldrew, C. (1998) *The Economy of Obligation: The Culture of Credit and Social Relations in Early Modern England*. New York.

Musgrave, E. C. (1993) "Women in the male world of work: the building industries of eighteenth-century Britanny," *French History* 7/1: 30–52.

Noy, D. (2000) *Foreigners at Rome: Citizens and Strangers*. London.

Nutton, V. (1995) "The medical meeting place," in van der Eijk et al. (eds.), 3–26.

Oberleitner, W. (1978) *Funde aus Ephesos und Samothrake*. Wien.

Ogilvie, S. (2011) *Institutions and European Trade: Merchant Guilds, 1000–1800*. Cambridge.

Olson, K. (2008) *Dress and the Roman Woman: Self-Presentation and Society*. New York.

Osborne, R. (1995) "The economics and politics of slavery at Athens," in *The Greek World*, ed. A. Powell. London: 27–43.

Oster, R. E. (1990) "Ephesus as a religious center under the Principate I. Paganism before Constantine," *Aufstieg und Niedergang der römischen Welt II* 18/3: 1661–728.

Patterson, O. (1982) *Slavery and Social Death. A Comparative Study*. Cambridge.

Peacock, D. P. S. (1982) *Pottery in the Roman World*. London and New York.

Pearce, T. E. V. (1974) "The role of the wife as CUSTOS in ancient Rome," *Eranos* LXXII: 16–33.

Pearse, J. L. D. (1974) *The Organization of Roman Building during the Late Republic and Early Empire*. PhD Dissertation, Cambridge University.

Pelizzon, S. (2000) "Grain flour, 1590–1790," *Review* 23: 87–195.

Pernot, M. (2004) "Des bronziers au travail dans leur atelier," in *L'artisanat métallurgique dans les sociétés anciennes en Méditerranée Occidentale: techniques, lieux et formes de production*, ed. A. Lehoërff. Rome: 171–91.

Perry, M. (2014) *Gender, Manumission, and the Roman Freedwoman*. New York.

Persson, K. G. (1999) *Grain Markets in Europe, 1500–1900: Integration and Deregulation*. Cambridge.

Petersen, L. (2003) "The baker, his tomb, his wife, and her breadbasket: the monument of Eurysaces in Rome," *The Art Bulletin* 85/2: 230–57.

Pfister, U. (2008) "Craft guilds, the theory of the firm, and early modern proto-industry," in Epstein and Prak (eds.), 25–51.

Piore, M. J., and Sabel, C. F. (1984) *The Second Industrial Divide: Possibilities for Prosperity*. New York.

Place, F. (1972) *The Autobiography of Francis Place (1771–1854)*, ed. M. Thale. Cambridge.

Pleket, H. W. (1987) "Labor and unemployment in the Roman Empire: some preliminary remarks," in *Soziale Randgruppen und antike Sozialpolitik*, ed. W. Ingomar. Graz: 267–76.

(1995) "The social status of physicians in the Graeco-Roman world," in van der Eijk et al. (eds.), 27–34.

Purcell, N. (2000) "Rome and Italy," in *The Cambridge Ancient History*, vol. IX, 2nd edn., ed. J. A. Crook, A. Lintott, and E. Rawson. Cambridge: 405–43.

Rankov, B. (2007) "Military forces," in Sabin, van Wees, and Whitby (eds.), 30–75.

Rathbone, D. (1997) "Prices and price formation in Roman Egypt," in *Économie antique: prix et formations des prix dans les économies antiques*, ed. J. Andreau et al. Saint-Bertrand-de-Comminges: 183–244.

(2007) "Military finance and supply," in Sabin, van Wees, and Whitby (eds.), 158–76.

(2009) "Earnings and costs: living standards and the Roman economy," in Bowman and Wilson (eds.), 299–326.

Rawson, B. (1966) "Family life among the lower classes at Rome in the first two centuries of the Empire," *CPh* 61/2: 71–83.

(1974) "Roman concubinage and other de-facto marriages," *TAPhA* CIV: 279–305.

Ray, D. (1998) *Development Economics*. Princeton.

Reith, R. (2008) "Circulation of skilled labour in late medieval and early modern central Europe," in Epstein and Prak (eds.), 114–42.

Richman, B. D. (2004) "Firms, courts, and reputation mechanisms: towards a positive theory of private ordering," *Columbia Law Review* 104: 2328–67.

(2006) "How community institutions create economic advantage: Jewish diamond merchants in New York," *Law and Social Inquiry* 31: 383–420.

Rickman, G. (1980) *The Corn Supply of Ancient Rome*. Oxford.

Riello, G. (2006) *A Foot in the Past: Consumers, Producers and Footwear in the Long Eighteenth Century*. Oxford.

(2008) "Strategies and boundaries: subcontracting and the London trades in the long eighteenth century," *Enterprise and Society* 9: 243–80.

Rockwell, P. (1991) "Unfinished statuary associated with a sculptor's studio." *Aphrodisias Papers* 2: 127–43.

Roebuck, D. (2001) *Ancient Greek Arbitration*. Oxford.

Roebuck, D., and de Loynes de Fumichon, B. (2004) *Roman Arbitration*. Oxford.

Rosser, G. (1997) "Crafts, guilds, and the negotiation of work in the medieval town," *Past and Present* 154: 3–31.

Roth, U. (2010) "Peculium, freedom, citizenship: golden triangle or vicious circle? An act in two parts," in *By the Sweat of Your Brow: Roman Slavery in Its Socio-Economic Setting*, ed. U. Roth. London: 91–120.

Royden, H. L. (1988) *The Magistrates of the Roman Professional Collegia in Italy from the First to the Third Century A.D.* Pisa.

Ruffing, K. (2008) *Die berufliche Spezialisierung in Handel und Handwerk. Untersuchungen zu ihrer Entwicklung und zu ihren Bedingungen in der römischen Kaiserzeit im östlichen Mittelmeerraum auf der Grundlage griechischer Inschriften und Papyri.* Rahden.

Rutherford, I. (2001) "Tourism and the sacred: Pausanias and the traditions of Greek pilgrimage," in *Pausanias: Travel and Memory in Roman Greece*, ed. S. E. Alcock et al. Oxford: 40–52.

Sabel, C. F., and Zeitlin, J. (1985) "Historical alternatives to mass production: politics, markets and technology in nineteenth-century industrialization," *Past and Present* 108: 133–76.

(eds.) (1997) *World of Possibilities: Flexibility and Mass Production in Western Industrialization.* Cambridge.

Sabin, P., van Wees, H., and Whitby, M. (2007) *The Cambridge History of Greek and Roman Warfare*, vol. 2. Cambridge.

Sallares, R. (2002) *Malaria and Rome: A History of Malaria in Ancient Italy.* Oxford.

Saller, R. P. (1994) *Patriarchy, Property and Death in the Roman Family.* Cambridge.

(2001) "The family and society," in Bodel (ed.), 95–117.

(2003) "Women, slaves, and the economy of the Roman household," in *Early Christian Families in Context: An Interdisciplinary Dialogue*, ed. D. L. Balch and C. Osiek. Cambridge: 185–204.

(2005) "Framing the debate over growth in the ancient economy," in Manning and Morris (eds.), 223–38.

(2007) "Household and gender," in Scheidel, Morris, and Saller (eds.), 87–112.

(2012). "Human capital and economic growth," in *The Cambridge Companion to the Roman Economy*, ed. W. Scheidel. Cambridge: 71–86.

Saller, R. P., and Shaw, B. D. (1984) "Tombstones and family relations in the Principate: civilians, soldiers and slaves," *JRS* 74: 124–56.

Samuel, A. E. (1965) "The role of *paramone* clauses in ancient documents," *JJP* 15: 221–311.

Scheidel, W. (1994) "Libitina's bitter gains: seasonal mortality and endemic disease in the ancient city of Rome," *Ancient Society* 25: 152–75.

(1995) "The most silent women of Greece and Rome: rural labour and women's life in the ancient world (I)," *G&R* 42/2: 202–17.

(1996a) "The most silent women of Greece and Rome: rural labour and women's life in the ancient world (II)," *G&R* 43/1: 1–10.

(1996b) *Measuring Sex, Age, and Death in the Roman Empire.* Ann Arbor.

(1996c) "Reflections on the differential valuation of slaves in Diocletian's price edict and in the United States," *MBAH* 15: 67–79.

(2001) *Death on the Nile: Disease and the Demography of Roman Egypt.* Leiden.

(2002) "A model of demographic and economic change in Roman Egypt after the Antonine plague," *JRA* 15: 97–114.

(2003) "Germs for Rome," in *Rome the Cosmopolis*, ed. C. Edwards and G. Woolf. Cambridge: 158–76.

(2005) "Real slave prices and the relative cost of slave labor in the Greco-Roman world," *Ancient Society* 35: 1–17.

(2007a) "A model of real income growth in Roman Italy," *Historia* 56: 322–46.

(2007b) "Roman funerary commemoration and the age at first marriage," *CPh* 102: 389–402.

(2008) "The comparative economics of slavery in the Greco-Roman world," in *Slave Systems: Ancient and Modern*, ed. E. Dal Lago and C. Katsari. Cambridge: 105–26.

(2009) "In search of Roman economic growth," *JRA* 22: 46–70.

(2010) "Real wages in early economies: evidence for living standards from 1800 BCE to 1300 CE," *JESHO* 53: 425–62.

(ed.) (2012a) *The Cambridge Companion to the Roman Economy*. Cambridge.

(2012b) "Physical well-being," in Scheidel (ed.), 321–33.

Scheidel, W., and Friesen, S. J. (2009) "The size of the economy and the distribution of income in the Roman Empire," *JRS* 99: 61–91.

Scheidel, W., Morris, I., and Saller, R. (eds.) (2007) *The Cambridge Economic History of the Greco-Roman World*. Cambridge.

Schmidt, A. (2011) "Labour ideologies and women in the northern Netherlands, c. 1500–1800," *International Review of Social History* 56/S19: 45–67.

Schwarz, L. D. (1992) *London in the Age of Industrialisation: Entrepreneurs, Labour Force, and Living Conditions, 1700–1850*. Cambridge.

Scullard, H. H. (1981) *Festivals and Ceremonies of the Roman Republic*. Ithaca.

Sewell, W. H., Jr. (1980) *Work and Revolution in France: The Language of Labor from the Old Regime to 1848*. Cambridge.

Shaw, B. D. (1996) "Seasons of death: aspects of mortality in imperial Rome," *JRS* 86: 100–38.

(1997) "Agrarian economy and the marriage cycle of Roman women," *JRA* 10: 57–76.

(2013) *Bringing in the Sheaves: Economy and Metaphor in the Roman World*. Toronto.

Sherlock, D. (1976) "Silver and silversmithing," in *Roman Crafts*, ed. D. Strong and D. Brown. London: 11–24.

Sijpesteijn, P. J. (1996) "A labour contract to build a boat," *ZPE* 111: 159–62.

Sirks, A. J. B. (1983) "The *lex Junia* and the effects of informal manumission and iteration," *RIDA* XXX: 211–92.

(1993) "Did the late Roman government try to tie people to their profession or status?," *Tyche* 8: 159–75.

(2002) "Sailing in the off-season with reduced financial risk," in *Speculum Iuris: Roman Law as a Reflection of Social and Economic Life in Antiquity*, ed. J.-J. Aubert and B. Sirks. Ann Arbor: 134–50.

Skocpol, T., and Somers, M. (1980) "The uses of comparative history in macro-social inquiry," *Comparative Studies in Society and History* 22: 174–97.

Smail, J. (2005) "Credit, risk, and honor in eighteenth-century commerce," *Journal of British Studies* 44: 439–56.

Smith, A. (1994) *An Inquiry into the Nature and Causes of the Wealth of Nations*, ed. E. Cannan. New York.

Smits, W., and Stromback, T. (2001) *The Economics of the Apprenticeship System*. Cheltenham.

Solin, H. (1971) *Beiträge zur Kenntnis der griechischen Personennamen in Rom I*. Helsinki.

Sonenscher, M. (1989) *Work and Wages: Natural Law, Politics, and the Eighteenth-Century French Trades*. Cambridge.

Staerman, E. M. (1976) "L'esclavage dans l'artisinat romain," *DHA* II: 103–27.

Stedman Jones, G. (1984) *Outcast London: A Study in the Relationship between Classes in Victorian Society*. New York.

Steffen, C. G. (1979) "Changes in the organization of artisan production in Baltimore, 1790–1820," *The William and Mary Quarterly*, 3rd ser., 36: 101–17.

(1984) *The Mechanics of Baltimore: Workers and Politics in the Age of Revolution, 1763–1812*. Urbana.

Storper, M., and Christopherson, S. (1987) "Flexible specialization and regional industrial agglomerations: the case of the U.S. motion picture industry," *Annals of the Association of American Geographers* 77/1: 104–17.

Strahilevitz, L. J. (2003) "Social norms from close-knit groups to loose-knit groups," *The University of Chicago Law Review* 70: 359–72.

Strong, D. E. (1966) *Greek and Roman Gold and Silver Plate*. Ithaca.

Styles, J. (1995) "The goldsmiths and the London luxury trades, 1550 to 1750," in *Goldsmiths, Silversmiths and Bankers: Innovation and the Transfer of Skill, 1550 to 1750*, ed. D. Mitchell. London: 112–20.

Talbert, R. J. A. (1984) *The Senate of Imperial Rome*. Princeton.

Tassinari, S. (1993) *Il Vasellame Bronzeo di Pompei*. Rome.

Taubenschlag, R. (1955) *The Law of Greco-Roman Egypt in the Light of the Papyri, 332 B.C.–640 A.D.* 2nd edn. Warsaw.

Taylor, L. R. (1962) "Freedmen and freeborn in the epitaphs of Imperial Rome," *American Journal of Philology* 82: 113–32.

Temin, P. (2006) "Estimating GDP in the early Roman Empire," in *Innovazione tecnica e progresso economico nel mondo romano*, ed. E. Lo Cascio. Bari: 31–54.

(2012) "The contribution of economics," in Scheidel (ed.), 45–70.

(2013) *The Roman Market Economy*. Princeton.

Tilly, C. (2005) *Trust and Rule*. New York.

Tilly, L., and Scott, J. W. (1987) *Women, Work, and Family*. 2nd edn. New York.

Tran, N. (2006) *Les membres des associations romaines: le rang social des collegiati en Italie et en Gaules, sous le haut-empire*. Rome.

(2007) "Les procedures d'exclusion des colleges professionels et funéraires sous le Haut-Empire: pratiques épigraphiques, norme collective et non-dits," in *Les Exclus dans l'Antiquité*, ed. C. Wolff. Lyon: 119–38.

(2011) "Les gens de métier romains: savoirs professionnels et supériorités plébéiennes," in Monteix and Tran (eds.), 119–33.

(2013) *Dominus tabernae: le statut de travail des artisans et des commerçants de l'Occident romain.* Rome.

Trebilco, P. (1994) "Asia," in *The Book of Acts in Its Graeco-Roman Setting*, ed. D. W. J. Gill and C. Gempf. Grand Rapids: 291–362.

Treggiari, S. (1969) *Roman Freedmen during the Late Republic.* Oxford.

(1975) "Jobs in the household of Livia," *PBSR* 43: 48–77.

(1979) "Lower class women in the Roman economy," *Florilegium* 1: 65–86.

(1980) "Urban labour in Rome: *mercennarii* and *tabernarii*," in *Non-Slave Labour in the Greco-Roman World*, ed. P. Garnsey. Cambridge: 48–64.

(1991) *Roman Marriage: Iusti Coniuges from the Time of Cicero to the Time of Ulpian.* Oxford.

Truant, C. M. (1994) *The Rites of Labor: Brotherhoods of Compagnonnage in Old and New Regime France.* Ithaca.

Tucker, C. W. (1982) "Women in the manumission inscriptions at Delphi," *TAPA* 112: 225–36.

Ulrich, R. B. (2007) *Roman Woodworking.* New Haven.

Van der Eijk, Ph. J., Horstmanshoff, H. F. J., and Schrijvers, P. H. (eds.) (1995) *Ancient Medicine in Its Socio-Cultural Context.* 2 vols. Amsterdam.

Van Minnen, P. (1987) "Urban craftsmen in Roman Egypt," *MBAH* 6: 31–88.

(1998) "Did ancient women learn a trade outside the home?: a note on SB XVIII 13305," *ZPE* 123: 201–3.

Van Nederveen Meerkerk, E. (2008) "Couples cooperating? Dutch textile workers, family labour, and the 'industrious revolution' c. 1600–1800," *Continuity and Change* 23/2: 237–66.

(2012) "The first 'male breadwinner economy'? Dutch married women's and children's paid and unpaid work in western European perspective, c. 1600–1900," in *Working on Labor: Essays in Honor of Jan Lucassen*, ed. M. van der Linden and L. Lucassen. Leiden: 323–52.

Van Nijf, O. M. (1997) *The Civic World of Professional Associations in the Roman East.* Amsterdam.

(2002) "Collegia and civic guards: two chapters in the history of sociability," in Jongman and Kleijwegt (eds.), 305–39.

Van Voorhis, J. A. (1999) *The Sculptor's Workshop at Aphrodisias.* PhD Dissertation, New York University.

Van Zanden, J. L. (2009) "The skill premium and the 'Great Divergence,'" *European Review of Economic History* 13/1: 121–53.

Venticinque, P. F. (2010) "Family affairs: guild regulations and family relationships in Roman Egypt," *GRBS* 50: 273–94.

(2015) "Courting the associations: cooperation, conflict, and interaction in Roman Egypt," in *Private Associations and the Public Sphere: Proceedings of a Symposium Held at the Royal Danish Academy of Sciences and Letters, 9–11 September 2010*, ed. V. Gabrielsen and C. A. Thomsen. Copenhagen: 314–40.

Verboven, K. (2002) *The Economy of Friends: Economic Aspects of Amicitia and Patronage in the Late Republic*. Brussels.

(2007) "The associative order: status and ethos among Roman businessmen in the late Republic and early Empire," *Athenaeum* 95: 861–93.

(2011) "Resident aliens and translocal merchant *collegia* in the Roman Empire," in *Frontiers in the Roman World: Proceedings of the Ninth Workshop of the International Network Impact of Empire (Durham, 16–19 April 2009)*, ed. O. Hekster and T. Kaizer. Leiden and Boston: 335–48.

Verboven, K., and Laes, C. (eds.) (forthcoming) *Work, Labour, and Professions in the Roman World*. Leiden.

Veyne, P. (2000) "La 'Plèbe Moyenne' sous la haute empire Romain," *Annales HSS* 55: 1169–99.

Von Petrikovits, H. (1981) "Die Spezialisierung des römischen Handwerks," in *Das Handwerk in vor- und frühgeschichtlicher Zeit, I: Historische und rechtshistorische Beiträge und Untersuchungen zur Frühgeschichte der Gilde. Bericht über die Kolloquien der Kommission für die Altertumskunde Mittelund Nordeuropas in den Jahren '77- '80*, ed. H. von Jankuhn. Göttingen: 63–132.

Wade, R. C. (1964) *Slavery in the Cities: The South, 1820–1860*. New York.

Waldstein, W. (1986) *Operae libertorum. Untersuchungen zur Dienstpflicht freigelassener Sklaven*. Stuttgart.

Wall, R. (1986) "Work, welfare, and the family: an illustration of the adaptive family economy," in *The World We Have Gained. Histories of Population and Social Structure. Essays Presented to Peter Laslett on His Seventieth Birthday*, ed. L. Bonfield, R. M. Smith, and K. Wrightson. Oxford: 261–94.

Wallace-Hadrill, A. (2008) *Rome's Cultural Revolution*. Cambridge.

Wallis, P. (2008) "Apprenticeship and training in premodern England," *The Journal of Economic History* 68/3: 832–61.

Waltzing, J. P. (1895–1900) *Étude historique sur les corporations professionnelles chez les Romains depuis les origines jusqu'à la chute de l'Empire d'Occident*. Louvain.

Ward, J. P. (1997) *Metropolitan Communities: Trade Guilds, Identity, and Change in Early Modern London*. Stanford.

Ward-Perkins, J. B. (1992) *Marble in Antiquity: Collected Papers of J. B. Ward-Perkins*. London.

Watson, A. A. (2000). *The Blacksmith: Ironworker and Farrier*. New York.

Weatherill, L. (1988) *Consumer Behaviour and Material Culture in Britain, 1660–1760*. London.

Weaver, P. R. C. (1972) *Familia Caesaris: A Social Study of the Emperor's Freedmen and Slaves*. Cambridge.

(1990) "Where have all the Junian Latins gone? Nomenclature and status in the early Empire," *Chiron* 20: 275–305.

Westermann, W. L. (1914) "Apprentice contracts and the apprentice system in Roman Egypt," *CPh* 1914: 295–315.

(1945) "Between slavery and freedom," *AHR* 50: 213–27.

White, K. D. (1970) *Roman Farming.* Ithaca.

Whitehorne, J. E. G. (1983) "A reinterpretation of BGU IV 1065," *Anagennesis* III: 331–9.

Whitman, T. S. (1997). *The Price of Freedom: Slavery and Manumission in Baltimore and Early National Maryland.* Lexington.

Whittaker, C. R. (2002) "Proto-industrialization in Roman Gaul," in *Ancient History Matters: Studies Presented to Jens Erik Skydsgaard on His Seventieth Birthday,* ed. K. Ascani. Rome: 11–22.

Wiedemann, T. E. J. (1985) "The regularity of manumission at Rome," *CQ* 35: 162–75.

Wild, J.-P. (1999) "Textile manufacture: a rural craft?," in *Artisanat et productions artisanales en milieu rural dans les provinces du nord-ouest de l'Empire romain. Actes du colloque d'Erpeldange, mars 1999,* ed. M. Polfer. Montagnac: 29–37.

Wilson, A. (2001) "Timgad and textile production," in Mattingly and Salmon (eds.), 271–96.

(2008) "Large-scale manufacturing, standardization, and trade," in *The Oxford Handbook of Engineering and Technology in the Classical World,* ed. J. Oleson. Oxford: 393–417.

(2009) "Indicators for Roman economic growth: a response to Walter Scheidel," *JRA* 22: 71–82.

Wipszycka, E. (1965) *L'industrie textile dans l'Egypte romaine.* Wroclaw.

Woolf, G. (1998) *Becoming Roman: The Origins of Provincial Civilization in Gaul.* Cambridge.

Wright, G. (2006) *Slavery and American Economic Development.* Baton Rouge.

Young, C. (1995) "Financing the micro-scale enterprise," *Business History Review* 69/3: 398–421.

Zelnick-Abramovitz, R. (2005) *Not Wholly Free: The Concept of Manumission and the Status of Manumitted Slaves in the Ancient Greek World.* Leiden.

Zenger, T., Felin, T., and Bigelow, L. (2011) "Theories of the firm-market boundary," *The Academy of Management Annals* 5/1: 89–133.

Zimmer, G. (1982) *Römische Berufsdarstellungen.* Berlin.

Zimmermann, C. (2002) *Handwerkervereine in griechischen Osten des Imperium Romanum.* Mainz.

Index